Voices of Diversity

CLINICAL SOCIOLOGY: Research and Practice
Series Editor: John G. Bruhn, *New Mexico State University, Las Cruces, New Mexico*

Voices of Diversity

Multi-culturalism in America

by

Mary C. Sengstock, Ph.D., C.C.S.
Wayne State University, Detroit, MI 48202

With contributions by

Arifa K. Javed, Ph.D., C.S.P.
Sonya Berkley, M.A.
and
Brenda I. Marshall, M.A.

 Springer

Mary C. Sengstock
Wayne State University
Department of Sociology
Detroit, MI
USA
m.sengstock@wayne.edu

ISSN 1566-7847
ISBN 978-0-387-89665-6   e-ISBN 978-0-387-89666-3
DOI 10.1007/978-0-387-89666-3

Library of Congress Control Number: 2009920954

Printed on acid-free paper

springer.com

The authors humbly dedicate this book to a man who represents, in a very special way, the diversity which is 21st Century America:

BARACK HUSSEIN OBAMA,

44TH PRESIDENT OF THE UNITED STATES

President Obama is consistently described as the first African-American President, and indeed he is. However, his great appeal across racial lines stems from President Obama's personification of the diversity which is so much a part of America.

The son of a white American woman from Kansas and a Black man from the African nation of Kenya, President Obama is multi-racial, like several participants in this study. He is Black, but was raised primarily by his Caucasian mother and grandparents. During his formative years, he encountered several religions: his stepfather was Muslim; while living in Indonesia, he attended both Roman Catholic and Muslim run schools; as an adult he is a member of a Protestant denomination. He was born and spent his adolescent years in Hawaii, where multi-culturalism and multi-racialism flourish.

As a consequence, President Obama, in a real sense, embodies all Americans. He is Christian, but his experience leads him to understand persons from other religions. He has numerous ties across racial lines. Like the respondents in this study, he has experienced the dilemma of defining a personal identity when faced with multi-racial and multi-cultural divisions. Who is better than him to lead America into the increasingly diverse 21st Century?

It is our fondest hope that the suggestions offered in this book will help the people of America deal more effectively with 21st Century diversity, under the leadership of their new President, who so vividly embodies this diversity.

Mary C. Sengstock, Ph.D., C.C.S.
Arifa K. Javed, Ph.D., C.S.P.
Sonya Berkley, M.A.
Brenda I. Marshall, M.A.

Acknowledgements

The author wishes to acknowledge the assistance of many people who helped to make this book a reality. First, I express my appreciation to my three co-authors, who contributed chapters to this book.

Dr. Arifa Javed's description of the workshops she has conducted with immigrant families and their children provides a valuable insight into the school problems of immigrant children, as well as techniques for dealing with them. While workshops for teachers, parents, and students are common, Dr. Javed's synchronized workshops provide a unique opportunity for teachers, parents, and students to work together in a coordinated effort to improve the educational setting for immigrant students.

The high school diversity program described by Sonya Berkley is one of many attempts to bring cultural and racial diversity into the classroom. However, her analysis provides a rare opportunity to examine the effectiveness of such programs from the perspective of participating teachers and students.

Rarely do we think about the manner in which societies other than our own cope with diversity. Brenda Marshall's analysis of the varying approaches to racial and cultural diversity which appear in different nations provides a unique international perspective.

The specific areas of expertise of these three authors add a valuable dimension to the work which I could not have provided.

Most important, I express my deepest appreciation to the thirty people who served as respondents in the study of multi-racial and multi-cultural families. At their request, their identities remain anonymous. However, without their cooperation, this book could never have been written. I am forever in their debt.

I also express appreciation to the Department of Sociology and College of Liberal Arts and Sciences at Wayne State University, for supporting me through a Sabbatical leave, which permitted me to conduct these interviews, and to three assistants who helped to conduct the interviews: Sonya Berkley, Kenneth Kelso, and Kathleen Sengstock. Appreciation is also due to Sara Miller Amberg, for her assistance in locating references and editing the manuscript.

Finally, I express appreciation to John Bruhn, Ph.D., who saw the need for a book such as this and provided a publication outlet, as well as to Teresa Krauss and Katherine Chabalko, of Springer Press, for their assistance in the publication process.

Contents

Part I
Theoretical Foundations: An Analysis of the Place of Race, Culture, and Diversity in American Society

Another book about multi-culturalism? Why? Has not enough been said about that subject? What does this one say that has not already been said? These are reasonable questions. Why should there be another book analyzing multi-culturalism in American society? And how will this book make a contribution which is different from its predecessors? The answers to this question provide the rationale on which this book is based.

This section will be composed of two parts, with the division based on a temporal distinction. Chapter 1 will provide a brief summary of the manner in which the diversity in race and culture has been viewed in American history, prior to the last few decades of the 20th century. Chapter 2 will take up the story from that time, focusing primarily on the dramatically different patterns which appeared as America moved into the 20th century.

Chapter 1
A Brief Review of American Views of Multi-culturalism

It is important to recognize the important roles that different cultural groups have played in American society. It is tempting for each generation and each era to view what is happening as unique – as though it has never happened before. For example, many people at the turn of the 21st century look at the cultural mix and insist that America has never had so great a diversity as exists today. They see the increase in immigration, multiple language groups, and very different religions – Muslim, Hindu, and Shintoism – the groups today are so different from the past. They wonder how a unified society can ever come of this mix. In order to place 21st century diversity in context, we need to look at the cultural context of previous generations of Americans. Is 21st century diversity really a unique phenomenon? Or does it follow a model established in the past?

The goal of this book is to examine these issues. That is not to say, of course, that these questions have never been dealt with before. And as we progress through our analysis, the views of these earlier studies will be examined. One of the most comprehensive analyses of the process of incorporating new groups into a society was undertaken by Milton Gordon (1964) over 40 years ago. The overall process of incorporation is called "assimilation," and Gordon pointed out that it has a variety of dimensions. "Acculturation" refers to the ethnic group's adoption of the dominant group's cultural patterns, such as speaking the language and learning ways to make a living. With "structural assimilation," the new groups are included in the social groups of the dominant society. Other dimensions refer to intermarriage between the groups, identification as a single group, absence of prejudice and discrimination between the groups, and the absence of conflict over power and values.

Most studies of assimilation focus on one or more of Gordon's dimensions. Most have also focused largely on *macro-* or *meso*-levels of analysis. Macro-analysis refers to the examination of broad societal patterns. Macro-analysis would examine how American society as a whole is affected by the existence of diverse groups within it. Such studies would analyze the impact of cultural diversity on the demographic makeup of society or the national political process, for example. Most studies which analyze American assimilation and acculturation patterns have been of this type. At the meso-level, the focus of interest moves to which might be called the "middle" level of analysis, for example, the impact of the existence of diverse groups on individual communities. A study which would look at the impact of an

M.C. Sengstock, *Voices of Diversity*, Clinical Sociology: Research and Practice, DOI 10.1007/978-0-387-89666-3_1, © Springer Science+Business Media, LLC 2009 influx of non-English-speaking children into community schools would be an example of this type of analysis.

The *micro*-level of social relationships refers to the very smallest of social patterns – the manner in which individuals relate to one another on a one-to-one basis. How do individuals of diverse backgrounds relate to each other? Or do they? In the past, these relationships have largely been ignored. It is as though there is an implicit assumption that such relationships do not occur. The major measure of this level of assimilation has been the presence or absence of intermarriage. Indeed, Milton Gordon's (1964) formulation suggests that such close associations do not occur until so late in the process of intergroup contact that most differences have already been eliminated.

Social scientists have long recognized intermarriage to be an indication of near total intermingling of two groups. One of the characteristics of multi-culturalism which began to be observed in the late 20th century was an increase in intermarriage between members of different cultural backgrounds. As Alba and Nee (2003: 91–94) report, the 1990 US census found that only about 20% of White Americans had married a spouse with exactly the same nationality background. In contrast, one-fourth had a spouse whose background included a portion of their own (e.g., an Irish-Italian married to an Italian-Polish woman). More than half of couples listed had no specific ethnic origin or had a spouse whose ethnic makeup bore no relation to their own. Intermarriage between Jews and Gentiles and Asians and Whites is increasing as well.

These data clearly indicate that relationships between people of different cultural backgrounds occur on the micro-level as well. On the one hand, it is tempting to conclude, as Gordon's (1964) assimilation theory suggested, that this means that all differences have now been eradicated. However, this is an empirical question. Research is needed to examine the families founded by couples such as these to determine whether they are indeed devoid of the cultural remnants of the backgrounds of the couples who established them. How do the members relate to each other? How do they relate to their respective families of origin? How do they raise their children? Do their children identify with the cultural backgrounds of their parents? If so, which parent's background do they choose and how do they make the choice? Such families offer us a valuable opportunity to examine the manner in which multi-cultural interrelationships occur on the micro-level. Previous research has largely ignored them.

Hence, this work focuses on three major goals:

1. We will examine the nature of American multi-culturalism in the past. How does the multi-cultural mix of the early 21st century compare with that which existed in previous generations?
2. It is possible that the diversity model, as compared with past generations, may exhibit *both* similarities and differences. If this is the case, these similarities and differences need to be sorted out.
3. The bulk of this study examines the cultural patterns of persons who grew up in culturally diverse families. How do they identify themselves? How do they relate

to the varying components of their extended families? This analysis will make up the greater part of this book.

Two Hundred Plus Years of American Multi-culturalism

The USA has been described as a nation of immigrants (Handlin, 1973; Parillo, 1994). While many Americans today seem to view immigration as a "new" issue, multi-culturalism has been an ongoing social reality in this nation since its colonial days (Parillo, 1994). As early as 1643, ethnic and religious diversity was obvious in the American colonies. Jewish refugees from Brazil as well as Quakers were accepted into the society as early as the 1650s. The colonies sought English immigrants, but many immigrants came from non-English sources as well. These included German speakers, French Huguenots, Quakers, Scots, Scotch-Irish, and Welsh. Religious diversity was not encouraged, and laws restricting Catholics' religious practices were passed by all of the colonies at one time or another (Schuck, 2003: 77).

Migration was reduced somewhat after the Revolutionary War, but it increased again during the 1830s. The number almost tripled in the 1840s, largely due to the Irish potato famine, as well as overpopulation and deteriorating economic conditions throughout Europe. At that time, Germans and Irish dominated US migration, followed by the English-Scots-Welsh group, and Scandinavians, as well as both English and French speakers from Canada.

Between 1890 and 1920, more than 18.2 million newcomers entered the USA. This period of immigration is viewed by historians as the watershed separating the "old" immigration from the "new" (Schuck, 2003: 82). Most of the immigrants during that period came from southern and eastern Europe, the Pacific, and the Caribbean islands. Italians, Hebrews, and Poles also came, as did Scandinavians, British, Irish, Canadians, non-Polish Slavs, Mexicans, Magyars, Greeks, and Japanese. Many unskilled laborers, tailors, Jewish tradesmen and merchants, and a few farm workers came as well.

Not surprisingly, this was also the period during which a considerable amount of opposition to immigration occurred. Americans were worried about the large number of new immigrants, many of them so different from the existing population. The widespread opposition of the American public led to a number of investigations and resulted in the passage of several laws restricting immigration.

The best known of these were a series of acts passed by Congress in the 1920s. This process began over a decade earlier, when Congress held a series of hearings on immigration, under the leadership of the Dillingham Commission, with Senator William Dillingham of Vermont as its chair (House-Senate Commission, 1910–1911). This Commission developed the major framework on which the restrictions on immigration, the so-called quota system, developed in the 1920s, were established. The Commission examined a copious amount of information, which led it to conclude that the "new immigration" of the later 19th and early 20th centuries was extremely bad for America. They saw the new immigrants as incapable of acculturating. As Parillo (1994; 2000) has pointed out, however, the assumptions on which the Commission based its conclusions included many errors, which he has referred to as the "Dillingham Flaw." One of these errors was the failure to recognize the lengthy periods of time over which earlier immigrants had become acculturated and assimilated into American society. In addition, immigrants who arrived at a later date had to cope with greater structural changes in urbanization and technology in the process of adjusting to their new homeland.

One of these, the 1921 Immigration Act, imposed an annual ceiling of 357,000 immigrants, with a per-country limit of 3% of the number of its foreign-born US residents. Some countries in Northern and Western Europe did not fill their quotas, which led to the Johnson-Reed (National Origins) Act of 1924. This law set an annual limit of 150,000 Europeans, completely prohibited Japanese immigration, and developed a series of quotas, based on the contribution of each nationality to the overall US population in 1890. Consequently, during the 1930s, only 500,000 immigrants came to the USA, and many of these eventually returned home. When the refugee issue arose in 1940s, the USA was reluctant to admit many of these displaced persons.

For some time, sociologists and anthropologists have studied the impact of acculturation and assimilation on ethnic groups and their members in the USA. This concern has even reached the applied professions, for we now have a recognition, on the part of medical professionals, social workers, counselors, and the like, of the fact that relatively recent immigrants may not share many of the cultural characteristics which we have come to expect in the so-called White (or WASP, or White Anglo-Saxon Protestant) segment of the population (McGoldrick et al., 2005a). There has even been some acceptance of the fact that some groups which have been in this country for a considerable period of time may not have accepted all of the dominant American culture.

However, the focus has largely been on groups such as Blacks, Hispanics, and Asians. There has been less acceptance, even among sociologists, of the idea that cultural differences may remain, even among some groups, such as WASPs or European Catholics, who have been in this country for a considerable period of time. However, some have suggested that the kinds of cultural differences which play a role in applied social settings, such as social work, medicine, or counseling, continue to exist in groups such as the Irish, British, or Polish, and may persist over several generations (McGoldrick et al., 2005a).

Particularly unrecognized is the fact that cultural differences exist even among groups which are widely assumed to be a single cultural group. The so-called Hispanics, for example, include all persons whose mother tongue is Spanish, which may include Cubans, Mexicans, Spaniards, and persons from the many south and central American countries; such persons may have Spanish as their national language, but may have quite different cultural patterns in other respects.

In this chapter, we will discuss the historical character of the USA as a "multicultural" or "pluralistic society": What does it mean to say that the USA is multicultural or pluralistic? Which cultural groups are included when we use the term? How do these groups compose themselves and how are they viewed by others? What is the impact on society as a whole? In short, we will attempt to place the notion of the USA as a multi-cultural society in historical perspective. We will begin with a discussion of the social context within which American cultural pluralism is viewed.

Who is NOT Part of Cultural Pluralism?

The historical perspective is particularly important in discussing the multi-cultural dimension or cultural pluralism. When people use such terms, they generally refer to the groups which are recognized *today* as representing "different" cultural groups. That is, they are referring to groups which are seen as "different" from what is believed to be the "majority" or "dominant" group in American society today. For example, a brief review of books or articles which focus on techniques for professionals working in multi-cultural settings generally focus on the characteristics of the "other" cultural groups, which professionals may encounter, and suggestions for techniques for dealing with persons from such groups.

They do not generally include an analysis of what is considered to be the "dominant" or majority culture. In effect, it is presumed that a general "American culture" exists and that the content of that "American culture" is widely recognized and understood. Most people – especially the professionals who are the target of these books and articles – are presumed to be part of that dominant group and to accept that culture. There is little attention given to the dimensions and assumptions of that dominant culture or even recognition that the "dominant" group actually has a distinctive culture. In short, the way of life of the dominant group is presumed to be "THE" appropriate life style and cultural pattern – "what everyone does." Indeed, it does not even seem to be seen as a "cultural" pattern, but simply as the way things are supposed to be.

Counseling handbooks are a good example. Most contain a series of chapters devoted to specific "ethnic" or "cultural" groups and their unique characteristics, which might have an impact on the counseling process. The groups included are those which would generally be called "minorities" as the term is applied today: Blacks or African-Americans, Hispanics, Asians, and Native Americans (Song and Kim, 1993; Ho, 1987; Mindel et al., 1998). Sometimes these are grouped together, as in the above list. Other authors recognize the diversity within these categories and devote chapters to each specific subcategory. Works of this type include chapters on Japanese-Americans, Chinese-Americans, and Korean-Americans, rather than a general chapter on Asian-Americans, and chapters on Puerto Rican-Americans, Mexican-Americans, and Cuban-Americans, rather than a chapter on Hispanic-Americans (Taylor, 1994; Locke, 1992; Mindel et al., 1998). These works take cognizance of the diversity that exists within each of these broad categories.

However, most works do not focus on the dominant culture, that is, the culture of presumed majority groups in American society: White (presumably Protestant) Americans. It is as though there is no recognition that group does have a culture which must be considered in order to examine the characteristics of the other groups and the differences between the two. Some works do include groups of European origin which are often ignored in view of the fact that they are commonly included in the "White" category. Examples are Irish-Americans, Polish-Americans, Italian-Americans, Jewish-Americans, and the Amish (Mindel et al., 1998). However, again there is the assumption that only these "different" European groups needs to be considered. For most authors, White Protestants are apparently "just Americans," whose culture is presumed. McGoldrick et al. (2005a) is an exception, in that it provides chapters on several White ethnic groups of European origin (see also Brislin and Yoshsida, 1994; Roberts et al., 1994; Ponterotto et al., 1995).

The Dominant White Group as Part of the Ethnic Mix

For anyone who has read about the history of "White" ethnic groups in the USA, the claim that they are "just White" or "just Americans," and have never been anything else, can seem somewhat amusing. For at the time of their arrival in the USA, most arrivals, other than the English Protestants, were viewed in the same manner as today's new arrivals. They were considered to have odd customs and language and unacceptable religious beliefs. Some were even thought to be a different "race" and were considered incapable of ever becoming part of the mainstream American society. It should be noted that the social scientific concept of race as a biologically distinguishable species of humans had not been developed, even as late as the 1920s (Jones, 1960).

Consequently, any unfamiliar new arrivals – even if they were visibly "white" – were the targets of discrimination and prejudice on the part of those who had already established themselves. Immigrants who could not easily be assimilated were unacceptable. No less a personage than Theodore Roosevelt, after his departure from the White House, was a vigorous supporter of Americanization, insisting that Americans had no room for persons who maintained a loyalty to their country of origin, and urging that English alone be taught in the schools (Roosevelt, 1919; Hart and Ferleger, 1989: 243). Indeed, the restrictions on immigration developed in the 1920s were established to keep persons who were not of the White race out of the USA. What is often not recognized, however, is the fact that many groups now considered to be "White," but of different cultures, were, at that time, considered to be different races, and were, therefore, not favored in the quota system (Ngai, 1999; Jacobson, 1998; Barrett and Roediger, 1997).

Hence, the concept of race has often been used by those in power to maintain dominance over others; the illogic of the categories has never been a major concern (Spikard, 1992). Intermarriage with persons of different cultures as well as races was considered repugnant by the early English and Dutch settlers (Fernandez, 1996)

English Protestants

The earliest White arrivals to this continent were English Protestants, chiefly Anglicans and Congregationalists, who arrived in either the Virginia or Massachusetts colonies. During the 17th century colonial period, they were joined by Baptists and Reformed Protestant groups. In colonial times, the religions also enjoyed financial support from government sources (Anderson, 1970: 2). At this early stage, the continent was sparsely populated, and most religious groups remained separated from each other. Though they might all be English Protestants, they were not in agreement about religious ideas. Anglicans conformed to the highly hierarchical structure of the English church, while Congregationalists believed in largely independent religious communities and held the "Popish" demeanor of the Anglicans in contempt. While these differences may be viewed in a rather benign manner by many Protestants today, this was not the case in colonial times.

Protestants from Other National Origins

The 18th century brought more diversity to the American population, in both religion and nationality. Lutherans and Presbyterians, together with some smaller sects, arrived, and Methodists increased to the point of becoming the single largest Protestant group (Lipset, 1963: 144). However, these newly arrived Protestants were quite different from their predecessors. Not only did they belong to a different denomination from the English (Lutheran), but they also had different nationalities and languages. Even though they were European and Protestant, their White Protestant predecessors did not always consider them acceptable neighbors. No less a figure than Benjamin Franklin is said to have worried about the new arrivals. Though he recognized that America needed their numbers, he worried about their unacceptable behavior and thought they might be too numerous (Cross, 1973: 4).

German Protestants

Discussions of the so-called German immigrants often include immigrants from other Germanic-speaking countries such as Holland, Austria, and Switzerland. These immigrants came in the colonial period and differed from the English in both language and religion. They also included a Catholic component, but most were Protestant, and Catholics as a group represented a relatively small segment of the population in colonial times (less than 1%), and could largely be ignored (Anderson, 1970: 2, 84). Hence, the major difference between the English and the German population involved language and a different brand of Protestantism.

While those Germans who chose could eventually move into the "White Protestant majority," many Germans did not choose to do so, and the German language remained in use in Pennsylvania well into the 20th century (Anderson, 1970: 82).

Religiously, the Germans also maintained their separate character. German Lutherans had an extensive school system throughout the 19th century. Interestingly, this religious identity persists today, with the German Missouri synod Lutheran denomination remaining one of the more resistant Protestant groups to the influence of other religious entities, including other Lutherans and Protestants. The Amish and Mennonites are other examples of this immigrant group which made considerable efforts to maintain their separate identity (Huntington, 1998). Thus, the early arrival of German Protestants did not guarantee that they would have – or even want – an automatic and easy assimilation into the so-called White Protestant majority.

Scotch and Scotch-Irish

Even Protestants from other parts of the British empire were not necessarily warmly received by their predecessors. Scottish immigrants from the Highlands continued to speak their unique language and wore their clan clothing, resulting in their being unwelcome in some parts of the Carolinas (Anderson, 1970: 40). Their lower class status, strange Presbyterian religion, and tendency to drink and use blasphemous language made them unacceptable to the proper English settlers who preceded them (Graham, 1956). Indeed, Scots and Scotch-Irish were banned from holding public office in the English colonies during the colonial period and were shunned in the military by "proper" Bostonians (Shipton, 1936).

During this period, Scotch-Irish Presbyterian churches were the target of vandals, not unlike the experiences of unpopular religions today (Jones, 1960). The Scots' reception was also dependent upon the area into which they moved. Some Scotch-Irish Protestants, for example, moved into Pennsylvania where their quick tempers, casual work ethic, and tendency to drink did not sit well with the more staid and religious Germans who had preceded them (Anderson, 1970: 36; Leyburn, 1962).

Scandinavians

Another component of today's White Protestant group is the Scandinavians, including immigrants from Sweden, Norway, and Finland. While there were immigrants from Scandinavia during colonial times, the majority arrived during the last quarter of the 19th and the first decades of the 20th century. These new arrivals from Sweden, Norway, and Finland were Protestant like the British immigrants who preceded them, but they did not share their Anglo-Saxon roots (Anderson, 1970: 32). Nearly all were Lutherans and practiced a particularly strict variety of that faith. Deviations from tenets of the Lutheran religion were viewed to represent undesirable Americanization and were handled severely by Lutheran pastors (Anderson, 1970: 49, 63).

Immigrants from Scandinavia required more time for assimilation than most British immigrants, largely due to their distinctive languages and their isolation in rural areas of the northern Midwestern states. Scandinavians did not know English and maintained their native languages within their communities. This was made easier due to their tendency to move into relatively isolated parts of the Midwest – Minnesota, Wisconsin, Ohio, and Michigan (Anderson, 1970: 48). Immigrants from Finland, in particular, reportedly remained an "out-group" among Wite Protestants longer than others (Anderson, 1970: 73–77). Like the Missouri Synod Lutherans, the Finnish Lutheran Church maintained a degree of distinctiveness into the late 20th century.

Marriage outside their respective nationalities almost always occurred with other Scandinavians prior to their eventual merging into the broader Protestant community. However, most Scandinavians eventually merged to become part of the White Anglo-Saxon Protestant group. Anderson (1970: 48) notes that "A distinctive Swedish subculture was rarely recognized beyond the second generation."

After two centuries of assuming that they were "just Americans," the increased diversity of the American population in the 20th century caused many Protestants to become more self-conscious of their Protestant identity (Anderson, 1970: 3). This enhanced Protestant identity has grown even greater since Anderson made his observation. Indeed, the family patterns of European Protestant groups remain sufficiently distinct to merit separate chapters in a manual for family counselors (McGoldrick et al., 2005a).

In summary, an analysis of the history of the reception of newcomers from various European Protestant groups reveals some surprising results. Certainly they exhibited more similarities to each other by today's cultural standards. At least they were all Europeans; nearly all were Christians; most were also Protestants. This marked similarity stands in contrast to the radical differences in nationality, language, race, and religion to the differences that exist among the newest immigrants of the late 20th and early 21st centuries.

What is surprising is the fact that they were often not viewed as similar by other Americans at the time of their arrival. Rather, they were often viewed as distinctive to the point of being inassimilable. Their religious differences were considered extremely important: they differed in their theological beliefs, and some believed in a hierarchical structure while others did not. Their national differences often perpetuated the division of Europe which immigrants brought with them. Language differences made communication difficult. Disagreements also arose over cultural differences, such as the strong work ethic of the English and Germans, as compared with the more casual life patterns of the Scotch and Scotch-Irish, not to mention differing attitudes toward alcohol, dancing, and other social activities.

Lessons from the White Protestant Immigration Experience

There are actually three lessons we should learn from the interchanges that occurred between the English and the Protestants who followed them. First is the realization that the differences between the original group and those that follow are not necessarily characteristics that would be obvious to an objective outside observer. From our vantage point, there was relatively little to differentiate the Scotch-Irish from the English – but the English colonists of the 16th and 17th centuries did not think so!

Second is the fact that intergroup exchanges go two ways. Not only must the receiving society agree to allow the newcomers in, but the newcomers must also want to be assimilated. Some incoming groups really do not want to lose their distinctive identity. Among White Protestants, for example, it is clear that some German Lutherans did not want to lose their distinct religious beliefs and become part of the broad "White Protestant" group.

Third, the history of White Protestant Americans also illustrates that religious and nationality groups can perpetuate themselves for quite some time. Again citing the example of the German Lutherans, they have managed to continue their distinctive community into the late 20th and even the 21st century.

For the most part, however, by the time of the American revolution, most English-speaking Protestants had largely become part of the dominant Protestant group. And most other Protestant Europeans from Germany, Holland, and the Scandinavian countries would follow during the 19th and early 20th centuries. To a great extent, it is likely that the increased acceptance they received as the 19th century progressed was largely due to the fact that others – even more different than they – were beginning to arrive. And all English-speaking Protestants were united in the recognition that, however much they disagreed with each other, these newcomers arriving in the second half of the 19th century were much more problematic.

The Irish: The First "Really Different" White Immigrant Group

If the English Protestants who founded this country thought their followers who were not English were strange, what they saw in them was nothing compared to what was to come in the mid-19th century, when the first "really different" White group – at least from the point of view of the dominant English Protestants – began to arrive. The failure of the potato crop produced extreme famine conditions in Ireland and led to a dramatic increase in both the size and type of Irish immigration to the USA. The first US census in 1790 showed less than 200,000 persons of Irish ancestry out of a total population of about four million; most of these were Protestants (Fallows, 1979: 19).

The Irish migration which followed represented a radical change. The 1830s witnessed the arrival of approximately 300,000 Irish; in the following decade, this number increased to 800,000 (Fallows, 1979: 14, 22–23). On some dimensions, these new arrivals resembled the Irish already here. For example, they were White and most knew English. However, there the similarity ends. This new group was abysmally poor and exhibited most of the characteristics the English did not like about the earlier Scotch-Irish: their perceived laziness, frivolity, and tendency to drink. Worst of all, they were Roman Catholic. This religious difference was particularly intolerable to the White Protestant population (Alba and Nee, 2003: 282–283).

While most Irish immigrants knew English, there the similarities ended. While the English colonists disagreed with their homeland on a number of dimensions, they did continue the strong anti-Irish prejudice of their home country, and this view was handed down to subsequent generations (Fallows, 1979: 6; Horgan, 1998). Most Irish lived in total squalor (Horgan, 1998). They were considered to be ". . .heavy drinkers, ferocious fighters, and loose in morals" (Anderson, 1970: 23). They were seen as extremely brutal and unable to think about anything but the present. Soon after their arrival, the American Irish established bars or "saloons," which continued the tradition of the Irish public house – or "pub" – as the poor man's neighborhood gathering place (Fallows, 1979: 50–51). These establishments soon became a target for the Yankees, more inclined toward abstinence.

The label, "Papist," was a particularly negative term applied to the Irish immigrants (Anderson, 1970: 23–24). It is difficult to overstate the importance of this religious difference in the social context of mid-19th century America. Anderson (1970: 100) goes so far as to call it "hatred." "It was not the national origin component of ethnicity, then, that automatically relegated the Irish to an inferior position, but the Catholic religious component which came to represent the critical factor making them seem strange, suspect, and therefore to be set apart" (Fallows, 1979: 6). McGrath (2007) observes that a major force for uniting Protestants throughout most of American history was their opposition to Catholics.

As early as colonial times, there were restrictions against Catholics holding office in America. These were eliminated after the American Revolution, but there was persistent agitation to reinstate them. Protestants saw Catholics as involved in a papal plot to undermine the American social order and the Protestant religion. These feelings were exhibited in the development of numerous social movements in the mid- and late 19th century, including the Know-Nothing Party, the American Protestant Union, Protestant Reformation Society, American Protective Association, and numerous others. Catholics were one of the earliest targets of the Ku Klux Klan (Anderson, 1970: 100–104; Alba and Nee, 2003: 283).

Protestants were particularly fearful of the Catholic authority structure, and the Catholic Church's position on confession, which, in their view, allowed believers to sin at will and receive forgiveness through the church (Anderson, 1970: 105). Anti-Catholic sentiment has been described as the most extreme religious prejudice and discrimination in American history (Kane, 1955: 43). Indeed, many Protestants did not consider Catholics to be Christians, even defining them as devil worshipers, views which also persist in some Protestant circles today (Mazzi, 2007; Shick, 2007; Chick, n.d.; jesus-is-lord.com, n.d.-a, b; Ankerberg and Waldon, 1995).

Because of their outward physical similarity to the founding English, together with their familiarity with the language, the Irish could have easily adapted to the American culture. However, the Irish who came to America carried with them vivid memories of the manner in which the Irish were treated by the English: their land taken and their people starving (Horgan, 1998). The Irish people had to reject their Catholicism in order to receive the educational and income advantages the English had to offer. Like no other European nation, the people of Ireland retained a particularly sullen resistance to co-optation by their conquerors (Fallows, 1979: 11–26). Having resisted such pressures in their homeland, the Irish were not about to reject their religion on their arrival in America; no other American religious group "...ever displayed such a militancy and belligerency," according to Kane (1955: 43). Their tenacious retention of the Catholic religion doomed them to be seen in a different manner by the American population. Their preference for the urban environment of the eastern seaboard, rather than moving toward the rural frontier, as had the

Scotch-Irish and Scandinavians, made their resistance to the Anglo-Saxon Protestant pattern all the more obvious (Fallows, 1979: 6–7).

As strange as it may seem today, when racial differences tend to be viewed as physical characteristics, the Catholic Irish were considered to be a different race from those who had preceded them (Fallows, 1979: 53; Alba and Nee, 2003: 132). Although the observed differences were largely social and cultural, "...the thinking of the time tended to interpret them as permanent racial endowments and to question whether any group so different could adapt to American life" (Fallows, 1979: 26). Eventually, the religious differences began to be seen as less important than the perceived racial differences observed with southern and eastern Europeans, and the Catholic Irish began to experience a grudging acceptance on the part of the broader American society. However, Protestant distrust of Catholics persisted into the 20th century, leading to the 1920s immigration quotas. It continues to reappear on occasion, notably when Catholics run for high political office, the campaigns of Alfred Smith, John F. Kennedy, and John Kerry being examples (Fallows, 1979: 46, 61; Anderson, 1970: 106–109).

The history of the reception accorded the Catholic Irish illustrates the absurdity of the position that no previous groups of immigrants have been so radically different from the American milieu as those coming today. It is not the objective differences between groups that matter. Rather, it is the *perception* of the groups involved – both the receiving society and the arriving newcomers – that defines a group as "too different" to be assimilated or not. Furthermore, as we noted with some German Lutherans, the Irish were not particularly anxious to become part of the American mainstream. Indeed, they were highly resistant – especially if it meant giving up the Catholic religion which they fought so hard to retain under British rule in Ireland.

More "Outsiders" Invading America's Shores

The fact that other groups arriving at the same time as the Irish also differed from the Protestant founders did not make the establishment of a unified society any easier. The new immigration of the late 19th and early 20th centuries included arrivals from southern and eastern Europe who also swelled the ranks of the religiously "different." They included Italian Catholics, as well as immigrants from Poland and other east European countries, some of whom were Catholics, others Jewish. Two of the groups, the Italians and Polish Catholics, were very similar in a number of respects.

Italian Immigrants

Most Italian immigrants to the USA came from the southeastern part of Italy. They were generally poor and spoke a different language. In addition, their dark hair and somewhat darker skin also distinguished them from the immigrants who preceded them. This made it easier for the dominant White society to identify and single them out for special discriminatory treatment. Hence, Italian immigrants were at a disadvantage in getting jobs, establishing themselves, and finding a place in the American milieu (Alba and Nee, 2003: 106).

Because Italians were Catholic like the Irish who preceded them, it could have been an advantage for them to enter a society where others from their religion had already established themselves. However, the brand of Catholicism the Italians practiced was radically different from that of the Irish. Italians valued Church rituals for their pageantry and contribution to family life, which was all-important to Italians. For the Irish, on the other hand, the Catholic Church was a rigid, authoritarian institution; Irish Catholics focused on rules of behavior and valued the Church as a means of avoiding hell.

Not surprisingly, the American Catholic Church reflected the Irish traditions of the ethnic community which had founded it. Italians entering American Catholic churches found them rigid, cold, and unwelcoming. They soon pressured church leaders to establish parishes and appoint priests from their own background (Giordano et al., 2005; Gambino, 1974; Nelli, 1980). As a result of these differences, Italian immigrants often had to accommodate to American society on two levels. On the one hand, like other immigrants, they had to adapt to American society as a whole. But unlike their predecessors who established their own churches, they did not have the comfort of a religious community of their own to serve as a temporary home in the meantime.

Like Irish Catholics and some German Lutherans, Italians have also been resistant to acculturation and assimilation. Italian immigrants urged their children to remain committed to the family, to marry other Italians, and to continue their "old ways." They were not always successful, of course, but the pressure to remain within the Italian community was strong. Italian-Americans have also been greatly affected by the reputation, widely believed in the USA, that Italians are connected to the Mafia and organized crime. Although relatively few Italians actually have such connections, this reputation has had an effect on the acceptance and advancement of Italians in America (Giordano et al., 2005: 619–620).

To a considerable extent, one might say that Italian-Americans have had the worst of both worlds. They have experienced restrictions of their acceptance into American society as a result of being foreign, speaking a foreign language, and belonging to the Catholic Church, which so many Americans find threatening. At the same time, they could not enjoy the comfort which these ethnic institutions could provide. For these, they had to establish their own institutions; to a great extent, their strong extended family structure served in that capacity. However, some found these same familial institutions to be oppressive in their limitations on advancement in America (Giordano et al., 2005; Papajohn and Spiegel, 1975). Although Italian-Americans today would be classified as "White" in most people's minds, there are still indications of resistance to their being accepted on an equal basis (Giordano et al., 2005: 619).

The Polish

Immigrants of Polish background began to appear in immigration records in the mid-1880s. There were considerable numbers of Polish immigrants until the quota limitations of the 1920s. Several factors make it difficult to identify with any accuracy how many Polish actually came to this country in the early years. In part, this is due to the fact that American immigration records listed the *nation* of origin of immigrants, and portions of Poland were under the domination of numerous other nations during this period. Consequently, many persons of Polish cultural background were recorded as Russians, Germans, or Austro-Hungarians. Since Jews were sometimes listed as Jews, other times by their national origin, it was difficult to determine how many Poles actually formed part of the Polish community as opposed to the Jewish community (Lopata, 1976: 34–35, 38).

While Polish immigrants were not physically distinguishable as were the Italians, there were many similarities. Polish Catholic immigrants were much like the Italians: They were poor, generally unskilled laborers, and did not speak English. The Polish language they spoke largely consisted of village dialects, making communication difficult, even with other Poles. Nonetheless, Polish immigrants were quick to form a solid set of businesses and other institutions within the ethnic community. Another significant dimension of the Polish community is the development of an extensive structure for status competition within the ethnic group; this structure was largely a re-creation of customs existing in Poland and served both as a source of strain and a unifying factor (Lopata, 1976: 4, 34, 43–47; Lopata, 1998).

From the point of view of religion, the Polish variety of Catholicism was much more like that of the Italians than the Irish. Like the Italians, they found the Irish brand of Catholicism to be strange. Poles had their own special ceremonies, were accustomed to using Polish in their religious ceremonies, and had their own group of saints whom they revered. They also resulted in early confrontation with the predominantly Irish-American Catholic church. The conflict became so severe that some Polish Catholics established their own independent Polish National Catholic Church (Lopata, 1976: 3–4).

Eventually, numerous Polish parishes were formed with their Polish-speaking priests, and these parishes were often the central focus of the local community (Lopata, 1976: 44). Dissatisfied with what they viewed as the overtly American content and lack of discipline of the public schools, Polish Catholics also developed a highly complex educational system, which included schools form the elementary level through college, as well as a seminary to educate Polish-speaking priests to serve the Polish community (Lopata, 1976: 50–52).

Like other immigrants, Poles were the target of prejudice and discrimination on the part of those who came before. Some changes in the quota acts of the 1920s specifically targeted Poles as a group deserving of restriction (Lopata, 1976: 36). Both Polish and Italians were specifically cited by Woodrow Wilson as groups whose characteristics and behavior made them undesirable American citizens (Gerson, 1953: 55). Poles were clearly aware of the way in which they were viewed by other Americans. To a great extent, they shared the negative sentiments; their response was to turn their backs on the dominant American society and devote their attention to the Polish community. When they could, Poles reacted with anger and frustration; others withdrew from involvement in Polish activities and made other efforts, such as name changes, to disassociate themselves from their Polish background (Lopata, 1976: 70–73; Lopata, 1998). While Polish-Americans may today largely be classified as "White," it is obvious that their entry into this category has been a long and arduous one.

Enter the Jews: The First White Americans Who Were Not Christian

Up to this point, all of the immigrant groups we have been discussing have belonged to one or another of the many denominations or sects that claim to be Christian. As we have seen, there are numerous disagreements among the groups as to which groups really deserve to call themselves Christians. However, with the arrival of Jews from eastern Europe came the first group that made a free choice to come to this country that did not make this claim. This, of course, does not include arrivals from Africa, who were not Christian, but also did not make the choice to come to America.

The earliest Jews to come to America was during the colonial period. Jews have come to the USA in three major waves. The first and smallest group was made up of Sephardic Jews from Spain and Portugal, who came to New Amsterdam where they were not very well received. There were sufficient Jews in Newport, Rhode Island, in the mid-1700s to form the first synagogue in America (Tauro Synagogue, 2007). The second wave consisted of German Jews who came during the middle of the 19th century. They were mainly merchants, and eventually many of them attained considerable success in business and finance (Farber et al., 1998).

However, by the last quarter of the 19th century, Jews numbered only about 200,000 people and remained a tiny proportion of the American population – less than one half of 1% (Goldstein and Goldscheider, 1968: 1). During the great migration in the late 19th and 20th centuries, this pattern was to change dramatically with the arrival of the third and largest wave of Jewish immigrants who came mainly from eastern Europe. These impoverished new arrivals practiced a more ritually orthodox version of Judaism than the Reform German Jews who preceded them; consequently, they received a less than enthusiastic reception. Eventually, the Jewish community expanded to include the various varieties of Jewish belief and practice (Farber et al., 1998).

The earliest of this great wave of Jewish immigrants were primarily lower class and unskilled workers; by the early 20th century, they were more likely to be skilled laborers (Sherman, 1965). Studies show that the occupational structure of the Jewish community moved from primarily industrial workers in the immigrant generation to much larger proportions of merchants, business managers, white collar workers, and professionals than the US population as a whole. Success and individual achievement were important goals in Jewish families (Goldstein and Goldscheider, 1968: 78–79; Rosen and Weltman, 2005). Indeed, the American Jewish population has proven to be so successful in adapting to the American economic structure that they have often been held up as the "model" American ethnic group, able to move from their initial poverty to attain success through their own industry and hard work, and other groups have been asked why they cannot do the same (Glazer and Moynihan, 1963).

Migration of Jews to the USA has been limited during the mid- to late 20th century. There was little migration prior to World War II, with an increase in Holocaust survivors following the war. In the last decade of the 20th century, another wave of Jews came to the USA, this group from Russia (Farber et al., 1998; Rosen and Weltman, 2005). Throughout the years, most Jews have been identified as Jews, rather than with the nation state from which they originated (Goldstein and Goldscheider, 1968: 11).

While they were attaining economic success in the USA, Jews were not ignoring their own ethnic community and its cultural institutions. Religious, educational, and other institutions were developed to ensure that members retained their Jewish cultural traditions and identity. Marriage within the Jewish community has remained high and families were remarkably stable; intermarriages which have occurred often result in the non-Jewish member becoming Jewish (Rosen and Weltman, 2005; Goldstein and Goldscheider, 1968).

Jews' identification with the Jewish community has been aided by their centuries-old tradition of self-consciousness, as well as their recognition that Jews have been persecuted in the past and may be again. And Jews have been subjected to considerable prejudice and discrimination throughout their sojourn in the USA. Just as American Protestants were not comfortable with Catholics, they were also uncomfortable with Jews. Again, the presence of the religious difference created considerable disturbance in the predominantly Christian population; Jews, like Catholics, became the target of groups like the Ku Klux Klan (Alba and Nee, 2003: 283).

Jews in the USA have been subjected to rejection in housing, social groups, employment, and educational institutions (Alba and Nee, 2003: 108). In the 1920s, for example, several Ivy League Universities established quotas on the number of Jews who could be admitted. They were concerned that the admission of too many ambitious and highly qualified Jewish applicants would discourage the upper class White Protestants on whom their status as an upper class institution, not to mention their fund-raising efforts, were so dependent. Alumni reportedly wrote to Harvard University administrators, urging that they devise a way for the institution to remain a "White man's college" (Klein, 2005: B13). Obviously, Jews were not considered to be "White" within the terminology of that era, and White Americans were convinced that Jews constituted a separate race (Alba and Nee, 2003: 132). Even at the turn of the 21st century, Christian anti-Semitism allegedly remains strong among some segments of Christians (Allen, 2007; Americans United, 2007). Again, being defined as "White" is a hard-won distinction.

The Special Position Reserved for People of Color

Some might wonder why I have waited so long to deal with the groups who are most negatively affected by American resistance to outsiders. After all, Blacks, Hispanics, Asians, and others who exhibit an obvious *physical* difference from the White Protestant majority are clearly the target of more negative sentiment and behavior than any of the groups we have just discussed. This delay has been employed for a deliberate reason: precisely to show that the prejudice and discrimination directed toward people of color is *not* uniquely different from the way other outsiders have been treated. It may be greater in degree. Indeed, it is much greater in degree. It is not, however, a manifestation of a new phenomenon and must be understood in that context.

African-Americans: Special Targets of Extensive Prejudice and Discrimination

Although all "strangers" have received unequal treatment in the USA, the position of African-Americans is indeed unique (Baldwin, 1963). No other group has received so high a degree of negative treatment for so long a period than Blacks.[1] Only Blacks were systematically brought to the USA as part of a forced migration and forced to live under slavery for 200 years (Pinkney, 1993: 1–3). Most immigrant groups included some members who did not come to America freely; these include indentured servants, as well as many women and children who were brought by their husbands and fathers. For Blacks, however, migration was not a free choice for the group as a whole. Blacks were also prohibited from citizenship from the very beginning of the nation. In 1790, Congress passed an act which limited citizenship to all who were not "free White persons" (Alba and Nee, 2003: 168).

The impact of forced migration is very different from that of free migration. Most free migrants do not come as individuals, but as part of the social network of their home country, or even their village. Consequently, free migrants often come with relatives; they also maintain contact with the home society after they leave, frequently assisting other members of the group who wish to follow them. Indeed, this is the reason why most immigrant groups are able to maintain their social traditions and culture in the new environment (Sengstock, 1976).

In contrast, forced migration totally separates the migrant from his/her former life. Africans brought to the USA under slavery were captured form a variety of geographic locations and social groups and intermingled indiscriminately. They were sent to whichever location would pay the appropriate price. If owners became aware that some slaves did know each other, or had developed social ties, they were deliberately separated in order to prevent the development of any contacts which might encourage slave uprisings (Pinkney, 1993: 5–6; Frazier, 1957: 12). Hence, slaves,

---

[1] Throughout this work, I will use the terms "Black" and "African-American" interchangeably.

unlike free migrants, were deliberately prevented from maintaining their previous social structure and culture in order to force them to be more pliable.

Once here, the treatment of slaves was brutal. They were subjected to forced labor and the most deplorable living conditions. Punishment for the even minor infractions was the most brutal that can be imagined. Such treatment was justified because Blacks were not considered to be human, a position which religious traditions helped to support. Because slaves were not considered human, they need not be accorded basic human rights (Pinkney, 1993: 2–9; Black and Jackson, 2005). Even free Blacks were subjected to severe legal restriction in employment, education, and even the right to hold meetings. These restrictions were not imposed on White immigrants, provided they give up their old ways (Roosevelt, 1917; Hart and Ferleger, 1989: 243).

Following the Civil War and the Emancipation Proclamation, slaves were technically freed, but it was not long before White Supremacy was reinstated, and the economic and social position of Blacks changed little. After the Civil War, Whites in the North lost interest in the status of Blacks. In the South, Jim Crow laws were imposed to continue the separation of the races in schools, transportation, and other public settings. Antimiscegenation laws were passed to prevent intermarriage between Blacks and Whites and to keep the White race "pure" (Nakashima, 1992). In World War II, 80 years after the Civil War, the military remained rigidly segregated. Court decisions supported these so-called "separate but equal" arrangements. However, the conditions were hardly equal, and these legally enforced restrictions on Blacks lasted until the Civil Rights movement of the 1960s and 1970s (Pinkney, 1993: 18–23).

The numerous social programs of the 20th century, which were designed to assist American citizens in recovering from the Great Depression and adjust to life after World War II, were deliberately structured so as to leave Black Americans behind, as Katznelson (2005) documents so effectively. For example, federal labor laws and the Social Security program, which provided worker protections such as minimum wages and regulation of hours and old age assistance after retirement, deliberately excluded domestic and agricultural work, in which most Southern Blacks were employed (Katznelson, 2005: 143–144). Federal mortgage supports helped persons with modest incomes purchase a home; red-lining and other bank policies made it virtually impossible for Blacks to take advantage of these programs (Katznelson, 2005: 163–164). Black veterans were also left behind by the GI Bill, which provided education, vocational training, and job placement for so many White veterans after the war (Katznelson, 2005: Chapter 5).

Was this failure because of a lack of interest on the part of Blacks? This was hardly the case. Members of Congress from the South used their positions in powerful committees to protect the segregated economy of the South and ensure that no federal measures, such as Social Security, protections for union organization, or the GI Bill, would decrease the supply of cheap labor for household and agricultural labor. This was accomplished largely by ensuring that individual states operated the bureaucracy which implemented the programs. In the South, this meant that local agencies dedicated to maintaining a segregated economy and social order were firmly in control and could discourage Blacks from applying or delay consideration of their applications if they did. These approaches were carefully crafted so as to accomplish their ends without targeting minorities by name; instead they focused on other categories, such as occupational categories or types of schools (which were segregated), as being eligible or ineligible for the special programs (Katznelson, 2005: 122–129, 160–162). In short, the New Deal and GI Bill were deliberately structured by Congress to assist Whites and exclude Blacks.

The position of African-Americans in the USA in the 21st century still bears the scars of this long history of second-class citizenship. Over the years, dominant White America has been somewhat open to the entry of some groups whom they perceive to be "different" into their hallowed circles. Obviously, however, for many Whites, skin color fits into a different category. The Civil Rights Movement of the 1960s improved the status of Blacks somewhat, particularly in the elimination of legal discrimination and the laws against interracial marriage. Many of these gains, however, were eliminated by actions of Presidents Reagan, Bush, and Bush Jr. (Miller, 1992). The 21st century Black population is also more diverse; however, in addition to descendents from the slavery period, it also includes more recent immigrants from Africa, South America, and the Caribbean. Blacks also vary in culture depending upon whether they have remained in the Southern rural areas, moved to the Northern industrial areas, and so on (Black and Jackson, 2005; Billingsley, 1968).

Native Americans

There can be no better example of White Protestant attitudes and behavior toward people of color than their treatment of the natives they encountered when they first set foot on lands they chose to inhabit. When the English colonists first came to North America, it was already populated by at least a million natives; some suggest there may have been as many as 18 million. Although they were categorized together by the early Spanish explorers, the "Native Americans" actually included hundreds of independent groups or "tribes," with at least 300 different languages and distinctly different cultures and social structures (John, 1998; Sutton and Broken Nose, 2005; Tafoya and Vecchio, 2005).

Anxious to settle in lands already occupied by the Natives, the first Europeans systematically removed them from their ancestral lands, forcefully herding them into reservations, a pattern which continued until the mid-20th century. Even the most humane actions taken with regard to Native Americans were condescending, sending missionaries, both Protestant and Catholic, to separate them from their indigenous cultures and convert them to Christianity (Sutton and Broken Nose, 2005). Native American populations were decimated by European diseases. Children were removed from their families and placed with White families or in boarding schools. Native Americans were forbidden to follow their centuries-old religious and social practices or speak their historic languages. This destruction of their culture and social traditions resulted in astronomical rates of alcoholism and suicide; the health of Native Americans is one of the worst of all American groups (John, 1998; Sutton and Broken Nose, 2005; Tafoya and Vecchio, 2005; Hooyman and Kiyak, 2005: 544).

A similar process of domination also occurred when Europeans took over the Hawaiian Islands, beginning with Captain Cook's explorations in the late 1700s. It continued with the decimation of the Hawaiian population, the take over of Hawaiian lands, and the subsequent absorption of the Hawaiian Islands as part of the USA (Kanuha, 2005). Not being accepted in the White and Protestant category has been an excruciatingly difficult experience throughout American history.

Hispanics

Hispanics, also known as "Spanish-Americans," "Latin-Americans," or Latins/ Latinos/Latinas,[2] represent the fastest growing segment of the population in the USA. An important factor to be noted with regard to the Spanish-speaking populations is their internal diversity. Most Americans are aware of the Mexican and Puerto Rican immigrants; they are less aware, however, of the other segments of the Latino population, which includes Cubans, the Dominican Republic, and the various countries of Central and South America. What most of them have in common is their native Spanish language, which is shared by all except the Brazilians, whose mother tongue is Portuguese. Hispanics have generally exhibited extreme consciousness of their distinctive character and have exerted considerable effort to maintain a unified ethnic community. Most often these are *separate* communities, however. Mexicans, for example, have been known to refer to themselves as "la Raza" ("the race"), but to apply this term only to Mexicans, not other Latins (Garcia-Preto, 2005; Moore, 1970: 134). And Mexicans have been known to reject the term "Hispanic" (Ramirez, 1996).

Hispanics exhibit some of the characteristics of White immigrants, as well as some of those which have plagued Blacks. Like Blacks, many Hispanics exhibit a wide variety of skin colors; hence, they generally were subjected to the same or similar discrimination on the basis of skin color (Alba and Nee, 2003: 14). This presents a particular problem for these groups. Hispanics tend to be rather evenly divided between those who identify as "White" and those who do not; most of those who do not identify as "White" prefer to be identified as "other" (Alba and Nee, 2003: 277). This most likely is a reflection of the fact that the original Hispanic societies are characterized by a high level of interracial social contacts and marriage; consequently, they are less likely to think in terms of "Black" and "White" (Moore, 1970: 1–2, 112; Fitzpatrick, 1987: 194–195; Alba and Nee, 2003: 133). Hispanics tend to be Roman Catholic rather than Protestant, although some Protestant denominations

---

[2] Throughout this work, the terms "Latins," "Latino/Latina," "Spanish-American," and "Hispanic" will be used interchangeably.

have made inroads into the Catholic domination of the Hispanic population, both in the USA and their nations of origin. Like Polish and Italians before them, Hispanic Catholics are often uncomfortable with the dominant structure and culture of the Catholic Church in the USA (Jones, 2000; Fernandez, 2000).

Like Whites, most Hispanics have been part of a free rather than a forced migration. I say, "most," because some Hispanics – Puerto Ricans and the earliest Mexicans – became part of the USA as a result of an American takeover of their land. The original Mexicans in the USA were living in the Southwestern border states when the USA took over these areas by means of a variety of maneuvers; Puerto Ricans became part of the USA when their home island became a territory of the USA as a result of the Spanish-American War (Moore, 1970: 2–3, 11; Fitzpatrick, 1987: 29–30, 115; Alba and Nee, 2003: 184). However, for both Mexicans and Puerto Ricans, the migration to the USA throughout most of their history resembles that of White immigrants. Mexicans, for example, often migrate as families and remain together in close-knit enclaves; hence, long-existing social relationships can be maintained (Moore, 1970: 54–55).

Latin-American immigrants have also experienced the prejudice and discrimination which plagues every other new arrival. The degree of maltreatment varies with the area in which they live, with those living in areas with smaller populations of Hispanics faring somewhat better than Puerto Ricans in New York and Mexicans in various sections of the Southwest. They have been a particular target in recent years, as various states have introduced limits on providing education, medical care, and other services to undocumented aliens, and English-only laws have restricted Spanish language programs in schools and other public centers (Garcia-Preto, 2005; Fitzpatrick, 1987: 114–115; Moore, 1970: 132–133). Because both Hispanics and African-Americans have been the targets of extreme discrimination, there have been some efforts for the two populations to work together for their joint benefit; however, these efforts have also been marred by feelings of competition between the various groups (Fitzpatrick, 1987: 114–115).

Immigrants from Eastern and Southern Asian Countries

The Asian continent has contributed numerous immigrants from a wide variety of countries and cultures to the USA. These include immigrants from a wide variety of areas in the Far East and southern and southeast Asia. The countries from which they originate include China, Japan, Korea, Vietnam, India, Pakistan, Indonesia, and the Philippine Islands, to name but a few. Most Asians have settled in the western states, not surprising in view of the fact that these were the closest to their homeland, but substantial numbers can now be found in other states as well (Lee and Mock, 2005a).

The first Asians to come to this country in considerable numbers were the Chinese; they still rank as the largest Asian group in the USA. Discrimination against Asians in the USA has been widespread since the earliest arrivals. As noted earlier, one of the earliest acts of the US Congress was to limit citizenship to Whites, effectively preventing Asians from achieving citizenship (Alba and Nee, 2003: 168). Not only citizenship but also migration of Chinese was hampered for many years by discriminatory legislation. These included the Chinese Exclusion Act of 1882, which prohibited Chinese Americans from bringing family members to this country (Lee and Mock, 2005a, b; Shibusawa, 2005).

When Chinese laborers could no longer be recruited, their place was quickly taken by Japanese men, who came to the USA in the late 1800s and early 1900s. Most Japanese-Americans are descended from these early immigrants. Japanese were also the target of discrimination: they were prohibited from becoming citizens and from owning land. The internment of Japanese-Americans in World War II, many of them American-born, is an extreme example of discrimination against Asians, which caused many Japanese to lose their homes and businesses. In recent years, there have been efforts to make reparations for these losses, including a presidential apology as well as some financial payments. Negative reactions to these efforts have reminded Japanese-Americans that anti-Japanese sentiment it by no means dead (Shibusawa, 2005).

Filipinos are second to the Chinese in the number of Asian immigrants to America. They differ from most East Asians in that they are predominantly Roman Catholic. Filipinos also differ from other Asians in their highly multicultural heritage, which includes Spanish, Malayan, Indonesian, Muslim, and American influences, in contrast with the more unitary cultures of China, Japan, and other East Asian countries. Filipinos also come to the US with a higher level knowledge of the English language than other Asians (Root, 2005).

Other notable East Asian groups are the Koreans and Vietnamese. Most Koreans and Vietnamese are relatively recent immigrants. Although some came in the very early years of the 20th century, most came as a result of the turmoil caused in their respective nations as a result of the end of colonialism and World War II. Many Korean and Vietnamese came to the USA as war brides after the Korean and Vietnamese wars (Leung and Boehnlein, 2005; Kim and Ryu, 2005).

Although many Americans think of "Asian-Americans" as a single group, they are clearly a highly diverse population. The Asian nations are not unified. They speak different languages, their cultures are different, the various nations have often been at war with one another. In this country, they generally do not intermarry or identify with each other. Both Korea and Vietnam have lived under the domination of their larger neighbors, China and Japan, for extensive periods of time. This has resulted not only in some blending of their cultures, but also in a degree of animosity and resentment (Leung and Boehnlein, 2005; Kim and Ryu, 2005).

In spite of their different origins, Asians share many cultural dimensions. Most place enormous emphasis on the family and community, which take precedence over the individual. This can extend to the point of not allowing members to discuss their achievements lest they offend others. This often places them at odds with American social traditions of individualism. Most also share religious and philosophical traditions which stem from Buddhism, Confucianism, and Taoist teachings (Lee and Mock, 2005a; Shibusawa, 2005). Asians also place great emphasis on history and ancestors, often manifested in ancestor worship, which is often continued even among converts to Christian religions (Leung and Boehnlein, 2005).

Immigrants from southern Asia, including India, Pakistan, and Bangladesh, make up the final category of Asian immigrants to the USA. Residents of the Indian subcontinent represent a highly diverse population. For example, people in India vary in skin color from very light to very dark. They include adherents of a variety of religions, including Hindus, Muslims, Sikhs, and several denominations of Christians (Pillari, 2005). Pakistan is predominantly Muslim and was formed as a result of a desire on the part of Muslims to be independent of predominantly Hindu India (Nath, 2005). South Asians share the family-oriented patterns of Asians from the Far East (Almeida, 2005). Pakistanis, who follow the Muslim faith, have been primary targets of deportation since the World Trade Center attacks (Nath, 2005). These groups represent a growing minority in the USA.

Immigrants from the Middle East

Another group which has experienced considerable migration in recent years is the Middle East, whose residents have benefited from the changes in the immigration law during the 1960s (Massey, 1995). This is also a highly diverse population. While the vast majority of Middle Easterners are Muslim and speak the Arabic language, there are small numbers of Christians living in the area. Indeed, the earliest immigrants from Middle Eastern nations, who came in the late 19th and the earliest years of the 20th century, were Christians, mainly from what is now Lebanon and Iraq. Recent Middle Eastern immigrants have included more persons who follow the Muslim faith (Abudabbeh, 2005; Sengstock, 1999; Sengstock, 2005).

While most immigrants from the area speak the Arabic language, there are also distinct regional differences in language, and the ancestral language of some of the Christian groups is not Arabic. Physically, Middle Easterners tend to resemble other Mediterranean peoples, being somewhat darker skinned than Europeans. The various groups from the Middle East, particularly those of different religions, tend to remain separate from each other. Discrimination against these groups has been considerable, particularly in the wake of the September 11, 2001, attack on the World Trade Center (Shibusawa, 2005).

Conclusion

Since colonial times, the USA has been an immigrant nation. Every group except the American Indian has come to these shores from "somewhere else." In short, they were immigrants. Even the founding English Protestants had come from Europe, but being the original immigrants, they saw the new land as theirs, with the accompanying right to establish it according to the image they envisioned. Consequently, they viewed all subsequent newcomers in light of the likelihood that they would "fit" into the society they were developing.

Most of the earliest newcomers were Protestants like themselves, and many were also from the British Isles. As such they were more acceptable, but even these presented problems. Germans spoke a strange language, and Scots were not appropriately industrious and temperate in their manners and use of alcohol. The Catholic Irish were particularly undesirable and represented the first of the long succession of radically different immigrant groups: Jews, southern and eastern Europeans. Many of these would eventually merge to think of themselves and be thought of as "just White Americans." But this would occur only after a long and arduous process in which both sides were to resist the process of assimilation into a larger whole. Throughout this time, there were other groups, Native Americans, Blacks, and Asians, who were always placed in a different category because of their different skin color. As a result, all of these groups were subjected to extreme prejudice and discrimination.

Immigration changed dramatically as a result of the altered immigration laws in the 1960s. This has led to the current increase in the number of immigrants from quite different areas of the world: East Asia, the Indian subcontinent, the Middle East, Africa, and a very large number of Mexicans. These immigrants bring with them very diverse languages, religions, and cultures. This has led many to surmise that these new arrivals are so different as to be incapable of being assimilated.

However, the purpose for undertaking this extensive historical description is to illustrate the manner in which earlier immigrants were viewed. Although they are viewed today as part of the broader "White" population, at one time they also were viewed as "too different" to be capable of assimilation. This perception lasted for several decades after their arrival. Indeed, many were considered to be a different race than "White." It is in this context that the newer immigrant groups of today must be viewed.

In the next chapter, we will proceed to examine the character of the American population at the beginning of the 21st century. What is the nature of American multi-culturalism and diversity? What is the impact on the society at all levels: macro, meso, and micro? What has been the response of the White American population to this diversity? And how will this book attempt to extend our knowledge of interrelations among the varying groups in 21st century America?

Chapter 2
American Multi-culturalism in the 21st Century

Whether the dominant American population likes it or not, the nation has become more multi-cultural as a result of movements that occurred in the last three decades of the 20th century. Largely, this was a result of the Immigration Act of 1965, which restructured the quota system of immigration which existed since the 1920s (Alba and Nee, 2003: 8, 174). As noted in Chapter 1, the 1920s immigration laws established a pattern in which the majority of legal immigrants admitted to the USA would be from the same Western European nations who came prior to the great waves of migration in the early 20th century. It was deliberately designed to exclude immigrants who were "different" from the White Protestant mainstream, and to make it easier for newcomers to become part of the dominant society.

The 1965 Immigration Act eliminated the long-standing national quotas, allowing greater numbers of immigrants from continents other than Europe (Schuck, 2003: 85–86). This change has had profound impact on American immigration, and on the US demographic structure generally. Asian immigrants increased from 21,000 in 1965 to 93,000 just five years later. Dramatic increases also occurred in the number of residents from the West Indies, most of them Afro-Caribbean. Immigration from Africa also increased, though not so dramatically. For the first time, there was a limit on immigration from Mexico, due to the imposition of a quota on countries in the Western Hemisphere. However, this led to the dilemma of "documented" as opposed to "undocumented" immigrants from Mexico, which has plagued US immigration authorities ever since (Alba and Nee, 2003: 175–176).

After three decades, it is clear that the impact of the 1965 change has been dramatic. The US Census of 2000, for example, found that one in five Americans (approximately 20%) were foreign-born or the children of foreign-born parents. Because most new immigrants tend to concentrate in certain areas, rather than be randomly distributed across the country, migration has a disproportionate impact on the areas in which the immigrants settle. Areas of entry, such as ports (New York) and border states (Florida, Texas, California), tend to absorb larger numbers of arrivals (Alba and Nee, 2003: 8–9).

Using California as an example, Alba and Nee (2003: 9) illustrate the change in the makeup of the population. Hispanic and Asian populations showed the greatest growth, with the Hispanic population increasing by one-third, and the Asian population by over 40%, replacing African-Americans as the largest minority group.

M.C. Sengstock, *Voices of Diversity*, Clinical Sociology: Research and Practice,
DOI 10.1007/978-0-387-89666-3_2, © Springer Science+Business Media, LLC 2009

In 2000, non-Hispanic Whites were less than half of the population, as opposed to over 60% in previous decades. This pattern was even more dramatic in areas such as metropolitan Los Angeles, where the largest numbers of new immigrants tended to settle. With such dramatic changes, it is no exaggeration for Alba and Nee (2003) to point out that we are "remaking" the American mainstream.

Not only does the new immigration increase the percentage of the population which is non-White, it also introduces more diverse cultural perspectives, particularly language and religion. The increase in foreign language speakers has resulted in numerous programs at city, state, and federal levels to provide translations in public places, as well as classroom programs for children whose native language is not English (Bloomberg, 2006; Caribworldnews.com, 2008). The increased numbers of foreign language-speaking immigrants is particularly difficult for the American population to accept, since it portends the possibility that another language besides English may become a medium of daily discourse (Alba and Nee, 2003: 184; Doucet and Hamon, 2007).

Furthermore, the influx of large numbers of Asians presents a dizzying array of both languages and unfamiliar religions. Asian immigrants bring with them over 30 different primary languages, not to mention numerous regional dialects, as well as a myriad of different religious beliefs, including the teachings of Buddha, Confucius, and Taoism (Lee and Mock, 2005a: 270–271). The increasing numbers of immigrants from India bring Hindus and Muslims, whose unfamiliar beliefs generate numerous negative stereotypes in the minds of many Americans (Almeida, 2005). Both Asians and Indians also include a number of different denominations of Christians. For the average American, the familiar cultural patterns of old seem particularly threatened.

The Resurgence of White Identity and Superiority

As was indicated in the previous chapter, the resistance of White Americans to the arrival of foreigners on their shores is not new, but neither is it dead. Surveys from the 1990s showed that more Americans were open to persons of different cultures than was true in the past, but this support is tempered by convictions that there should be limitations on these groups, in particular, that certain parts of the dominant culture must be maintained and accepted by incoming groups (Alba and Nee, 2003: 141–143). Intense discrimination and prejudice still appear against groups who differ from the American mainstream, particularly if those groups exhibit physical or religious differences.

Indeed, there are some indications that the dominant White population is making a determined effort to reassert their position as the rightful dominant group in American society (McDermott and Samson, 2005). As Parillo (1994; 2000) has pointed out, some of the errors which characterized the Dillingham Commission in the early 20th century continue to be applied to the current groups of new immigrants a century later.

Observations are that the American population as a whole is becoming more conservative (Pinkney, 1993: 224–225). While recent research seems to show that people are less likely to be *openly* prejudiced, indications are they have simply become less overt about their racial attitudes and their discriminatory behavior (Quillian, 2006). In general, people are supportive of equal rights in theory but often not in specifics: when specific types of programs are described, they may not receive support, even in the face of previously stated liberal attitudes (Krysan, 2000). Often Whites who were not part of the original English Protestant group are some of the most strident supporters of this new Americanization movement. These include descendents of the early German and Scandinavian Protestants, and Roman Catholics from Ireland, Italy, or Poland. All of these were the targets of severe discrimination and prejudice upon their arrival. Yet their descendents today have become supporters of Americanization.

This should not be surprising. In their efforts to move ahead, many of these groups took pains to "prove" their "Whiteness" by differentiating themselves from Blacks (Alba and Nee, 2003: 132). Furthermore, today's descendents of White ethnics were not actually the targets of the discrimination; their grandparents or great grandparents were. Often they know nothing of these experiences, and probably do not believe it if they hear about it. If they do know about it, they may be more even anxious to support the Americanization programs. After working hard to get into the dominant White group and enjoy its privileges, why should they now have to watch these advantages disappear in an effort to assist newer arrivals?

Often the movement is not framed in discrimination terms. Rather it is framed in terms of defending traditional American culture. There are several manifestations of this effort, including resistance to immigration; the move to make English the official language; resistance to programs, such as affirmative action, that assist minorities; and the reassertion of Christian fundamentalism, often phrased in terms of a return to "traditional American values."

Resistance to Immigration

Since the passage of the 1965 immigration law, a number of actions have occurred to indicate that support for restrictions on migration are alive and well. Surveys illustrate that Americans are ambivalent about the entry of large numbers of newcomers. For example, the 1994 General Social Survey found that nearly three-fourths of the respondents expressed their discomfort with the increased numbers of immigrants entering the country, believing it might make it "harder to keep the country united" (Alba and Nee, 2003: 143).

It has been suggested that the framers of the original law did not anticipate its far-reaching impact. Because the law included provisions for family immigration, it was thought that the resulting migration would not alter the racial or ethnic makeup of the American population. However, the numbers of Asians who took advantage of the new provisions was far greater than expected. Furthermore, the 1965 law and a subsequent 1976 act both placed limitations on immigration from Western

Hemisphere countries, without recognizing the difficulty of managing immigration from Mexico, with its extended border and a large population desiring immigration (Alba and Nee, 2003: 176).

Indeed much of the opposition to immigration in recent years has focused on the waves of "illegal" or "undocumented" immigrants. Consequently, there is considerable discussion about the need to prevent illegal immigration and the need to secure US borders, particularly the border with Mexico, to prevent their entry (Krauthammer, 2006). This has taken the form of proposals in Congress to limit immigration, particularly of illegal or undocumented immigrants. Whenever such actions occur, considerable effort is exerted by members of both political parties to avoid offending either the opponents of immigration or those who support it (Kiely, 2006).

While the federal government assures the nation that their highest priority is to ensure that unauthorized persons do not enter the USA, efforts to ensure that this is the case has not been persuasive (US Customs and Border Protection, 2006). Consequently, many states have expressed annoyance with the federal government for not preventing illegal immigrants from entering the USA; some state governments and individuals have attempted to take matters into their own hands and introduce their own efforts to prevent border crossings. In these efforts, immigrants who lack proper documentation are sometimes referred to by means of various euphemisms, such as "human trafficking." Not surprisingly, these states are primarily located along the Mexican border (Invasion USA, 2005; Democracy Now, 2005; Lucas, 2005; Brezosky, 2007; Robbins, 2007; Gazelem, 2007).

Opposition to immigration has also manifested itself in resistance to provide public services to illegal immigrants. The most obvious of these was Proposition 187, passed by the state of California in 1994 (Lucas, 2005; Mailman, 1995). This law, much of which was subsequently found to be unconstitutional, declared illegal aliens ineligible for any state services, such as health care, education, and social services. Unfortunately, actions directed against illegal immigrants rarely are limited solely to this group. Since it is often difficult to distinguish between legal and illegal immigrants, the actions often attack both groups indiscriminately. Anti-immigration efforts have not gone unnoticed by immigrant groups, who are well aware of the negative sentiments aimed in their direction. A poll of legal immigrants found that two-third of respondents perceived sentiments against immigrants were increasing in the USA today; a majority felt these sentiments were having a deleterious effect on them and their families (Bendixen and Associates, 2006).

English Language Movement

A major dimension of this sentiment to maintain cultural unity is the insistence on the use of English. Public opinion surveys throughout the last quarter of the 20th century consistently show that there is strong support for encouraging, or even forcing, immigrants and their children to learn English, and to learn it as quickly as possible, though this does not usually appear as strong as it has been at some periods in the past (Boulet, 2001). For example, in a 1994 study, nearly half of the respondents believed that classes in the students' native language should be allowed only for a few years, until they were able to learn English. Over one-third of the sample rejected any use of languages other than English in schools (Alba and Nee, 2003: 142–143).

This sentiment regarding the importance of English as the dominant American cultural language is manifested by the strong movement to establish English as the official language of the USA. This movement has resulted in efforts to eliminate bilingual programs in schools, as well as to prevent the use of other languages in public places, such as businesses or hospitals. Several states (California, Massachusetts, and Arizona) have already passed "English Only" requirements for schools. This movement now even extends to the need for immigrants to reduce or eliminate any "accent," so that their speech sounds more like Americans; proponents suggest this will make them successful in business and more comfortable in their social contacts (ARI, 2008; ELT, 2008; Luongo, 2007; Swift, 2007). (Periodic updates on the success of the various federal and state legislative efforts to pass English language requirements can be found at English First, 2007; US English, 2005.)

Although it has not been described as a program to establish English as the official language, portions of the federal "No Child Left Behind Act" of 2001 had the same effect. By imposing corrective actions on schools which failed to meet certain overall standards, these requirements represent near-insurmountable barriers for schools with large programs teaching English as a second language (Crawford, 2006). The reluctance to permit schools to teach classes in the students' native languages is considered unfortunate by linguistic experts, who contend that the children's education, including their eventual fluency in English, is furthered by offering classes in their native tongue in their early years in this country (Crawford, 2004a, b; 2006; 2007).

Resistance to Affirmative Action

Perhaps no area is more indicative of Whites' resistance to the assimilation of Blacks into society as a whole than the continued opposition to the so-called affirmative action. Affirmative action consists of the maintenance, especially by government agencies, of specific policies or programs designed to ensure that minorities are accorded certain rights. Included are programs which require that colleges and universities ensure that members of the targeted minorities are assured of a certain number of admissions, or requirements that government contractors take specific measures that guarantee that a specific number of jobs or subcontracts go to minorities (Alba and Nee, 2003: 57, 155).

The assumption underlying affirmative action is that minorities have been prevented from achieving to the level of their ability in the past and that the resulting disadvantage is cumulative (DiPrete and Eirich, 2006). Upper and middle class Whites are born into families which have both financial and social resources allowing them to provide their children with opportunities that minority families lack;

consequently, the disadvantage for members of minority groups accumulates with each successive generation.

Affirmative action programs go back several years, as does opposition to them. Through the 1960s and 1970s, several programs were developed, and courts supported them. In 1978, the Supreme Court considered the case of *Regents of the University of California v. Bakke*. By a slim 5–4 majority, the court agreed that the use of quotas for admission had violated Mr. Bakke's rights, and he was entitled to admission; however, at the same time, the Court declared that decisions using race as a factor could be employed appropriately if done properly (Katznelson, 2005: 152–153; Pinkney, 1993: 223). In retrospect, the *Bakke* case might be seen as a sort of watershed for affirmative action programs in education, showing as it did how closely divided the Court was, as well as its willingness to consider limitations on affirmative action programs.

Research has shown that, over the years, the population as a whole has become more accepting of diversity in principle. With reference to specific programs such as those mentioned above, it is also clear "…that whites have been much more reluctant to accept many state interventions to enforce racial equality, especially where these might interfere with what they see as their own rights…" (Alba and Nee, 2003: 57). For example, many Americans express opposition to the use of racial or ethnic categories in a variety of situations which the surveys mention, affirmative action programs being one such option (Alba and Nee, 2003: 143). There is also a common belief on the part of Whites that discrimination against Blacks has decreased to the point that no further action to combat it is necessary (Katznelson, 2005: 167). Opponents often frame their opposition in terms of an unfair favoring of minorities over poor Whites, who often have equally disadvantaged backgrounds. This opposition has advanced to the point that one study suggests that affirmative action is "under siege" (Alba and Nee, 2003: 155).

The resistance to affirmative action can be seen not only in surveys but in political and legal actions. Shortly after the *Bakke* decision, many of the programs going back to the New Deal, the Civil Rights Act of 1964, and the Voting Rights Act of 1965 were reduced or dismantled during the Reagan administration. States were informed that the Reagan administration sought to overturn existing affirmative action programs in employment programs. These policies were continued by the first Bush administration (Pinkney, 1993: 221).

Affirmative action in higher education has been a particular target. In 1995, the Board of Regents of the California system of higher education eliminated programs requiring the inclusion of minorities in admissions decisions. The next year, the University of Texas Law School's admissions policy giving preference to Blacks was ruled unconstitutional in the *Hapwood* decision (Alba and Nee, 2005: 155). More recently, the Supreme Court's rulings in cases involving the University of Michigan, *Grutter v. Bollinger* and *Gratz v. Bollinger*, have exhibited mixed support for affirmative action. In summary, the Court seems to be saying, by narrow margins, that programs encouraging the inclusion of minorities are legitimate, but numerical formulae are not. Seeing this opposition on the part of both the courts and the public, politicians at the national level and in several states have responded by catering to the negative public opinion and developing laws against affirmative action (Katznelson, 2005: 167).

Since many of these programs focus on providing opportunity for persons who have not had such advantages before, they often place the minority applicants in opposition to Whites who may themselves lack previous advantages. It is not surprising then that Whites may see these programs as a treat to their long-standing beliefs in White superiority and resist the outcomes they represent (Winant, 2000: 179). Indeed, opponents have been extremely effective in developing their arguments and defending their opposition in the language of the Constitution. In defending their position, opponents of affirmative action use the language of the 14th Amendment itself, since it guarantees "equal protection of the laws" and forbids the government from violating an individual's rights without due process (Katznelson, 2005: 153). Clearly, this argument cuts both ways: if Blacks are guaranteed equal protection of the laws, then so are Whites, and actions to assist Blacks cannot be conducted in such a manner as to violate the rights of those Whites who are also in contention for the same competitive situations.

To summarize, Katznelson (2005: 153–154) points out that all government programs and policies are based on distinctions between categories of people. Certain categories of taxpayers are given advantages over others, for example, or some industries receive trade advantages which others lack. In the case of affirmative action, however, it is a racial group which is singled out for social treatment. And the American public is clearly divided over the question of whether this kind of distinction is appropriate. They are also clearly uncomfortable with the problem of reconciling the rights of minorities as a category with the rights of specific individuals. In short, is it appropriate to impose disadvantages on some individual Whites today in order to remedy the harm done to specific groups in the past? As the late Justice Thurgood Marshall once pointed out, in reference to the *Bakke* decision, "It is more than a little ironic that, after several hundred years of class-based discrimination against Negroes, the Court is unwilling to hold that a class-based remedy for that discrimination is permissible" (quoted in Katznelson, 2005: 154). Katznelson (2005: 167) concludes that affirmative action is "legally and politically insecure." And the security of White privilege is likely to be maintained.

Reassertion of Christian Fundamentalism

For White Protestants, the disturbing changes in American society are more than simply changes in the color of its residents. In the influx of new immigrants and the increase of people of color, they see a threat to their whole familiar way of life: their conservative Protestant theology, their religious beliefs, and their conservative moral traditions. If the early Scots and Irish immigrants, with their poor work ethic and tendency to imbibe, seemed strange, how much more strange must the religious traditions of India and East Asia appear? It is not surprising, therefore, that the movements to reassert the traditional Protestant values have developed at this point in time.

Analysts of religious fundamentalism have suggested that the social changes have developed as the world has become more "modern." With the industrial revolution also came a revolution in the social order. No longer were people spending most of their lives in close connection with their families and others like themselves, as Durkheim and Marx both pointed out. The development of the industrial economy divided social relationships into separate spheres (Bruce, 2000; Emerson and Hartman, 2006). No longer did individuals spend their working hours with their families and neighbors. Instead, they went off to factories where they encountered people very different from themselves. Sometimes these were located miles away, and they were separated from the familiar social environment for days, weeks, or even months.

As Emerson and Hartman (2006: 129) point out, "Social life would no longer be a cohesive whole. . . ." People found their lives divided into separate spheres. In the home sphere, they were surrounded by family, friends, and neighbors, who shared the familiar traditions and values they had received from their parents and grandparents. In the work setting, however, for the first time people encountered people radically different from themselves: people with different religions and values, as well as languages and skin colors.

Under these conditions, the role of religion in social life becomes dramatically altered. With so many different religious perspectives coming into contact, the industrial modern world changes the manner in which social life is regulated. In place of divinely proclaimed rules of behavior, modern industrial societies impose empirically derived rules and laws, as Max Weber pointed out (Emerson and Hartman, 2006: 129). In effect, the role of the divine disappears. The impact this has upon the role of religion in society is dramatic. In a unitary society, the common religion provides a set of shared concepts about the appropriate way in which the members of the society are to relate to each other, as well as the manner in which the society as a whole interacts with the Divine. As Emile Durkheim conceived of religion, these shared beliefs and expectations serve as a unifying factor for society as a whole, or what Peter Berger called a "sacred canopy" which protects the whole of social life (Berger, 1967; Emerson and Hartman, 2006: 129–130).

The modern world brings with it a plurality of religions, as opposed to a single society-wide religion, and this powerful unifying role of religion is lost. People increasingly are governed by the laws of society, rather than divinely determined commandments, and the role of the divine in social behavior is diminished, if not eliminated. Religion also loses its ability to unite society, since the members no longer share the same religious ideology and rituals. In short, religion is reduced to the level of individual beliefs. And religion, once the overarching institution in society, is reduced to the level of being just one of the many spheres into which social life is divided (Berger, 1967; Smith, 1998; Emerson and Hartman, 2006: 129–130).

What impact does this religious pluralism have on religion itself? Of course, this depends on one's perspective. Some have suggested that religion beliefs and practice become stronger in societies under pluralism (Finke and Stark, 1992); other evidence raises questions about this contention (Olson, 1998; Chaves and

Gorski, 2001). It is clear, however, that this whole process "...squeezes out religious influences from many ... spheres and greatly reduces religion's role in the others" (Emerson and Hartman, 2006: 130). Seeing religion thus removed from many spheres of life has an immense impact on religious leaders and on persons who are very religious. They decry the loss of religious influence in social life; they demand a return to a communal belief in the divine and a restoration of religious values and rules to the control of social behavior. Thus, religious fundamentalism is basically a militant reaction to the decrease in the importance of religion in society (Almond et al., 1995; Bruce, 2000; Emerson and Hartman, 2006).

Why the term, "fundamental"? The term apparently comes from a series of pamphlets published in the early decades of the 20th century, in which conservative religious leaders delineated a series of "nonnegotiable" aspects of the Protestant faith. At the time, the major audience of the conservative religious leaders was not members of other religions, such as Catholics, Jews, Muslims, or the nonreligious. It was other Protestants whom they felt were diverging too far from the true Christian message (Emerson and Hartman, 2006: 132).

What are the characteristics of fundamentalist religion? Research has shown that fundamentalism across a variety of religious traditions tends to share several patterns of ideology and organization. Ideologically, fundamentalists tend to do the following: view the world as good versus evil, react vigorously to the marginal character of religion in modern society, have specific traditions or texts that are considered to be divinely inspired and inerrant, select out certain aspects of society for particular concern, and perceive human society as having a specific divinely ordained end (the Millennium). Organizational characteristics include a select membership; clear boundaries *vis-a-vis* the rest of society; a clearly defined leader, often charismatic, who is often viewed as being specially chosen or gifted; and specific behavioral requirements for members, such as dress, sexual behavior, drinking, family patterns, and so on (Emerson and Hartman, 2006: 134).

In the USA, Fundamentalist Protestants share to a considerable degree all of these characteristics. They see themselves as defending the good and the modern world as evil. The Bible is the inspired world of God and must be accepted as the literal Truth. Critical matters to be emphasized include the emphasis on the patriarchal family with clearly defined roles for men and women; closely related is their intense opposition to abortion and homosexuality. Religion is always preferred over science, as evidenced in the desire to replace the scientific study of evolution with the teaching of creationism. Fundamentalists draw a clear distinction between themselves as the elect and the rest of the world as the damned and look forward to the "Rapture" as the arrival of the Millennium (Emerson and Hartman, 2006: 135). In recent years, the Fundamentalists have increasingly sought to restore their version of religion to what they consider to be its proper place in the social order, resulting in the emergence of all of the above issues onto the American political scene.

Of course, the restoration of religion requires a factor which is simply *not* present in a multi-cultural society: a unitary religion. How can the beliefs and values of religion become the unifying principle of a society, when the members of that society hold so many varying religious beliefs? This question is answered very simply by

Fundamentalist Protestants: since their traditions were the founding traditions of American society and since persons who identify at least nominally as "Christians" constitute a substantial proportion of the US population, clearly the unifying religion should be Christian.

There are, however, two major difficulties with this position. The most obvious problem is the increasing presence within the nation of non-Christians, including Jews, Muslims, and Asian religions, not to mention persons who have no religion at all. Less obvious but equally important is the undeniable fact that the single unifying factor for many American Christians is the title. Beyond that, they agree on little else. What the Fundamentalists consider "fundamental" is not accepted by many of their fellow citizens, even those who claim the title, "Christian" (Myers and Scanzoni, 2005). Conversely, Fundamentalists themselves would deny the right to be called "Christian" to persons who reject their views on the fundamentals. With this absence of common traditions and beliefs, establishing a common religion would serve little more than a nominal purpose. It certainly would not constitute the overriding unifying factor or the "sacred canopy" that Durkheim and Berger envisioned.

The Future of America as a Multi-cultural Society: Is Assimilation Possible?

Where does this leave us? For better or for worse we are a multi-cultural society. Many – perhaps most – Americans may wish it to be otherwise. But the die has already been cast. Over 80% of the immigrants of the last two decades of the 20th century trace their origins to places other than the traditional European nations which formerly contributed to the American population (Farley, 1996: 162). Many of these newcomers are non-White and practice religions at variance from the previous US population. The diversity of ethnic groups represented in the 2000 census "...has made the USA arguably the most ethnically diverse country on the planet" (Alba and Nee, 2003: 214). However, they also point out that assimilation can occur even with physical differences, as has been shown with the Asian population (Alba and Nee, 2003: 131).

Americans can pressure Congress and the executive branch to impose restrictions on immigration. We can dismantle affirmative action programs that provide special advantages to minorities. We can insist on use of the English language and force schools to eliminate English-as-a-second-language programs. Religious leaders can use their political influence to develop laws based on fundamentalist Christian tenets, as opponents are concerned that they will (Boston, 2006). For all these reasons, some assert that today's immigrants are not capable of being assimilated (Alba and Nee, 2003: 125)

This will not change the situation, however. Indeed, some of these activities listed above are already in place. Affirmative action is already being reduced, for example. And we do not need English-Only policies to induce immigrants to learn English; within two or three generations, most newcomers become fluent in the English language (Alba and Nee, 2003: 218). Fundamentalist religious leaders can attempt to impose their views on large-scale social policies. However, in the long run, none of these measures will make the diversity of cultures go away. Short of imposing capital punishment or deportation on anyone who disagrees with the dominant views – ideas which probably sound appealing to many – there is no way people can be forced to adopt any particular cultural pattern. After all, not all dissidents are new immigrants or minorities! Many of them are citizens and voters and have been so for several generations!

So, America is becoming multi-cultural: more diverse in race, national origin, language, and religion. What is its future? Is the concern about our becoming a hopelessly divided society a valid one? Is there no way to bring us together? The major premise of this work is the contention that the diversity of today is not *essentially* different from the diversity of the past. The types of immigrants coming today may *look* very different from the immigrants of the past. Their languages may seem stranger – they may use a different alphabet or be written right-to-left instead of left-to-right. They may bring religious beliefs and traditions that vary greatly from the Judeo-Christian tradition. However, as was shown in Chapter 1, the immigrants of the past looked equally strange to the Americans of their time. Yet over time, these groups, for the most part, assimilated into the dominant society and became a part of it – to the point that some have become among the staunchest supporters of "traditional American values" today.

So the "American mainstream" is already being "remade," as Alba and Nee (2003: Chapter 6) suggest. Their macro- and meso-level analysis examines several measures of assimilation, including adoption of the English language; "transnationalism," entry into the economic structure; advancement in education; broad spatial distribution across the country; and entry into social relations with the dominant society. Perhaps the strongest example of ethnic acculturation is use of the English language, with the best measure being language use in the home. Anyone who has contact with immigrant families has noticed the common ethnic language pattern, in which the immigrants speak to their children in the ethnic language, and the children respond in English. Hence, immigrant homes tend to be bilingual. In the second generation, however, more than half report they use English exclusively at home. Using English proficiency as the measure, most new ethnic groups are "acculturated," in that they use English rather quickly.

English language use is usually of greatest concern with the Mexican population, because they are such a large group, and their homeland is so close, making language maintenance easy. Consequently, many Americans are concerned that Spanish may become the dominant language in portions of the USA along the Mexican border. Even with this group, however, over one-third of the American-born report using English exclusively at home. Even if one looks only at Mexican-Americans in the border areas, there is little evidence that Spanish is supplanting English. These young people may become bilingual, but their proficiency in English is not diminished by that fact.

Perhaps, the most dramatic difference between today's immigrants and those of previous eras is the issue of "trans-nationalism." This refers to the interaction between immigrants and the homeland from which they come. Immigrant groups have always exhibited a considerable degree of trans-nationalism. Many of the great wave of immigrants in the late 19th and early 20th centuries maintained a considerable degree of contact with their homelands. Some came to the USA expecting to return home after making a fortune, which a few of them did. Even larger numbers sent money back to their families and villages (Alba and Nee, 2003: 145 ff.). The process of "chain migration" was also a major source of contact with the country or origin, as early immigrants, usually men, returned to their homeland to choose a bride from among their townspeople (Sengstock, 1999; 2005).

However, many authorities consider trans-nationalism today to be considerably different from that of the past. A century ago, travel to the homeland was by steamship and took weeks at best. Communication was only by letter, which also traveled by the same laborious method. Both letters and personal visits were necessarily infrequent. Advances in the communication and transportation industries have dramatically altered this pattern. Email and cell phones keep immigrants in daily contact with relatives in the homeland. And visits all over the world can literally take place over a weekend. Interviewing in Detroit's Middle Eastern community during the 1991 Gulf War provided a stark example of this intimate contact, as respondents would interrupt the interview to follow the ongoing events, often before they were seen on American television (Sengstock, 2005). Such contact is likely to cause the immigrant communities to retain closer ties to their homelands than was feasible in the past.

With regard to the remaining areas, Alba and Nee (2003: 246) find that there is no clear evidence as yet that recent immigrants are moving ahead rapidly. They believe there is cause for "cautious optimism," however. All of these are areas in which it is difficult to measure advancement in the short period of one or two generations. It takes considerable time for groups to gain education, move into the economic structure, and disperse throughout the society, as was true with ethnic groups in the past. Overall, a cautious conclusion is that more time is needed in order to evaluate the success of assimilation in most areas. How does this process occur? A major factor is related to the "multi-linear" nature of acculturation. That is, immigrants frequently add elements of the new culture without giving up their own cultural patterns, as Gibson (1988) pointed out in a study of Sikh high-school students. This is not unique to the current immigrant groups, but was characteristic of immigrants in the past as well.

The picture at this point is unclear, but evidence suggests that assimilation has already begun and will occur with the current population of immigrants, just as it did with the immigrants of the past. As Alba and Nee (2003: Chapter 6, 218 ff.) point out, the impetus to maintain ties with the country of origin comes from the immigrant generation, while their children and grandchildren prefer to think and behave as Americans. For them, their parents' and grandparents' national origins are at most a matter of mild historical interest. As was true in the past, today's immigrants will eventually lose the ability to control their children's assimilation.

Assimilation on the Micro-level

The preceding analysis has focused on macro- and meso-issues. *Macro*-issues analyze the level of society. Problems on this level would examine the manner in which
the entire society is organized. For example, what is the political structure? How
are new ethnic groups included in it? When Alba and Nee (2003) ask how new ethnic groups fit into the economic structure or how they are distributed geographically
across the country, they are asking questions at this level. The *meso*-level moves one
step down. It focuses on the makeup of major social organizations and institutions,
such as the economy and economic institutions, or the educational institution and
its component schools and colleges. Studies which examine the differential participation of children from different ethnic groups in specific schools in a community
or the hiring practices of corporations are looking at meso-level data. Most research
on ethnic group relations have been on one of these two levels.

While these are important analyses, they do not provide insight into an equally
important dimension of social relations: the *micro*-level. Analysis at this level
focuses on the manner in which individual members relate to others who are not
a part of their own segment of society. For example, in each of the situations mentioned above, if members of different ethnic groups are working or going to school
together, these individuals must interact with members of different ethnic groups to
a greater or lesser degree. How does this occur? How often? What is the nature of
their interactions? Do individual Whites relate to Blacks or Asians differently from
the manner in which members of each group relate among themselves? These analyses would focus on issues such as the amount of interaction the participants have,
the kinds of issues they discuss, the degree to which they exercise an influence on
each other, and so on. A particularly important dimension would involve what we
might call the "tone" of the interaction: are their contacts formal or informal? Are
they polite and pleasant or nasty and rude? Do participants from both sides of the
ethnic barrier see them in the same way? While macro- and meso-analyses are valuable and necessary, the picture will not be complete until we analyze the individual
interactions which constitute the micro-level as well.

Perhaps the lack of attention to such issues is based on the assumption that
inclusion in these types of social relationships does not occur until the process
of inclusion is nearly complete, as (Gordon, 1964) suggested. However, at some
point, there must be individual contacts between individual persons from different
groups. If immigrant children are to attend school or college, at some point they
must encounter persons from groups other than their own. What happens? Similar
questions could be asked with encounters in the world of work, political gatherings,
or neighborhood meetings. As Gordon (1964) pointed out, if assimilation is really
going to occur, minority groups must eventually become part of the intimate social
structure of society: small face-to-face social groups and ultimately, marriage. What
I am suggesting here is that studies of assimilation must begin to analyze in some
detail the manner in which members of ethnic groups interact across ethnic lines

and that an analysis of families made up of people from different ethnic groups is a good place to start.

Multi-cultural Families as a Micro-analysis of Assimilation

Decades ago, Gordon (1964: 80) suggested that marriage was the ultimate evidence of assimilation. It was assumed that once persons from a different ethnic group were accepted into the informal social groups of the dominant group – the play groups of children, the cliques of high school, the college fraternities and sororities, and the informal social clubs of adults – it was inevitable that members of these groups would begin to view each other as potential mates. Once intermarriage had occurred, he believed it inevitable that the individuals' sense of identification with their original groups would cease and the original groups would be indistinguishable. Once the acceptance of members of a different group as appropriate partners in a relationship as intimate as marriage occurs their acceptance into all levels of social structure could be assumed. Gordon's view is echoed by Alba and Nee (2003: 90–91, 283–284).

Some questions might be raised as to the inevitability of this process. For example, one might imagine two groups of quite unequal status in which the lower status women are accepted, perhaps even preferred, as marital partners for the men in the higher status group. However, their role in the marriage might be simply to provide servile work and children, who would become members of the fathers' group, with the mothers' group being largely ignored. In general, however, particularly in societies where marital choice is a relatively free act on the part of both parties, Gordon's view is probably correct. Marriage between members of different ethnic backgrounds can be a mark of a high degree of interethnic assimilation, at least for the individuals participating in the marriage.

It should also follow that studies of the families founded by such couples can be equally valuable as examples of what actually does happen when assimilation at that level occurs. One might, for example, examine the claims of Gordon and of Alba and Nee concerning the manner in which members of these families view each other and their group identities. Hence, Gordon suggested that an assimilated individual's sense of identity would change to fit the new social group affiliation. With a spouse and perhaps also children, who are not part of the group to which the parent she originally belonged, the assumption seems to be that the parent would no longer identify in that manner either. Similarly, their children would assume a new identity as well. In any event, the presumption is that the separate identities of the original partners would disappear. There is little research, however, to indicate whether this is what actually happens.

In-depth analyses of intermarried couples are relatively few, but a few studies have made some suggestions concerning this issue. The most common approach assumes the "Triple Melting Pot Theory" introduced decades ago by Kennedy (1944), which asserted that assimilation in the USA tended to follow a pattern which followed religious boundaries. Hence, Protestants who married outside their denominations tended to marry other Protestants; intermarriage among Catholics usually implied marriage within the Catholic religion but to persons from different nationalities; and when Jews intermarried, they chose persons from different national origin or divisions within Judaism.

Many such studies simply assert the fact of intermarriage as evidence of assimilation, although some assert the likely consequences, such as the increase in mixed ancestry and the consequent reduction in the likelihood of identification with the ethnic group (Alba and Nee, 2003: 94). Several studies make brief references to the fact that their generalizations cannot apply to all members of the group because some no longer participate or identify with the community. For example, Squiers and Quadagno (1998: 111), studying the Italian family, comment that marital homogeneity among Italian-Americans has decreased. Lopata (1998) points out that many second- and third-generation Polish-Americans change their names, no longer identify as Polish, and are lost to the Polish community.

Only studies of Jewish-Americans seem to analyze the issue in more detail, describing varying patterns of family life for Jews. In contrast with homogeneously Jewish couples, the authors observed two categories of intermarried couples. When the non-Jewish partner converted, the couple tended to adopt Jewish traditions, though often at a somewhat lower level than homogeneous couples. In other instances, the intermarried couples adopt aspects of both traditions (such as having both a Christmas tree and a Passover meal) or give up such religious traditions altogether (Farber et al., 1998: 440).

Waters' study (1990) goes into greater depth in this area than most. She was particularly interested in the manner in which the respondents identified themselves in response to the national ancestry question on the US Census. She interviewed Catholics who lived in ethnically mixed areas, the suburbs of San Jose, California, and Philadelphia, Pennsylvania. Hence, they were likely to be somewhat assimilated, nearly half having mixed national origins; and she could control for the influences of race and religion. She found that the respondents exercised a considerable degree of choice in their chosen identification. Some persons of mixed ancestry listed several identities; others identified with a single origin, and the reasons for the choice varied greatly, from being the one with the most numerous ancestors to being told they "looked like" that nationality or having a particular preference for that group, or many other options. This research raises questions concerning the presumed assumption that individuals in ethnically mixed families necessarily give up ties to their original ethnic identities. While some may identify with a more general category, such as "White" or "Catholic," others may choose to identify with one of the original ethnic groups, and still others may claim several of their ethnic ties.

What is missing from the literature is an analysis of the process by which the individual makes these choices. As George Herbert Mead (1934) told us, the individual's view of him or herself is a social product, influenced by the manner in which we are treated by others. Hence, one of the reasons why young people within an ethnic group identify as they do is the fact that they are reminded of their group membership at every turn. A child of Italian immigrant parents, for example, is frequently told by his/her parents to be proud of their Italian ancestry. Extended family members may also remind them of their Italian origins. Even outsiders may reinforce this view by noting that they look or act "Italian." These reminders may be positive, negative, or a mixture of both; either way, the individual cannot escape the message that this is the group to which they belong.

With persons of mixed ancestry, the process is more complicated. In what way does such a person decide how to answer the survey's identification questions? Persons who are half Italian and half Polish, for example, are likely to be told by one parent that they are Polish and by the other that they are Italian. The same mixed messages occur when they encounter members of their extended families or outsiders. How do they decide which to accept? Initial responses suggest that physical appearance or surname are possible answers, but the process, as Waters (1990) suggests, is likely to be much more complicated.

For example, Howard (2000) suggests that some people are more likely to make fine distinctions concerning their own ethnic identity, but hold more generalized assumptions about the identities of others. Thus, many persons of "Hispanic" origin do not like the generic identification of "Hispanic." Instead, they prefer to be identified with their own subgroup (Cuban, or Mexican, or Salvadorian, for example). When speaking of persons from *other* Spanish-speaking groups, however, they tend to use the more general "Hispanic" categorization. Similar patterns may be found among Blacks, Whites, and other ethnic groups. Howard also notes that people have many different identities, such as age, gender, or class, and that these play a role in self-identification in addition to ethnic origin.

Finally, it is possible that some may actually choose a more general identification of "mixed," as was exemplified by a student in my ethnic studies class some years ago. This young woman came from a family which included persons from a variety of Black, White, and Native American backgrounds. She deeply resented being forced at many turns to identify herself by a single ethnic choice, feeling that any such choice forced her to reject one of her many valued personal identities. In a society which valued being "Black and proud," or "Hispanic and proud," or "Jewish and proud," she was frustrated by the fact that she could not be "mixed and proud" (Sengstock, 1999: 221).

Her frustration has received considerable attention in recent years due to the attention focused on prominent multi-cultural individuals. First was the athlete Tiger Woods, the golf superstar with African-American, American-Indian, Chinese, Thai, and Caucasian ancestry. Like my student, he refused to accept a single identity, inventing the term "Cablinasian" to refer to his multiple heritage and being the target of criticism by some Blacks for rejecting his blackness (Gaskins, 1999: 4). Indeed, it has been suggested that Tiger Wood's refusal to allow himself to be forced into a single racial category did much to establish the legitimacy of the use of a mixed racial identity (Rockquemore and Laszloffy, 2005: 1–2).

Most recently, multi-culturalism and multi-racialism has gained even more attention from the election of America's 44th President, Barack Obama, who was born in Hawaii of a White mother from Kansas and a father from Kenya. His anthropologist mother made him keenly aware of cultural diversity (Behar, 2008). He also lived for several years with his stepfather in Indonesia, before returning to Hawaii to live with his maternal grandparents (Obama, 1995). It is difficult to find a more dramatic multi-cultural and multi-racial experience than that of President Obama.

Research on Persons from Mixed Racial Backgrounds

In the past, social scientists have largely ignored the circumstances of ethnically mixed individuals and the process by which they define who they are. Only recently, with the growth in the number of multi-*racial* (as opposed to multi-*cultural*) individuals, has this topic received attention. This should not be surprising, given the recent growth in numbers of non-Whites due to immigration as well as the extreme emphasis on racial background in the USA. In such a setting, we would expect multi-racial individuals to be more likely to raise this issue than multi-cultural persons. Hence, recent research has focused on studies of multi-*racial* respondents, rather than examining the issue in broader cultural terms (Root, 1992; 1996; Rockquemore and Laszloffy, 2005).

The US Census now allows respondents to classify themselves in more than one racial category. In the Census Bureau's 2006, American Community Survey, 2.1% of the American population exercised this option. The percent of mixed race individuals was highest in Hawaii (21.5%), followed by Alaska (8.1%), Oklahoma (6.1%), Washington and California (3.3% each), and Nevada and New Mexico (3.2% each), and Oregon (3%). In all other states, less than 3% claimed a mixed racial heritage (US Census Bureau, 2006).

The lack of attention to persons who breach intergroup boundaries, whether by race or by culture, should not be taken as an indication of the degree of importance of the issue – both now and in the past. As we have previously indicated, the USA is a society in which ethnic divisions are extremely important and have been so for most of its history. People are reminded at every turn of the importance of ethnic identity. When children are registered for school, the forms invariably ask the parents to check a box indicating the child's race. Forms often ask for religious preference. Children hear different languages and learn about people from different countries. They meet other children at school or in their neighborhoods who have different ethnic origins than their own. Sometimes their own ethnic or racial origins are questioned or even demeaned.

In such settings, it is impossible for children not to become aware of ethnic and racial differences at a fairly young age. Inevitably, they must ask questions about their own origins. How do parents who come from different race and ethnic backgrounds define these origins to their children? How do the children process this information? How is this information used to develop the child's sense of "who I am"? In particular, it is important to place these issues in historical perspective. How do the experiences of today's "ethnically different" children compare to the "ethnically different" children of past generations? It is difficult to believe that their experiences are unique, given the fact that past eras also had their ethnic divisions and animosities, some of them even defined in "racial" terms, as we have shown.

What lessons can be learned from the experiences of the past that can help deal with the difficulties of today's multi-cultural individuals?

A major problem with our knowledge of multi-racial people is the fact that they are not included in major research studies. Their relatively small numbers ensure that they will not appear in large surveys. Furthermore, most research does not allow mixed race or mixed ethnic people the option of identifying themselves in this manner. The US Census long resisted the inclusion of mixed race options, even to the point of requiring a personal visit by a census taker when a "mixed race" response was submitted (Root, 1992b: 9; Thornton, 1992: 323; Fernandez, 1996: 26). Furthermore, prior to the mid-1980s, social scientists accepted the "one-drop" rule of racial definition; anyone with a single drop of Black blood was considered Black (Rockquemore and Laszloffy, 2005: 2).

In the past decade, several works have appeared which deal with the problems and perspectives of persons from mixed cultural backgrounds; many of these works have been initiated by the multi-cultural individuals themselves. The titles of the books themselves exemplify the issues which multi-cultural individuals confront: *Half and Half* (O'Hearn, 1998), *What Are You?* (Gaskins, 1999), and *Does Anybody Else Look Like Me?* (Nakazawa, 2003). These works focus on the individuals' experiences as they grew up in multi-cultural settings and as they continued to deal with multi-ethnic difficulties in adulthood. In *Half and Half*, for example, the editor introduces her series of essays by biracial and bicultural writers with a personal anecdote: being called a "half-breed bitch" by a total stranger on a New York street (O'Hearn, 1998: vii).

These books are filled with accounts of similarly disquieting experiences of multi-racial and multi-cultural individuals: being asked – numerous times – "What are you?" or "Where do you come from?" (Gaskins, 1999: 5); having to "Check one box" on forms, forcing you to choose among your ethnic identities (Gaskins, 1999: 5); having siblings who look dramatically different from each other – one looking very "Chinese," the other quite Caucasian (O'Hearn, 1998: ix); hearing your friends make derogative comments about people from one of your heritage groups (O'Hearn, 1998: xi); encountering criticism from members of both of your ethnic groups when you express an affiliation with the other, even when you "don't look it" (See, 1998: 136–137; Gaskins, 1999: 4–5); the enjoinder from students in the schoolyard to "Go back to where you came from!" because you look so different (Alvarez, 1998: 144); seeing the expression of dismay on your Asian-American child's face at being the only black-haired child in the class (Hongo, 1998: 4); and trying to comfort your children when their friends express shock at their multi-racial appearance or the fact that family members do not resemble each other (Nakazawa, 2003: ix–x).

Much of the social scientific literature also focuses on the difficulties encountered by multi-racial children during their formative years (Nakazawa, 2003; Rockquemore and Laszloffy, 2005). The focus on the multi-racial issue is not surprising in view of the fact that racial differences are physically visible, while cultural issues can be hidden (Nakashima, 1992: 170). Some of the issues analyzed are how to assist a preschool child in dealing with cruel comments from other children on the playground (Nakazawa, 2003: Chapter 1); dealing with school officials – or even passersby on the street – who refuse to accept the parent–child relationship of multi-racial families (Nakazawa, 2003: Chapter 2); handling the special dating problems of multi-racial adolescents (Nakazawa, 2003: 133 ff.); and, in general, helping your child to accept the "many selves" which make them who they are (Nakazawa, 2003: 64–65).

The few studies which do focus specifically on mixed race people are generally conducted by researchers who are themselves multi-racial. They tend to be based on small, selective samples, which limit the degree to which they can be generalized to other populations and other settings. They are largely interdisciplinary and focus on multiple dimensions of multi-racial people's lives. They may also use measurement tools which have been developed for the dominant group and may not be valid for persons from different cultural backgrounds (Root, 1992c: 182).

The issue of their self-identification is a common topic for the studies of multi-racial people. This issue is particularly critical, given the fact that the multi-racial category has been denied, or even demonized, for so long. "Please Choose One" category has been the expectation for mixed race people in all settings (Valverde, 1992: 150). Even as late as the 20th century, the "mulatto," or mixed blood individual, was perceived to be unstable, biologically inferior, and psychologically tormented (Nakashima, 1992). It has long been suggested that mixed race young people have more severe conflicts and a more intense identity crisis than single-race individuals, while others have disagreed with this issue (Gibbs and Hines, 1992: 224–226). Anyone who identified as mixed was considered to be confused and have mental problems (Rockquemore and Laszloffy, 2005: 2). Many groups, such as Native Americans, have long been suspicious of persons who have mixed ancestry (Wilson, 1992). Biracial Blacks have long been pressured to identify themselves as "Black" (Gibbs and Hines, 1992: 224; Rockquemore and Laszloffy, 2005: 51–52).

The research itself raises serious questions concerning the validity of these long-standing assumptions about multi-racial people. Multi-racial people themselves resist the negative implications of their multi-racial status (Gibbs and Hines, 1992). When multi-racial people are allowed to speak for themselves, it is clear they do not accept the assumptions of the broader society concerning who they are. In a study of over 200 persons of Black-White parentage, it was found that less than 20% identified as either exclusively Black or White; a large majority chose to identify themselves as "mixed" (Rockquemore & Brunsma, 1998). While most studies focus on a single combination (such as Black-White or Asian-Black), some researchers recognize the applicability to other mixed race combinations (Rockquemore and Laszloffy, 2005: xiv).

A study of Black-White adolescents in the San Francisco Bay area found that these young people were generally comfortable with their mixed identity (Gibbs and Hines, 1992: 232). Similarly, a study of Black-Japanese in Los Angeles found that one-third of the sample chose to be identified as "other," an indication of their comfort with their multi-racial status (Hall, 1992). Furthermore, the self-esteem ratings of those who identified as "other" did not differ significantly from those who chose to identify as either "Black" or "Japanese" (Hall, 1992). This study suggests that multi-racial people openly recognize their intergroup identity and are more comfortable with it than has typically been assumed; it has been confirmed in other studies which have found that the psychological adjustment of biracial children does not differ significantly from other minorities (Cauce et al., 1992: 218–220). As a result of these studies, authorities have begun to consider mixed identity as the only healthy identity for mixed race people (Root, 1992; 1996; Gibbs, 1998; Poston, 1990).

When multi-racial people choose to identify with one or the other of their parental groups, what kinds of factors precipitate this decision? It has been suggested that physical appearance plays an important role in this process. However, the nature of this influence is not altogether clear. Research on persons of Black-Asian heritage, for example, found that some persons who were quite dark skinned did not automatically identify as Black, nor did lighter skinned ones identify as Asian (Williams, 1992: 291). Other factors seemed to play an important role. In another study of Black-Asians, only one respondent identified as "Japanese"; this woman had lived in Japan most of her life (Hall, 1992: 254). Clearly, there are instances in which cultural issues can override physical differences.

Many mixed race people also report that they feel like they are not accepted by either group. In the Los Angeles Black-Japanese study, for example, over half felt this way (Hall, 1992). Similarly, a study of American-Japanese at a US military base in Japan found that mixed race persons felt that their Japanese relatives did not really accept them, nor did they feel comfortable with their American relatives due to their having lived in Japan for so long. Most preferred to have other mixed race persons as their friends, including dating and marriage (Williams, 1992: 288–289). This study also found that language played a particularly important role in the identity development of American-Asian individuals. Most were fluent in both languages and had spent much time translating for their parents. Hence, they could express themselves in both languages and could communicate better with persons who shared this "mixed" language (Williams, 1992: 292–295).

This brings up another critical issue in the identity development of mixed race individuals: the importance of the social setting in which they live. There is no question that their biracial background has the potential for producing problems, including feelings of ambivalence. Consequently, it is important that biracial children be introduced to multi-ethnic communities which will help them to see that their biracial character is normal, as well as assist them in dealing with their feelings of ambivalence (Jacobs, 1992: 205). Families also should be comfortable with the mixture of races and cultures which they represent and be ready and willing to answer any questions their children may have, as well as dealing with problems their children may encounter in the wider community (Cauce et al., 1992: 212–213).

It has also been suggested that multi-racial people need a "label" which uniquely applies to them. As biracial people in an ethnically focused world, they will necessarily be asked to respond to the question, "What are you?" On the one hand, it is important that a biracial child be able to recognize and be comfortable with the fact that his/her heritage includes *both* the race of the mother and that of the father. On the other hand, this child is actually the race of *neither* the mother nor the father. Rather this child is both and needs a statement which exemplifies this fact (Jacobs,

1992: 204). Unfortunately, our society, in its eagerness to divide itself into "White" and "Black," has not provided any labels which encapsulate such a joint identity.

Despite the problems, it is reassuring to note that so many multi-racial individuals are generally well-adjusted and comfortable with their mixed identity. However, this process is not an easy one, and it has been noted that successful biracial or bicultural identity development is the culmination of three stages. The first stage, which occurs from approximately age 3–10, is a period in which children are made aware of the differences among people; this stage may be characterized by a degree of dissonance as biracial or bicultural children become aware of the fact that they are different from other people, many of whom have only a single racial or cultural heritage. The second stage, beginning around age 8 and lasting through the teens, is characterized by a struggle for acceptance. While this period is problematic for most children, it can be greatly complicated for those who are perceived by their friends as "different" in any respect, including biracial or bicultural. The support of parents and other adults is *particularly* critical for children who are perceived as "different." The third stage is generally reached only after high school, when young people are able to accept themselves and their biracial heritage (Kich, 1992).

Adding the Voices of Persons from Mixed Cultural Backgrounds

What is true for multi-racial identity development can be said of multi-cultural identity as well (Kich, 1992; Williams, 1992). Some researchers who study multi-*racial* individuals recognize the applicability of their issues to the multi-*cultural* population. While most of these studies tend to focus mainly on the discrimination experienced by persons with minority heritage, the cultural differences are also of importance. For example, Stephan (1992: 58) discusses the fact that children from families of "mixed heritage" are likely to be "bicultural." That is, it is the presence of different *cultural* traits, rather than simply different *racial* characteristics, which may present problems for the growing child, who is presented with multiple options in establishing an identity, and may also be exposed to conflicting socialization experiences. This study focused on different *cultural* traits, such as personality traits, social contacts with the individual's heritage groups, attitudes and world views, and so on. All of these are characteristics of culture, as opposed to race.

While cultural differences are observed between the various races, these are not the only cultural differences that exist and should be studied. Within each of the races are numerous subcategories which themselves have different cultures. For example, within the racial group categorized as "Asians" are Japanese, Chinese, Koreans, Vietnamese, and numerous others; no one would question the fact that these different nationalities have different cultures and different perspectives on life. Indeed, such differences illustrate what Spikard (1992: 12) has called the "illogic of American racial categories." The importance of the cultural dimension, as well as the racial dimension, is also illustrated by the fact that the first organization of representatives of multi-racial groups in America, formed in 1988, chose to call itself the Association of Multi-Ethnic Americans (Fernandez, 1996: 25; Brown and Douglass, 1996: 337). While most of the groups represented multi-racial people, this name choice focuses attention on the critical importance of "ethnic," or cultural differences, rather than simply race.

An initial effort in the direction of recognizing the importance of cultural (including racial) differences in family patterns can be found in a few works on the family (McGoldrick et al., 2005a; Baca Zinn et al., 2007; Trask and Hamon, 2007). These authors represent the forefront in the movement to bring cultural diversity in families to the attention of society and social leaders, including sociologists. As the editors of one work on family diversity state in their "Preface," their book ". . .consciously emphasizes cultural aspects over racial impacts on family life so as not to reinforce the myth that race is a biological truth" (Trask and Hamon, 2007: viii). However, the literature on the cultural diversity in families tends to downplay or ignore the cultural differences which exist within the broad category of "White" Americans. This is unfortunate, since it tends to perpetuate the myth that the critical differences are racial, as opposed to cultural.

It is not surprising that the diversity within White families is ignored today, because most of these groups have moved into the third, fourth, or subsequent generations past immigration, at which point a great deal of adaptation to American society has taken place. However, as we have shown, when these groups originally came, their differences were critical, just as those of the largely non-White immigrants are today. The family is also an area in which cultural differences are particularly evident. Indeed, some can still be seen three or four generations later. The American model of the family was the European nuclear family (Stewart and Goldfarb, 2007: 4). Yet even this is an overstatement. This model was at most a northern and western European model, not shared by Europeans from southern and eastern Europe. Polish and Italians, for example, were both more likely to include extended relations in the family makeup, as were some religious minorities, including Jews, Amish, and Mormons. Families who did not conform to the nuclear family model, with the husband employed and the wife at home to care for home and children, were considered deviant and even defective, and efforts to change them were necessary (Stewart and Goldfarb, 2007: 5).

Recognizing an extended family model, as opposed to a nuclear family one, automatically imposes a number of family characteristics which differ between numerous White ethnic groups and the supposedly dominant White model. The status and role of the elderly in the family is a particularly important example of the manner in which numerous ethnic communities are at variance from the nuclear family model. Polish, Italian, Jewish, Middle Eastern, and other "White" ethnic groups are much more likely to include older relatives in the family structure (Karasik and Hamon, 2007; Usita, 2007). Ethnic families' inclusion of the elderly is often a bilateral pattern, with the family providing care for the elderly, but the elderly also playing active roles through assisting with child care, financial assistance, and advice (Greder and Allen, 2007: 124).

Similarly, ethnic families are often poor or working class, and the role played by women and children in such families is quite different from that of women and children in upper or middle-class families. The process of immigration presents financial hardships for most families; consequently, they cannot afford to allow women and children to remain at home in nonproductive roles. Many immigrant women play important roles in their family businesses, and many children in these families are expected to participate in the family business or provide assistance in the form of care for younger siblings (Kim and Woolfolk, 2007; Allen and Beitin, 2007; Trask and Koivunen, 2007). This is true of today's immigrant families, but it was also true of women and children in the families of White immigrants in earlier waves of immigration.

The differences among immigrants from different European nations were considered so extreme that most groups segregated themselves from each other demographically and tried to maintain their own individual cultural patterns. As the nation developed, the English group became dominant and imposed its own views on others. As a result, American governmental policies have tended to reflect the views of the original English and did not recognize the diverse patterns of family and social life which were brought by immigrants from other European nations and had already become established here. However, these variations have continued to affect our law in many ways, including privacy rights, the rights of parents to direct their children's education, the right to select a marriage partner, grandparent rights, the rights of women and children, and numerous others (Henderson, 2007: 229). What all this suggests is that analysis of the problems of multi-*racial* families and children looks at only a part of the issue.

The critical issues to examine include those which multi-racial families share with persons from multi-cultural settings in which race is not a factor. While the recent literature contends that race is a largely meaningless category and that ethnicity is more useful in determining people's identification and social patterns, the focus nonetheless has largely remained on multi-*racial* people (Spikard, 1992; Root, 1992: 4). As indicated earlier, Alba and Nee (2003) have suggested that today's multi-cultural people are more likely to come from different racial backgrounds, rather than different nationality backgrounds. Does this make their experiences essentially different from the experiences of multi-ethnic people in past generations? Or are there some experiences which they all share? If so, are there lessons from the experiences of past generations which can be used to simplify the lives of today's multi-cultural and multi-racial people?

A New Focus of Analysis: Multi-cultural Persons

We know very little about what happens when people from different cultural backgrounds form families together. This includes not just racial differences, such as Black-White, Asian-White, or Asian-Black, but also people from the same racial background. For example, what happens when Asians from Japan and China marry and form a family? Or Blacks from Africa and the Caribbean? Hispanics from

Mexico and Puerto Rico? Or White Europeans from Poland and Italy? What kinds of family patterns result? More critically, what happens to the children?

Most research to date has focused on the problems of children in multi-racial families: How do they define themselves? What difficulties do they face? How are they received in society? These issues, while important, do not tell the whole story. First, they do not consider the problems in multi-*cultural* families in which the participants happen to be from the same race. As some of the examples given above illustrate, cultural differences can be as important – perhaps more important in some circumstances than racial differences. Second, these studies generally do not examine the family patterns which exist in these families. As many experts have shown us, there is no institution more dramatically impacted by culture than the family. However, nearly all discussions about the family begin with the assumption that each family "derives from a single culture."

As noted earlier, early works on the family – and even some today – assume that "The Family" is a unitary institution that transcends all cultures. More recent works have recognized the variations in family patterns which derive from different cultures (Baca Zinn et al., 2007; McGoldrick, et al., 2005a). However, we have yet to examine an important question: How are families structured when they have origins in two different cultures? If husband and wife come from the perspectives of different cultures, with their varying views of the family, how does this impact the way in which they establish a family of their own? How do they raise their children? Do they adopt the family cultural patterns of the father or of the mother? Or is their family pattern a blending of the two sets of family customs?

This possibility raises an additional issue. If multi-cultural families are a blending of two family types, then the children of these families are not just children with two (or more) cultural *backgrounds*. They may indeed be people with two *cultures as part of their personalities*. Or more accurately, they have a culture – but it is a mixture of two cultures. Are they really divided individuals, as our view of them seems to have been? Or are they in fact integrated individuals with a unique culture of their own? If so, what is the nature of that culture? Is it more likely to be the father's culture or the mother's? Or is it comprised of elements of both cultures from which they originated? Do all children in a multi-cultural family derive their cultures in the same manner? The issues which multi-culturalism in a family suggests seem endless.

We get some hint of the patterns exhibited by such multi-cultural individuals from a few studies which have been conducted on children from multi-racial families. As noted earlier, studies have found that Black-Japanese adolescents were quite comfortable with their heritage. Many identified themselves with one group or the other, while others preferred a "mixed" identity. Most had a positive self-image and were comfortable with their social relationships (Hall, 1992; Gibbs and Hines, 1992). Dating choices were a problem for some, but positive comments about their "mixed" cultural background were more frequent than negative ones (Hall, 1992). More important, many of these individuals were themselves bicultural. That is, they were not simply products of a bicultural environment, which many have suggested produces a mixed-up individual. Rather, they had internalized elements of both cultures and were, in fact, most comfortable with others who shared their common joint culture, including their ability to express their ideas and feelings in both of their ancestral languages (Williams, 1992).

It appears then that children who grow up in multi-cultural families may actually be *multi-cultural persons*, that is, some persons who have internalized the cultures and identities of both of their origins. These people are not, in fact, fighting an internal battle between their two cultures of origin but have accepted these cultures as a single culture with which they are quite comfortable. Is this a common pattern among people from multi-cultural families? Are many of these children integrated multi-cultural persons? Or is this a rare occurrence, happening with only a few of these multi-cultural individuals? Research to date suggests this pattern is more common than previously thought. However, only further research on more people from a variety of multi-cultural backgrounds will indicate the conditions under which such integrated multi-cultural persons may originate.

The character of the culture of people who are products of multi-cultural families will be the focus of the present study. That is, we are interested not solely in the family patterns of people from different cultures. Rather, our focus will be on people who themselves are engaged in interactions – on the most intimate basis of the family – with people whose origin is a culture different from their own. As noted earlier, we are interested in analyzing the micro-aspects of the multi-cultural society – the interactions of persons whose close, one-to-one relationships are with persons from different cultures than their own. How do people who come from different cultural perspectives, which necessarily include different approaches to social roles and behaviors, manage their interactions with each other? As noted earlier, studying families composed of persons from different cultural perspectives is a way of analyzing this issue.

In this work, we propose to analyze this issue based on interviews with a sample of persons who were raised in multi-cultural homes: homes in which two or more cultural perspectives prevailed. How did they cope? Looking back from the vantage point of adulthood, how do they view their childhood multi-cultural experiences? What problems did they encounter growing up in such a setting? What did their families or communities do to help? Were their problems or difficulties resolved? Or did they remain unresolved dilemmas?

Given the fact that multi-culturalism is not a new phenomenon and that ethnic groups in the past have experienced discrimination and prejudice similar to that which multi-racial people report today, it seems likely that some of the experiences of multi-cultural people in the past may also be similar to the experiences reported by multi-racial people today. Hence, the multi-culturalism which will be studied here includes all varieties of cultural patterns, including people from similar racial categories, such as two Whites from different nationality or religious groups or two Blacks, one of whom is from Africa, the other from the American South.

We will seek to determine whether there are similarities in their experiences that persist across multi-cultural as well as multi-racial groups. Have multi-cultural people in the past experienced similar problems to those which multi-racial people experience today? How are they the same and how are they different? Are there hints we can gain from these experiences to help improve the lives of today's multi-cultural people? Of particular interest to this study is the process by which people from different cultural backgrounds manage to maneuver among their different cultural perspectives within the close confines of the family. Do they manage to become a single, relatively harmonious group? Or is there always a degree of tension among their different cultural perspectives? If there are tensions, how are they resolved?

Answering these questions may perhaps give us a hint of the manner in which ethnic groups have, over time, come together to establish the pattern of assimilation which has occurred in many communities. How, for example, did the English, Scotch-Irish, and German Protestants manage to overcome the antagonisms which clearly existed among them in the early years of the American experiences to become "just WASPs" they are today? How did the Irish, Italian, and Polish Catholics come together in spite of their different views of religion and culture? Learning the answer to such questions can possibly help us to determine how we, as a multi-cultural society, can manage to live harmoniously with each other today.

The individuals who served as the respondents in this study of multi-cultural family patterns are persons who spent their childhood years in families which were a mixture of cultures. They were of Black, White, and Asian racial origins. Some were of mixed racial as well as cultural backgrounds, while others were from a single racial group. At the time of the interviews, they ranged in age from 18 to over 70 years; consequently, the eldest spent their childhood years in the 1940s and 1950s, while the youngest grew up in the 1980s. What do these people – so different in age, nationality, religion, and racial origin – have in common? What provides a unifying experience for all of them, raised, as they were, in different families, different geographic environments, and different historical periods? The one characteristic they shared is the one factor in which we are most interested: All were raised in families which they themselves viewed as having more than a single cultural pattern.

As noted, some of the cultural differences were racial in origin. Many were from different nationality cultures within a single race. Some of these different cultural patterns were derived from religious differences, mainly Protestant-Catholic or Christian-Jewish differences. All were attracted to the study because they perceived themselves as having experienced a mixed family culture during childhood. Hence, they provide us with an opportunity to examine the experiences they recalled from their childhood which stemmed from these cultural differences. Their stories can help us to see the roles which cultural differences play in a family, the problems – or advantages – which may arise. Their racial diversity can also help us to sort out the patterns which may be derived from *cultural*, as opposed to uniquely *racial* characteristics. In the next chapter, we will describe these individuals more thoroughly, as well as the manner in which they were selected, and how the interviews were conducted.

Part II
Data Analysis: Hearing the Voices of Persons From Culturally Diverse Families

As I have shown in the two previous chapters, the experiences of multi-cultural individuals can be daunting. Persons who are "different" are not always received hospitably by those around them. What is it like to be placed in this situation? More critically, what is it like to grow up in an environment in which many of the people you encounter consider you to be odd at best, or evil at worst? The only way to understand the perspective of people in this situation is to hear their voices. In this section, we will do exactly that: hear the voices of people from diverse cultural backgrounds, and attempt to understand the experience of growing up in a culturally diverse environment.

The section will be divided into five chapters. In Chapter 3, I will introduce the respondents in the study who described their multi-cultural childhoods. Chapter 4 will focus on the problems they described and will attempt to classify them into types. Chapter 5 will focus on a major dimension of multi-culturalism: the need to reach a sense of identity – a sense of "who I am" – in the face of many other people who are demonstrably different. Chapter 6 focuses on the social environment and its impact on the problems of multi-cultural individuals, and shows how their experiences varied greatly, depending on the setting in which they lived as they were growing up. Finally, Chapter 7 will focus on the families in which these multi-cultural respondents lived: How did these families cope with the environment? Were they able to raise their children to be healthy and productive individuals, in spite of the often inhospitable social environments in which they lived? What was useful and what was not?

Chapter 3
Sources of Multi-culturalism in Families

Encouraging people from different cultural backgrounds to get along peacefully with each other has long been a concern in American society. With a wide diversity of racial, ethnic, religious, linguistic, and other cultural dimensions present in its population, the USA has lacked the advantage of a broad common culture. Unifying such a society and preventing the development of widespread conflicts over cultural values have been American problems for the better part of its history, particularly spawned by the immigration of so wide a variety of cultural backgrounds in the late 19th and early 20th centuries (Gordon, 1964; 1978; Greeley, 1971; 1974).

These diversity issues – how to get people from different backgrounds to cooperate on projects of joint interest; how to prevent misunderstandings resulting from variances in language and gestures; and how to prevent violence when such misunderstandings occur – have all been major concerns in a variety of settings (Fritz, 1985; Fong and Gibbs, 1996; Gallagher and Nahan, 1997; Gills and White, 1997). Few sources are available to provide solutions to these difficulties. Many groups and leaders grope in the dark and hope their efforts will attain some measure of success.

At the same time, there are some people who serve as a sort of natural experiment in the manner in which intercultural groups can operate. US statistics (McNamara et al., 1999) show an increasing rate of marriage between persons from different groups, including interreligious, interethnic, and interracial marriages. These couples and their children have had long years of experience living in an intercultural setting. These experiences provide a wealth of information on the manner in which intercultural interaction occurs and how it can operate successfully.

Past studies of interethnic, interreligious, or interracial marriages have concentrated primarily on the marriage partners (Waters, 1990; McNamara et al., 1999). They have inquired about the manner in which these partners have been received by their families and communities, what problems they have encountered, and how they have coped with them. However, the children of intercultural marriages represent an untapped source of information. These people have lived most of their lives in a multi-cultural setting. They offer an opportunity to examine the possibilities of living and working with persons from different cultures.

M.C. Sengstock, *Voices of Diversity*, Clinical Sociology: Research and Practice,
DOI 10.1007/978-0-387-89666-3_3, © Springer Science+Business Media, LLC 2009

Methodology of the Study

The data on which the analysis is based are derived from a study of multi-cultural families conducted by the author from January 1998 through February 2003. The sample consisted of 30 individuals whose parents were from different cultural backgrounds. Interviews were open-ended and were conducted by the author and three assistants.[1] Most were carried out in conjunction with the author's sabbatical leave in Winter term, 1998. The methodology of the study and the interviewing process were reviewed and approved by the Human Investigation Committee of Wayne State University.

The sample was a convenience sample: Persons known to the author to be from mixed cultural backgrounds were asked to participate. In addition, notices were placed in newsletters in two settings: a faculty newsletter at the Detroit area institution at which the author teaches, asking the faculty to refer themselves and/or their students who qualified; and a multi-cultural religious congregation in the Washington, DC area. Respondents were also interviewed at a conference in the Washington, DC area. Of the 30 persons who eventually agreed to be interviewed, 10 were from east coast states, interviewed in the Washington, DC area, and the remaining 20 were from Michigan. Michigan respondents were not only from the Detroit metropolitan area, but also from surrounding areas within the southeast and south central parts of the state. The location denotes the area of residence of the respondents at the time of the interviews, not necessarily where they grew up.

Whether or not a respondent's background was "multi-cultural" was based on the respondent's own perception. In short, if the respondent defined him/herself as multi-cultural, it was presumed that s/he had experiences which were worthwhile examining in light of the goals of the project. Hence, respondents were largely self-selected – if they believed their families were multi-cultural, then they were. Because of the self-selected nature of the sample, it cannot be assumed that the respondents are in any way "representative" of persons from multi-cultural backgrounds. Indeed, their self-selectivity may be an indication of their satisfaction with their multi-cultural heritage. One might presume, for example, that persons who were uncomfortable with their multi-cultural background might hesitate to volunteer to discuss it.

Not only were respondents from a wide variety of cultural backgrounds, they also differed in age and gender. There were more women (19) than men (11). The youngest respondents (6) were between 18 and 29 years. The largest group of respondents (17) included those between 30 and 60 years of age. At the other end of the spectrum, the oldest respondents (3) were in their 60 s and early 70 s. Five respondents gave no information about their age.

Interviews varied from about 40 minutes to over 2 hours, with most lasting approximately 1 hour. All interviews were tape recorded and transcribed.

---

[1] The author would like to express appreciation to Sonya Berkley, Kenneth Kelso, and Kathleen Sengstock, who provided assistance with interviewing.

Confidentiality of the respondents was guaranteed. The interviews focused on a number of issues, including the racial or cultural backgrounds of both parents; which race(s) or culture(s) the respondent identifies with; how other people tended to identify the respondent and the respondent's reactions to this; child-rearing practices in the respondent's family; respondent's contact with members of both extended families, both as a child and as an adult; respondent's experience with ethnic festivals, foods, and other ethnic activities; and respondent's perception of his/her siblings' experiences in the same family setting. (See Appendix A for a complete list of the issues raised in the interviews.)

In the data analysis, several issues were considered, including how did the members of the family get along? How did they "maneuver" their varying cultural differences? Did they tend to follow one cultural pattern more than another? If so, how was this selection made? How did the children adjust to the multi-cultural dimensions – especially in a world which often assumes a single culture?

Yesterday's Multi-cultural Inequity as a Model for Today's Multi-racial Inequity

The sample, as described, includes respondents from a variety of racial and cultural backgrounds, who grew up in various parts of the USA over a 50-year period, from the 1940s through the 1990s. What they have in common is that all had parents who were from different racial or cultural backgrounds, and all were raised with varying degrees of contact with these different backgrounds. What is the value of such a study? What can so diverse a group have in common? What can they tell us about the characteristics and needs of people in the early 21st century? Are any experiences they had relevant to today's world?

Multi-culturalism and multi-racialism are relatively new phenomena. Today's children have more experience with mixed settings than earlier ones. If today's world has more experience with multi-cultural settings, how can people from an earlier era provide assistance? Furthermore, the multi-cultural relationships of today are likely to be different from those of the past. Today, multi-culturalism often means multi-racial settings; yesterday's multi-cultural relationships were more likely to develop between people from the same race, but different nationalities or religions. Do the multi-nationality or multi-religious relationships of the past have anything to say to today's multi-racial world?

The experiences of these respondents are relevant in two respects. First, social relationships of highly divergent types can often be summarized into similar types. As we indicated in Chapters 1 and 2, societies have long placed people into groups on the basis of whether they were "acceptable" or not. Indeed, various nationalities, including Italians, Jews, Polish, Irish, and others, who today are seen as "just White" were viewed as different races in previous eras. Ethnic and religious discrimination were quite prevalent in the past, in addition to racial discrimination; indeed, some aspects of this still persist today. The assumption of this study is that the experiences of persons from mixed racial backgrounds in today's society are likely to be similar in many ways to the experiences of persons from mixed religions or nationalities in the 1940s, 1950s, and 1960s. Hence, the lessons learned from these earlier settings can help families, schools, and counselors provide a more hospitable environment for the mixed heritage people of today.

Second, as persons who have experienced the manner in which people viewed as "different" were treated in their communities, indeed, in their own families, these respondents can tell us about the way in which this treatment made them feel. They can tell us what the problems were, and they may be able to suggest what could make the experience more pleasant. They also may be able to suggest ways in which communities and families can help people to operate in multi-cultural settings and establish communities which are more hospitable to multi-culturalism.

In particular, we are interested in the impact which being multi-cultural or multi-racial has during an individual's most formative years. This is the period in which a person is defining him or herself in relation to others. Who am I? Who are the people most important to me? Of what group am I a part? How do we, as a group, relate to other groups in society? These are all critical questions that must be answered by children in every age. All children must learn their culture, their society's rules and expectations, the roles they must play, how they relate to others, and so on. When the community is homogeneous, the options presented are basically unitary. Only a single set of options is presented. In a homogeneous community, a child is not confused by the presence of people with a different culture, traditions, or rules.

For this reason, many parents deliberately select an educational setting for their children which mirrors the child's home environment: they choose to live in a community of persons from similar religious, racial, class, and ethnic backgrounds as themselves; they exercise their influence over the local school board to ensure the school's program reflects their values. Witness the efforts of parents to ensure that creationism is taught in the schools versus evolution (or the reverse). When parents become concerned that their children are being exposed to unacceptable cultural patterns, they often resort to sending the child to sectarian schools or even educating the child at home.

However, single-culture settings are becoming increasingly scarce in the modern world. The isolated community is becoming a thing of the past. International contacts are numerous – even as close as the living room television. Rural areas are disappearing as these communities are incorporated into large metropolitan areas. Communities increasingly consist of numerous groups quite different from each other. Nearly all families come in contact with people from quite different backgrounds. Presenting children with a unitary cultural pattern is increasingly difficult.

Obviously, the questions presented above must still be answered by children in mixed cultural settings: Who am I? What is my group? What do we believe? What rules and expectations does society have of me? But unlike the child growing up in a small, homogeneous community, children in a multi-cultural setting are presented with a variety of options which greatly complicate the task of understanding society's expectations and developing a set of values and rules.

Although they grew up in different historical eras and with different types of groups surrounding them, the respondents present us with a valuable resource. They grew up in the multi-cultural settings of a previous era. Their experiences can provide us with information about the problems – and advantages – of such a setting. What was it like to grow up in a multi-cultural environment? What problems did they encounter? How did they cope with them? How were they assisted by those around them? What did they wish had been available to help them? What worked and what did not?

The respondents, both male and female, come from a variety of racial, ethnic, and religious backgrounds. They have experienced multi-culturalism or multi-racialism, not only in the context of the community in which they lived, but also within their own families, which were composed of persons from different cultural origins. Hence, they encountered different cultural possibilities intimately on a daily basis. They also come from different age groups. The eldest were growing up in the middle of the 20th century. The majority (16) experienced their formative years during the tumultuous years of the 1960s and 1970s. The youngest respondents are today's young adults, growing up in the last decades of the 20th century.

But they all have one thing in common: all know what it is like to encounter different cultural options at an early stage of life, even in the intimate setting of the family itself. Their experiences can help us to understand the process of developing a sense of personal and group identity and learning society's norms and expectations in a setting where a variety of options are presented. I propose to use their experiences to tell us what the problems of such settings are and, hopefully, suggest ways this process can be more a positive one for participants. In addition, this discussion may also remind members of the so-called dominant White population that their predecessors in earlier generations were treated in a discriminatory fashion. Perhaps, it may lead the White population to a greater sensitivity to the aspirations and needs of the minorities of today.

Description of the Respondents

Who are these people from mixed cultural backgrounds? What kinds of backgrounds did they have? Initially, it was assumed that respondents would be persons who had parents from two different cultural backgrounds. However, it was soon discovered that this represents only one dimension of family multi-culturalism. Just as there are families with multiple cultures, so also there are multiple ways of achieving this multi-culturalism. In this section, I will examine the roads to multi-culturalism followed by the respondents in the study.

Nine respondents were multi-racial, which included Black-Caucasian, Black-Asian, Caucasian-Asian, European-Native American, and Black-Native American. Three were from multi-religious marriages, all of them were marriages between Christians and Jews. Thirteen respondents were from multi-nationality marriages. Eight of these were from mixed European backgrounds, such as Polish-Irish, English-Scottish, Austrian-Irish, or Irish-Italian. Two respondents were

from European-Middle Eastern backgrounds. Two included nationalities from the
Western Hemisphere, such as European-Mexican or Mexican-Puerto Rican. One
respondent was of mixed Asian nationalities (Chinese and Korean). A few respondents were combinations of these, such as mixed nationalities and religions. They
were assigned to these categories based on the issues which appeared to be most
salient in each of the respondent's views. A summary of the respondents' backgrounds has been provided in Appendix C.

Multi-racial Backgrounds

Of the ten respondents from multi-racial backgrounds, two were of Caucasian
and Native American heritage. Peter,[2] a college student, had a French-English
mother and a Paiute father. Grace had an English-Irish Father and a mother whose
background was diverse, but included Cherokee Indian. Deanna had an African-
American father and a Korean mother; she was one of several respondents who
were the children of war brides. Karen's father was of German background; he met
her Korean mother when he served there in the war. Derek's father, who was Black,
was also a military man, who met and married a German woman while stationed
there. Carlos had a Salvadorean-Spanish father and a mother whom he described as
"German and indigenous." Teresa's father was African while her mother was White.
Leslie's father was Filipino and her mother Caucasian. Ken, a college student, had a
highly diverse background, his father being Black, Irish, and Native American while
his mother was Guatamalan and Chinese. Adam's mother was African-American;
he had never had contact with his Caucasian father.

In summary, the interracial respondents included three persons who were Black
and Caucasian (Derek, Teresa, and Adam), one who was Black and Asian (Deanna),
two who were Caucasian and Asian (Karen and Leslie), three who were European
and Native American (Peter, Grace, and Carlos), and one who was Black and Native
American (Ken).

Multi-religious Backgrounds

Three respondents described themselves as being from multi-religious backgrounds.
All of these were the offspring of Jewish-Christian marriages. Sarah is a teacher
whose father's family was Greek orthodox and Polish Catholic; her mother was
of Jewish, European, and Romanian background. Vickie, also a teacher, was the
daughter of an Irish father and a Jewish mother. Jeff's father was the son of an
Orthodox rabbi, while his mother was the daughter of a Methodist minister. There
were also several respondents whose parents were from different religions, such
as Catholic-Protestant, different varieties of Protestant, or Christian and no religion. However, these respondents did not view the religious difference as the most

---

[2] All names are pseudonyms.

important aspect of their multi-culturalism. Consequently, they have been listed within the categories which they considered most salient to their background. For most this was nationality-based.

Multi-nationality Backgrounds

Fourteen respondents described themselves as being from multi-national backgrounds. Most (9) were from different European backgrounds. They included Robert, who had an English father and a Scottish mother. Nichole's mother was Irish and her father French and German. Peggy's father was Irish and her mother Belgian. Betty's father was Polish while her mother was Irish, German, and English. Ted described his background as "generalized European," including an English, Irish, German father and an Austrian, German, Polish mother. Francine's father was Czech and her mother Italian. Margo had a Sicilian father and a French-Canadian and Austrian mother. Sam's father was Italian, and his mother Irish. Finally, Yvonne's father was Scottish and Swedish, her mother French-Canadian.

Two respondents were products of European and Middle Eastern parents. One was Jeanette, with an Irish father and a Lebanese mother. The other was Ida, with a British father and a Lebanese mother. Two respondents listed their ancestries as being from different parts of the Americas or from European and American combinations. Gary had a Mexican mother and a Lithuanian and Polish father. Anita had a Mexican mother and a Puerto Rican father. One respondent (Evelyn) was from different Asian backgrounds; her father was Chinese, and he met her Korean mother when he served in Korea.

Several of these multi-national combinations sound like similar backgrounds to the casual observer. Robert's English and Scottish background, for example, or Ted's multiple European national origins would simply be described as "European" by many. Similarly, Anita's Mexican and Puerto Rican background would be viewed as "Hispanic," and Evelyn's Chinese-Korean heritage might be considered 100% "Asian." However, these judgments belie the very different cultural traditions represented. They may even ignore long-standing political conflicts between the component cultures. Anita, for example, was emphatic in her description of Puerto Rican and Mexican as different cultures, not generalizable to "Hispanic." Similarly, Evelyn noted the differences between Chinese and Korean cultures, as well as the fact that the two nations have frequently had unfriendly, even hostile relations. England's long-standing hegemony over both Ireland and Scotland, for example, may create difficult cultural conflicts for persons whose parents originated from these backgrounds, although Robert did not appear to see any difficulty.

To summarize, the multi-national respondents consisted of nine persons from varying European backgrounds, two persons who were European and Middle Eastern mixtures, two whose parents were of European and American origin or from different parts of the Americas, and one whose parents came from different Asian nations. The reader will note a relative lack of respondents in the sample of persons whose backgrounds represent the newest groups of immigrants to the USA. There were no South Asians, and only two respondents traced their origins to Middle Eastern nations. Is this a flaw in the sample? Why did we not find more respondents from these areas?

While including respondents from these areas would certainly be desirable, we should not be surprised that no such respondents could be located. It takes considerable time for a group to reach the level of inclusion in American society which is represented by intermarriage, as Gordon (1964) pointed out. Indeed, intermarriage has long been used as the ultimate measure of assimilation. Once members of a group intermarry with members of the dominant group, they are considered to be completely integrated into the society at large. Furthermore, to be multi-cultural, as we have defined it, one must not only have parents from different cultural or racial groups but must also have reached adulthood. It is not likely that very many south Asian or Middle Eastern communities will have been in this country long enough to have become assimilated enough to have intermarried and produced children who are now adults. Indeed, the two representatives from Middle Eastern culture, Ida and Jeanette, both had mothers who were members of the single Middle Eastern nation, Lebanon, which has had immigrants in the USA for the longest time.

Other Routes to Multi-culturalism

As indicated earlier, a person can become multi-cultural in other ways than being born of parents from different cultures. Regina, for example, had parents who were both Polish; indeed, they were highly committed to their Polish heritage and involved with the Polish community. However, they had been refugees after the World War II and had lived for some time in Brazil, where Regina spent her early childhood years. While her parents were not multi-cultural, Regina was and considered the Brazilian culture to be an important part of her heritage. Carol's parents were from a general European background; hence she did not view herself as being multi-national. However, her parents were from widely disparate social class backgrounds: her mother from the old Southern aristocracy and her father a working-class man. Carol recognized the very different cultural patterns represented by these two heritages. Brian's parents were both of Irish background, but his mother died when he was very young; eventually his father remarried to a German woman, who introduced a very different cultural pattern into her stepson's life.

Continuing a Tradition of Multi-culturalism

Finally, several respondents pointed out that they had achieved an even greater level of multi-culturalism than appeared on the surface, largely through their own marriages to persons from other cultures. Jeff, Derek, and Yvonne, all of them raised in multi-cultural backgrounds, had married persons from still different cultural backgrounds. Thus, Jeff was from a Jewish-Christian background, identified as Jewish, but married a Christian. Derek was from a Black and German background and married a Filipino woman. And Yvonne, whose background included Swedish, Scottish, and French-Canadian married a man from Africa.

Summary

Respondents were assigned to these various categories based on the issues which appeared to be most salient in each respondent's view. Nine respondents were multi-racial; three were from multi-religious marriages. Fifteen respondents were from multi-nationality marriages; ten of these were from mixed European backgrounds, and the other five were from mixtures involving other parts of the world. Some of the mixed nationality backgrounds also were multi-religious marriages, but this was not the most important dimension for them. Some were aware that others might consider their backgrounds not to be multi-cultural. However, they hastened to point out that the cultures were indeed quite different. Finally, three respondents achieved their multi-cultural status through means other than their biological parentage. These mechanisms included immigration and being raised in another culture, stepparent-age, and the influence of different social class backgrounds.

Drawing Lessons from Multi-cultural Settings

This brief summary of the respondents' heritage illustrates not only the diversity of their backgrounds, but also the variety of means to achieving this diversity. Most diversity originated, as expected, from the marriage of two people from different racial, religious, or national origins. The resulting families can draw upon the cultures of both parents in developing their family structure, traditions, and values. However, cultural diversity can itself occur in diverse ways. Different social classes present their own variety of cultural diversity. If the family lives in another culture, especially during a child's formative years, diverse cultures are introduced. The addition of a stepparent to the family – or indeed, the addition of any other individual, such as an adopted child – contributes to the diversity of cultures.

Although the sample does not include representatives of the newest groups of immigrants to the USA, the attempts of earlier immigrants and their children to become integrated into American society can serve as a model. Their experiences can assist us in seeing how acculturation and assimilation can proceed more effectively. Hopefully, these earlier generations of newcomers can serve as the "natural experiment" which can assist both society and the immigrants themselves in finding effective ways to integrate the various segments of society more effectively.

Most of these respondents did not choose to live in culturally diverse settings. It was forced upon them by the accident of their birth and family background. Indeed, some of them expressed the wish that their family origins had been more traditional. However, most eventually came to terms with their multi-cultural heritage, even to the point of enjoying it. Some even sought out multi-cultural contacts, including, in some instances, their own multi-cultural marriages. It is their adaptation to these culturally diverse situations which make these respondents interesting to study. They can provide us with valuable lessons as to how to maneuver the profusion of cultures which occur in modern industrial society. In the pages ahead, I will draw upon their stories to illuminate some of the techniques they and their families employed in their multi-cultural journeys.

Comparing Multi-racialism and Multi-culturalism

Throughout this work, we plan to analyze the experiences of these respondents as though they are representative of a common pattern, that is, the manner in which American society treats people who are from mixed backgrounds. Throughout, we will use "multi-cultural" as a generic term, which includes both multi-cultural and multi-racial. After all, racial groups nearly always exhibit different cultural traits as well, a point which several of our respondents mentioned. That is, we will generally be treating the experiences of respondents who are of mixed *racial* backgrounds as though they are generally similar to those of mixed *cultural* backgrounds.

However, it might reasonably be questioned whether this is an appropriate assumption. Are there important differences between the experiences of persons from *multi-racial* backgrounds as opposed to those with *multi-cultural* backgrounds? Since we are discussing the impact of the community on children during their formative years, we must confront directly the differential manner in which these many different communities treat racial and cultural issues. As we suggested in Chapters 1 and 2, social scientists view racial differences and ethnic differences equally; furthermore, as we also showed in those chapters, American society has historically treated ethnic groups and racial groups in the same manner.

A question remains, however, as to whether their treatment is *experienced* in the same way by members of ethnic and racial groups. Do racial minorities experience the treatment they receive in a different manner than persons who are ethnically/culturally different but not racially different? What special difficulties might occur in these families as they try to establish a sense of identity in their children? At this point, we will discuss the degree to which the community may have different impact on respondents who exhibit racial diversity, as opposed to ethnic diversity. Because of the enormous importance of skin color in the USA, it seems likely that this might be the case.

US Preoccupation with Skin Color

The role of race in American society is of such importance that others pale in comparison. The USA is so preoccupied with skin color that even small variations are noticed. Furthermore, many people feel free to call attention to an individual's skin color, even in relatively casual situations, and to mention it to the individuals involved as well as to others. This is true even of relatively sensitive persons who would normally be hesitant to discuss others' personal characteristics in public settings. With race, even they may feel entitled to raise questions. Consequently, individuals are often questioned about their racial background and expected to identify themselves with whichever group the questioner presumes they represent. Often the questioners are not willing to accept any identity other than the one they expect. What are some of the consequences of this for persons whose origins are *racially* disparate as opposed to *culturally* disparate?

Several patterns emerged in the interviews which illustrate the ways in which racial and cultural diversity are handled in a different manner. We will discuss six dimensions of this "different" experience which these respondents discussed: the observable character of racial differences, the greater likelihood that outsiders insert their views into the identification process, the absence of any possibility of "hiding," the distinctions tend to be made for the purpose of exclusion rather than inclusion, the persistence of these problems throughout life, and finally, the fact that individuals cannot escape even when alone. We will discuss each of these issues in turn.

The Observable Character of Physical Differences

It is perhaps belaboring the obvious to note that the physical character of racial differences ensures that they are constantly observable, even to the casual onlooker. Only people with racial differences *look* different – *all* the time. Karen, for example, reported that she always felt out of place in her community. Only when she visited Hawaii, with its broad racial spectrum, did she feel "That I wasn't being looked at as different ... that I didn't feel that I stood out to any extent walking down the street or hanging out ... or whatever."

Even the White, multi-cultural respondents recognized that people with racial differences fell into a different category than people with cultural differences. For example, according to Robert, little notice was taken of cultural differences in his community. He says:

> The social economic structure that I grew up in – I grew up in a small rural, southern, Kentucky, southern town. It was very segregated ... This is the late, mid 50's, so the segregated are race and Black children went to a separate school for a long time ... It was all white kids, we were all a bunch of white kids from working class families and I don't think we were aware of anyone's heritage or culture. It was not an issue. No one spoke with an accent; no one spoke any differently than each of us did. ... a very homogeneous White Anglo Saxon Protestant structure.

Hence, anyone who "fit" within an obvious racial category could "get away with" appearing to be part of the group ("passing"). Peggy, whose background was Irish and Belgian, commented on this when she reported that she could easily have "passed" as Irish if she chose. Both Peggy's and Robert's comments illustrate their recognition that there was a distinct difference between the cultural differences they themselves exhibited and the racial differences of others. People whose differences were cultural could, if they were careful, hide these differences from others and "pass" as part of the community as a whole. Indeed, a common complaint of the multi-*cultural* respondents was the fact that they had trouble getting others to recognize their cultural differences. In short, their concern was that people expected them simply to "pass" as "White" when they wanted others to recognize their distinctive ethnic character.

In contrast, persons whose *racial* characteristics were different did not have this freedom to disappear into the general population, even if they chose to do so. They were always reminded of their differences, as Karen complained. Hence, a major distinction between persons with racial, as opposed to cultural, differences is that their distinctiveness is ever present. It cannot be escaped. Whenever they move outside their racial community and into the population as a whole, they are always "visibly different." They can never experience the comfort of being just like everyone else.

Furthermore, people who *appear* to be of a different race are constantly treated as though they were members of that group, even if they do not identify as such. Ken, whose background included Guatemalan, Black, Native American, and Chinese, provides a good illustration of the dilemma of the multi-racial, as opposed to multi-cultural, person. He usually preferred to define himself as "mixed" or sometimes to list all of his several identities. However, he reported several incidents in which he was singled out for discrimination on the basis of his appearance. This discrimination could go both ways. That is, he was not welcome in certain neighborhoods because he was assumed to be Black, including an incident in which he was held for questioning by the police. On the other hand, he felt that some Blacks felt that he was, ". . .not Black enough." He reports he usually ". . .found more acceptance with Hispanics or certain white people. . ." than from some Blacks.

Greater Likelihood that Outsiders Insert Their Views into the Identification Process

When differences are based on physical characteristics, people seem much more likely to raise questions and express their views openly. Respondents complained that persons outside of the family constantly felt they had the right to intervene in their self-identification. As noted earlier, the one thing that these people wanted was the right to define themselves. However, outsiders – including members of both ethnic groups involved and the society as a whole – frequently felt free to tell the individual who s/he was. This seemed more likely to happen if the individual was multi-racial than multi-cultural.

Karen, whose parents were Korean and Caucasian, described the situations in which attention to her race caused concern: ". . .what usually happens . . . [are] the questions about race or my background when someone of white background approaches me with a question like that. I take it a little offensively. . . . I get a little offended by it. . . . Especially when it's the first question that comes out of their mouth when I run into them." She goes on to note that she is offended when Caucasians ask the question, but not when Asians do so. She explains: "When a person of Asian descent asks me . . . they are trying to figure out if I am the same as they are. Am I Korean too? Am I Japanese too? . . . if they are Korean and they discover that I am Korean, it's a joy or a similarity." In contrast, with Whites, her impression is the opposite: ". . .when someone of non-Asian descent asks me that, it is usually because they are trying to establish . . . based upon how I am different."

In short, she perceives the questions people asked about her background as stemming from an attempt to differentiate her from them, to set her apart, to exclude her, or to determine that she need not be considered. She concludes: "Yes, I am being marked as different rather than as the same, and that is why I had that differential reaction. I figured that out after years of dwelling on it." She is suggesting that persons from different racial backgrounds constantly feel they are being reminded that they are "different" and do not "belong." Their easily observable *physical* differences make it more likely that they will experience such open confrontations, which people with distinctive *cultural* characteristics can frequently avoid by virtue of the fact that cultural differences are not always obvious.

The identity issue is perhaps most poignant for Teresa, the youngest respondent, age 18, at the time of the interview, who was closest to the trauma of having to develop a sense of identity as a mixed race individual. Asked how she identifies herself, Teresa clearly prefers to view herself as racially mixed. She says: ". . .on a census, I usually check both boxes. Both the White and Black box. So I always identify myself as a 'mixed' child. Not one over the other." She goes on to say that she identifies with *both* her parents' cultures: ". . .I'll say I'm African-American, which is, my mother's American, and my father's African, so I identify with both that way."

However, she is quite concerned about the response she gets from others when she identifies in that manner. She complains: ". . .they don't know me, or even if they know my background, they usually say, like, 'Oh, you're just Black,' or 'Anything mixed with Black, is Black.' So people usually identify me as Black." She continues: ". . .I really don't like it because I'm not – even though I was born here – I'm not Black-American. My father is African and my mother is White. I'm not taking any side over the other. And I don't like to be associated with, like, the Black-Americans, either mixed or African-Americans – either one of those." Asked if "African-American" and "Black-American" mean something different, she says: "Yes, to me it does, because Black-Americans . . . most of 'em, . . . their cultural backgrounds are from . . . the United States. And my Daddy's African – he knows an African dialect. He speaks French. My mother also speaks French. So I don't like to put myself with Black-American. I always make the distinction." Teresa's complaint has also been documented in other studies of multi-racial individuals (Rockquemore & Laszloffy, 2005: 51–52).

So to Teresa, the term "African-American" gives her the opportunity to claim both her mother's and her father's heritage. The terms, "Black" or "Black American," are generally associated with persons whose families have been in the USA for several generations, and do not give her the opportunity to claim her father's African heritage. In another portion of the interview (quoted elsewhere in this work), Teresa also complained that teachers in school consistently refused to accept her self-definition of herself as "mixed" or listing two origins, reclassifying her as "Black."

Clearly, she did not believe these terms defined her true identity. She wanted to be clearly associated with her father's African culture and her mother's heritage, which included several cultural strains, but which Teresa preferred to summarize as simply "American." She clearly felt uncomfortable with others' persistent pattern of forcing the definition of "Black" upon her.

Derek, whose mother was German and his father African-American, viewed the entire process from a somewhat different perspective, being approximately 20 years older. But he too recognized that his physical appearance was a major component of his self-identity: "I know because of my light coloring that I am identified with other different races. But I identify with Black because it's more prevalent." By this he means: "...my skin color, and my features, my hair, things like that." Although he was otherwise quite comfortable with his mixed heritage and had good relations with both sides of his family, he recognized that the Black component was the dominant one and would be viewed as such by others. He gave no indication how he felt about this during his formative years, but at the time of the interview he was comfortable with the Black identity.

Possibility of "Hiding" is Absent

Multi-cultural individuals usually have a major advantage which multi-racial persons do not. Outside of the individual's family and friends, where people do not know their origins or background, multi-cultural individuals can frequently "hide" if they choose to do so. Multi-racial persons – or anyone with even a slight physical difference – do not have that luxury.

Of course, some multi-cultural persons choose *not* to hide. They wear their cultural symbols – such as a cross, the hijab (veil), or Star of David to indicate their religion, or show their pride in knowledge of a foreign language. But this is their choice. It is usually not forced upon them, as occurs with people from a different race. Indeed, some multi-cultural individuals made the point that they were offended when people did *not* recognize their distinctive cultures of which they were very proud. I have already discussed Regina's desire that people recognize both her Polish and her Brazilian heritage. And Ted went into considerable detail about his pride in his extensive knowledge of his broad European heritage and his knowledge of European history and the German language. However, it was their *choice* that people recognize their heritage. In contrast, recognition was usually forced upon people who exhibited racial differences, and this recognition was constant, in every type of social setting.

Exclusion Rather Than Inclusion

This raises another distinction that may often appear between racial and ethnic minorities. When members of the dominant White society point to others as racially distinguishable, they are usually doing so to exclude them from social groups rather than include them. The minority group members are being reminded that they are really "not part of us." This is different from telling a person who claims French ancestry, for example, that s/he is really "European like the rest of us" or "just American."

Thus, Karen noted that she always felt "out of place," always felt people were reminding her she was "different." Only when she visited Hawaii as an adult did she feel part of the group. During the trip, she encountered a woman who ". . .asked 'So what are you? So what's your mix?' or something very similar to that." As indicated earlier, this was a question to which she had become very sensitive. She reacted in what she calls an "irate" manner, until she realized that this woman was

> . . .a mixture of Hawaiian, Afro-American, Chinese and she was like a mix of every racial group. But the thing that was nice about this racial experience was just not her asking but the visit to Hawaii. It was the first time in my life that I didn't feel like I stuck out. That there was so many mixed people and that my mix was probably a minimal mix compared to most of the people I met on this Hawaiian vacation. And so, I really found that to be, not so much a bonding experience, like I didn't feel bonded to these people, but I felt at ease. That I wasn't being looked at as different, and that's the first time that this has ever happened to me in my life to the extent that I didn't feel that I stood out to any extent walking down the street or hanging out or being with my brother or whatever.

This exclusion factor is true of some ethnic minorities as well, particularly if they are seen as radically different. The manner of treatment accorded to Muslims and Arabs at the turn of the 21st century is an example of exclusion. But for persons with observable physical differences, the exclusion process seems to be on-going, which leads us to the next difference to be discussed.

Persistence

A major difficulty which persons exhibiting racial differences experienced, which was less so for persons from ethnically diverse backgrounds, was the persistence of these problems. None of the problems they experienced were situations which they could "deal with," or come to terms with, and then forget about. They were present forever and could reassert themselves at any time. Even people who had long since become comfortable with their multi-racial background and identity could be reminded months – or years – later that they really did not belong. This was largely due to the fact that the physically obvious character of their differences did not disappear, as well as the fact that so many people in the community as a whole felt free to question their identity and comment upon it.

This could occur when they least expected it and in all types of situations. Karen reported the constant reminder that she was different and did not fit in. Anita attended a conference and was accused of denying being Black. Deanna went to work at a store and was reminded by a total stranger that anything that was even a little bit Black was Black. Most of the racially mixed respondents reported experiences such as this. Over time, most of them came to terms with it. How did they deal with it? Deanna is an example. She says:

It doesn't bother me. I know some people react differently to it, but it doesn't bother me, 'cause I know who I am. And OK, fine, society says that, because I have a little bit of Black blood in me, I'm considered Black, that's fine. But I know who I am.

Similarly Anita has concluded:

...well, I guess it just, the older I got, the more comfortable I became with who I was, and found a place for myself, . . . the less people challenged who I was. So I think a lot of it had to do with how I carried myself, and how I . . . chose to explain or not to explain who I was or what I was.

That the process is not an easy task is illustrated by Karen's analysis:

...there was a time in my life when I was growing up and I think that in my teen years going through high school and looking back at it now, I was very depressed about a number of things and this issue [race and being different] was one of them. . . . There was a kind of a transformational point in my life when I realized that I had to, it was kind of the path was very clear that if I go this route I get depressed, and I would go kill myself. But if I go this route, that I start standing up for myself and basically I made an assessment that my interests and values and opinions were as important as if not more important than these other people who might be making an issue of things and that was the transformational point in my life of moving me towards being much more assertive and not caring what other people think. . . . It is more important for me what I think and do . . . .

Although she is technically not from a different race, Jeanette and her siblings also illustrate this issue. As the offspring of a Lebanese mother and an Irish father, they were constantly aware of looking different from other children in the largely Irish or Polish neighborhoods in which they lived. She experienced such trauma from the process that she went into therapy as an adult. At the time of the interview, when she was 57 years of age, she still appeared to be recovering from the trauma and seemed unable to find any redeeming features in her multi-cultural heritage.

So racially mixed people constantly encounter questions and comments about their racial makeup, and they must come to terms with this fact. For their own peace of mind, they must also reach a point at which they do not let these comments bother them and recognize that they must be comfortable with their own opinion of themselves and their identity. And they must not let the views of others disturb their sense of themselves. However, this can be an extremely disturbing process for younger people or those who have not yet reached that level of comfort.

Individuals Cannot Escape Even When Alone

A final dimension of racial, as opposed to ethnic, identity formation is the inability of racially distinct persons escape from the problems of "being different" from others even when alone. People who exhibit physical characteristics which differentiate them from others are always aware of this fact. There is no escaping from it, and the pressure of how to deal with it is always there.

This was noted by several of our respondents, and we have discussed some of these comments before. Karen said she never felt like she belonged until she went to Hawaii. She also discussed at some length the fact that her parents could not help her with the problems she faced: her White father because of his conviction that racial differences were no more important "...than having big ears" and her Korean mother, "...because it hurt her too ... when you make fun of her children." So, as a child, she had little support in dealing with her problems and was left alone to try to work them out.

Similarly, Jeanette and her siblings knew that they looked different from the other children in their neighborhood, where most children were Irish or Polish. About her experience in one particular Irish Catholic school, she says:

> I felt different there. ... the difference was through my mother, but I didn't know it then. But my sisters and ... We would talk about who had the Irish skin or the Lebanese skin or who looked Irish and who looked Lebanese. Then we would compare how the Lebanese were different from the Irish. I can remember thinking, I wish that I was all Irish, to be like those kids in the public school, that had Irish mother and father. ... it was just I wanted to fit into that.

Hence, even when she should have been in the comfort of her family, Jeanette and her sisters were constantly discussing how they were treated, the differences they perceived, why they were important, and trying to figure out where they fit. Persons who did not have a physical difference to cope with are often able to ignore these issues when they are alone or with members of their own family or group.

Summary of the Impact of Physical Differences

To summarize, we have delineated six characteristics of racial differences which place the multi-racial individual in a different category from persons from multi-cultural backgrounds. These make the identity formation process different for them in significant ways. First and foremost among these distinctions is the highly observable character of racial differences, making it difficult or impossible for people to ignore. We have also suggested that there appears to be a greater likelihood that outsiders feel free to insert their views into their interactions with persons who exhibit noticeable physical differences, which they normally would not do if the differences were not so obvious. With obvious physical differences, the possibility of "hiding" is clearly absent; hence multi-racial individuals do not have the luxury of "passing" if they wish to do so. Respondents also noted that, with racial minorities, recognition of the distinction between racial minorities and the dominant group usually is made to exclude them from a group rather than to include them. We have also noted that, for physically different individuals, these problems tend to persist over an extended period of time, never allowing the individuals to put the problems behind them. Finally, the experiences of our respondents suggest individuals find it difficult to escape these problems even when alone or with their closest friends and family; in these settings, the problems were a common topic of conversation.

Furthermore, physical differences also played a role in the identity formation of some Whites, primarily those with darker skin. Most significantly, it applies to persons from Middle Eastern or southern European groups, such as Lebanese,

Italians, or Spanish; people from Central and South America; and persons of Native American heritage, all of whom have slightly darker skin color than Whites of northern European backgrounds. All possess some physical characteristics which may differentiate them from the Caucasian population; they can, therefore, be easily differentiated. All are likely, therefore, to experience, at least to some degree, the difficulties we have outlined which are experienced by multi-*racial*, as opposed to multi-*cultural*, individuals. Theoretically, we might hypothesize that these issues may also apply to anyone who is physically "different," such as the disabled.

Consequently, there is no doubt that, in the USA, outwardly observable characteristics play an important role in the community's definition of its members. It is also likely that these characteristics will also be used by the community in influencing its members to accept the definition which the community prescribes. However, outwardly observable characteristics include more than simply physical differences. It may also involve surnames, foreign accents, and other factors that can easily be noticed, such as religious symbols (the Muslim *hijab*, or veil, the Jewish Star of David, or the Sikh turban). Such outward symbols may be employed with regard to persons who do not differ in physical appearance from the dominant White population.

Furthermore, our major concern throughout this work is not to focus specifically on the racial or cultural characteristics of the respondents per se. Rather, the focus will be on their experiences as persons from *mixed* backgrounds, that is, persons whose origins include more than a single cultural or racial heritage. Our assumption is that the experiences of people from mixed backgrounds may bear similarities to others with the same experiences, whether that mixture be racial or culturally based. There may be points at which the issue of race, as opposed to culture, may be relevant. When that issue appears to be relevant, we will bring out this point.

To a great extent, however, the mixed background respondents reported relatively similar experiences in their encounters with the communities in which they lived. As we shall see, these encounters were largely related to whether their backgrounds were viewed as "normal" or "different." Sometimes the basis of these differences were racial and sometimes cultural. Hence, we will assume that, for the most part, the experiences can be considered together. In most instances, they created problems for the individuals involved. A discussion of these problems appears to be an appropriate way to begin our analysis. Hence, this will be the topic of the next chapter.

Chapter 4
Growing Up Painful: Problems of Multi-cultural Socialization

Many of the respondents described problems which they had encountered as a result of their multi-cultural family backgrounds. One even described the experience as "painful." Since this issue of childhood problems related to multi-culturalism appeared so frequently in the respondents' descriptions of their childhoods, a discussion of these problems appears to be a reasonable place to begin our analysis. In later chapters, we will discuss several of these problems in greater depth, and analyze how the parents and their offspring handled them, or, in some instances, failed to do so. We will also suggest ways in which the experiences could have been less painful.

This discussion of childhood problems, even painful ones, should be understood in the context of the respondents' general perception of childhood. Indeed, one of the most encouraging aspects of the interviews of these multi-cultural respondents was their overall optimism and generally positive outlook on their multi-cultural background. Most of the respondents seemed happy to have the opportunity to talk about their multi-cultural experiences, and the conversation was pleasant and congenial. Most respondents felt that they had done reasonably well in life, and looked upon their multi-cultural experience as a positive aspect of their lives. They often pointed to their experiences as important dimensions for consideration in a multi-cultural society such as the USA. While they often talked about problems from their childhood, they looked back upon it as a growth experience which had placed them in a position to develop their skills and make the most of their adult lives.

However, while nearly all of the respondents described problems related to multi-culturalism, there were a few who seemed to focus almost entirely on the problems. What stood out in a few respondents' memories were the difficulties they faced. Many (though not all) of these were younger respondents, for whom the unpleasant experiences were more recent and had not yet faded from memory. Since problems were mentioned by so many respondents, these problems clearly deserve attention.

Nowhere were the problems more clearly delineated than in the interview with a woman I call "Jeanette." In many ways, Jeanette's interview was quite different from any of the others. Three dimensions in particular stand out. First, Jeanette's interview was undoubtedly the most disorganized of any of the respondents. While all interviews were conducted in an "open-ended" fashion, allowing the respondents to direct the progress of the discussion, most were quite content to move from one

M.C. Sengstock, *Voices of Diversity*, Clinical Sociology: Research and Practice,
DOI 10.1007/978-0-387-89666-3_4, © Springer Science+Business Media, LLC 2009

topic to another in a fairly organized fashion. Jeanette's interview, however, was different. She jumped rapidly from one subject to another. There were dramatic changes of focus from one topic to another and back again. For example, in one early section of the interview, while describing her family, Jeanette interrupted the discussion several times, as the mention of another family member brought to mind another problem she wanted to mention.

Peter, whose parents were Native American and Caucasian, and Karen, whose parents were Caucasian and Korean, were other respondents who mentioned many problems. Both talked frequently about being rejected in various settings because of their mixed ancestry; however, both also interspersed their complaints with descriptions of the more pleasant aspects of their lives. Peter particularly enjoyed the times he spent with cousins on the reservation. The contrast was obvious: other respondents were able to focus on the socialization experience as a whole. For Jeanette, however, the focus was always on the problems. Her interview appears highly disorganized on the surface, unless one recognizes that, for Jeanette, the underlying theme is always her recollection of the problems.

The difference between Jeanette and the other respondents was also obvious in Jeanette's constant use of negative words to describe her life growing up. For example, she used the word, "painful" several times to describe her socialization. She also employed other terms such as "ashamed," "hated," "awful," and "worse." In contrast, other respondents, even those who described many problems in their childhood, did not generally use such negative terms (or similar ones, such as bitter, depressing, disturbing, or sad) in describing their experiences growing up.

Finally, Jeanette's approach to the interviewing process focused much more on her need or desire for self-analysis, a point which she specifically mentioned on more than one occasion. Most respondents, when they learned about the study, told me they would like to be interviewed because they were interested in the topic, they felt multi-cultural people were an important group to study, and they wanted to share their experiences with others. Jeanette was the only one who specifically said she welcomed the opportunity to deal with issues which still remained in her mind as a result of her childhood.

Consequently, it appears that an analysis of Jeanette's "painful" experiences might be a useful mechanism for examining the negative aspects of a multi-cultural childhood. What was it about her growing up in a multi-cultural setting that she found so painful? Was this unique to her? Or did other respondents have similar experiences? If so, why did she (and a few others) focus so much on the painful aspects, while most of the respondents did not? This topic will be the focus of this chapter.

In reviewing the issues Jeanette described as "painful," two different types of issues appear to be involved. On the one hand, some of the issues appear to be distinctly related to the family's multi-cultural nature, that is, the fact that persons from several different cultures were part of the household. The specifically multi-cultural issues were three in number and included relating to the diversity of cultures and people in the family, developing a sense of personal and family identity, and the perception of nonacceptance in the larger community.

However, other issues which were described as "painful" stemmed from more general problems. These problems would be familiar to many families which are not multi-cultural. They would be characteristic of any family which exhibits characteristics which are "different" from the surrounding community. Two of these more general issues could be delineated. They are problems which stem from the nature of a lower class, immigrant family; and problems which stemmed from the specific ethnic group in the home.

I will discuss these two different types of issues separately. I will reserve discussion of the specifically multi-cultural issues to the second part of the chapter. In the next section I will discuss the factors which seem not to be essentially multi-cultural. Rather, these are characteristics which these families shared with other, single-culture families. In these instances, the families exhibited a single distinct cultural pattern which placed them in a disadvantaged position with regard to other members of the community.

General Issues for All "Distinctively Different" Families

In this category are characteristics these families shared with all families or individuals who do not "fit" very well into the community in which they are located. An issue which arose very early in the interviews with these multi-cultural respondents was the importance of the social environment in which they were raised in determining their satisfaction with the experience. This issue will be discussed in detail in Chapter 6. In this chapter we will focus on the specific patterns which set these persons and their families apart from their communities. We have already indicated in Chapter 3 that racial differences set people apart from the community. Cultural differences often do the same.

Communities which are not accepting of persons or groups different from themselves are likely to engender difficulties for children in their midst. Children from multi-cultural families are likely to have problems, but so also will children from a single racial or cultural background, if it is not one of those preferred in the community. In such communities, children from poor families, immigrant families, or other culturally distinguishable families are likely to experience distress. Any family or individual exhibiting these differentiating characteristics would be likely to experience difficulties in these communities. There were two types of characteristics in this category, one of them class-related, the other ethnic/cultural in character.

Problems Which Stemmed from the Nature of a Lower Class, Immigrant Family

The nature of life for most children of lower class background or of immigrant origins (not to mention both) is necessarily a painful one in most communities, particularly if other members of the community are more prosperous or are from native-born families. Again, Jeanette's experience is most illustrative. She lived with her maternal grandmother for the first 11 years of her life. The house was very small, and the household included grandparents, aunts, uncles, and cousins, in addition to her parents and siblings. The family used any means available to provide financial support. They had a goat in the yard, and her grandmother ran a store from the living room. Syrian and Lebanese relatives from other parts of the state would come to work in the area and would live with them:[1]

> A lot of the Syrian and Lebanese relatives . . . my father was getting them jobs in the factory . . . We had a three bedroom rural home, they were in one room, all the kids in another room and then my parents. . . . Especially one, my mother's sister . . . and her three children, we grew up with. . . . We were all in one bedroom . . . there were two cribs in there, two double beds, and a single bed. All the girls were in there. It wasn't like this was my side of the bed, or this is my bed, it was who got in bed first. . . . in fact I went back to look at it a few years ago . . . and it was so small. And I thought, how did we do this? How did we all come out of this little house? It was very poor, in terms of class and environment. [But] we had clothes and food and we were taken care of. . . .

Hence, Jeanette's memories were of a too-small house with too many people living in it, constant scratching to make a living, everyone involved in the activities of supporting the family. These are not special problems which are unique to a multi-cultural family. These are common issues in immigrant families, in which there is constant migration from the country of origin, and families are expected to provide living space and financial support for these new arrivals whenever possible. In Jeanette's case, this included not only people arriving from Lebanon, but others who might have been living in other parts of the USA, but who were able to find better jobs near them. Hence the embarrassing household patterns: overcrowded living arrangements, numerous rooms being converted into bedrooms, conversion of the living room into a shop, and keeping goats and chickens in the yard.

Jeanette expressed the view that these extreme measures were not necessary since several household members had jobs, but this view either was not shared by her grandmother, or she was so used to doing this that she could not imagine life otherwise. But to a child who wanted to have activities of her own and time for herself, it was "painful": ". . .I didn't like it . . . I wanted my own room. I wanted to bring friends home. I wanted to be active in school."

Hence, one factor which created problems for these multi-cultural individuals stemmed not from the multi-cultural character of the family, but from the fact that the family as a whole was radically different from others in the community. In this instance, the difference was economic: they were poor. In poor families, making a living takes precedence over all other issues. And the interest of children – in school, sports, socializing with friends, or any other activity – had to take second place, and second place often meant it was never considered at all. Children from any low-income family, or any family which included a large number of persons in the household, would very likely have felt out of place in this setting, regardless of their

---

[1] Throughout the book, longer quotes have been edited to omit extraneous material without altering the integrity of the original content.

ethnic origins. So the first factor which appears to have created problems for these multi-cultural families is the fact that some of them were from poor backgrounds, which put them at a disadvantage in the community.

Robert was a particularly interesting case in this regard. As noted earlier, he was adamant that nationality-based ethnic differences did not matter in the southern town where he grew up. At the same time, however, it was clear from some of his comments that there were negative experiences which stemmed from the family's economic status. In his case, it was not because his family was poorer than others in the area, but because the community as a whole was poor and unable to provide adequate resources for the education of the children. Robert commented:

> I enjoyed school tremendously. . . . I loved my teachers, and I learned a lot. . . . I was a good listener. . . . I do remember in Kentucky, in 1960, that when you went to high school you had to buy your own books. . . . It was like free public education stopped at the end of the eighth grade, which was against the law. So here I am, a freshman in high school, now I've got to buy books. And it was a lot of money. It was probably $30–$35.

So Robert may not have felt out of place because of his nationality background. However, to a boy with college aspirations, he did feel much of the same discomfort that Jeanette mentioned, due to the economic status of his family and community.

Peter echoed the same feelings of discomfort in describing his experiences growing up in southern California, where his Native American culture came into conflict with the predominant materialistic culture. He reported: "I'm plain and I'm not very American, I guess, in the sense that Americans have a lot of things, having a nice car, having ambitions, stuff like that." As a result, he had the same sense of not being accepted that Jeanette reported: ". . .it was strange because a lot of people didn't want to be friends with me, being in California." Hence, several multi-cultural people had experiences related to the fact that their families often experienced economic difficulties which made them uncomfortable in the communities in which they lived. Whatever their source, being financially disadvantaged relative to others in the community can be painful for children and youth.

It should be noted, however, that not all respondents who grew up in households which practiced a pattern which was ethnically or economically different from the surrounding community were particularly bothered by the situation. Regina, for example, speaks of her childhood as a child of Polish refugee parents growing up in Brazil. Her mother was a seamstress and made all of her clothes by hand, using traditions which she had brought with her from Poland as well as years of living in Germany. They were beautifully hand-stitched, but dramatically different from the clothes which her Brazilian schoolmates wore. However, rather than feeling out of place, Regina only recalls being "very in awe" of the artfulness of this handiwork. Apparently, being "different" does not necessarily make a child uncomfortable. The impact it has is largely dependent upon the manner in which the family handles it, as well as the character of the surrounding community. We will return to these issues at a later point.

Problems Which Stemmed from a Specific Ethnic Cultural Pattern in the Home

Another set of problems not related specifically to a family's *multi*-cultural character stemmed from the specific ethnic group which predominated in the home. Jeanette grew up in a home which was largely dominated by the grandmother's Lebanese culture. While the members might marry persons from other backgrounds, as her mother had, these "outsiders" soon became part of the household in which Lebanese culture predominated: "...when people marry in, you're part of the family then." As a result, the whole family exhibited the characteristics of Lebanese culture which made them conspicuous in the local community; here again this difference was negative.

Five dimensions of culture appear in the respondents' discussion: use of ethnic languages, the "loud" character of some ethnic cultures, gender differences, the oppressive nature of family responsibilities, and lack of concern for the children's interests.

Ethnic Language Usage

Again Jeanette's memories are significant. She was embarrassed by the use of ethnic languages in the home. She remembers that "...there were lots of languages," since several of her aunts had married men from different nations. But her grandmother's language was predominant:

> There was the Arabic, but it wasn't called that, it was Lebanese. Because Arabic, when I was growing up, Arabic was very negative, it was like a bad word. ... When I was growing up people used the term Mohammed. ... I don't remember saying it, but that's what that meant. [The men] would get into arguments ... and they were yelling at each other, and like the worse thing you could say is that you're an Arab ....

Hence, there was a constant undertone of belonging to a group which had a highly negative association in the community, with Arabs and the followers of Mohammed.

Language-related issues were mentioned by other respondents as well. Sarah, for example, recalls frequent experiences in which they would be told, in a very rude manner, that they were unwelcome in the community. While it rarely happened to her directly, her mother was often insulted because of her foreign accent. Sarah says:

> ...not so much me personally, because ... by then I was fluent in English, but I would go to the supermarket with my mother, and someone would cut in front of us and my mother would tell the woman, "I was here first," ... and the response was, "Go back where you came from." And a fairly regular basis. This was not an isolated incident.

Ted, whose family background included Austrian, German, and Polish, recalled his parents' stories:

> [being] ...called "Hinnes and Huns and Krauts" and spit upon occasionally. And occasionally kids threw rocks at them for being non-American. So my grandfather, 20 odd years later, forbade, really he couldn't forbid my mother, he said as the patriarch of the clan he would not address us ... in anything other than English...

Hence, a family rule was established that they did not use their foreign language facility in order not to appear different in the community. Other respondents also indicated their families stressed the use of English, especially for the children, even if the adults used the ethnic language themselves. Jeanette noted that the men of the family often used foreign languages to keep their conversations private, but would get angry if the women failed to use English. And Francine reported that her mother and grandmother often spoke to each other in Italian, but did not teach it to the children, apparently to enable the adults to keep their personal conversations private. Hence, foreign language use appeared to be used in some settings to keep conversations private and also to keep certain members, such as the women and children, "in their place."

Some respondents never mentioned their family's foreign language usage as creating a problem. Anita, for example, stressed the fact that her parents tried very hard to ensure that their children learned Spanish; however, she never viewed it in a negative way and only saw it as a desirable trait that she was fluent in Spanish. But for many of the respondents, the presence of a foreign language often made the family conspicuous and placed them in an uncomfortable situation.

Loud Ethnic Speech Patterns

Another language-related problem focused on the manner in which language was used. Middle Eastern culture, like other Mediterranean cultures, tends to be somewhat loud. This is the case whether they are speaking in the ethnic language or in English. This pattern has created problems between Middle Easterners and their American neighbors for some time (Sengstock, 1999). Jeanette remembers the men arguing and insulting each other in loud voices: "Grandpop and the five guys . . . . They would smoke, drink, and eat and fight and argue. Now it sounded loud. . . . I say fight but they would yell at each other. It sounded loud probably because it was in Arabic."

Hence, loud arguments in languages she did not understand were part of Jeanette's painful memories, especially so in view of the fact that she remembers herself as, ". . .a very quiet child." This loud use of language is not unique to Middle Easterners. The reader will recall, for example, our earlier discussion of the discrimination experienced by early Scottish and Irish immigrants from the English colonists, who considered them boorish and rude. Their use of a strange variety of English – loud and with an unusual accent – probably played a part in this perception. Discrimination on the basis of language patterns considered "improper" is obviously still practiced in American culture today. Again, these differences can be embarrassing to children, who fear that their friends will make fun of them because of the manner in which their family is viewed by the community.

Ethnic Gender Differences were Painful

The next issue illustrates another aspect of the culture of immigrant families which several of the respondents considered problematic. As indicated earlier, the majority of the respondents were female (19 or 63%). Since many ethnic cultures tend to be more "traditional" than American culture, many of the women in the study expressed dissatisfaction with the gender discrimination they encountered in their families. Two cultures in particular seemed to convey this view: Asian and Middle Eastern.

Evelyn, with a Chinese father and a Korean mother, reported on the problems which she perceived in a home which was dominated by the Korean culture of her mother. The male-dominant character of the culture was unmistakable, and in Evelyn's mind, unacceptable. She reported:

> There's so many differences, you know, conflict, that goes on in this house ... we don't know ... how we were supposed to act. ... no arguing back at your parents, ... from a girl's perspective, I'm supposed to take care of the family   the whole family ... like chores ... pick up after my brothers ... feed them ... like my family comes first. ... in their eyes, it doesn't matter if I pursue a career or a vocation because I'm going to get married someday and someone's going to take care of me. So my duties are to be what they feel a woman should be. In their culture – a homebody, I guess.

Since Evelyn has three brothers and no sisters, her role is to care for all three of them, "...regardless of age ... I have a brother, the youngest is 20 and I'm still supposed to ... tend to him ... I'm 30!" Of course, in the eyes of her family, being 30 and not yet married is also inappropriate:

> Yes, I hear that from my mom all the time. ... It is difficult for me even to bring someone into this house, because of my parents, their ways. ... It probably wouldn't be accepted. ... because they would be non-Asian. ... And that would have a lot to do with it. ... And from past experiences, I won't do it again! [Like what happened?] ... my mother disowned me. I mean, you know, I had to leave the house. ... I was out for ... almost 2 years. [Q: Oh, you moved out?] Yeah, well they kind of like kicked me out!

Hence, Evelyn was unable to accommodate to the extreme gender discrimination which she perceived in her family, to the extent that her family, in her words, "kicked her out." Eventually she moved back, but only after nearly two years of being estranged from the family.

Jeanette found the same depressing patriarchal tradition in the Middle Eastern culture of her grandmother. Again, it was the female side of the family which prevailed, but that did not lessen the degree of male dominance. Jeanette says:

> I hated it .... It was just awful. The men were ... just kings of the house. Everything centered around them. The hierarchy of age was very important among the Lebanese. The first cousin was a male ... and he was the king. ... She [e.g., her grandmother] would make this cake ... and then it would sit there because ... nobody could have a piece of cake, the women, the ones who did all the work, until he had the first piece. It was just cooking and cleaning. ... They never did any cleaning. ... [my cousin and I] we were discussing this ... I remember we were saying, we don't even count, but our sons do. ... That whole ... the men, the line ... Carrying that name and having sons. ... My mother ... found out she was going to have twins. ... when my father came home and told us that they were both girls, ... my brother had an ice cream cone and he threw it from the front door and it went through all three rooms and hit the back kitchen wall, he said he was never going to live in this house with all the girls. ... and in fact they had the name [e.g., for the boy] picked out. ... Yes, they were pretty much the bosses. ... and they didn't do any housework, nothing, nothing. ...

Having the men be "kings" and having to serve them in everything was not the only gender dimension which bothered Jeanette. The other side of the coin represented the deprivations which came with being a girl. In particular, Jeanette liked athletics and found this also was an area reserved for her brother. The family purchase of a bike represented a particularly unpleasant episode:

> So I remember . . . my parents bought a bike. This really made me angry. . . . they bought a boy's bike because there was one bike for everybody. Because a boy could not ride a girl's bike, but a girl could ride a boy's bike. But we couldn't ride the boy's bike because we had dresses on. . . . and I didn't express my anger, it was all internal. I didn't speak out, but my sister . . . used to.

Hence, another distressing component of being part of an ethnic family involved some dimensions of the culture which placed one portion of the family at a disadvantage as related to other members. In the example which Evelyn and Jeanette describe, this is a gender-related issue. Girls and women held a different status in the family from men and boys. This placed the girls at a great disadvantage with reference to their fathers and brothers. While it has been shown that American families also show significant gender differences, these differences are often more extreme in families of foreign origin (Segal, 1998; Min, 1998; Sengstock, 1999; 2005).

Again, this places the members of these families in a different and often embarrassing position with reference to the rest of the community. Jeanette and Evelyn both felt they could not do what other girls their age could do: have free time, go to school, engage in sports, have dates with boys they chose, and so on, due to the expectations of their families. For them, the differences were gender-related. However, immigrant family patterns might involve other cultural expectations as well. Some immigrant families, for example, expect to control the occupational choices of their children, both boys and girls (Sengstock, 1999; 2005). And this has been known to create difficulties as the children are frequently left with unresolved aspirations.

The Oppressive Nature of Family Responsibilities

As suggested in the previous section, closely related to the gender aspect of much ethnic culture is the extreme focus on family responsibility. While family responsibility is imposed upon both men and women, the responsibilities for each are different. From both Jeanette's and Evelyn's point of view, the women's responsibilities were more extreme. Women were required to carry out many responsibilities. In Jeanette's case, the traditional Middle Eastern hospitality was an important part of this, and her grandmother was the model, and the girls were responsible for carrying it out:

> . . .you know the ritual – hospitality. Behind the scene, I with my sisters would be doing all the cleaning, the percolator, washing the dishes, emptying ashtrays, watching the twins. . . . to me there was just work, it was intolerable. But people loved our house. . . .

Much to Jeanette's dismay, she soon learned that she was also expected to take over the role her mother and grandmother had played, of caring for all family members in need:

> And then I was taking that over. I couldn't believe it was happening. . . . My brother lived with me before he went to Vietnam after my father died. My sister . . . came and lived with me with her daughter in between her divorce. My mother came and lived with me in between her marriages. My sister . . . she was a teen and had a drug problem, I went down to Florida got her, brought her back, took her to rehab. . . . I was by [a major interstate], so . . . whatever . . . [was], going on in the area, they would get off the turnpike and come to my house and I would be expected to be my mother. . . . that's when I realized . . . what I would be doing for the rest of my life and I left.

Hence, the extreme focus on family and carrying out responsibilities toward the family were other aspects of immigrant culture, in this case, Middle Eastern culture, which Jeanette found unacceptable. As noted earlier, Jeanette's views were echoed by Evelyn's complaint that in Korean culture, she was expected to take care of her brothers, regardless of their relative ages. To young girls growing up in the USA, with friends who had the freedom to choose to do school work, engage in sports or play, and choose their own activities, living in a family which favored their brothers over them was oppressive. They longed to be like other girls they knew at school, whose families let them have some freedom and engage in some activities of their own, without imposing a great many responsibilities on them simply because it was a girls' duty to take care of the family, even of their own siblings who might be younger than they, but who were accorded a special status simply because they were male.

Lack of Concern for the Children's Interests

The final aspect of ethnic culture which some respondents resented was their parents' lack of concern for the kinds of issues which their children considered important. For several respondents, this issue focused on education. This was true of Robert, who would eventually become a teacher. He reported that he was generally good at school. However, he sounded somewhat bitter when he recalled that his parents showed little interest and provided no support for his school activities. He says:

> I don't recall my father or my mother ever going to a parent teacher conference. . . . I pretty much learned I was on my own. . . . I just pretty much took care of my own stuff. I had a job, a little bit of money from working in the stores in town. I had a paper route as a kid. I had saved some money and that's how I bought my clothes and . . . my books and . . . my baseballs and stuff. I learned to count on myself.

For the women, such as Evelyn and Jeanette, this issue also became involved with the gender issue. Like Robert, both were interested in school. And both complained that their responsibilities to their families often made it difficult or impossible to pay attention to schoolwork. Had they been boys, their parents might have been more willing to indulge their interest in school. However, in a community which sees little value in education in the first place, education for a girl seemed particularly useless. Jeanette was excited by newspapers which her uncles would bring home and was particularly thrilled when she discovered the existence of a library: "I remember I spotted this building and it said library and I went in and I found out that you could join, and you could take out books." However, for a young girl who wanted to learn, and who would eventually go on to do graduate work in college, it was difficult to read and study under the constraints of a family structure which did not accommodate these interests:

> That was probably the most painful because I loved school. . . . I remember my father talking about you're supposed to get good grades . . . but there was no place to do homework at our house. . . . the main thing was survival and not really study.

Furthermore, when she established a particularly satisfying experience at a new high school, "It was cutting into my service at home, so they pulled me out and put me in a [another] school so that I could help my mother at home and work at my uncle's store."

In summary, much of the stress these respondents felt in their home environment was not primarily related to the fact that the family was multi-cultural in character. Rather, it was related to the fact that a foreign culture which was brought from another country was dominant in the family. There appeared to be no major disagreements about culture or ethnicity within these families. Instead, there was a single cultural pattern which prevailed, but it was a pattern in which the interests of the children were subordinated to the concerns of the adults. Robert, Jeanette, and Evelyn all grew up in families which were primarily concerned with the necessity of making a living. They had little time or interest in assisting or even allowing their children to develop and pursue interests they could share with their friends or on which they could build a future. All of these respondents seemed aware of the fact that these particular problems stemmed from the particular characteristics of their family pattern and not from the fact that it was multi-cultural.

In the case of both Evelyn and Jeanette, they grew up in families which were structured around a fairly clear ethnic pattern. For Jeanette, Middle Eastern culture predominated; for Evelyn, it was Korean culture. But in both instances, men dominated and women had numerous responsibilities toward the family. The requirements of the women's role were particularly cumbersome and oppressive. They prevented the girls from doing all of the things which they found interesting and exciting: study, learning, and living an independent life. However, these problems did not originate in the multi-cultural nature of the family setting. Rather they would have been experienced by any child in a family of immigrant origin with a culture which placed them at odds with the surrounding community.

Indeed, Jeanette's multi-cultural background actually added a special character to the stress of an oppressive ethnic family. Although her family clearly followed a Middle Eastern patriarchal culture, she also was able to view, second-hand, the experiences of her father's Irish relatives. She reports looking with envy on the experiences of her Irish cousins; these young women were afforded much more freedom than her Lebanese family culture allowed her. She says wistfully: "when we would visit or have my … Irish cousins visit … they were totally different. They were older than I was … my female Irish cousins, some of them went to college, they were athletic. They just had the kind of life I would have wanted." Hence, the multi-cultural character of the family gave her a close-up view of an alternative life style which she would have preferred. Being multi-cultural came to represent to her how things could be, were it not for the oppressive family patriarchy.

In Robert's case, he did not have to be concerned with the gender responsibilities, but he still was concerned that his family culture did not allow him to engage in the activities he preferred, namely, his interests in school and learning. In a way, however, he was somewhat fortunate, in that his family allowed him to retain his earnings from odd jobs. Since his mother did not work and his father was an alcoholic and not always a dependable provider, some families would have expected him to contribute his earnings to the family instead of retaining them for himself. This pattern is not unknown in ethnic families, even with the boys, who are often expected to go into the family business and often to work without remuneration as Jeanette found to her dismay. From his perspective, Robert insisted that the different cultural backgrounds of his parents made little difference in the family. He simply saw their family as a poor Southern, White family while segregation was still in force.

Distinctly Multi-cultural Problems

At this point, we move to the remaining three issues, all of which deal directly with the multi-cultural character of the family and the way its members dealt with it. They are unlikely to be encountered by other families in which a *common* cultural pattern prevails, even if that pattern differed from that of the surrounding community. While the previous issues are difficulties which multi-cultural families share with other lower income, minority, or immigrant groups, these problems would be unique to the multi-cultural family experience. These three issues include coping with the diversity of cultures and people in the family, developing a sense of personal and family identity, and coping with the perception of nonacceptance of their multi-culturalism in the larger community.

Dealing with the Diversity of Cultures and People in the Family

By virtue of their existence in a multi-cultural family, all of the respondents in the study had to cope with diverse cultures as a part of their daily lives. It would have been extremely difficult for these people to avoid noticing that different members of their families had different ways of doing things. Many of them heard different languages spoken in the household. Many were introduced to different religious traditions and ideas about raising children and the relationships between men and women. Even if the family united around a particular cultural pattern, as some of them did, they came into contact with others in the extended family who felt differently. How did they view these differences? How did they react? How did their parents deal with these differences? This will be the focus of this section.

As I have previously indicated, Jeanette seemed more aware of these issues than any of the other respondents. Her awareness may have been due to an unusually sensitive nature. Or it could have been related to the fact that she was really somewhat unusual in the number of cultures she had to cope with, as well as the relative lack of knowledge about these cultures which her family provided her. These two issues – the extreme diversity and the lack of information – appear to have had a role in creating the painful feelings she experienced. Whatever the reason, her observations are a useful place to start.

Her mother and her mother's sisters had married an Irish, a German, and a Polish man, respectively. Jeanette recalls being confused by this diversity:

> And it just seemed so big, it seemed so big. And my memories of it are just like . . . that was the world. . . . I remember German, Italian and French. Not African-American. . . . But when we moved . . . That's when it included more Italians than ever. . . . when, when I say about painful . . . it just seemed so busy, and so confusing, so many different languages.

Furthermore, the differences were not only present but emphasized, with stereotypes to fit each group. What brought the whole group together? She felt the only thing that pulled people together was eating together, with Polish, Irish, Lebanese, Germans, and Italians all contributing their special dishes. Hence, Jeanette's memories are almost a jumble of people from a wide range of nationalities, all of whom were appropriate once they became part of the extended family network; of intermarriages that were all right – as long as they were from the same religion; of religiously mixed marriages that were spoken of in hushed tones; of her Irish father and her Polish and German uncles eating her mother's Lebanese kibbe; Italian neighbors who brought in food to the house.

Many of them could have been relatively pleasant memories – of people eating together, cooking food for each other. Yet there is a strong undertone of distress to her memories, as though there is a lack of understanding and resentment about the experiences. It is as though she has never been able to come to terms with and accept her childhood. Nor was there ever any attempt on the part of her family to assist her in doing so. At one point in the interview, with no apparent basis, she exclaims, "You're jogging memories! . . . This is fantastic! . . . I've been [talking about] this for years with all my relatives. This is helping me piece things together."

Like Jeanette and Evelyn, most other respondents also reported problems in dealing with their family diversity and the issues which arose. In contrast, however, most did not express the same level of distress. Sarah, for example, had a family background which included Greek, Rumanian, Eastern Orthodox Christian, and Jewish. She also reported having had contact with both sides of her family. And Teresa said she often wished she were either all-Black or all-White. They could easily have been as confused by these many cultural dimensions as was Jeanette. For the most part, they were not.

To summarize, one problem of multi-cultural families is the presence of a variety of cultures in the environment, including the immediate family. However, some respondents found the encounter with these diverse cultures to be confusing and even disturbing. Others seemed to take these experiences in stride. Apparently some individuals were able to understand the diversity better than others. Or perhaps some families were able to explain the differences in a way that the children were more comfortable with their differences and better able to assist their children in dealing with them. We will return to this issue in Chapter 7. In the next section, we turn to another issue which many respondents found difficult: determining the nature of their own ethnic identity.

Identification Problems: Developing a Sense of Personal and Family Identity

If there is a single issue which nearly all of the respondents had to confront as they grew up in a multi-cultural family, it was the question of their identity. As George Herbert Mead (1934) pointed out so effectively, a major developmental problem of childhood is finding a sense of self. This process inevitably involves three closely interrelated questions: "Who am I?" "Who are these people around me?" "How do we relate to each other?"

When children are exposed to a single cultural pattern in all aspects of their lives, this process is considerably simplified. Everyone they encounter – parents, older siblings, extended family members, neighbors – all present to them a common response to these questions. For example, a child who was born in the USA in 1940s would very likely have experienced a highly ethnic childhood and would have had little difficulty understanding who she was. Her parents most likely were of the same racial and nationality background and they would have lived in a largely ethnic neighborhood. She would have attended a school in which the other children were of the same background, and many of her teachers would also have shared that background. She probably would have received a similar response to any of her questions from everyone she encountered.

If she were of Italian origin, she would have been reminded of this at every turn. Of course you are Italian! We are all Italian! We are proud of our Italian heritage! And she would be informed numerous times of what was expected of a proper young Italian-American girl. Polish, Black, Irish, and Mexican children of other groups would have the same experience. That is not to say that *understanding* who she is and who these people are would necessarily be easy, but the message she would receive would be the same from the majority of the people she encountered. Everyone would have reinforced the same messages: "Who you are." "Who we as a people are." "What we as a people believe in and do."

In contrast, for children from a multi-cultural background, the process is much more complicated. If their social environment is culturally mixed, then they will receive mixed messages as to who they are, who their people are, and what are the appropriate ways to believe and act. Sarah, with a Jewish mother and a father who was Orthodox and Catholic, received mixed messages as to "who she was." She comments:

> ...I got a lot of stuff from both sides of the family. Fairly subtle. I didn't know what was going on because I was a kid, and I didn't know I was being manipulated in this little game of power between the two sides, where I would go to my father's relatives and they would say, "you're a Christian because it goes by the father." And I'd go to my mother's relatives and declare I was Christian because it goes by the father, and they'd say, "oh no, no, no, religion is always on the side of the mother." Uh, and my Jewish relatives were always reactive – they never initiated any of this discussion. They would only answer things that I would bring up that my father's [relatives] would sort of send me home with.

Hence, Sarah's vague memories as a little girl present a clear division within her family. Some relatives were Christian, others Jewish; some believed that a child should follow her father's faith; others insisted she should follow her mother's. How different this was from a family in which everyone followed a single religion and there was no distinction between the religion of the father and that of the mother! At an early age, no clear answer was presented to her about who she was, nor what religion her parents were. Was she Jewish, like her mother? Or Christian, like her father? Very early she would come to realize that her father and mother were different, at least in this area known as religion. Clearly also, her relatives on both sides of the family were different from each other in ways that each side considered important. Hence, the answers to the important questions of identity were not receiving clear-cut answers. As indicated earlier, Sarah's parents did not make an issue of religion, so there was no confrontation over whether or not she should be baptized or become an active member of either faith. But for Sarah, the message is quite different from the message received by the hypothetical Italian child mentioned earlier. For Sarah, there was no clear message as to who she was, no indication that her entire family shared her identity, nor that they all had a common perspective on the world, or what we commonly call a "culture."

While Sarah was not bothered by the obvious display of a religious division in her family, the same could not be said for Jeanette. The need to find an identity with which she was comfortable was definitely an area which she described as "painful." When I originally asked how she identified herself, it was not an answer that came quickly or easily. She responded with: "That's a tough question. Now? How do I identify myself now?" After some thought she commented, "I'd have to have time to think about it." She then went on to say that, "It shifts, as I'm understanding this myself." By "shifting" she meant that it changes, both through time and in different places. She first tried to come to terms with the sense of identity as a child. At that time, she found it difficult to figure out who all the people in her environment were:

> When I was growing up, that, I think, was for me the most painful. Who are we? I don't think as a kid you think, who am I? Who are we? Who are all these people? It was very confusing to figure out are we Syrian or Lebanese, and then there's the Irish father, and then we were in this extended house and then there were, I had a German uncle, Polish.

Hence, the bewildering variety of people from different cultures – all of whom were identified as different, but all of whom lived in the same house and were part of the same family – left her unable to come up with a sense of identity. As she indicates, her question, as a child, was not "Who am I?" Rather, it was "Who are we? Who are all these people?" That is, she was trying to get a sense of the identity of the total group, not just herself. Until she came to terms with the group's identity, she was unable to some to terms with her own sense of being.

The mixture was particularly distressing in view of the fact that other people in the community were not from mixed ethnic families, nor did she receive any information about one component of her heritage: "Because my cousins . . . we tried to figure out who the Lebanese were. . . . Because . . . you didn't get that in school." Hence, a major problem which she encountered was the fact that the primary origin of the family, Lebanese, was one which she and her cousins did not encounter in school. There were few other Lebanese children, the school curriculum probably never mentioned Lebanon, and the teachers focused on the dominant ethnic group in the school. At the same time, however, it was impossible to ignore the ethnic differences:

> That was confusing and it seemed to me that the Irish, the Italian, the Polish, and even the German, and the Jewish community – there were some Jews in public school. . . . But to be mixed was, at that time, I didn't think it was comfortable. . . . Now that I'm older . . . I can appreciate the diversity now, because we're in a historic period where diversity is celebrated, but then I remember it being something to be ashamed of, and it wasn't just me. . . .

Hence, being mixed might present problems of identity, but particularly so in a community in which others were from a clear ethnic identity. This was an issue which several other respondents also raised.

Jeanette's experience suggests that a special identification problem exists when both ethnic identities are visible. Clearly her darker skin, inherited from the Lebanese side, bothered her. But her father's ethnic identity was also obvious, in view of her Irish surname. In addition, the Catholic parishes in which she attended school were also identified as Irish. What was the impact of that? Couldn't she find a sense of belonging from being Irish? On this issue she commented:

> . . . I remember I would say I was Irish, because my last name was [Irish] and that made sense when I was in the Irish/Catholic Parochial school system. [But] . . . I felt different there. . . . I think the difference was through my mother, but I didn't know it then. But my sisters and I were taught, because they felt that too. We would talk about whom had the Irish skin or the Lebanese skin or who looked Irish and who looked Lebanese. Then we would compare how the Lebanese were different from the Irish. I can remember thinking, I wish that I was all Irish, to be like those kids in the public school, that had Irish mother and father. . . . I wanted to fit into that. . . . I didn't know what Lebanese was.

Hence, Jeanette had the sense, shared with other mixed culture respondents, of feeling left out because of their mixed backgrounds, and of wishing that were clearly part of a single cultural identity. Most respondents reported that they were not comfortable claiming just one – Jeanette and her sisters could not simply say they were "Irish" in an Irish Catholic School, and let it go with that. They had to come to terms with the varying aspects of their heritage.

The parents of some respondents were able to present to them a shared identity which made sense to them and with which they were comfortable. Sarah certainly was comfortable with the diversity in her family, which was discussed at great length in her home. Unfortunately, Jeanette was not so fortunate:

> I think I told you . . . I was asking my mother about Syrian and Lebanese and she said we should just say we're Irish, just say you're Irish because no one would understand. Then when we moved to [another town] and we were in the Italian community, I lied, my sisters did too, this is not just me. What I would say was my mother had some Italian, because if I said Lebanese you were a camel jockey or an Arab . . .

Thus, Jeanette's childhood identity was a painful mixture of different ethnic heritages, none of which she understood, with which she and her sisters and cousins were uncomfortable, and which her family did little to help her understand and accept.

As Jeanette became an adult, her awareness of the dimensions and their implications grew. She reports that she did not really start to identify as Lebanese until she was in her late 30s, had married and was raising four children, had taken college classes, and had been in therapy. Hence, her Lebanese heritage was a late revelation to her. As an adult who has been through extensive therapy, she believes she would probably identify herself as ". . . American with Lebanese/Irish heritage." But then she adds that it would also depend upon where she was or who asked. Her voice trails off, without completing the thought. As an adult, her self-identity is still not clear. As she said, finding her identity was ". . . for me, the most painful."

Clearly, the issue of self-identity is a major issue for children of mixed cultural heritage. Some learn to cope with the issue at an early age, either because they have supportive parents and other family members who assist them in understanding the various dimensions of their cultural origins or through their own devices. For others, the process is resolved only with great difficulty, if at all. For them, the question of personal identify remains a painful memory for years afterward.

Dealing with the Perception of Nonacceptance of Multi-culturalism in the Larger Community

Closely tied to the question of individual and group identity was a sense of acceptance by others in the community. Several interviews are filled with references to the fact that the respondents did not feel that they and their families were accepted by others in the community. To some extent this perceived lack of acceptance appears to be related to other factors discussed here: the socioeconomic or immigrant status of the family, specific ethnic customs which the family practiced, such as gender discrimination or lack of attention to school issues, which made the children seem "out of step" with their friends. The problems were particularly intense when the family's culture was considerably different from that of the surrounding community; Jeanette's family's dominant Lebanese culture is a major example in this regard.

Particularly salient for our purposes, however, are the instances in which it is specifically the multi-cultural characteristics of the family which make the family "stand out" in the community. That is, the respondents perceived that they were rejected because of the variety of different ethnic cultures in the family, or the family's lack of a single cohesive identity to present to the world. All of these issues come together in the minds of the respondents as factors which made them see themselves and their families as unacceptable to the community as a whole.

The lack of acceptance of her and her family was a major component of Jeanette's pain. It was often not clear why, but Jeanette and her sisters were pretty sure that they and their family were not accepted. Perhaps this was because they were poor and had so many children in one room; or because they had too many other relatives living with them; perhaps it was because they had all these different cultures and languages going on; or because the girls had to work at home and in the family store; perhaps it was because they really didn't "look Irish," with their darker colored skin. Whatever the reason, they were not accepted. Better to lie and say you were Irish and part Italian to explain the darker skin. They could not say they were Lebanese, in part because they did not know what that was, but also because there was this sense that it was not accepted: Lebanese were Arabs, "Mohammeds," "camel jockeys." That her family as a whole shared this sense of nonacceptance was clear from the fact that her mother would tell her to "just say we're Irish, just say you're Irish because no one would understand." But there remains, in the mind of the little girl, a long term feeling that all of this was very "painful."

Several of the respondents accepted their "mixed" backgrounds and were anxious to have this recognized. However, they also found that being "mixed" was not acceptable to the larger society. Often the occasion for this sense of rejection occurred when they had to fill out a form. Deanna, whose mother was Korean and her father African-American, preferred to identify herself as "mixed." To a considerable extent this might have been related to the fact that she ". . . didn't look a certain race. . . . I don't recall having too many problems with Asians because I look Asian . . . I think I had more problems with African-Americans." Deanna often felt that she was ". . .just being cast aside because I wasn't Black or considered Black."

A concern shared by several respondents was the dilemma they faced on the many occasions on which they were expected to respond to questionnaires or applications. Deanna spoke for several of them when she said:

> . . .when it's time to, time to fill out applications, . . . questionnaires, or something like that . . . that's never on there. . . . Mixed. That's never on there. It's one or the other. . . . they always tell you to choose one. I believe that's the only time when I feel like I'm forced to make a decision. And most of the time I check "other."

Deanna's objection to the necessity of choosing one of her identities on questionnaires was shared by Teresa, whose father was African and her mother Caucasian. Teresa is frank in her disdain for these questionnaires:

> . . .the census things that they do, I think that they're really wacky, because everything that you can possibly think of from Alaskan, for this and that – there's no box for mixed children, which is kind of annoying . . . Because on a lot of them they'll tell you, check one box. . . . And even though, I mean, this'll be wrong to say, but uh, my mother's raised me more, so if anything, I have more of a stronger American or White influence . . . in my life. But because of the color that I am, I wouldn't be able to check the White box. And I don't feel White, but, you know, . . . I wouldn't be able to do that. I'd have to check the Black box, and I just don't think that's fair!

Teresa makes an important point when she notes that many of these forms have a place for numerous ethnic categories, but they provide no option for persons whose background includes several ethnic or racial categories. She was bothered not only by the questionnaires themselves, but by the response she received from others when she filled them out. Since she chose to have a "mixed" identity, she dealt with the situation by checking both boxes. However, in many settings this response was not accepted. School experiences were particularly annoying, as we will discuss in Chapter 6.

It is important to note that the feeling of nonacceptance extends not only to the individual but to the family as a whole. Teresa's comments indicate she was also concerned about the manner in which her mother and father were perceived:

> ... they were thinking like, "What is this White lady doing with this Black guy? And what is this Black guy going out with this White lady? Or um, who do those kids think they are?" ... Things like that. ... in fact, that's what I know they were thinking. But they wouldn't say it because I was so young ... And the adults wouldn't say it to my parents because ... they probably didn't think it was their place to say anything. But you would hear it more from the kids.

Karen, whose parents were Korean and German-American, shared Deanna's and Teresa's discomfort at being "different" and having her mixed background not accepted. She first recognized the lack of acceptance "Very young, probably when I first started going to public schools ... First or second grade." Some of the comments were quite obvious, others less so, but they gave a clear indication that she and her family did not "belong": "... someone would call you a name like Chink, that was a pretty obvious one ... adults would go by and comment on how cute you were .... So I grew up for a distaste for the word, 'cute.' So it became noticeable ... not really knowing what that meant but knowing there was a difference...."

A particularly interesting situation in Karen's family concerned a nephew of her father's who was adopted into the family at a young age. She describes the situation:

> I have a brother who is actually my cousin originally ... blue eyes and curly blonde hair. When he was adopted into our family, he was a very young age, he was an infant. ... white kids don't usually go to minority families but this was a family member. ... We were at Sunday school playing outside on the playground the yard outside ... And people were making fun of us for some reason or other and my brother screamed at them ... to stop making fun of us and just because we are Asian. And here's this little kid, blonde hair, blue eyes and very, very light complexion and we just looked at him and said, No you are not Asian. I think it was a revelation to him and that he was not.

Hence, Karen's family was multi-cultural and multi-racial in several respects, but they saw themselves as a family. Her younger brother was defending his family, whom he had obviously heard described in a negative manner as "Asians." He was unaware of the meaning of the term, nor did he realize that he was not "Asian," although his mother and siblings were. Having their family perceived in that manner was clearly a disturbing experience for all of them.

Karen, Deanna, and Teresa all found that their "mixed" racial identity was not accepted by the surrounding community. In their cases, the differences between their parents were racial. None were satisfied with being defined within a single category; all preferred to be known as "mixed." Yet all felt that there were numerous circumstances in which others did not accept them in the manner which they preferred. How to deal with these circumstances? Obviously their responses differed at various points in their lives. At times, Teresa found that the situation was so upsetting: "And a lot of the times I would wish ... not that I didn't love my mother, and that I didn't love my father, but I wish I was just Black, or I wish I was just White," depending upon which group predominated in the setting in which she happened to be.

In contrast, Deanna, who is a few years older (24 to Teresa's 18), is less concerned. Asked if the reactions of others bother her, Deanna says:

> Occasionally.... [but] it's not too much. ... It doesn't bother me. I know some people react differently to it, but it doesn't bother me, 'cause I know who I am. ... society says that, because I have a little bit of Black blood in me, I'm considered Black, that's fine. But I know who I am. ... I don't look Black, so, no, I'm not all Black. ... even if I told people that I was all Black, they would [say] ... no, you're not. ... Even the same ones that say, if you got a little bit of Black in you, you're Black ... So I can't win! [laughs] So ... I don't bother with it. I don't worry about that too much.

Eventually, most had come to terms with their distinctiveness, compared with the community as a whole. Karen summarizes:

> ... it is funny because ... there was a time in my life when I was growing up ... I was very depressed about a number of things and this issue was one of them. ... The issue of race or being different in a way that I really didn't understand too much .... There was a kind of a transformational point in my life when I realized ... the path was very clear that if I go this route I get depressed, and I would go kill myself. ... basically I made an assessment that my interests and values and opinions were as important as, if not more important, than these other people who might be making an issue of things, and that was the transformational point in my life, of moving me towards being much more assertive and not caring what other people think.

Although none of them used Jeanette's term, "painful," clearly Deanna, Teresa, and Karen all had moments which could be described in that manner. Some of the distinctions they all faced focused on physical differences in the family – issues which would commonly be called "racial" in character. Three came from families in which the parents were of visibly different races. Even Jeanette came from a family in which there were visible physical differences, her father being Irish and light skinned, her mother, Lebanese and darker skinned. In Jeanette's case, there were also cultural distinctions which distinguished her and her family from the surrounding community. All of them found the distinctions between themselves and others disturbing. All had to come to terms, some more successfully than others, with the fact that they and their families were not accepted by the community as a whole. Not "belonging" is a very difficult experience, particularly for a child.

The four respondents we have been describing in the preceding section were all dealing with a multi-*racial* as opposed to a multi-*cultural* condition. That is, all had obvious physical characteristics which distinguished them from the surrounding community, to a greater or lesser extent. This raises a question about the problems of respondents who were strictly multi-*cultural*. Did they experience the same kind of problems as the multi-racial respondents? An examination of this issue is in order.

Multi-cultural distinctions can also be difficult. Earlier we described Sarah's experiences with her mother in which they would be told to "Go back where you came from." Both Sarah and her mother were of east European background, living in a community which was largely East European as well. However, her mother's foreign accent identified them as outsiders, prompting the taunting retort. Other respondents with unusual cultural patterns reported similar experiences. Peggy, for example, found that reminding people of her joint Irish and Belgian heritage caused her to be left out: ". . .because I looked Irish and had an Irish name, I probably could have become part of the Irish group. . . . [but] the Irish girls knew I was not all Irish, and so I couldn't be in the Irish group. . . ." Hence, cultural differences can be as effective as physical appearance in setting people apart from the community as a whole.

Indeed, some of the respondents made the point that cultural differences could create more difficulties than physical or racial differences. Deanna, for example, reported concerns she had with people identifying her as Chinese rather than her actual origin, Korean. She says:

> . . .there's not enough knowledge on the Asian Culture, so everyone is grouped as Chinese. Which offends me. . . . A lot of people call me Chinese. It doesn't matter if I'm not, I'm considered Chinese. And whenever there's a confrontation, there's an argument, that's the first thing that people throw at you, is: "You're different. You're Chinese." So I've had a lot of that, a lot of jealousy. . . . This is mostly from African-Americans. There's a lot of jealousy. I used to have very long hair when I was growing up. . . . People would pull my hair and all those kind of things. And literally get into fights because I was not considered one of them. . . . I can remember that more than anything, being called Chinese . . . .

The reader will recall that Deanna was distressed at being rejected because she was not considered "Black." However, it is clear that the persistent pattern of identifying her as Chinese rather than Korean was also bothersome.

The cultural difference between Chinese and Koreans was even more poignant for Evelyn, whose background included both groups. Because she exhibited the physical characteristics associated with being "Asian," she did not have the problem of being misidentified racially. However, she felt herself caught between the Korean and Chinese cultures, a problem which occurred primarily with other Asians. She reports that "Americans" (i.e., people who are not of Asian background) rarely raise an issue when she says she is Chinese and Korean:

> because they all feel that it's the same thing – they don't know that there's a difference . . . between the two. . . .but when it comes to other Asians, . . .they find that odd, because Chinese and Korean don't get along . . . You know, the two countries themselves, they don't think highly of each other. *They* [i.e., Asians] find it odd.

So Evelyn is placed in the difficult position of having non-Asians see her as a generalized "Asian," without distinguishing between the two cultures she represents, while persons of Asian background, who are aware of the nature of the two cultures, find it "odd" that she has roots in both cultures and identifies with them. At the same time, however, she feels more comfortable with "Americans" than with Asians.

Asians, I think the majority of 'em that I know, like my parents' friends, feel that my behaviors aren't . . . to their standards – that I'm not the way I should be. . . . whereas Americans – like my friends are all Caucasians – they don't even see me as being Asian. I've always asked them that . . . 'cause I act as . . . the American people – so I don't feel that other American people feel that I'm any different.

Hence, Evelyn feels more rejected by Koreans and Chinese, both of whom see her as an unacceptable representative of their specific culture. She provides numerous examples of situations in which her parents or their relatives would have fights and argue about the negative aspects of the other culture. Americans, on the other hand, view her as primarily "American." Although they know she is Asian, they see her as following American culture and accept her as an American. For her, the cultural differences are more salient.

Evelyn's view of the importance of cultural characteristics was shared by Anita, whose father was Puerto Rican and her mother Mexican. Anita was particularly offended when people used the generic term "Hispanic" to refer to persons from Spanish-speaking cultures. She says:

That's totally wrong. The Mexican and Puerto Rican cultures are totally different. . . . I would go so far as to say that even the racial composition of the groups are very different. Um, on my mother's side of the family [Mexican] there's much more Indian . . . with European. On my father's side of the family [Puerto Rican] . . . there is European . . . Venezuela to the Canary Islands back to Spain. . . . but also . . . there was intermarriage with an African escapee.

Throughout her interview, Anita frequently mentions situations in which she was made to feel considerable discomfort from the lack of acceptance of her Mexican cultural characteristics by her Puerto Rican relatives and vice versa. Anita also experienced considerable antagonism from Blacks, many of whom openly resented her identification as Mexican, when her dark skin indicated to them that she should identify as a Black-American.

Summary

This chapter has presented five types of experiences described by people who grew up in a multi-cultural setting. I have divided these issues into two major categories. In the first category are issues which do not appear to be directly related to the multi-cultural character of the family. Rather, they stemmed from other characteristics which made the family appear "different." These are issues which these families could share with any group which did not "fit" into the community, whether due to unusual racial or cultural patterns. Many single-race or single-culture groups have experienced such difficulties. The Black or Asian family living in a neighborhood made up of primarily Caucasians would experience the same kind of problems. So would the Polish family in an Irish neighborhood, or the Jewish family in a Christian neighborhood.

The differences may be physical in character, what we would usually call "racial" differences, or they may be cultural. In the area of cultural differences, we have described families which were of lower income status, and so did not have the same advantages as other members of the community, placing them at a distinct disadvantage; or they might have followed a culture in the home which made them highly visible to their neighbors, such as having a large number of people living in the house or running a business from the home, or engaging in practices which placed some members, especially the women and girls, at a disadvantage compared with other community members. However, these patterns are not specifically related to the multi-cultural character of the family. They have been seen many times before as people from different racial, religious, or nationality backgrounds who have moved into the American scene. Since these issues have often been described in other studies of ethnic differences, we will not consider them further.

Three other issues do appear to be related to the presence of multi-cultural and/or multi-racial characteristics within the family. These are issues which the family encountered specifically because of the fact that the family itself was a mixture of different races and cultures. These are the issues that give these families their unique character, and these problems will be the major focus of the remainder of this book. These include the difficulty of coping with the diversity of cultures and people in the family, problems of self-identification and identification of the group, and the perception of nonacceptance of the family and its members in the larger community. Throughout the discussion, it has also appeared that some respondents seemed better able than others to deal with the difficulties they faced.

The remaining chapters of this section will deal with all of these issues in greater detail. In Chapter 5, we will focus our attention on the manner in which these respondents developed a sense of personal and group identity and came to terms with their "mixed" background. We will pay particular attention to the issue of the similarities and differences between specifically *racial* as opposed to *cultural* differences in reaching a sense of identity. Chapter 6 will focus on the impact which the larger social environment had upon these issues. In short, did the social setting in which the respondents lived play a role in making it more or less difficult to be multi-cultural? Chapter 7 will focus specifically on the multi-cultural families themselves. How did these families assist their children in dealing with their multi-cultural or multi-racial character? Were some families better at this task than others? Are there some types of family structures and processes that could be recommended as more successful in this regard?

Chapter 5
Developing an Identity Out of Multiple Options

An important issue for persons from mixed cultural backgrounds is their source of identification (Harris and Sim, 2002; Gaskins, 1999; Gibbs, 1998; Gibbs and Hines, 1992; Hall, 1992; Poston, 1990; Root, 1992a; 1996; Waters, 1990). Where family background is important, as it is in the USA, people are often asked to provide information on their origins. Such questions appear in the census, in school records for children, and in other questionnaires as well. Associates often ask questions about ethnic origins as well, sometimes as a matter of simple interest, but often in a rude or intrusive fashion.

How do persons with a mixed ethnic background respond when asked a question about their origins? As we indicated in Chapter 4, several respondents found the experience unsettling. Many wanted to identify as "mixed," but found they were often forced to "choose one" category, which some saw as a rejection of other parts of themselves. Particularly offensive was the fact that some teachers or interviewers refused to accept their response, replacing their identification choice with their own evaluation.

Sources of Identity and How They Are Employed

An analysis of the interviews of ethnically mixed respondents indicates that numerous factors play a role in an individual's definition of her or his sense of personal identity. Certainly, the individual's personal views of who she or he is are important. However, the social environment also plays a critical role in these definitions. As Anselm Strauss (1959: 26) has noted, "...classification and evaluation are not merely private acts but are usually, if not predominantly, public concerns." George Herbert Mead (1934) focused on his belief that the "self" was really composed of two parts: the "I," through which the individual takes an active role in defining who she or he is and what values are important, and the "ME," which consists of the social environment's imposition of itself onto the individual, expressing its demands and attempting to ensure that the individual "fits in" with the demands of the group.

Charles Horton Cooley (1922) went into great detail in his discussion of what he called the "social self," emphasizing the fact that the self is developed in a social context. While recognizing that the self had an important relation to the physical body, he contended that the individual's concept of the self will vary with the social conditions under which it develops. His very clever notion of the "looking glass self" illustrates his view that children only learn who they are by seeing their views of themselves reflected in the social groups which surround them. He even notes that the sense of "we," the child's recognition of the group to which s/he belongs, is an equally important part of her/his notion of self. This view was specifically mentioned by Jeanette, who felt that a definition of the *group* to which she belonged was an important part of a child's sense of identity.

Hence, Cooley would predict that the development of a sense of self would be different for a child who grows up in an environment in which there is a mixture of cultural identities. Since such children are surrounded by people from different cultural backgrounds, they are constantly reminded of these differing cultural groups. The image they will see in the "looking glass" of these social groups will be very different from those of a child with a singular background.

Most critically, they are likely to encounter *questions* as opposed to *affirmations*. That is, the child from a singular background is reminded at every turn that: "This is who we are" and "you are one of us too!" For children from mixed backgrounds, however, the process is quite different. Some members of the group are telling them they belong to one group; others say they are part of another group. The case of Sarah, whose father was Greek Orthodox and her mother Jewish, is a good example. The reader will recall that her father's family constantly reminded her that she was Christian because children take the father's religion, while her mother's relatives insisted that she was Jewish because religion followed the mother. Still others, observing these differences, may simply ask, "Well, what *are* you?" For persons from mixed backgrounds, Cooley's "looking glass" is quite blurred.

So the question remains: How does the child of mixed background come to a sense of "Who s/he is?" We shall begin this discussion by delineating some of the dimensions of identity which the respondents discussed. While numerous characteristics might be mentioned, three appear to be of major importance. These are physical appearance, surname, and a variety of cultural patterns, such as language religion or national origin. We will discuss them in that order.

Physical Characteristics as the Basis for a Sense of Identity

The most obvious basis for defining personal identity is the presence of physical characteristics which distinguish the individual from other members of the community. What is the role of personal appearance? We live in a society which is often very superficial. People often focus on outward appearances which are easy to recognize. Other characteristics, which may be more important but less visible, are often ignored. What is the role which obvious physical characteristics play in defining an individual's conception of self?

In the USA, skin color is the major example, being the source of the dramatic racial divide between Blacks and Whites. Other physical differences might also be mentioned, such as gender or gender preference, obesity, unusual height, or the presence of some physical disability. All of these are often the basis for social distinctions and a resulting sense of personal identity. Physical differences are difficult to ignore, making it possible, or even likely, for others to focus on this difference in their relationships with others.

In this study, the primary physical difference we will discuss involves race as a dimension of personal identity. People from a minority race are reminded on numerous occasions by a wide variety of people that one looks "different" – Black while others are White or Asian while others are either Black or White. When skin color is persistently mentioned in contacts with others, it is nearly impossible for a person to escape the definition of him/herself as belonging to a category defined on the basis of skin color. This is particularly so for an impressionable child. As indicated earlier, Teresa commented that she constantly felt out of place with her two sets of relatives and often wished she was "just Black" or "just White." And Karen and her siblings were constantly reminded of their Asian heritage in a predominantly White community, such that it was difficult for her "White" brother to understand why everyone thought he was different from the rest of his family.

As we also noted, the use of physical differences to define group boundaries can be much more complex than the simple issue defined by Black, White, and Yellow. Much more subtle skin color differences are also employed. Hence, Mediterranean peoples (Italians, Greeks, Spaniards, and Arabs) whose skin color is somewhat darker than north Europeans, but considerably lighter in tone than Africans, have frequently been categorized on the basis of this color difference, as we noted in the case of Jeanette. Furthermore, characteristics other than skin color are also used in defining group boundaries. The eye fold in Asians, lip size in African-Americans, or the facial patterns of Native Americans, Alaskan Natives, and Pacific Islanders are other examples.

Surname and Personal Identity

Assignment to groups is often made on the basis of nonphysical differences as well. While somewhat less obvious than physical characteristics, the name is another visible dimension of appearance. Among Caucasians, family surname is an example of a nonphysical characteristic which is often used to identify someone as Polish, Italian, Irish, or Greek, based on the sound of the name. It would be difficult, for example, for someone with the surnames "Murphy" or "Pulaski" to avoid being identified as Irish or Polish, respectively. Peggy, for example, commented that she could have become part of the Irish group in her school because she "looked Irish and had an Irish name," thus combining the impact of both her physical appearance and her surname. Sam, who preferred to be seen as simply "American," usually identified himself as Italian-American, because his surname sounded Italian and most people expected him to identify in that manner. Given names might also serve the purpose of identification if the name is known to be associated with specific ethnic groups.

In the USA, assignment to the "Hispanic" category is usually made on the basis of family name, as indicated by use of the term "Spanish-surnamed," to determine eligibility for certain government programs (Leonetti and Muller, 1976; Pollinger, 1972). However, as Phinney and Rotheram (1987: 11) point out, one's surname is often an inaccurate indicator of ethnic identity. Use of the Spanish surname to categorize Hispanics illustrates the fallacy imbedded in most classifications of people. Many "Blacks" or "Whites" who have no tie to the Hispanic community are Spanish-surnamed. This is particularly true of women, who may carry the name of a husband – or even an ex-husband. Using the surname definition, one could reach the anomalous conclusion that a woman who marries a Spanish-surnamed man and takes his name has the right to any advantages accorded to Hispanics, even though she has never spoken Spanish, never grew up in a Hispanic neighborhood, and never experienced any of the problems encountered by many Spanish-speaking persons in the USA.

Surname and the Importance of the Mother's Culture

Use of the surname to define an individual's identity and culture involves another problem in a society such as the USA. In a clearly patriarchal society, such as some nations in the Middle East or Africa, this might be a reasonable approach. In such societies, children automatically belong to their father's lineage, are raised in his culture, and inherit only from him. When a woman marries, she may leave her father's home and join the household of her husband, but she remains a part of his lineage. However, our society has had a bilateral family system for decades (Triandis, 2002). That is, children are considered to be a part of both their father's and their mother's families and may inherit from both sides. Consequently, it is impossible for them to be considered part of only one culture, since they are likely to have considerable contact with both sides and encounter both cultures.

Indeed, children are likely to be closer to the mother than the father. Ours is a society in which children are reared largely by the mother, while the father may be an absent or disengaged figure. Sisters are more likely to remain close in adulthood than brothers. Hence, the children tend to encounter their mother's family culture more often than the father's: her views of child-rearing are likely to predominate, her relatives tend to visit more often than his, and so on (Bank and Kahn, 1997; Connidis, 2001; Uhlenberg, 1996; 2004). Hence, the loss of the mother's identity may be particularly painful in view of the fact that the *mother's* influence may be the primary one for many children. This is true even of highly patriarchal cultures. Shakir (1991–1992), studying the identification patterns of Arabic men, noted that the mother was the most important influence on their sons.

In spite of the increased role played by fathers in the household today, studies show that the mother still does the great bulk of the child-rearing (Lindsey, 1990: 123–124, 139–140). It is reasonable to assume that, absent a major effort on the part of her husband to alter the pattern, she raises the children according to her culture, which she received from her mother and maternal grandmother. In identifying mixed culture people by their surnames, we are depriving them of the identity which may represent the most salient part of their backgrounds. The author is aware of a man whose surname associated him clearly with his *father's* culture, with which he did not identify; this pattern finally became so uncomfortable that he changed his surname to his mother's maiden name.

The special salience of the mother's culture and family background is illustrated by research which has shown that the closest, widest-ranging ties between adult siblings tend to be among sisters. Their interactions include home visiting, communication, mutual aid, and membership in the same organizations, to mention a few (Adams, 1968: 106–108). Furthermore, except for blue-collar males, cousins who feel closest to each other are more likely to be the children of sisters. In the middle class, even males are closer to their mothers' sisters' children (Adams, 1968: 136–139). This same closeness of relations through sisters was noted by Schneider and Homans (1955). Some have also noted that the interaction may even take place at the home of the mother (Willmott and Young, 1960: 78, 81) (see also Bank and Kahn, 1997; Connidis, 2001; Uhlenberg, 1996; 2004). Hence, it is not unreasonable to hypothesize that sisters, through their frequent visiting and socialization, transmit the *maternal* culture to their children and that this culture may in some instances be even more salient than the father's culture. Teresa, for example, noted that she was raised primarily by her White mother, although everyone associated her with the Black race of her father. In any event, it is reasonable to assume that it is likely to represent a major force in the individual's life and identity, at least rivaling the importance of the father's surname.

The characteristics which an individual receives from the mother's culture may, in fact, be of greater importance in the individual's life than his/her sense of identity. Whether or not one "feels" close to the culture represented by his/her surname and wishes to be identified with it may indicate a sense of ethnic pride. However, the mother's role as socializing agent, together with the close association with the mother's family, even in adulthood, may result in the ethnically mixed individual adopting the mother's culture with its unique characteristics, even though s/he is identified with the father's culture through the surname. Indeed, these characteristics may be more important for the individual in determining his/her style of life. As Phinney and Rotheram (1987: 23) point out, there are numerous underlying behavior/life style characteristics which culture incorporates into the individual. These include a tendency to focus either on the group or on the individual, an active or a passive orientation, a tendency to be either expressive or restrained in the demonstration of affect, an authoritarian or egalitarian approach to relationships, tendency to be either overt or covert in relationships, and a tendency to view humans as either good, bad, or neutral. All of these are factors which play a substantial role in the individual's manner of relating to other persons.

Personal Identity and Other Cultural Characteristics

Religion, language, nationality, and other cultural characteristics also play a role in society's process of identifying individuals. As discussed in Chapters 1 and 2, religion has long been used in the USA to target Jews, Catholics, Muslims, and others who do not practice one of the dominant denominations of Protestantism. Similarly, speaking a foreign language or even speaking English with an unusual accent can also set people apart (Boulet, 2001; Alba and Nee, 2003). Other cultural characteristics, such as customs of dress, may have the same effect. The dress patterns of the "plain people" (Amish and Mennonites), use of the "yarmulcha" (head covering) by Jewish men, and wearing the hijab (veil) by Muslim women are all examples. Thus, Sarah recalled being rudely treated in the supermarket when people noticed her mother's foreign accent, and Peter felt out of place because his Native American heritage did not encourage the materialistic patterns of middle class American culture. When children grow up in a setting in which they are singled out for some aspects of the culture, it cannot help but impact on their development of a sense of self.

Inaccuracies in the Use of Simple Classifications

As we have noted, most of these classification systems tend to be unitary in nature. Classifications which use such simplistic variables as physical differences and surnames fail to recognize the cultural dimensions of differences among groups of people. Thus, classifying all persons from the Far East as "Asians" fails to recognize the major differences among the cultures of Japan, China, Korean, Vietnam, and other quite distinct Asian societies. Similarly, the "European" classification ignores the fact that German, French, English, Italian, and other European cultures are anything but equivalent, especially since most of them involve language differences and many generations of dispute and even warfare.

Neither do African-Americans exhibit a single culture. The so-called "Black culture" is never very clearly defined. But even a cursory examination of the culture of Blacks in the USA will indicate that there are many different cultural groups within the Black community (Billingsley, 1968; Pinckney, 1993). Southern Blacks, for example, have a quite different culture from those who have lived in the Northern cities for several generations. Blacks from Louisiana have historically had a different culture, very closely allied with the French culture of the area. Recent Black immigrants from Africa or the Caribbean islands clearly exhibit different cultural patterns from Blacks with a long family history in the USA. Indeed, this difference is sometimes the basis for considerable dissatisfaction among American Blacks, who are unhappy when African or Caribbean Blacks receive the advantages of special treatment for minority groups which American Blacks often believe should be reserved for the descendants of US slaves. On the other hand, one Black woman cautioned her children to respect all other cultures, because, she said, "They're all yours!"

Pressure to Accept Externally Defined Identities

Social pressure to accept these "obvious" identities can be extremely forceful. It can be particularly uncomfortable when presented by professional counselors, who espouse views that require conformity to ethnic boundaries. On a recent talk show, for example, the topic focused on interracial dating. The "expert" stressed the view that persons who engage in interracial dating are rejecting their own heritage. Recently, I interviewed a woman who lives and works in an ethnically mixed environment; she discussed with me her experience with a counselor who forced a group of white participants in a counseling group – none of whom had ever met before – to embrace and share their group experience. The woman was most uncomfortable, commenting: "They weren't 'my group'! What made her think they were 'my group'? Just because we all have the same skin color? That doesn't make us a group!" She found the experience extremely stressful; it bothered her for months afterward.

The Added Complication of Cultural Mixtures

Particularly lacking is research on the cultural patterns of persons, like our respondents, who come from mixed cultural backgrounds. The position of mixed culture persons has become more important in recent years, as some have requested special definitions in census data. What of a man whose father is Hispanic and his mother Italian? Or a woman whose mother was English and her father was Black? Or a person whose father came from the Caribbean Islands, while his mother was born and reared in the American South? With which culture do these people identify? In which cultural traditions were they raised?

Indeed, there seems to be an assumption, beginning with Milton Gordon (1964) many years ago, that marriage is an indicator of a single culture. Gordon believed that "marital assimilation," or marriage across ethnic lines, was an indicator of complete assimilation. This leaves an open question, however: Assimilated into what? What culture is exhibited by the intermarried couple? That this is an important question has been alluded to by some of the literature on religious intermarriage, which has suggested that some religious groups are "winners" and some "losers" in the game of religious intermarriage (Greeley, 1974). That is, when religious intermarriage occurs, some religious groups are more likely to gain converts while others lose members.

Religion, however, is not the only aspect of culture which must be studied in order to understand the cultural patterns of intercultural families. Particularly important are those differences which are subtle and may not appear except in intense interaction or counseling. Examples are: Do you talk about problems and feelings or hide them? How should children be raised? Who do you visit? How often and under what circumstances? How formal should visiting be? Which holidays are celebrated? How and with whom? Is it appropriate to just "drop in" for a visit? Or is a formal invitation required? (Greeley, 1971; Lopata, 1976).

Importance of Recognition of the Multiple Dimensions of Culture

In the previous section, I have noted the critical role played by the mother's culture. Further analysis may reveal other dimensions of culture which may play an important role in an individual's development. If these cultural factors play the important role which I have suggested, they are crucial issues for applied sociologists and other professionals to consider. Many professionals in a wide variety of fields recognize the importance of considering the ethnic backgrounds of clients, students, or workers in counseling or advising them, planning their work or student roles, or evaluating their performance. They realize that the cultural patterns with which one grows up are not easily lost, but continue to influence us throughout our lives. However, the emphasis on obvious physical characteristics or the paternal name as the basis for ethnic identification causes us to lose sight of the major cultural influences on individuals in mixed ethnic families.

Other dimensions of the family make-up are likely to exert considerable influence on the development of culture and identity. It is critical not to allow ease of classification to obscure an important component of an individual's ethnic heritage. These issues were the major impetus for the study of multi-cultural families which is the focus of this book. It quickly became apparent that the situation was far more complex than a simple choice between the mother's culture and identity and that of the father. Thus, one's ethnic *identity* may be likely to come from those characteristics which can be most easily observed by others. For Blacks and Asians, this is likely to be race. For Whites, the surname is the most obvious, making the father's ethnicity most salient. Hence, Whites are reminded of their father's identity each time they use their surname, and are likely to perceive society as a whole as identifying them in this manner. *Cultural* patterns, on the other hand, may be more likely to come from the mother, due to the mother's role in socializing the children and the closeness of many individuals to the mother's relatives. Hence, a pattern of *identity* from one parent and *culture* from the other may be common.

Self-Identity: A Personal Choice or Socially Imposed?

To summarize, the process of defining one's own identity, as well as defining the group to which s/he belongs, is a social rather than an individual process. Children reach a sense of who they are by seeing themselves mirrored in the eyes of those they encounter. These include members of their families, children and teachers they meet at school, the surrounding community, and society as a whole. When a child grows up in an ethnically limited setting, most, if not all, of the people s/he encounters give the same message as to who s/he is and the group with which she is associated. However, children from mixed backgrounds encounter conflicting definitions of their identity. Teachers, neighbors, and even different members of their own families give them divergent messages. Consequently, for them, defining "Who I am" becomes more complicated. In this chapter, we will examine the experiences of respondents from mixed backgrounds to determine what messages they received about their identity and how they resolved the issue.

A second issue we will examine involves the relative importance of the various factors in the individual's personal choice of a self-identity. We know that both the social environment and individual choice play important roles, but what is the relative importance of each? To what extent is the sense of personal identity the individual's own choice? Do they feel their identity statement was one they freely chose? Or do they believe their choice was actually enforced by others? With regard to the role played by others, who plays the more critical role? What is the role of families, for example? What role is played by teachers in school, other officials, or other members of the dominant society? What role is played by ethnic groups themselves? For example, do Blacks or Italians or Asians put pressure on their members to identify themselves as members of the group?

The issue appears to be much more complex than any single simplistic answer can provide. A major problem which appeared is the resistance of ethnic groups themselves to allow their members to discontinue their association with the group. Some families were more directive than others in exercising influence over their children's choices in this regard. The process of self-identification is the subject of this chapter, with special attention to a comparison between the role of physical and cultural differences in this process. In Chapters 6 and 7, we will go on to examine specific influences on the process. Chapter 6 will examine the pressures brought by the surrounding community in the process, and Chapter 7 will look at the way the multi-cultural family can influence the process to make it easier for their children.

Observing the Respondents' Experiences

As we have noted, early on it became apparent that there were more possibilities than a simple choice between identifying with the father's culture or the mother's. Many respondents developed multiple cultures and identities, which they employed in different settings, as they found them useful. Multi-cultural children proved to be highly creative in the ways in which they combined the cultural heritages they inherited. We begin the discussion with an analysis of the simplest case – the respondents who chose to accept a single self-identification, specifically the one that was generally expected of them by others.

The Simplest Choice: A Single Identity as Defined by One's Surroundings

Many people in American society would probably wonder why there is a problem with self-identification. After all, isn't it obvious who one is? If you look Black, then you are Black. If you look White, you are White. If your name is Polish, you are Polish. What is the problem?

A few respondents were indeed comfortable with this approach. Their approach is best exemplified by Adam, who grew up in a large midwestern city in the 1980s. He reports that his birth certificate lists his father as Caucasian, but he had never met him and knew little about him. Like Adam, his mother was also racially mixed, since her mother was African-American and her father was Native American. However, Adam notes that she was "...dark complected, she was raised African-American ... [and] would be considered African-American." In response to a question about his own self-identity, he says he is:

> African American, because I've grown up in the African American culture. Although I realize that there are some parts of me, some of the Caucasian comes out, like I like some White music (laugh). But primarily African American just because of the way I was raised.

With further questioning, Adam explains why he believes he identifies so strongly with his African-American background, although it represents only one-fourth of his heritage:

> ...my mother was basically a single mother. I never knew my father. I grew up in foster care quite a bit, and I was actually ... about half the time I was in African-American foster homes and half the time I was in Caucasian foster homes. But ... they looked at me as Black, African American, because while I am light skinned, I am not White, I am not pale in any sense of the imagination. ... I guess you could say that I was placed in that ethnic group ... because of my mother's family. You know they took me and they raised me ... with their own cultural identity, and when I went to foster homes, they looked at me as African American.

In addition, Adam describes an experience which occurred when he was in early grade school, which clearly focused his identity in his mind. The experience to which he refers occurred when he attended a predominantly White grade school, and he and a White girl decided they would be boyfriend and girlfriend. He continues:

> The little girl said I want you to meet my parents. So, I am standing by the curb at school. They pull up and they look at me, and they look at their daughter standing next to me and her mother opens the door and snatches her daughter in the car, and they peel off – like burn rubber on the spot ... kicking up dust and dirt while pulling away from the curb. And I was like, oh my God what happened? And the next day ... [she] came to school and said ... "I can't go with you anymore – my parents don't like you." And that was it.

As a result of that incident, Adam says: "...I can tell you the exact point and time that I realized that I was Black. ... it was in the first grade when I experienced racism."

Regarding more recent periods of his life, he again notes that other people assume he is African-American, "...because of my complexion, because of my haircut you know ... I think most people identify me as [African-American]." Unlike some of the other respondents, defining himself in the manner which others expect of him does not seem to bother Adam. "I don't ... have an issue with it, again because of the way I was brought up. ... and since I look at African-Americans as my race, and I look at us with pride, I really don't have an issue with being looked at or perceived that way."

As a result, Adam identifies as African-American for a variety of reasons. His mother, the major parental force in his life, was considered African-American, although she was actually half Native American. He was raised in homes that were largely African-American and was introduced to the African-American culture throughout his early life. Although he is light skinned, he believes he clearly looks African-American. His contacts with the Native American and Caucasian components of his background were minimal or nonexistent. Perhaps more important, the contacts he had with Caucasians were not supportive. In the Caucasian foster homes as well as in school, he found that these people also defined him as African-American. He has experienced discrimination because of his African-American heritage. Consequently, he accepts his identity as African-American, even though it represents only one-fourth of this background. Adam's self-identity appears to be based on a variety of factors: his perception of the way he looks and the way others think he looks, his rearing in the African-American culture, his experience of discrimination by others because of his African-American background, and his pride in what being African-American means.

Are there others who share his approach to self-identity, accepting with little complaint the definition which others have of them? At the other end of the racial spectrum is Robert, who grew up in Kentucky in the 1950s, with Scottish and English parents. He described many distressing childhood experiences, as indicated in Chapter 4. However, it was difficult to get him to discuss the issue of identity at all. Although he recognized that his parents were of different nationalities, he did not consider these nationality differences to be a major factor in his difficult childhood. Asked if the nationality differences between his parents created problems in his family, he commented:

> No. If I understand your question, it wasn't like my mom had fundamental beliefs about certain ways to raise children which were in conflict with my dad's . . . in a lot of respects of it, the culture I grew up in was very homogenous. I was not in a situation where I was in competing cultures. English, Scottish, and Irish cultures are very compatible I think.

Robert was also asked whether he felt people in the larger community ever noted the fact that his parents were of different backgrounds; again he attached little importance to the issue. Instead he refers to the character of the community in which he was raised, and the fact that the major defining factors of that community focused around the issue of race, in a section quoted in Chapter 3. So while he had numerous problems in his childhood, they were not related to issues of identity. As discussed in Chapter 4, he attributed his childhood problems primarily to his parents' inept parenting skills as well as to economic difficulties. His personal sense of identity was not a problem. He felt the cultures in his family were quite compatible and thus unimportant. More critically, he pointed to the dominant character of the town: its racial makeup. While he did not use the term "identity," he clearly defined himself as one of the working-class "White kids" in a setting in which only race mattered. Like Adam, Robert's identity was easy to define. He grew up in a family and community which focused on race alone and did not recognize nationality differences. It was not difficult for him to understand where he fit into the picture, even to the point of finding it difficult to understand questions about the impact of these differences.

It is interesting to note that, in spite of the racially segregated character of his childhood, at the time of the interview, Robert was employed in a multi-cultural and multi-racial setting and seemed to work quite comfortably with it. Indeed, he made a point of noting that his first encounters with cultural diversity occurred when he became an adult and left Kentucky to move to a northern city for college. This was his first opportunity to hear people speaking different languages or deal with Blacks in a nonsegregated environment.

Other respondents also reported having a single identity which fit well into the American pattern. Ida, the daughter of an English and Scottish father and a Lebanese mother, is an example. Throughout the discussion she reports relatively frequent contacts with her mother's family, including occasional attendance at the Lebanese Maronite Catholic Church. She recalls her mother's family as having ". . .a little darker skin and . . . hair, and . . . they seemed to talk a little different." However, asked about how she identifies herself, Ida reports:

> Usually I identify myself as American . . . I guess because I look and feel that way – I was born here and I think that's the most accurate. . . .other people identify me as American. . . Sometimes people seem . . . yeah, a little surprised if I tell them about my Lebanese background.

While she recalled their reactions to her being Lebanese as largely a positive experience, it apparently had little impact on her. Here is a woman who appears to have received only infrequent and ineffective messages from either her parents or extended family concerning their cultural origins. Most people she encounters think of her as American and seem surprised her mother is Lebanese. She too reaches the conclusion that she is just American. Like Adam and Robert, her "mixed" background plays little role in her sense of self.

A final example of a respondent with a single-identity pattern is Brian, whose family provides an illustration of another source of multi-culturalism in the family – the introduction of a new member, in Brian's instance through his father's remarriage when he was 8 years old:

> . . .she came from a very strong German culture . . . we were taught to be Irish. . . . we knew Irish history and we felt Irish. And my [step]mother felt German because that was what she was raised in. She spoke some German and her family spoke some German. . . . And uh, it was a helluva of a clash of cultures. First of all, there was a clash of an orderly person who didn't want 2 little, utterly undisciplined little rats running around the house. . . . my German stepmother came to this household, which still included my [Irish] grandmother, which was a difficult bone of contention too. . . . initially . . . there was a lot of tension, because we had never been faced with that sort of discipline before, so there was a lot of screaming and yelling, and my stepmother would, and, as you might expect, here was the grandmother who had been in charge, at least nominally, oh, for 6 years, now being a klutz! . . .

Hence, Brian's family illustrates the conflict which can occur in a family due to the addition of a new member whose culture differs radically form that of the others. His new German stepmother's well-structured approach to child-rearing was radically different from the rather casual approach to family life, as represented by his Irish father and grandmother. The initial clash of cultures was a dramatic component of his early school years. He notes:

> ...there's no question, the way they lived, the values they had, came from that German Catholic background. ... the biggest differences, and I'm not sure this is true across other families, but it certainly was true in my family, in a German family, apparently the father is the center of attention, and everybody is, things are organized to be helpmates of the father.... In the Irish family, the kids are the center.

He credits his German stepmother for having had a considerable influence over his life. However, she came on the scene after several years of influence of his vigorously Irish Catholic family and had little influence over his sense of identity. Eventually, he became close to his stepmother and many of her relatives, while still maintaining a strong tie to his Irish background. All of these examples illustrate the fact that an individual's self-identity is easy to define when all or most of the people in the individual's environment, especially in their earliest years, are sending the same message.

Brian's experience also suggests another source of multi-culturalism in today's families, however: the addition of a new member. Karen's Asian-Caucasian family experienced such a change when her parents adopted her father's all-Caucasian nephew; as we previously noted, this boy was confused to learn that he was not Asian like his adopted siblings. Multi-cultural adoptions are increasingly occurring in the USA, as families adopt children across racial or ethnic lines or in other countries. These will also produce multi-cultural and/or multi-racial families. It is interesting to note that two of the respondents in our study were involved at the time of the study in the process of adopting children from other countries. One of them commented that her multi-cultural family was going to become even more multi-cultural. Already more open to multi-cultural experiences, these people may be more open to this type of adoption than others.

These examples illustrate a variety of ways that a family can become multi-cultural. Even if the parents have the same ethnic origins, the children may experience different cultures by virtue of living for a time in another culture and speaking a different language. Other family members, such as a new stepparent or an adopted child, can bring in a new cultural pattern. Even social class can produce a clash of cultures in the family or in the surrounding community. It is important to stress this fact, because these families are likely to experience some of the same culture clashes as the respondents in our study. These families should also be aware that their children may encounter the same type of problems in the broader community which our respondents described.

Developing a Single Identity Out of Mixed Options

The fact remains, however, that most children in multi-cultural families do not receive a unitary message about their identity. Instead they receive a variety of messages from parents, extended family, neighborhood, school, the community at

large, even governmental agencies. What is the impact of such messages? How did
the respondent deal with them? How do these mixed background individuals reach
their decisions about identity in the face of these competing views they receive? In
this section, we will describe several examples of individuals from families with a
mixed racial or cultural background and let them explain how they and their siblings
developed a sense of identity.

Anita's background would be considered "Hispanic" by most observers, since
her mother was Mexican and her father Puerto Rican. However, she quickly points
out:

> That's totally wrong. The Mexican and Puerto Rican cultures are totally different. ...
> I would go so far as to say that even the racial composition of the groups are very dif-
> ferent. Um, on my mother's side of the family there's much more Indian. ... On my father's
> side of the family there's um, there is European. We can trace our family back um from
> Venezuela to the Canary Islands back to Spain.

Asked how she identifies herself, Anita says:

> I identify myself as multi-cultural, multi-racial, of Hispanic, or of, you know, of Latin Amer-
> ican background, or something like that. Because it is, I can't say that I'm Mexican, can't
> say that I'm Puerto Rican. I'm not Americanized enough that I feel comfortable saying I'm
> American. Um, and although my birth certificate says I'm white, I'm obviously not that. So
> I consider myself multi-cultural, multi-racial.

In a sense, Anita contradicts herself, since she insists that "Hispanic" is not a
single identity, but at the same time she includes it as a part of her complex definition
of who she is. At another point, however, she indicates a more specific identity when
she says, "My heart is Mexican, it really is."

In describing her childhood, Anita provides numerous examples of contact with
both Mexican and Puerto Rican culture: frequent visits to both countries, sometimes
lasting the entire summer; use of the Spanish language in the home; observance of
numerous Mexican and Puerto Rican festivals; and a remarkable array of foods from
both countries. Even today she describes her frequent visits to Mexico, where she
even purchased her mother's family home.

Is this the common pattern among her siblings? Would they respond to the
identity and culture questions in the same way that she did? Her response was
immediate:

> Very differently. I have – my older brother . . . has very strong Puerto Rican identity. . . . he
> went back and married his sweetheart from Puerto Rico. He has never been back to Mexico,
> but he's been back to Puerto Rico quite a bit.

She goes on to describe other members of the family and their patterns of identity
and culture. About a younger brother she says: ". . .the brother that's behind me identifies very Mexican. Even through he's the one we call 'the white boy.' . . . 'Cause
he's fair, and . . . his Spanish is the worst of everyone." She goes on to describe how
he was the only one of the siblings to Anglicize his first name, married a Caucasian,
and only goes to Mexico to visit the big resorts. A sister went to high school in Mexico and was described as "very Mexican" in her speech and other cultural aspects.
However, she married a man from Jamaica and has borrowed some Caribbean Island

cultural patterns from him. Her youngest brother is also described as having a Caucasian wife and identifying primarily as American, although he often does business in Mexico and speaks rather fluent Spanish.

A similar pattern appeared in the family of Vickie, whose father was Irish Catholic while her mother was Jewish. Vickie had a brother and sister. Asked how she identifies herself, she says, "I identify myself as Jewish. But my siblings are different. . . . I've identified as Jewish since I was a little kid. I can't say exactly why." She goes on to describe a family in which religion was not viewed as important. Neither parent was a practicing member of his/her respective faith, and extended family members did not place much pressure on them to practice the religion. At approximately the time she started school, she notes that: ". . .people were nagging my parents, 'You can't raise children without religion' . . . So my father had met this cool hippie Protestant minister that he liked, so we became Protestants. It was a middle ground."

Consequently, at about the age of 6, she and her brother, who was a few years younger, were enrolled in a Protestant Sunday School. The experiment met with little success, however. Vickie continues:

Yeah. And my brother and I just couldn't buy one word of this stuff. You know, we had been raised without anything, so we didn't have a deity to believe in. We didn't have any practices to believe in. And we just thought it was bunk. So we got thrown out of Sunday School. Both of us – within weeks of each other.

This is also the point at which Vickie's interest in Judaism began to develop. She says:

Well, yeah, I became – even as a little kid I was fascinated by Judaism. And when I found out that there was such as thing as Hebrew School, I wanted to go, but I knew not to ask. Because there was sort of a little prohibition against religion in the house. And so I never asked, but I hung out with the Jewish kids in town, 'cause I wanted to know more. And I got my grandmother to tell me things, and when my grandmother would do the few little practices she still did, like lighting candles on the anniversary of people's [death] and stuff, I would do that with her. And when it was Passover, I would force her to make me food . . . that went along with Passover, and I would read books. . . . so I always have called myself Jewish. . . . I never [told my parents]. Pretty much it was . . . my private thing. . . . I would say [from about] 6 [years].

At another point Vickie also notes that being a practicing Jew and celebrating Jewish feasts could be difficult when she had a very Irish-sounding surname and physical characteristics which many people associate with being Irish.

Hence, Vickie's is a fascinating story. At a very young age, she obviously picked up some information about the Jewish religion and became interested in it. She became particularly close to Jewish families in her neighborhood and joined her grandmother in various religious practices. She does this quietly because she recognizes that her parents are not supportive of religion. But the interest is sufficiently strong for her to develop what becomes a life-long commitment to the Jewish faith, in spite of her parents' opposition to religion. Given the propensity of children to engage in the forbidden, one might wonder if her interest in the Jewish faith might not have been sparked, in part, by her parents' obvious opposition to religion, an opposition which continues as she has become an adult. Vickie notes: "...my mother is very uncomfortable with this. ... And I don't know exactly why, I mean, she'll say to me, 'You're not getting religious, are you?' ... I don't know why she's so uncomfortable with it."

The story becomes even more interesting as Vickie describes the identification patterns of her siblings, both of whom have followed a quite different path. About her sister she says:

> ...she was drawn to Christianity when she – from earliest childhood ... she wanted to be a Christian. ... And I think part of that was because we had a neighbor across the street who was very young ... and had little kids. This woman was one of these effusive, grandmomma, you know, can't get enough of everybody's children, loving, wonderful woman. ... and my sister was always bothered by my parents' age ... embarrassed by it. And so she was very drawn to this woman who was a very, very religious Catholic. And I suspect that that's part of the whole picture. She always wanted to be a Christian ... she used to make herself little crosses and stuff, and my grandmother would have a fit about it. "Oh, you're Jewish," ... so that they'd occasionally come to blows over that. And my parents hated it, because they didn't want her to be Catholic.

Vickie concludes by reporting that her sister grew up to marry in the Catholic Church and became a very religious Catholic. Her brother, on the other hand, has adopted their father's Irish culture, visiting Ireland on several occasions, studying and becoming fluent in the Irish language and raising his child to identify as Irish. However, she says he "...doesn't do religion, so he mocks both of us." Hence, Vickie's family really brought together three cultures, the Irish, the Catholic, and the Jewish. Each of the three siblings has chosen one of them and made it his/her own, sometimes to the dismay of their parents, who did not identify closely with any of them. In both Anita's and Vickie's families, different members of the family developed a single sense of identity out of the various options provided in their family. But each member chose a somewhat different identity from that of their siblings.

When Culture is a Taboo Topic

In contrast with the families of Anita and Vickie, some multi-cultural families never discussed the various cultures present in the family. Karen's and Jeanette's families are examples.

Karen's parents met when her father served in the Korean War. Her mother was Korean and she describes her father's background as "White European," primarily German, Austrian, and French. Asked how she identifies herself, Karen says:

> If someone asked me bluntly, what are you, which is a typical way that people ask, I always say, because I know what they are trying to get at even though they are not doing it very eloquently, that I would say that I am Asian and White European descent. I consider myself more Euro-Asian, essentially. But that's how I identify myself. I don't consider myself Asian, and I don't consider myself to be White. If anything, I consider myself to be the "Other" category in a census.

Hence, her identity is Euro-Asian or "Other." Indeed, she expresses surprise at learning that a cousin, who is also half Korean and half White, unhesitatingly identified herself as Asian, without any reference to her European heritage. Clearly, her multi-cultural, multi-racial heritage is important to her. However, she is also firm in noting where her self-definition came from. Asked whether her mother had told her how to identify herself, she says "...we were told by the community how to identify ourselves, not by our mother ... when you get ethnic slurs passed your way ... kids are not very nice." Hence, Karen feels that her identity was, in a sense, forced upon her by the community, which consistently, even rudely, made it clear that she was Asian. We will return to the issue of the broader community's role in defining identity in Chapter 6.

Karen and her siblings found this situation particularly difficult since they had not been prepared for it by the family. Karen's description of her childhood provides a picture of a family which tried very hard to deny its multi-cultural nature. There were few indications of the family's various cultures. As a child, she and her siblings rarely saw members of either of their parents' families. About her father's family, Karen says:

> ...I don't know, I suspect, although my father would never say this, his mother I believed ... was very upset because he married an Asian woman, but he would never say this. There was some falling out between him and his mother.

Asked whether her parents ever discussed their cultural differences, Karen explains:

> ...my parents came over here when there was very much anti-Asian, especially anti-serviceman-marrying-Asian-women attitude. And they moved into a very White community. And this was after World War II when men came over with Japanese brides, and ... after the Korean War. ...I grew up in a very small community in Massachusetts. And so I think my mother's intent was to try to make us as American as she could. So she didn't talk Korean around the house; she very seldom cooked any Asian foods; and she didn't dress in any Asian dress style. And didn't tell stories in growing up in her life. And I didn't notice or understand the absence of that until I was older. ... no, my parents didn't deal with cultural issues, and ... my father just assumed because he was fine with it ... that everyone was fine with it. But of course, that wasn't the case.

As an adult, she reports having a "rather close relationship" with her father, to the point of having a "pretty intensive conversation" with him about the racial differences in the family and their impact on her and her siblings. In the end, Karen seems to have to have come to terms with her parents' lack of attention to multi-cultural issues: "So my father was a good father in many ways. There were areas where he was not. The area of race was not the area that he was strong on. ..."

Hence, Karen's family provided very little information about their racial differences or cultural backgrounds, nor any support to their children, about dealing with comments they might encounter from others. Instead, they were left largely on their own to deal with these problems. That the children did not deal with the issues well is illustrated by the fact that Karen had to reach adulthood to understand the meaning of all this. As indicated in Chapter 4, the most dramatic impact was not on Karen and her Euro-Asian siblings, but on the blond, blue-eyed nephew who was adopted into the family as an infant. It took a rude confrontation in Bible School to confront him with the realization that he was not Asian like his siblings, which Karen describes as "...a revelation to him ... that he was not [Asian]."

This revelation lead to a difficult period for the child, who was forced to confront his adoption and his difference from his siblings, issues for which his parents had clearly not prepared him. The incident also illustrates the problems which often ensue if children are not prepared for comments they might encounter in the larger community, a topic to which we will return at a later point.

A similar lack of recognition of cultural differences was found in Jeanette's family, which was described at length in Chapter 4. She and her siblings received little information about all the people and cultures who made up the extended family. As a result of living in these confusing surroundings, Jeanette's self-identification also seemed to suffer from a lack of focus. Asked whether she identifies herself as Lebanese or Irish, she had difficulty responding, indicating that her identity "shifted" at different periods in her life or with the setting or who was asking the question. She and her sisters frequently discussed what it meant to be Lebanese, but from their parents they got little information or support. Her mother's only suggestion was to "...just say you're Irish...." Jeanette also reported that she often lied and said her mother "had some Italian" to explain their somewhat darker skin without getting into the issue of being Lebanese, which raised the embarrassing association with being "a camel jockey or an Arab."

Karen and Jeanette provide an interesting comparison for children from families which do little to describe their cultural differences. For both, growing up in a multi-cultural family was clearly a distressing process. And both reported going into therapy at later points in their lives. To summarize, when families tried to ignore the various cultural and/or racial patterns which were present in the family, they left the children confused and uncomfortable. The children needed their parents' guidance and assistance in sorting through the various dimensions of the family's ethnic and racial makeup. This was particularly true when the family lived in a setting where the children were likely to encounter questions about their background, which was almost always the case. When parents avoided the question of ethnic and racial differences, as did Jeanette's and Karen's parents, the children had nowhere to turn.

Consequently, they were constantly questioning their identities. Jeanette reported that she used to change her definition of identity with the setting or the person asking the question. And for her, this was not a simple response to whatever happened to be convenient at the time, but a psychologically stressful attempt to deal with what she perceived to be, in her words, a painful situation. And her mother's suggestion that she "just say you're Irish" did little to help her. Both Karen and Jeanette reported having gone into therapy as adults to try to deal with the problems caused by their uncertain sense of identity. Even Karen's brother, who was White rather than Asian, was confused as to why he was not considered Asian when his siblings were. Unlike the children whose parents had often discussed their family's racial and cultural patterns – sometimes "at length," as Sarah suggested – respondents such as Karen and Jeanette were constantly uncomfortable with their cultural identity, a pattern which often lasted into adulthood, and sometimes never ended.

Up to now we have mainly been discussing persons who primarily identified with a single racial and/or ethnic group. They came to this determination through several different methods. Despite the fact that these were all people from multi-cultural or multi-racial backgrounds, some, like Robert and Adam, grew up in a setting in which they were presented with a single pattern. Hence, Adam never met his father and was reared in his mother's African-American culture. And Robert lived in a community in which the nationality differences of his parents were considered unimportant: he was just one of the White kids in a town where only racial differences mattered.

Others, like Vickie and Anita, were raised in families in which the varying cultural backgrounds were quite clearly delineated, and children seem to have felt free to select from among the cultural options their parents presented to them, with different siblings selecting different patterns. Still others grew up in families in which the parents chose to be uninvolved in their children's definition of a cultural self, often leaving the children uncertain as to who they are and how they and their families fit into the broader scheme of sociocultural patterns in the community, a pattern which they often found distressful. Karen eventually came to a definition of herself as Euro-Asian or "Other," while Jeanette's identity continued to "shift" even as an adult.

Identifying as "Mixed"

Persons from multi-cultural or multi-racial backgrounds can also choose to be identified as "mixed," and some respondents did choose to be identified in this manner. We turn now to a discussion of the way they reached this option. Individuals who deliberately wanted to be known as "mixed" appear to be at the other end of the spectrum from the respondents described above. They provide an interesting contrast to most of the others in the sample. Given the fact that being "mixed" in American society is relatively recent and rare and that so many forces are aligned against it, it is interesting to know how someone would come to this definition of themselves. After all, one concern that many respondents mentioned was the necessity of "choosing one," whenever they filled out an application or responded to a questionnaire.

As we have noted with several respondents, they often received messages from others concerning their identity, but usually it was a message suggesting that they belonged to one specific group. Often this was presented in a context which deliberately negated other identity patterns, and sometimes it was stated in opposition to what the proponents knew was a message they were receiving from other agents. Thus, Jeanette's mother told her to "just say she was Irish." Teresa's teachers consistently changed her "mixed" response on student forms to "Black." Even as a small child, Sarah was aware that her Christian relatives expected her to identify as Christian, while others wanted her to identify she was Jewish.

In the face of what are often vigorous messages indicating that they owed allegiance to a single group, how did some respondents persist in choosing a mixed identity? Initially, it should be noted that there are two ways of identifying as "mixed." Some respondents actually used the term "mixed," while others took pains to indicate the nature of the "mixture," specifying the various ethnic or racial components which made them "mixed." For the most part, these are all individuals who seemed to take considerable pride in their various racial and/or cultural backgrounds and were anxious to have this aspect of their identity recognized by others.

Deanna, whose mother was Korean and her father Black, is an example. Asked how she identifies herself, she says:

> ...um, I always say that I'm mixed. I never just say that I'm Black or Korean. I always tell people I. Uh, me and a girlfriend of mine, we call ourselves Amerasians. 'Cause we're part Americans and part Asians. We never just, uh, well, I never just um, identify with one race. I identify with both. So I consider myself biracial rather than just one race.

In response to a direct question regarding whether it "bothered" her to be identified as "mixed," she says:

> It doesn't. It doesn't. Not now. I mean, I don't think it ever really did, but growing up I think it was like something that was always on, on my mind, that I was mixed, because of all of the teasing and all of that thing, all of those natures, but now it doesn't. It doesn't bother me at all that I'm mixed. It doesn't bother me at all....

As we indicated in Chapter 3, Regina's "mixed" heritage had very different origins. She was multi-cultural through their own personal immigration experience, rather than having parents whose origins were different. Regina's parents were both Polish, but she was born in Brazil while her parents were refugees there after World War II. She still has relatives in Brazil; she rarely visits, but communicates regularly, largely through email. As an adult, Regina retains aspects of both cultures. Since she went to school in Brazil, she learned the Portuguese language; she also knew Polish because her parents insisted they speak Polish at home. She keeps contact with the Polish culture through keeping some of the religious traditions, the annual Polish Christmas celebration, and eating Polish food. Her ties to Brazil also remain strong:

> I belong to the Brazilian culture club in Detroit, and I was editor for their little magazine that they publish. I was the Portuguese interpreter for the Brazilian soccer games when they were here in 1994, so that was exciting. ... I still like to talk to my friends in Brazil.

Hence, Regina has a rich multi-cultural experience which she still retains as an adult. It comes, not from having parents from different cultures, but from having been born and raised in the Brazilian culture, which was different both from the Polish culture of her parents and that of the USA in which she now lives. As an immigrant and a multi-cultural individual, Regina experienced frequent problems as a child, particularly from members of the Polish community in which her family lived. She says:

...when I came to this country I was really ostracized. . . . where we lived [people] actually would point to me and call me DP . . . I had to learn what DP was – displaced person. But we weren't displaced – we were here by choice. And then when I would try to explain that, they would say no, you are DP. And I thought that was really weird. . .

Another example was Grace, whose background was a combination of English, Irish, and Native American. Grace insisted that she herself did the identifying – not anyone else. Asked how she identifies herself, Grace focuses on her ability to look at the "lighter side" of the issue of ethnic differences. She says:

I'm a jokester anyway, I like playing around, so I consider myself Heinz 57. I tell them I'm English, Irish, and Indian; which I am. But I usually go Heinz 57 because that's what most people say, so that's what I tell them.

When the interviewer commented that some respondents had not been successful in getting others to accept a "mixed" identification category and wondered if she had had this problem, Grace responded:

No, because I tell them what I am, and who I am. And I hope they will respect that enough. But like I said, I joke around so much, they say Heinz 57, and I say yes. Just go get me mad cause I'm going to pow-wow. I've always done stuff like that, because I'm a jokester, I like playing around and teasing . . . I haven't found anyone that would tell me that I'm not Indian or English, or Irish. So I'm pretty lucky that way.

Like Jeanette and Karen, Grace also came from a family that did little talking about their cultural heritage. However, unlike them, she was able to ask questions and get answers. She says:

I have a hard time going way far back. So I'll go back when I was a teenager when I can remember when I started asking what my heritage was. That's when they told me. And it really excited me, I got really excited about it because I find it interesting. I'd like to know more about it because I find it interesting. . . . Of course it took me quite a few years to figure out that I do want to go in my past, and I want to go through my family tree album. But I do want to do that.

Another example of a person with a strong "mixed" identity was Ted, whose family included a mixture of several European backgrounds, including Irish, English, Austrian, German, and Polish. He also describes his family as being "staunch Catholic." His parents and grandparents also spoke several languages, a matter in which he takes great pride. He is particularly proud that his mother even knew enough Yiddish to converse with the shopkeepers in the largely Jewish neighborhood in which he grew up. However, his family was also very sensitive to the impact of the two World Wars on the American population and concerned about being identified with the German nation. Consequently, they tended to identify under the general Catholic "umbrella." When asked to identify himself, Ted described his identity as "multi-cultural and multi-European."

One characteristic which all of these "mixed-identifying" individuals seem to have in common is a considerable degree of interest and pride in the varying dimensions of their backgrounds. They all seem to have grown up in families in which their parents and other relatives discussed rather openly the different cultures present in the family. Hence, these differences did not appear as a matter of embarrassment or secrecy. Instead, they chose to select all (or at least, several) of the options. This is not to say that identifying as "mixed" was always a pleasant experience for some of the respondents. As noted in Chapter 4, Peggy found herself "left out" of the important social networks in her high school because she insisted on indicating her "mixed" ethnic origins.

Grace's experience may suggest a clue as to why at least some respondents found the "mixed" identity appealing. In part, it appears that Grace's comfort with her "mixed" heritage may come from viewing this identity as a means of avoiding another, less positive identity to which others appeared to want to assign her. She reports having been "...in a lot of fights with kids in the neighborhood ..." in order to "...protect my family." Asked to explain, she indicated that:

> ...they [neighborhood children] were trying to – they would call my sisters, brother and my mom and dad names. They would call us white hillbilly trash and we weren't. We weren't trash, we were just as good as everyone else. They didn't have the right to say that. And they would call us foul names and I wouldn't take it, I'd just go bust them in the face and fight with them, because I didn't think they had the right to call us that. That was degrading to us. We weren't white trash, we were white human beings. We were just as good as anyone else.

For Grace, it appears that taking pride in being ethnically "mixed" was a means of avoiding the more onerous epithet of "white hillbilly trash." Hence, she found it interesting and exciting, and something she wanted to identify with and learn more about.

Indeed, for all of the "mixed" identifying persons, this pride in the multiple dimensions of their backgrounds appears to have been an important characteristic. Grace found it "interesting" and wanted to know more about these different cultures. Peggy had numerous stories to tell of the Irish and Belgian cultures of her parents and the way they had influenced her childhood. Ted seemed to take great pride in the multi-cultural Catholic European background of his family, including their facility with languages. And Deanna is proud to be "Amerasian," which recognizes both her American and her Asian background and also recognizes that her father was Black. These are all people who have confronted the several dimensions of their heritage and embraced them all. In effect, they are saying, "I am all of these!"

As indicated in Chapter 2, this preference for identifying with all, or at least several, of their ethnic origins has been found to characterize persons of mixed backgrounds in previous studies. Thus, Waters (1990) found that many respondents in her sample of multi-nationality Catholics chose to hold multiple identities. And Howard (2000) notes that people often have multiple identities, such as race, gender, age, or class; why could not also have multiple ethnic identities as well? However, it has also been noted that they there is often considerable pressure to force multi-cultural and multi-racial people to "choose one" category (Gaskins, 1999; Rockquemore and Laszloffy, 2005). At times, this even goes to the point of suggesting that persons who insist on choosing a "mixed" identity are somehow psychologically confused or unbalanced (Nakashima, 1992; Gibbs and Hines, 1992; Rockquemore and Laszloffy, 2005; Wilson, 1992; Gibbs and Hines, 1992). Clearly, these "mixed" respondents did not think of themselves in that manner!

Summary: How People from Multi-cultural Families Define Themselves

In this chapter, we have been discussing the identity patterns described by persons from mixed racial and cultural backgrounds. We have focused on the different types of identity patterns they developed. As we noted, the individual's sense of identity is not developed in a vacuum. Rather, as Strauss (1959), Mead (1934), and Cooley (1922) pointed out, the concept of "who I am" is developed in a social context, with the child's social contacts playing a very active role in the development of the child's sense of self. A major concern which several respondents mentioned is that they were often forced by various social agents to "choose one" of their cultural backgrounds with which to identify. When they refused to do so, they were often faced with others who would alter their chosen response for them. While children from a single culture are reminded of their identity by everyone they meet, multi-cultural children are more likely to encounter questions as to who they are, as well as hearing different responses from different segments of the family and community.

We noted three major characteristics which are often used to define social categories: physical appearance, surname, and cultural characteristics such as language religion or national origin. In the USA, the physical characteristic of skin color, or race, is a major source of identification. Blacks and Asians are constantly reminded that they are "different," as a result of their skin color; however, other groups with more subtle differences, such as southern Europeans or Middle Easterners, are also defined on the basis of their darker skin color. Surname is another mark of identity, and some respondents reported being pressured to identify with the ethnic group with which their surname was associated. This is particularly true of Hispanics, for whom "Spanish-surnamed" is sometimes the basis for assignment to programs designed for persons of Hispanic background. Use of the surname can be problematic as a mark of identity, since names are often changed at immigration or marriage. Use of the surname also eliminates the possibility of being identified with the mother's culture. Since mothers do most of the child-rearing, many people remain closer to their maternal relatives, even in patriarchal cultures.

Religion, language or accented speech, dress patterns, and other observable cultural patterns may also be the basis on which people are defined by others. Simplistic classification systems which use single variables like physical differences and surnames tend to ignore these cultural differences, such as the nationality differences among various Asian, Spanish-speaking, or European nations, as well as variations among African-Americans. In particular, these generalizations often discount the impact of the mother's culture, which can be particularly important in view of the mother's role in the rearing of the children.

However, pressure from the so-called experts, as well as the community at large, to accept these predetermined definitions can be very strong, not to mention very disturbing to persons from mixed backgrounds, who believe they should be free to define themselves in a manner which recognizes what they personally believe to be the most important components of their background. We will discuss this impact of the broader community on the self-defintion of these multi-cultural respondents in greater detail in Chapter 6, with particular emphasis on the respondents' reactions to this pressure.

In this chapter, we recognized that the development of a sense of identity was a complicated process and showed that children from mixed cultural backgrounds might receive mixed messages concerning their sense of self. We examined the respondents' definition of "who they were," both in terms of how they defined themselves and how they developed this definition. We found that these respondents frequently receive mixed messages concerning their identity, from members of their own nuclear families of parents and siblings and from their extended families of grandparents, aunts and uncles, and cousins, and from the community at large. In this chapter, we placed greatest emphasis on the impact of the family.

As we compared the experiences the respondents reported, it became obvious that no simple hypothesis, such as outward physical appearances or the impact of the mother's culture as opposed to that of the father, could account for differences observed. We noted that respondents were highly creative in the manner in which they evaluated and assimilated their parents' cultures. Some chose the mother's culture, some the father's; others combined the two; and still other families included several siblings who each identified with different aspects of the cultural dimensions their parents presented to them.

Some respondents chose to identify with a single culture. In some instances, this occurred because they were raised in a setting in which a single cultural identity made sense. If you were born of parents from mixed racial or cultural backgrounds, but one parent disappeared soon after your birth and you were reared by the remaining parent and his/her relatives, you easily identified with that background. Similarly, if your parents were of different nationalities, but the community you grew up in only defined race an as an important factor in defining one's position in society, then it was fairly easy for you to define yourself in a unitary manner. In effect, such persons may technically have been of "mixed" backgrounds, but for all practical purposes, their socialization process had been focused on a single race or culture.

The most interesting cases, however, involved respondents for whom both parents and both cultural backgrounds were present throughout their formative years. These people received a number of messages about their identity. Some families appeared to provide fairly clear descriptions of the various cultures. Others were somewhat secretive about their respective backgrounds. Each approach produced different results in their children's identity formation. In this chapter, we were primarily concerned about the outcome, that is, what pattern the children eventually chose.

While many respondents did identify with a single ethnic or racial background, some deliberately chose to identify with several or all of the ethnic groups which made up their background. One way of doing this was simply to identify as "mixed." Another approach was to specify all or several of the different components. Several respondents mentioned that this approach could be problematic, since this response was not acceptable in some quarters. Questionnaires often did not permit this response, and some complained that their "mixed" response would even be altered by others who wished to force them to "pick one category."

Since choosing a mixed response was apparently highly unacceptable, it is perhaps surprising that some respondents went to considerable length to force the issue. People who took this approach were usually people who took great pride in their various cultural backgrounds and were proud of the diverse components of their mixed heritage. Hence, they were reluctant to dismiss any part of what they considered to be parts of themselves. Most reported having had some problems claiming their multi-cultural heritage but considered the result to be worth the extra effort.

One of the issues which has arisen at various points throughout this chapter has been the fact that the identity patterns of multi-cultural and multi-racial individuals are considerably influenced by persons outside the family. These people were constantly reminded by others in the community that they were "different" and often questioned about "who they were." In this chapter, we have concentrated on the impact of the multi-cultural families on the identity formation of their children. We have referred only briefly to the outside influences but have not described them in detail. In Chapter 6, we will discuss in greater detail the ways in which persons outside the family attempted to influence the identity patterns of multi-cultural people and the effect it had. Chapter 7 will focus specifically on the impact of the family.

Chapter 6
"It Takes a Village": Critical Role of the Social Environment on Identity Formation

If the family is not the sole entity involved in defining children's sense of ethnic identity, who is? Karen's father seemed to feel that racial differences were unimportant – no more important than "big ears." However, the fact remains that there are many forces in society which do not agree that racial, religious, or nationality differences are unimportant. Strauss (1959: 26) even went so far as to say that classification and evaluation of its members are "...usually, if not predominantly, public concerns." Hence children are likely to encounter comments in the larger community which remind them that they are indeed "different." An African tradition says that it "takes a village to raise a child" (Clinton, 1996). Santorum (2005), on the other hand, insists that raising a child is a task for the family. This chapter will focus primarily on the "village" influence.

If the village axiom is true, then the villages in which these respondents spent their childhood years were, in one way or another, nonsupportive of their growth and development. Several respondents mentioned the fact that their multi-cultural heritage could be greater or lesser, depending upon the social milieu in which the family lived (see also Harris and Sim, 2002). Some social environments appeared to be open to people from different cultures, others, less so. Presumably, in communities that were more supportive of multi-culturalism, the offspring experienced relatively few problems. Indeed, some were not even aware of being multi-cultural until their later lives. Others experienced disapproval, censure, or even ridicule from friends and neighbors.

Recalling the small, primarily White community where she grew up, Karen commented that "...kids are not very nice," and she and her siblings would "...get ethnic slurs passed [their] way." They were constantly reminded that they were Asian, and "...it didn't make any difference if you were half or whole." Similarly Peter, who spent his early years in California and his teen years in Michigan, commented that in California, being Native American was less stigmatized, but income differences were very important. In contrast, when he moved to Michigan, his Native American heritage was less accepted. Sarah lived in two different communities in

Portions of this chapter were originally presented to the Sociological Practice Association, San Francisco, CA, August, 2004

Michigan, one a small isolated town, the other a large suburb of a major city. She found it odd that she was more accepted by the residents of the small town than in the suburb, where she and her mother were often told to "go back where you came from."

Hence the various communities of which these respondents were a part clearly played a role in their identity formation. In this chapter we will discuss the different social settings in which these respondents lived and the ways in which they exercised this influence. We will begin by discussing the various meanings of community.

Placing Identity Formation in the Community Context

In order to move from the family setting into the larger community context, we must first cover two important matters. The first matter is the definition of what constitutes community for the individuals, particularly young people, who are in the process of identity formation. How is "community" defined? What are its components? What are the different types of community? We will then go on to discuss the role of the community in defining the dimensions of culture which that community considers relevant in distinguishing among its members. Finally, we will discuss different dimensions, in addition to race and nationality, on which communities may base their distinctions.

Defining Community

When we speak of the influence of the "community" on the development of a sense of identity, the term "community" actually has multiple meanings. As we noted in Chapter 4, respondents described numerous problems, many of them unique to persons with a diverse heritage. The various groups which impacted on their lives may be considered to be part of the "community" – or "communities" – which played a part in their identity formation. These communities include the society as a whole, the local community, as well as segments of the local community with which the individual comes into contact. We will discuss each of these in turn.

Perhaps the most obvious community which exercises an influence is the society as a whole. While this may seem vague and distant at first glance, there were obvious indications that these distant social entities played an important part in producing problems for these multi-cultural individuals. A common complaint was the constant demand that they list their identity on questionnaires or applications which originated from various bureaucratic organizations at the national, state, or local government levels; the fact that this requirement usually involved a single identity was particularly distressing. So society as a whole, acting through its representatives, is the first community which must be considered.

The second community which influences the individual's sense of identity is the city or town in which the individual lives. The nature of that community – its ethnic and racial makeup, its public bureaucratic structure, the way its members view persons from different backgrounds, all will play a role in the identity formation of children in the community.

Finally, every community is made of various segments; many of these are actually communities in their own right. For example, cities are made up of neighborhoods, which play a role in the development of the children who live there. Individual schools, together with the children, their families, and the teachers and administrators who work there, also play a role. The same might be said of churches or other religious institutions, the business community, and so on. Each of these components may play a role in the development of children's sense of identity. If businesses or religious groups act in a discriminatory manner toward certain ethnic or racial groups, this will have a different impact on the children of the community than another community in which religious groups or businesses are more open to diversity.

In addition, the various ethnic groups in a town or neighborhood are also likely to influence how children in the community view themselves and those around them. For example, a child whose parent is Mexican is much more likely to learn about the Mexican culture and community if s/he lives in a community with a large and active Mexican component. In this chapter, we will examine the respondents' tales concerning the impact which these groups of varying types played in their childhood experiences.

Community Role in Defining Relevant Dimensions of Multi-Culturalism

Several respondents emphasized the importance of the communities in which they lived in making them aware of different aspects of their backgrounds. Those who had grown up in social settings in which racial, religious, or nationality differences had been emphasized, were much more conscious of these issues. They were reminded at every turn that they belonged to a particular group, even if they or their families did not view that group as important. This awareness played an important role in determining which of the several aspects of their background children would be likely to emphasize.

Perhaps the most dramatic finding in the data was the impact which the social setting had upon these respondents' awareness of whether they were multi-cultural. Individuals could view themselves as multi-cultural – or not – depending on the manner in which their communities viewed them and their families. Some communities emphasize the importance of specific groups, and define other group distinctions as unimportant. Such settings will exert a profound influence on whether a child will define himself or herself as having a mixed background. Unquestionably, the most important environmental aspect mentioned was the degree and nature of the prejudice or discrimination which the individual encountered. It is no great surprise to sociologists that persons whose environmental experiences included a racial component were more likely to be sensitive to these differences than those whose family patterns did not include a racial component. As we have shown in previous chapters, several respondents, both Black and White, commented on the importance of the racial issue.

Robert, of Scottish-English background, who had very negative memories of his childhood, did not attribute them to the cultural differences between his parents. In fact, he stated he was really not aware at the time that these cultural differences even existed. He attributed this to the racist character of the rural area in southern Kentucky where he grew up. Of this region, he said: "Whites and Blacks, that's what it was." Hence Robert was raised in an area in which race was the only difference that mattered. As long as you were White and Protestant, everyone was seen to be the same. Any other differences did not matter.

Derek, whose father was an African-American who married a woman from Germany, viewed the world from the other side of the racial divide. He made a point of comparing several areas in which he or other members of his family had lived. Initially, his commanding officer did not want to give the required approval for the marriage. When they returned to the Washington, D.C., area, racial tensions were difficult, exacerbated by the fact that his mother was unfamiliar with the language and culture. He notes: "my mother had a hard time . . . And, of course, people see the children together . . . people called names." In contrast, he remembers good relations with his mother's family during his teens when they lived in Germany. When they moved to a military base in Texas, he notes that the family "experienced some Klan activity. . .," as well as ". . .name-calling and stuff like that. . . . People called us zebras, uh, crows, things like that. Weird names, because of our mixed heritage." He also commented on the differential manner in which mixed racial people are viewed ". . .even within the Black [community] . . . being lighter skinned, people thought that we received better treatment than others."

Still, he contrasts his experience with the negative experiences described by members of his father's family in Louisiana. In contrast: "I never experienced anything malicious. I never . . . experienced any of the really dramatic, overt acts of prejudice that were prevalent back in the . . . 60s, and things like that, during the civil rights era. . . . most of my growing up was in Texas, in the South." However, ". . .having a chance to be exposed to different military bases, you know, going to school with a lot of people with different ethnic backgrounds," he felt made the racial experience less negative. Actually, he believed there was more discrimination against Mexicans in Texas: ". . .Growing up in Texas, you're either American, Black and White didn't matter, or you're Mexican. . . . So . . . on the whole, I'm very fortunate in the fact that I didn't have to suffer any racial indignities that a lot of people had."

Hence Derek provides a detailed description of the differential treatment his family experienced, depending upon the setting. They were more warmly received by his relatives in Germany than in the USA; they received better treatment on the military bases in Texas than his relatives from Louisiana remembered; lighter skinned Blacks are generally treated better than darker skinned ones. Hence multi-racial Blacks are likely to receive better treatment. Derek also appears, however, to be the type of person who does not allow the attitudes of others to affect him greatly; hence, he is able to see Mexicans as having more difficulty in Texas than Blacks, and shrugs off the epithets of "zebra" and "crow." His experiences illustrate not only the regional variations in treatment of multi-racial families, but also the individual variations in their handling of it.

Other respondents had lived in different areas, and they also found the reception to their cultural backgrounds to vary, depending on the area. Peter, for example, described how social class was important in California, where he spent his early childhood, but being Native American was more difficult in Michigan, where he went to high school:

> ...it was very different [in Michigan]. Money wasn't that important [as in California]. . . . it was nice, I like it a lot because I didn't have to dress up nice and stuff like that. Everybody else seemed to dress the same. . . . I was more at ease because my clothes were not a big issue anymore.

However, he continues:

> I guess here [i.e., in Michigan] race really was an issue. That's when I got more identified with being a Native American than being back in California. . . . Pretty much anywhere I went around here [e.g., in Michigan], people are meaner . . . If you're not the same as them, they kind of exclude you. Because I'm not Black I wasn't very much invited. . . . Because I knew how to surf, I picked up skate boarding and I kind of met up with the group that knew how to skateboard. And these were different types of people, one guy was Filipino, one guy was Irish, another guy was African-American. We were all kind of like interracial.

Peter's experience of differential treatment in different social settings was shared by Sarah, whose background involved both religious and nationality mixtures. She was born and spent her earliest years in Europe during and following the Second World War. She came to the USA with her mother at the age of 14. She compares her early years in the USA in a small, rural town in southern Michigan with her later experiences in a large suburb of Detroit. Sarah felt that she and her mother were much more accepted in the rural area:

> ...interestingly enough, my reception in a small town in Michigan was . . . in a sense . . . less hostile, less resistant, more welcoming, . . . genuine curiosity, than it was when I came to [the suburb] 2 years later when I was fluent in English, and all that. . . . in [the small town], of course, we were exoticized . . . But I found friends very quickly. . . . I was involved in a lot of school activities. I didn't feel left out, even though I had to be taught lots of things all the time about cultural differences.

She contrasts this broad acceptance in the small town with the suburban area:

> ...it was a working class neighborhood, but they're very hostile to anybody that they suspected of being intellectual . . . I was a very good student which was resented. I was seen as having leftist politics, which of course I did.

As we noted in Chapter 4, she felt this antagonism not only in school but in other areas as well, where perfect strangers would tell them, ". . .to 'go back where you came from.'"

In the instances described above, the distinctions were based on fairly clear characteristics: race, immigrant status or language, even social class. In some instances, however, the distinctions were not nearly as obvious as these. Some settings appear on the surface to be similar to Robert's: everyone appears to be from the same cultural background, but because the participants see it differently, individuals will experience it differently. Peggy's experience in a Catholic high school is an example.

Since she was Catholic, she assumed that she was part of the group, but was consistently reminded that she was not. In retrospect, she realized that what she assumed was an all-Catholic setting was actually quite divided by nationality. The school had large groups of girls from Irish and Polish backgrounds, with a smaller group of Italians, and an even smaller group of what she described as "everything else." Since Peggy's mother was neither Irish nor Catholic, she was not accepted. She felt her mixed nationality background "...always opened the door to the fact that I didn't belong anywhere." She goes on to describe the rigidity of the divisions in the school:

> ...the girls I was most anxious to be friends with I found out later were in the Polish group, and I used to hang around them. ... finally one of them took me off to the side and said, "Why don't you leave us alone? Don't you know you don't belong here?" ... no, I didn't know I didn't belong there. And at the time I didn't know why I didn't belong there. ... I don't think any of us would have realized it was ethnic. ... As I look back, the ones I ended up being friends with were in this other ... the very small group of people that didn't belong anywhere! ... As a matter of fact, one of the girls in that group ... was Polish. ... But she was Polish from Poland. ... Which made her different from the "real Polish." ... Polish-Americans is what they were, and she didn't belong there either because she was Polish from Poland and she wasn't one of the kids who grew up in ... the Polish neighborhoods. ... she really wasn't one of them. It was interesting, now that I think of it, that someone that was really Polish didn't belong in the Polish group.

Here was a setting in which some of the members thought they were part of the majority, but the group made clear distinctions about who belonged and who did not. This illustrates the need for parents and teachers to become sensitized to the distinctions which children make about each other, in order to assist children in dealing with them – even if, to the casual observer, it appears as though all of the children are the same.

Vickie's experience in her Irish–Catholic–Jewish family illustrated another way in which the community can emphasize one aspect of a family's multi-cultural identity. As described in Chapter 5, neither of her parents practiced or expressed any interest in their respective religions. However, her sister became attracted to her father's Catholic background through an unusual aspect of community happenstance, their living across the street from a very devout Catholic family. She became very close to the family, and eventually became a Catholic, much to the dismay of the rest of her family, who did not want her to be Catholic. Vickie, in contrast, was very close to her maternal grandmother, and developed an interest in the Jewish culture which the grandmother shared with her.

These examples illustrate the fact that the community to which children are exposed as they grow up plays a very important role in defining the components of their heritage which they will define as important. Their choice among the several cultural options they are offered is largely dependent upon the social experiences they encounter. If race is emphasized, children will be very conscious of their racial backgrounds. If they live in a community in which religion is very important, with many churches, synagogues, or mosques, and watching people attend services regularly, children will grow up being very conscious of their own religious heritage. If the community considers only racial differences to be of importance, then all other differences pale into insignificance. On the other hand, if the members of the community think ethnic or nationality differences are critical – even if they are not aware that nationality is the basis for these distinctions – then these differences will affect the way in which community members are treated.

Different Communities – Different Factors Prevail

An important issue to be considered in the context of the role of the community is the fact that there are as many meanings of multi-culturalism as there are communities to define it. Each community emphasizes the characteristics it defines as important in differentiating among its members. With respect to social class, we previously discussed the example of Peter, who experienced different treatment in Michigan and California, where his social class was an issue. Another example of social class differences comes from Carol, who defined her family as "multi-cultural" on the basis of the social and economic class differences between her parents. Both parents were born and reared in southeast USA. She stresses the differences between their backgrounds:

> ...my mom's family was very well-to-do. They were part of the last of the old southern aristocracy ... her dad was a plantation owner, and he owns a cotton mill ... and I don't know what all else. ... and my dad came from more of a working class sawmill family. ... So the cultural difference is not because they came from different parts of the world, but because they came from different social and economic backgrounds ... you know, if you've ever seen "Gone with the Wind," my mom was Scarlett O'Hara ... You know, large house, maids, and my mom always had a maid...

Carol commented extensively on the differences between the cultures of these two different social classes. She noted that there were constant disagreements in the family because her mother wanted a larger house and had frequent concerns about the family not engaging in the "appropriate" behavior in various social settings. She says: "My Mom ... was always, you know, sort of picking on [my Dad] to talk right, act proper, and all that kind of stuff." Carol identifies more closely with her working class father: "I feel like an alien in her world. ... I don't know ... the social stuff and parties and bridge club and golf course and all that kind of crap. ...." In contrast, her brother has a life style which resembles that of her upper class mother. As adults, she and her brother have little in common and rarely see each other. Her experience of clashing social class requirements was also mentioned by Peter, who found the social class demands of his California community more stressful than the ethnic discrimination in the school he attended in Michigan.

Both Carol and Peter illustrate the manner in which social class may serve as a discriminating factor in communities. Other groups may be alienated from the community for similar reasons. Both Regina and Sarah indicated that their status as immigrants, and perceived to be "DPs," or displaced persons, exposed them to greater discrimination than their status as multi-cultural persons. Both spoke of others rejecting them because they were outsiders and did not belong in the community. For Regina, the experience was particularly painful, since it occurred in a Polish neighborhood, where she and her family thought they would be accepted.

The Influence of Community on Identity Formation for Mixed Background Individuals

The major focus of the interviews with the multi-racial and multi-cultural respondents was the way in which they defined who they were. In particular, they were asked if they usually identified themselves, or if others often forced an identity on them. Their responses to these questions will be the focus of the following discussion. An analysis of the comments which the respondents raised with regard to their experiences suggests that there were several types of problems these multi-racial and multi-cultural persons encountered in their contacts with various agencies or institutions.

The areas they mentioned can be summarized as follows: assuming or forcing a single identification; pressure from various ethnic and racial groups in the identification process; identifying individuals by outward appearances; a general lack of recognition or respect for different cultural patterns; and a lack of acceptance of their cultural backgrounds from the respondents' own groups. We also compare the development of multi-racial identity with multi-cultural identity. Several respondents mentioned issues which had particular reference to school policies. Since the respondents were discussing their childhood experiences, and the school is the critical institution in the socialization of children, these issues will be discussed as a separate concern.

Assuming or Forcing a Single Identification

Perhaps the single, most common concern raised by the respondents concerned their perception that they were often forced into a single ethnic identification. The most obvious situation in which this occurred was at the society-wide community level. In a complex society such as the USA, there is an almost constant requirement to fill out forms. These include census forms, questionnaires for work or school, or surveys. The sheer number of situations in which people are required to respond to these forms makes this annoyance unending.

The process was painful to many of the respondents, since it forced them to select among their individual identities, to the exclusion of the others. And the stress was experienced almost equally by persons who were multi-racial and those who were multi-cultural. As Sarah commented, there is no real recognition of diversity or multi-culturalism in the USA. Anita (of Mexican and Puerto Rican background) agrees and notes that diversity in the USA is "not a positive thing." Affirmative Action programs can cause particular concerns for people from multi-cultural backgrounds. Karen, whose father was Caucasian and her mother Korean, was a University employee, and noted that administrators consistently tried to categorize her and inquired about which category she belonged in. Ken, whose mother was Guatemalan and Chinese, and whose father was Black, Irish, and Native American, also objected to being forced to choose a single category in filling out forms, or to choose a general category, such as "Hispanic." He said he preferred to list "all" – an option which was rarely allowed.

Nearly all respondents would have been happier if these questionnaires had a space for "multi-cultural," as suggested by Regina. When she attended a university, she was asked her national origin. When she tried to claim both Polish and Brazilian, she was informed that "there was so space for that." Hence she was asked to pick between the two. Most respondents found this a painful experience. As Leslie (Filipino and Caucasian) put it, other people did not "get it – what it felt like for someone to put a label on you that didn't fit." Like the others, Leslie considered herself to be both, and did not like to identify with only one or the other. Unfortunately, according to Leslie, people would always tell her to "Check one – and only one." She went on to say: ". . .if I could have checked 2, then that would have been OK . . . so I thought they should . . . have, like a multiracial option, or multicultural option."

Yet in most settings, the "multi-cultural" option is not available. Even people whose options *appear* to be available may be resentful of the options offered. Anita (the Mexican/Puerto Rican woman) is an example. Most questionnaires offer the "Hispanic" option, and most people would think of her as Hispanic. However, Anita was adamantly opposed to being forced to assume a single identification as "Hispanic," since she was well aware of the quite different cultures which Mexico and Puerto Rico represented. In her mind, to identify as "Hispanic" forced her to reject the breadth of her cultural background. Other respondents also objected to the requirement to check a single box. For example, both Sarah and Regina could easily check "white" or "Caucasian." Both objected to selecting an identity which did not accurately describe their complex cultural background.

To summarize, a major concern which these multi-cultural respondents faced was the necessity of identifying themselves in questionnaires which did not include an option which correlated with the manner in which they defined themselves. How did they respond to this problem – especially since many encountered this problem at a very early period in their lives when they had little preparation for dealing with it? Several said they chose to identify as "other." Says Leslie: "They did have . . . this 'other' box with a line next to it." Her solution was: "I would check 'other' and then I'd explain." Karen also indicated that she did not want to be either European or Asian, so she also checked "other" in the census – and put "whitish-yellow" down as her description. As indicated in Chapter 4, Teresa also had the problem, and dealt with the situation by checking both boxes. However, she also noted that her multiple responses were often not accepted, particularly in school; we will return to this issue again later in this chapter.

It was not only in surveys or questionnaires that multi-cultural individuals faced problems. Many of them recounted social instances in which they were pressed by their companions to select a single focus of identification. Ken, with his highly diverse background, recalled a work setting which included a Filipino, Mexican, White female, and himself. The woman asked, "What are you guys?" When they joked around about the question, she continued to press the matter to learn their ethnic background. Some of the men found the questioning unpleasant and rude.

Perhaps the most striking incident was mentioned by Anita, who was Mexican and Puerto Rican, and quite proud of both. She recalled an unpleasant incident in an interaction with her own family. A favorite cousin on the Puerto Rican side of her family invited her to a social gathering. As they arrived at the party, he suggested that she should "not mention the Mexican part," which was the side of the family to which she felt closer. She objected to the expectation that she change her ethnic identification in different settings.

A few respondents were not bothered by the expectation that they assume a single ethnic identity. For example, Ida, who was of British and Lebanese background, stated that she usually identifies herself as simply "American." Most people see her that way, and she is content with that identity. Similarly, Adam, whose background included African American, Native American, and Caucasian, is usually identified as African American and does not have a problem with having people identify him that way: "I don't think I have an issue with it, again because of the way I was brought up. Um, and since I look at African American as my race, and I look at us with pride, I really don't have an issue with being looked at or perceived that way. I don't have a problem with it."

In general, people who did not object to the labels thrust upon them were generally people for whom the forced identity was identical to their chosen one. In addition, they tended to be individuals who had strong social connections with one of their component identities, to the exclusion of the others. Adam, quoted above, is an example. He had no contact with his father and was raised in the African-American community of his mother, who apparently had no connection with her Native American parentage. Hence there was little opportunity for Adam to encounter anyone who would provide the seeds of an alternate identity – or any impetus for Adam to establish an allegiance with it.

In many instances, however, it may not be clear which came first – the individual's personal choice or an imposed label. Ida, for example, preferred to identify simply as "American." Was this her choice after considering and rejecting the Lebanese and British identities of her parents? Or was this essentially a "non-choice," because the other ethnic identities were never presented as practical options, as in the case of Adam? It might also be the result of a painful process of rejection of identities which had been found traumatic and unpleasant in the past. Jeanette, whose Lebanese-Irish background was very similar to Ida's, remained highly resentful, years after her family's insistence that she "just say you're Irish." As Mead so eloquently reminded us, personal identification is more a *social* process than an *individual* one!

In summary, most respondents shared a sense of resentment for being forced to assume a single identification pattern. Karen recognizes that most people try to impose a single category because it "makes it easier for them." All the same, she says, "I still find it offensive." It is less offensive when other Asians ask, because she thinks they are trying to find out how they are the *same*, but she thinks that Whites have another agenda, i.e., to see how they are *different*. So the first issue which was a concern to these persons from diverse backgrounds was what they viewed as a constant pressure to choose among their diverse identities. In effect, they felt they were constantly forced to reject a part of themselves in order to please others. For those who tended to identify with only one of their origins, this might not be a problem, provided the label applied to them coincided with the one they preferred. However, in the words of Leslie, people often ". . .didn't understand what it felt like for someone to put a label on you that didn't fit. . .."

The Special Role of Ethnic and Racial Groups in "Claiming" Their Own Members

It is important to recognize that racial and ethnic groups are among the major role players in influencing the self-definition of ethnic identity. Most racial and ethnic communities want to maximize their membership. They want to be able to show others the strength of their respective communities. And strength, with regard to human communities, is usually measured, at least in part, through membership size. Consequently, such groups are constantly trying to expand their groups by encouraging – or pressuring – as many persons as possible to claim membership in the group. In the USA, the importance of the race issue ensures that this will be particularly true of racial groups.

Most respondents who exhibited physically different characteristics had experienced pressure to identify with the group, even if they did not consider it to be their chosen identity. Often this pressure came from the wider community. However, some respondents indicated the strongest messages came from within the ethnic group itself. As noted earlier, Teresa was often told she should identify as Black, rather than as mixed. She recalled that teasing seemed to come more from Black children, who seemed to resent her focus on being mixed. She says: "The Black kids would call me names. Like oreo or zebra. Or they'd ask me, 'Was I White or Black?'" Racially mixed respondents, such as Teresa and Derek, were usually the ones who reported that others liked to ridicule their background with epithets such as these.

Similar stories were told by Anita and Deanna, both of whom were of mixed race. Deanna, who was half Korean and half Black, reported on an incident which occurred in the Korean store in which she worked. She was operating the cash register when a Black woman came to the counter. The woman assumed she was Korean until she spoke, and her accent exhibited the speech patterns of African-Americans.

At that point, she notes, "Their whole attitude changes!" She describes one woman as being:

> ...so started she almost dropped her purse! ... she couldn't believe it. She looked over at me with big eyes. it was like, "Oh my God! You sound like one of us!" She said that! She said, "You sound like one of us!" And I'm lookin' at her like, what does that mean? "You look Chinese but you sound Black!" And that's when it may come out, yeah, yeah, I'm mixed. [They say] "Oh I can tell now; I can tell." But most of the time it's when I talk. . . . I get it all the time. . . . The change is so obvious. . . . It's so obvious, the change, when they find out that . . . I'm mixed.

What is more important is the comment which usually follows. Deanna says:

> ...most of 'em do tend to say, well because you're Black, you're Black. You have a little bit of Black in you, you're Black. . . . When I tell them that I'm biracial, . . .I've had a couple of customers tell me, "No, girl, you're Black."

Hence Deanna has found that Blacks who learn of her mixed heritage insist that she is Black, even though they realize she is of mixed heritage. Their conclusion is, "You have a little bit of Black in you, you're Black."

Anita, whose parents were Puerto Rican and Mexican, had a similar experience in school. Anita exhibited the somewhat darker skin characteristic of many people of Mexican or Puerto Rican backgrounds, and considered herself to be "multi-cultural and multi-racial." She reported two incidents, one in college and one in a workshop setting, in which she was attacked for not identifying as an African-American. She describes the workshop incident:

> ...there was ... a self-identification exercise, and I didn't step into the [group] that was African-American. And one woman [an African-American] in the exercise says, "Well, I think there's someone in this room who should have stepped in that didn't." ... And I'm sure it was directed at me because every other person of color stepped into that and people just assume that I'm African American or biracial, African American and Caucasian, or something like that.

Elsewhere she says:

> I was always challenged with, "Oh no, you're African American. You're just trying not to be." Or something like that. Uh, or "you're trying to deny that you're African American." ... I used to put a lot of effort into trying to come up with a good answer that, African American is a culture, it's not a race. African-American is a separate culture which I don't know anything about.

Concerning the college incident, she was particularly distressed that the instructor allowed the other student to attack her without coming to her defense.

Hence a theme which appears with many of the respondents who were, or appeared to be, Black was that they had to identify themselves as such. There was considerable pressure exerted over them, most often by Blacks, to define themselves as Black, coupled with considerable rancor if they resisted the pressure. Deanna was told, "If you're a little bit Black, you're Black." Teresa and Derek were called "oreo" or "zebra" when they claimed their mixed heritage. And Anita was accused of trying to deny her Blackness. Clearly members of racial communities are not very accepting if they feel that people they perceive to be "their" members are not willing to accept the appropriate designation.

Ethnic community pressure was not only experienced by multi-racial respondents, though perhaps it was more severe in multi-racial settings. In some instances the ethnic group influence was seen as a positive sense; in other cases it was viewed as negative, as in the instances of Deanna and Anita described above. Sarah is an example; she carried the surname of her Greek father, but identified more closely with her Jewish mother. On numerous occasions she had been approached by other persons of Greek background, many of whom wanted to know why she did not know the Greek language and considered her to be a traitor to her heritage.

All of these respondents were frequently placed in stressful situations by members of the ethnic groups to which they *appeared* to belong. I say, "appeared," because in some instances, they did not even have ties to the ethnic community of the questioner. In Anita's case, she was not Black but Mexican and Puerto Rican; however, this did not stop Black people from confronting her and accusing her of betraying the Black cause. In other cases, there was some reason for the respondents being considered a part of the ethnic group in question: Deanna's father was Black; Sarah did have a Greek surname. In all instances, however, the respondents defined themselves in terms of some other aspect of their multi-cultural or multi-racial background. Either they identified with another of the ethnic communities involved, or they preferred to claim all of the groups together. In either instance, the pressure of one or another of the ethnic groups to be "true" to the ethnic group's cause was strong.

On the positive side, Peter is an example of someone whose experience with his ethnic community led him to make a strong commitment to his father's Native American heritage. This occurred even though he spent his late teens with his Caucasian mother and her second husband. Peter's parents came from very different backgrounds. His mother was French and English and a Catholic. His father was Native American and a nonpracticing Mormon. He attributes their divorce to their considerable cultural differences. He knew few of his mother's relatives. As young children, he and his two siblings had spent considerable time during the summer with his paternal grandmother and several paternal cousins on the tribal reservation. He recalls these as very pleasant memories, and recognizes its impact on his life. His father's family was very active in the tribal community, a fact which caused a strain in his parents' marriage but also had a considerable influence on him. He speaks the tribal language and values the tribe's emphasis on having "patience and listening." As an adult, he still makes semiannual visits to the opposite side of the country to visit his paternal grandmother and his numerous cousins. His fond memories of the reservation include not only the family contacts but also the physical environment:

I remember the air around my Reservation, it's just such a distinct air, that it just smells great, just a different smell. . . . This is in the mountains, and the area, you can really identify yourself with that. I can just remember all of us as just looking around and just being kids and stuff like that. I remember all of us just playing out in the wilderness, or out in the desert, what ever you want to call it.

Clearly, Peter's Native American heritage constitutes the major component of his identity. Interestingly, however, he sees his identity as something less than a free choice, since "...most everybody identifies me as Native American once they found out. If they don't find out, they just say I'm exotic." By "exotic" he explains that people who meet him generally recognize that his culture does not follow the White, middle-class, American culture. He says:

> I'm not normal, in American terms, I'm not materialistic. I'm kind of a grudge, not really grudge. I'm plain and I'm just not very American, I guess, in the sense that Americans have a lot of things, having a nice car, having ambitions, stuff like that. So people just see me as different or exotic.

Hence Peter was strongly influenced by his Native American background and is not unhappy about being identified with it. He also recognizes that his identification with Native Americans is partly imposed on him by others, who recognize him as "different" (in his term "exotic"), and are looking for an explanation for this cultural difference. At no point does Peter suggest that he experienced pressure either from his father's family or from the reservation to identify himself as Native American. Certainly their strong impact on him during his formative years led him to become the committed member of Native American society and culture that he is today.

One cannot help but be struck by the contrast between Peter's experiences, on the one hand, and those of Deanna, Anita, Sarah, and Peggy, on the other. Perhaps the difference stems from the fact that the Native American experience of Peter was a long-term and highly supportive one. For the others, the experiences tended to be short-term contacts with people they barely knew, and usually assumed an accusatory tone. In none of these instances did the commentator have the impact she or he intended to have. They only served to reinforce the respondents' commitments to their respective mixed backgrounds, or to some aspect of it other than the one the commentator wished.

These respondents complained about the narrow-minded view of the ethnic groups who refused to accept their mixed heritage at face value. We noted earlier how distressed many respondents felt about being forced to "pick just one." When the pressure to "pick one" came from members of one of their own groups, or even, as in Anita's case, from a member of her own family, the negative experience was even greater. They seemed to feel that these people, at least, should be more sensitive.

Community Identification by External Appearances

The reader should recall that the focus of this entire chapter is the impact of the *community* on the identity formation of mixed race of culture individuals. If the focus is on the *community*, then the issues which are most important would have to be the issues which are considered important by the community in which the individual lives. Nearly all communities in the USA have a sizable component of people who consider race to be an important consideration in their evaluation of others. We have already recognized the importance attached to external appearances in our comparison of racial and ethnic minorities.

However, this issue is broader than simple physical differences, and the broader issue of outwardly observable differences was mentioned by both multi-racial and multi-ethnic respondents. All were annoyed by the tendency of many people and agencies to identify others based on outward appearances. Apparently, for many Americans, the assumption that prevails is: "Whatever you look like, that's who you are!" So it is important to understand what outwardly observable factors are considered to be important in a particular community's evaluation of others.

Some cultural factors are often the basis for discrimination in America as well, as we noted in Chapters 1 and 2. Religion, immigration status, and national origin are obvious examples. As we have noted, each of these can sometimes be "hidden" if the individual is careful. However, this may sometimes be impossible; even if a person is "careful," and manages to keep his/her "embarrassing" cultural characteristics "hidden," they constantly run the risk of being "discovered." The knowledge of this possibility of disclosure can generate its own kind of fear. And some communities may be particularly offended by certain cultural patterns, and may deliberately target people who exhibit them. As Chapter 2 suggested, religion, immigrant status, and foreign language use have often been the basis for cultural discrimination, often to an extreme degree. Several respondents discussed examples of this.

Three external dimensions were mentioned by respondents: physical appearance, surname, and sociocultural contexts, such as family background, cultural patterns, or the area in which someone lived. Sometimes these issues were interrelated; at other times they were not. And special problems seemed to appear when there were conflicts among these factors.

We will begin by analyzing the manner in which the most obvious characteristics – clear racial or other physically identifying characteristics – impacted on these mixed race or culture respondents. As noted earlier, Karen believed that community identification was a racial issue – it did not matter if you were half White. You were automatically assumed to belong to the minority race. Adam said that most people identified him as Black or African American. When physical appearance was unclear, that could become a more sensitive factor. Derek and his siblings, as well as Teresa, all complained that they were called "yellow" or "crows," or "zebras," because of their mixed heritage and lighter skin. While Derek perceived these comments as a "term of endearment," other respondents considered the comments to be more insulting.

Derek also experienced quite conflicting identification patterns, depending upon the setting in which he was placed and whom he encountered: ". . .even now, because of my complexion, I've been, had people approach me thinking I was Hispanic, . . . Egyptian, Ethiopian, a lot of things like that." Identification is also complicated by the varying appearances of members of his family. For example, he believes his youngest sister's experiences are probably different from his, ". . . 'cause she's very, very fair-skinned. In fact, a lot of people think she's White. And she married a White . . . guy, and the children are both, you know, very, very fair-skinned, White, I guess." This dramatic outward difference is probably also related to the fact that this sister has moved away and no longer has contact with the family. In general, Derek said he basically identifies as Black because "it's more prevalent" – that is, his skin color, features, and hair make him appear Black, even though he is light skinned and often could be mistaken for other races. While he was not bothered by these designations, others did not agree.

Anita, for example, said it bothers her when people base their evaluations on outward appearances. In particular, she did not appreciate it that she was often described as Black, African American, or a "n – r," even though her background is Mexican and Puerto Rican. Another respondent who objected to her forced identification was Deanna, who worked in a Korean business with many Black customers. Their reactions often disturbed her:

> ...because they naturally assume that it's all Koreans in the beer store, or all Chinese, whatever they want to call us, . . . when they walk in, they immediately . . . it's almost like they talk down to us because they feel like, we don't understand, there's nothing you can do to stop us, we can do this if we want to. So they come in immediately and talk down to us.

However, Deanna had lived most of her life in African-American communities in the USA. As a result, she spoke with a distinct African-American accent. Results were sometimes amusing when customers compared her speech with her appearance. She relates:

> Most time you can hear it in my voice. They can hear it in my tone. I don't know what that, "you sound Black" means, but, I've, I've had that. You can hear it in my tone. You see me from . . . good example, I was ringing up a customer, and she was looking, she was in her purse trying to find some money, and I hadn't said a word, at this time. . . . She assumed I was Asian . . . I was ringing her up, and one of the employees called me and asked me for a price, or something. And I hollered across the store and I told them what they needed to know. And this girl . . . She, she couldn't believe it. [laughs] She looked over at me with big eyes. it was like, "Oh my God! You sound like one of us!" [laughs] She said that! She said, "You sound like one of us!" And I'm lookin' at her like, what does that mean? "You look Chinese but you sound Black!" And that's when it may come out, yeah, yeah, I'm mixed. . . . But most of the time it's when I talk. . . . I get it all the time. Because they, and it's so, so obvious. The change is so obvious. . . . They come in one way, and by the time they leave out they're a completely different way. It's so obvious, the change, when they find out that I'm, that I'm mixed.

Furthermore, as noted above, when Black customers realize that she is of mixed background, most of them insist that she is Black or African American, not Asian or mixed. Deanna goes on:

> . . .most of 'em do tend to say, well because you're Black, you're Black. You have a little bit of Black in you, You're Black. Most of 'em – I've had a couple of customers tell me that. When I tell them that I'm biracial, I've had . . . a couple of customers tell me, "No, girl, you're Black." And um, and I don't argue.

Similarly, Leslie, whose parents were Caucasian and Filipino, complains that other people tend to identify her based on her multi-racial appearance:

> . . .people tend to identify people based on their appearance, and act towards them or treat them . . . based on that assumption, whether it's correct or incorrect. And a lot of people assume that I'm Hispanic, and . . . I've had like some negative treatment . . . based on that assumption. . . it bothers me when people identify me as something other than . . . what I am.

Leslie recalled an incident which occurred when she was in high school. One of the Spanish teachers saw her in the hall and began speaking Spanish to her, although she is not Spanish and does not know the Spanish language at all. While she says she does "... not necessarily ... feel more Filipino than American, because I don't feel either way about it," she is more likely to identify with her Filipino father. As she says, "... being Filipino is more of a minority than being Caucasian, and so ... if you were to ask me whether I felt I was more of a majority or more of a minority, I would definitely say more of a minority. Because ... I think that I, you know, people would assume that I'm a minority and treat me that way." As noted with other respondents above, Leslie's identification choice is really not a choice – but one which has been forced upon her by the manner in which others in society treat her.

While these experiences seem to be most common for persons with mixed *racial* backgrounds, the experience is not unknown among persons of totally Caucasian backgrounds as well. This is partly because there are recognized physical differences even within racial groups. Margo, for example, was Sicilian (Italian), Austrian, and French Canadian; however, she was constantly identified simply as Italian, because of her dark hair and eyes. While Margo reported she generally did not mind the assumption, other respondents did not agree.

Physical appearances were not the only external means which communities used to distinguish their members. A common method of classification is the use of surnames, and some respondents objected to this categorization. Sam, who was Italian and Irish, summarized the frustration of many of them. He grew up in an Italian neighborhood and had what he called "this very ethnic-sounding" Italian name. By default, he reported that he usually identified himself as Italian-American. "But I just wish – I would prefer just being an American. Cause I – I really don't speak Italian and uh, any other – I don't do any of the cultural Italian things that my grandparents would do. I feel more Americanized." Like it or not, however, he was defined as Italian. His annoyance was shared by Margo, who generally did not mind being identified as Italian, but complained that, since she was viewed to be Italian or Sicilian, everybody also assumed that her family was rich and part of the mob.

Generations of American immigrants have avoided this method of identification by the simple process of changing their surnames. Hence "Lewandowski" became "Lewis" or "Leonard," and "Antonelli" was shortened to "Anton." Identification by means of surname presents a particular problem for women, many of whom bear a husband's surname, which may have no relation at all to the wife's ethnic identity. Peggy mentioned this issue, and expressed an objection to people assuming a woman's married name represented her ethnic origin.

Of course, physical appearance and surname can be combined. In such cases, the identification is more difficult, if not impossible, to avoid. Vickie shared Sam's dissatisfaction. Her physical appearance, as well as her surname, easily identified her with her father's Irish background. However, Vickie identified closely with the Jewish traditions of her mother. She found others' constant identification of her as Irish troublesome. Particular problems were experienced by people whose surname and appearance did not "match." Jeanette, for example, had an Irish surname, but the dark hair and olive skin of her Lebanese mother. The constant questions about the conflict between her appearance and her name she found disturbing, to the point that she seemed more distressed by her childhood experiences than any of the other respondents.

Cultural patterns are the final outwardly observable dimension which can be distinguished. Few respondents exhibited these. As noted above, many respondents were far removed from the ethnic characteristics of their parents and did not want to be identified with these cultures. The respondents who were most likely to exhibit such characteristics were those whose parents were foreign born, or were themselves foreign born. The most common cultural pattern to be exhibited was the use of a foreign language or presence of a foreign accent. Their experiences illustrate the problems of anyone in the USA who is not fluent in English. Sarah complained that people would hear her mother's foreign accent and tell them to go back where they belonged.

Deanna was born in Korea prior to her mother's immigration to the USA. She came to the USA about the time she started school, and spoke no English. In an effort to improve her English, her teachers constantly sent notes to her mother, urging her not to speak to her daughter in Korean, and totally ignoring the fact that her mother spoke little English. Hence mother and daughter could barely communicate with each other. Because of her closer ties to her father's family, Deanna grew up speaking English with a Black accent. As we noted previously, this surprised many Blacks who patronized the Korean store where she worked.

All of these instances illustrate the prominence of outwardly observable characteristics in the process of community identification of its members. Most respondents found that the settings in which they lived or worked were most likely to identify them by the obvious whether that be their skin color, surname, or the language or accent they exhibited. This is not surprising, since these are the characteristics which people will observe first. However, to people who are from mixed backgrounds, and may be very proud of or attached to some groups which are less visible, it can be a painful experience. Many of these respondents longed to be viewed by the less obvious dimensions of their heritage.

Lack of Recognition/Respect for Different Cultural Patterns

The fourth concern focused on a different dimension. While the earlier issues focused on the manner in which they felt they were identified by others, this issue focused on the lack of recognition or respect which others showed for the cultural patterns which their diverse backgrounds represented. Respondents seemed to feel that Americans expected everyone to operate from a single perspective, to think and act the same as everyone else. Their diverse origins, however, meant that they had different ways of perceiving the world, as well as different approaches to life. They were resentful if these perspectives were not respected. And they described many instances in which their unique cultural perspectives were not accorded the respect and acceptance to which they believed they were entitled.

Regina complained about the rude treatment she and her parents experienced when they first came to the USA – by immigration authorities, by teachers in the schools, nurses in hospitals, even by neighbors. She says: "...I was really ostracized... people ... actually would point to me and call me DP, which I had to learn ... was displaced person. ... and the children in school ... they would come to me and touch me and touch my hair. They wondered why I was blonde and white because they expected me from Brazil to be a native, like a Brazilian – dark." Carlos, who was an immigrant from El Salvador, felt that the USA made more distinctions among people than people in his home country, where everyone was considered to be "the same thing" (e.g., El Salvadoran).

Religion is another aspect of culture which often forms the basis for discrimination. This was keenly felt by multi-cultural respondents, especially those who were the product of mixed religion marriages. Yvonne was the daughter of a French Canadian mother whose family was devoutly Catholic; her father was Scottish, Swedish and Protestant. Her parents were not married in the Catholic Church, which was very distressful to her mother's family. She recalled a time when her father wanted to take his children to his church. She remembers being frightened about going to church with her father because she had been told by the nuns in school that going to a Protestant Church was wrong. She told him, "No, I can't! It'll be a mortal sin!" When he insisted, "...I said to the nun, 'Will I go to hell?' And she said, '... just don't take communion.'" She recalls the experience of attending the Protestant service as very painful, as she was afraid she and her little brother were committing a sin by going to church with their father.

Peggy's father was Catholic and her mother nonreligious; she did not mention overt references to the religious difference. However, she noted that, in retrospect, she thought some of the aspects of her childhood that she found odd might have been due to the religious difference. For example, they were much closer to her mother's family than her father's. Invitations to visit her father's family cottage were always rejected, much to her dismay. Peggy says: "I used to pester them, 'let's go, let's go.' My mother would never go. ... I could not understand why she didn't want to go, but ... in retrospect, I think she wasn't comfortable ... because most of these years she was not Catholic. ... I've never actually been told that my father's family didn't like him marrying a non-Catholic, but I always suspected that they kind of wished that ... he had married the 'right kind of girl.' And he didn't."

The mixed Catholic–Protestant marriage was mentioned by other respondents as well. When Jeanette was asked how her mother's Lebanese relatives felt about a marriage to an Irish man, she says: "...I asked that question, and what I was told was that what was important was that he was Catholic ...." Similarly, Brian, whose Irish father married a German woman after the death of this first wife, stressed the importance of religion in Catholic families. About his Irish Catholic family he comments:

> ...they were so Irish Catholic, that to them, ... a mixed marriage would have been a marriage between an Irish and German Catholic. A marriage to a Protestant is something that would have been a huge impropriety – and negative.

Moving to the issue of Jewish–Christian marriages, Jeff discussed his experiences as the son of a Methodist mother and a Jewish father. This created little difficulty within the marriage itself, because neither of his parents was particularly religious. However, he noted that his paternal grandfather, an Orthodox rabbi, was never told that his son had married a non-Jewish girl. These comments suggest that religion is a cultural difference which created significant difficulties for respondents who were involved in mixed religion situations, whether they appeared in the family or in the school or community. It was often made clear to mixed religion children that they were "different" or "out of place," and that they did not belong to the community as a whole.

In a broader sense, some respondents were critical with regard to the manner in which Americans deal with people in general. Most of these comments could have come from any child or even adult, who has experienced rudeness from others. Or perhaps these respondents, with their multi-cultural background and already heightened sensitivity to the perceptions of others, were more aware of the way others treated them. For example, Peter, who operated from a strong Native American cultural component, complained about a severe absence of "patience" in American society. He felt that the failure to listen to others' problems and point of view was particularly hard for persons from Native American backgrounds, whose culture considered patience to be a valued component; most Americans, he felt, were very rushed and impatient. Ted, Peggy, and Robert all complained that American society showed little concern for the rights and perspectives of others, particularly children. One wonders whether their experiences as children growing up in a multi-cultural setting played a role in their sensitivity to this issue.

Lack of Acceptance from Their Own Ethnic Communities

Up to this point we have focused on the attempt of most ethnic communities to *retain* the allegiance of people who they believed shared their heritage. However, there were some exceptions. A particularly painful aspect of being from a mixed background is that mixed heritage persons are often rejected by members of one of their identity groups because of another group to which they belong. Even within the extended family, their multi-cultural or multi-racial origins were not accepted. Karen related how she was never accepted by her father's mother because of her Asian background. This lack of acceptance went to the extreme of the children being left in the car on a rare occasion on which he visited his mother.

Some respondents were rejected by their groups because they were not seen as really a part of the group. Perhaps the best example is Regina, who learned that her status as Brazilian and Polish would be a problem when her father tried to enroll her in the local Polish Catholic school. A confrontational discussion in Polish took place in her presence:

> And the nun said ... school is almost over like in June [this was in March] and we don't have any room. And my father said well I don't understand it, what do you mean you don't have any room. ... And she said we don't have a place for her, we don't have enough chairs ... and my father said I will bring a chair. And this is in Polish .... That was one of the reasons why my father took me there, because he felt they would know Polish and at least I would be able to adapt easier to somebody I could communicate with and she said no.

Hence the nun in charge of the school refused to accept this Polish-speaking child from Brazil. Apparently they felt she did not "belong" to the Polish community as they viewed it. The reader may recall that Peggy also mentioned the case of her Polish-born friend who was not accepted into the Polish subgroup of her class because she was a Polish *immigrant*, rather than being brought up in the local Polish community.

Sarah described several instances, both when she lived in Europe and after her arrival in the USA, in which she was not accepted because of her cultural background. She felt that children from diverse origins were really targets of hate for many reasons and by different groups. Some people did not like her because she was Greek; others because she was Romanian, and still others because she was Jewish. She says: "...the irony of it is that the groups they didn't like also didn't accept me, because I wasn't sufficiently Greek, or sufficiently Jewish ...." In short, multicultural persons were not accepted by anyone. The larger community rejected them because of one or another of the origins, and each of the ethnic communities rejected them because they were not sufficiently like them.

A few respondents found that they had difficulties in their relations with the various groups to which they belonged, due to the fact that some of the cultural groups did not seem to "fit together" well. These problems had their origin within the ethnic groups themselves, rather than in the dominant American society. While many people see racial distinctions as more critical than cultural ones, some people, even those with a multi-racial heritage have a different view. In particular, several Asian respondents pointed out the extreme variation among Asian cultures.

Karen related a discussion she had with a cousin, who, like her, was half White and half Korean. According to Karen, the cousin "...was recalling a story where she goes into this Korean restaurant and she gets treated very rudely.... And I said to her ... that there is probably a couple of reasons why you are treated so rudely, one is because you are half White. The other one is ... that they thought you were Japanese, part-Japanese. She said, 'Oh, I never thought of that!'" Karen concludes: "I get the rudest treatment in Korean restaurants if they think I am Japanese." Hence a major problem which some Asians experience is discrimination from other Asians because of the cultural differences among the various Asian countries. While this may seem strange to Caucasian or Black Americans, it recalls the long-standing animosities among the various European nations for many centuries.

As discussed in Chapter 4, Evelyn reported similar problems with her Chinese and Korean background. While Americans often considered Chinese and Korean equivalent, other Asians found her background "odd," since they were aware that the two countries, China and Korea, "...don't think highly of each other." She spoke for many of the multi-cultural respondents when she described her feeling that people from her two cultures did not "get along." She went on to describe how her Korean mother was, "...jealous that we veer towards the Chinese way," which she saw as "more Americanized," because the women were more likely to smoke, get divorced, and lack respect for the elders. When her mother would get angry, she would remind her children: "...you're just like your father and his side of the family ... they have no brains." Of course, many people whose families are of a single culture have members who will blame the other side of the family's ways when someone behaves badly. However, when there is a cultural difference, this is very likely to be seen as the cause of the problem.

Of course, some of these mixtures can be both multi-cultural and multi-racial. In such instances, it is difficult to sort out the source of any animosities. Leslie, as the daughter of a White mother and Filipino father, has a cousin whose parents are also Filipino and Caucasian. She describes what it is like to be involved in social relationships with members of both the Filipino and the Caucasian sides of the family. As she grew older, she began to notice that large family gatherings with all the relatives present could be difficult at times. She says:

> . . .it was like the family took sides, really, it was like, you know, even my mom, and . . . my uncle, the Caucasian uncle, and her sister, and my grandmother were all on my uncle's side. And it was like me and my . . . Filipino aunt, were on my cousin's side. . . . I don't know if it was because my uncle was the father that they took his side but it felt like – my cousin was right . . . he didn't do anything wrong – my uncle got mad at him for no reason and that's why they got into an argument. And so it was like they took my uncle's side even though he was wrong. . . . And my grandmother . . . I just noticed that she treated me differently than my other cousins. . . . it's hard to explain – it's just like when I'm there I feel like an outsider in a way – me and my cousin . . . and my [Filipino] aunt . . . actually my mom's family is pretty rough on her – and so, like they talk down about her behind her back, and stuff like that, and . . . I think part of it has to do with her being Filipino.

Leslie found the experiences so unsettling that she says, ". . .I don't know . . . after all that, I'm not gonna go to Thanksgiving . . . anymore. Because I was kinda disgusted by it all." Were these negative experiences a result of multi-cultural animosity? Or multi-racial conflict? Or simply normal family disputes? It is difficult – if not impossible – to tell.

Like Leslie, Deanna is both multi-cultural and multi-racial. She felt that the multi-cultural dimension was more important than the multi-racial one. She had believed that her mother had given up much of her Korean culture for her husband, as Korean culture required. She points out:

> I remember telling my mom one time that, . . . although I don't oppose interracial relationships, I almost oppose intercultural relationships. . . . I don't have a problem with Whites and Blacks, . . . with Hispanics and Blacks, or whatever, because we all live together. You all pretty much grew up learning the same thing. But . . . when it comes to other cultures, it's so different. . . . one person almost always have to give it up [i.e., their culture]. . . . I saw that happen with my mom.

Hence Deanna considered cultural differences so difficult to deal with that multi-cultural people should not marry, although multi-racial marriages were all right. Cultures structure the entire way in which we think and work and relate to each other. Without a common culture, it is almost impossible for people to get along. Deanna thought that one partner would have to give up his or her culture to make the relationship work, as she felt her mother did to be submissive to her husband, as Korean culture required. She associated her parents' divorce with her mother's eventual refusal to continue her cultural submissiveness.

Multi-Cultural Identity as Compared with Multi-Racial Identity

As we discussed in Chapter 3, several multi-racial respondents observed that being of a different race was usually a mechanism for exclusion. This was less the case with White respondents, who generally viewed themselves as part of American society as a whole. For them, their multi-cultural background was an interesting component of their heritage, often one of which they were very proud.

White respondents, who did not "stand out" for some other obvious reason (such as a distinctive foreign accent), were less likely to report being singled out in society or feeling uncomfortable, as did the multi-racial respondents. For example, Nicole, whose background included Irish, French, and German, asked if having a multi-cultural mixture had been a problem, comments: "No, where I grew up I don't remember nationalities or any of that being terribly important. You were just whoever you were and had nothing to do really with nationality." Betty, whose background was Polish, Irish, German, and English, says she identifies herself as "100% American." She had no memories of ethnic differences being important in her childhood. Indeed, if there was a problem it was the fact that people at her college expected her to identify with a culture, and did not accept "American" as an acceptable choice.

Most White multi-cultural respondents were more likely to have the opposite problem, in terms of identity, from the multi-racial respondents. That is, rather than having people constantly remind them of their differences, some of them complained that they had difficulty getting others to recognize their distinct culture. Ted, for example, was very proud of his extensive European background. He had been close to his grandparents, learned a great deal from them, and believed it enriched his life. But others seemed to resent his knowledge of Europe and interest in education; indeed, some teachers resented his bringing these issues up and complained to his parents that he was "spoiled." So while racially distinctive persons were concerned because they were constantly singled out, the concern of White respondents was how *not* to be dismissed as "just White." In a sense, this illustrates again the dominance of the skin color issue in the USA. It affects both Whites and other races – all are pressured by various segments of society to identify primarily with what *others* define as their racial category, and individuals are subjected to criticism if they resist following these dictates.

We have already discussed the dismay of Deanna, who found that African Americans constantly reminded her, "Girl, you're Black!" However, she believed that she resembled both Black and Asian races, was proud of her Korean background, and missed the ability to identify as Korean or Asian. She noted that it was "hard to be mixed" in our society. She was constantly assumed to be either one or the other. But she really wished to identify with both of her backgrounds, and resented the absence of a "mixed" option. While she and her relatives might think of themselves as mixed, others did not. Furthermore, the "mixed" option tended to have negative connotations – such as people who taunted her and her brother, calling them "mutts" because of their mixed racial background. She noted that friends who were of mixed racial backgrounds, whether Black and White or Black and Asian, experienced the same problem. She noted also that this was not unique to the USA – when they were in Korea, the same discrimination occurred.

These experiences were not unique to people with mixed racial origins: Evelyn was of a single race but different – often radically antagonistic – cultures (Korean and Chinese). Among Asians she noted that people frequently thought the mixture was "odd," because Koreans and Chinese in the old country "don't think highly of each other." Vickie chose to think of herself as Jewish, but found others identified her on the basis of her Irish name and appearance. Peggy wanted both her Irish and Belgian backgrounds recognized. In all instances they constantly were pressured to adopt the unitary definition of their backgrounds as defined by others, rather than by themselves.

In contrast to these respondents, who wanted their diverse background recognized, some persons chose to have a unitary identity but this was denied them. These were people who no longer felt as though they were "mixed." Instead, they had given up identification with any ethnic group. Betty, for example, had traces of Polish, Irish, German, and English in her background. However, she had long since ceased to identify with any of them. Instead she resented being forced to have an ethnic identify "...when you feel 100% American!" Yet she was often asked to claim an ethnic origin. Her sentiments were shared by Sam, who wanted to be "American," but even within his family he was pressured to adopt an ethnic identity, his father insisting they were Italian-American, and his mother claiming they were Irish-American, but never, he noted, in front of his father!

Specific Issues Related to School Policies

In preceding sections, we have been discussing the identity experiences these multi-racial and multi-cultural respondents had as children. Our interviews focused on the years in which they were just beginning to develop their sense of identity and their relation to their families, their community and group connections, and society as a whole. Hence it is reasonable that experiences at school might have been an important component of this process; critical issues involve administrators, teachers, and other children (Rockquemore and Laszloffy, 2005: Chapter 5). Many respondents mentioned school-related experiences. Because of the critical role which school plays in the socialization of children, it is appropriate to focus on the ways in which the school community played a role in the identity formation of mixed background children.

For several respondents, their first introduction to the idea that they were "different" because of their mixed race or mixed culture background came when they began school. Perhaps the first event that occurs upon enrolling in school is the need for registration. Leslie, who was Caucasian and Filipino, recalled her mother enrolling her in a school which included a broad range of Blacks, Caucasian, and Asian children. Still, "...when you enroll in school you don't really get a choice – you have to pick one or the other. And my mom enrolled me as Filipino or Asian. So that's how I was listed. . . . It kind of bothered me that I didn't get a choice." So even schools with a diverse student body insisted that children "...had to be put in one category.... Check one. And only one ...," as Leslie states. Although she does not specifically say it, Leslie is also obviously hurt that her mother listed the category for her, without giving her a choice.

Teresa, the youngest of the respondents at 18 years of age, also remembers what it was like to have to identify herself, not only at registration, but on many other occasions:

> ...I don't know if I was enrolling for school – there was something with school, and ... in fact, there were a lot of times with the school, where they would give you these ... things to fill out, and you'd have to fill out which sex you are, which race you are, and sometimes I'd check the "other" box and I'd put White and Black, or I'd check both boxes, and ... things that you have to fill out, like cards that you have to give to the guidance officer, the office, and they usually go by what you filled out on this paper ...."

For multi-racial or multi-cultural students, however, they did not always go by "what you filled out on this paper." As a multi-racial child, Teresa continues:

> ...what they'd do is they'd give you back papers... And every time I'd get mine back, they have a big "B," which I'm assuming stands for Black, on these cards. ... There's never been any time which they haven't. So even though no one comes to back to me, you can tell like, "Foolish! She's made a mistake! And we know more so, she's Black – so we'll just put this 'B'."

The incidents described by Leslie and Teresa involve official school actions. The forms they described were required by the school, and teachers, principals, and other administrative officials were responsible for carrying them out. Two issues are present here, and multi-racial children were bothered by both of them. The first is the school officials' insistence that they had to be classified in "one, and only one" category. In other words, children who were of mixed backgrounds were forced to select the heritage of one of their parents, and ignore the other. The official requirement was that "one and only one box" be checked. There was no option allowed for mixed background children; they were forced to choose the heritage of one parent and ignore the other.

However, the second requirement is even more offensive than the first: the option selected had to be the one which the official requesting the information expected. They were equally offended by the fact that the choice was obviously not theirs to make. Regardless of Teresa's attempts to assert her multi-racial background, the authorities who solicited the information insisted on reassigning her to the category which *they* had already selected for her. She knew they were not accepting the option, "White," so she listed "Other." But this was not acceptable. Teresa was clearly aware of the insult which was implicit in their action: the teacher's judgment that she was a "foolish" child who had made a "mistake." The critical attitude was clearly as offensive as the action. School officials were certain they knew the child's proper classification better than she did. Not only the official actions themselves, but also the manner in which these actions were performed, were insulting to children of mixed background.

Official school actions were not the only difficult aspects of school for multi-racial and multi-cultural children. Behaviors of teachers and other children could also bring about unpleasant experiences. Teresa remembered that it was sometimes embarrassing to her as a small child, since she looked Black but her mother didn't, and "...a lot of the kids make fun of you. They call you different types of names when you're mixed."

Ken, whose background was mixed both racially and culturally, provides a good example. He recalled an incident in early grade school, when all the children were asked to identify themselves. As noted earlier, Ken's background included Guatemalan, Black, Irish, and Native American. He comments:

> I do remember, I think it might have been first or second grade ... They were talking about ethnic differences and discrimination and all that stuff within in the school and they asked people who are of White to stand up and actually I don't think I stood up then. But when they said Black, I stood up and then they would say are there any Hispanic kids or whatever ... Chicano – the term they were using at the time and I stood up for that. And some of the kids ... knew my mother and ... there was some snicker. You know Oriental and I stood up for that, Native American and I stood up for that and I do remember that was probably the first time I remember feeling different and that it wasn't necessarily a good thing. All the kids were laughing and stuff.

Hence another difficult aspect of school for mixed background children was the interaction with other children, who could be "mean," or "not very nice," as Peter and Karen both said of their school experiences. Unfortunately, relatively few teachers do anything to prevent or mitigate the consequences of such actions on the part of children.

The distinctions could be cultural as well as racial. We have already described the experience of Regina, who was refused admittance to the Polish Catholic school because the principal did not consider her appropriate to their school. She told Regina's father to take her to the public school down the street. Regina's experience is similar to a comment made by Peggy about the Catholic school she attended, where the one child who was actually from Poland was not accepted by the Polish-American girls. Regina reported that the public school was considerably more accommodating:

> ...there were three teachers that spoke Polish and [the principal] called one of them ... so that I could communicate and ... I was kind of frightened. ... I have to really give them a lot of credit for the public school ... so these teachers would take turns with me on their own time after school ... and they would go over the day's assignments with me. And I thought that was very dedicated....

However, there were also numerous incidents, even in the public school, in which her multi-cultural background was problematic. Regina had the blond, blue-eyed appearance typical of her Polish parents, and was constantly questioned about her appearance: Since she was from Brazil, why did she not have dark hair and complexion? Teachers found it difficult to comprehend the disparity between her appearance and language problems. She did not look South American – How could she know only Portuguese? One teacher even ordered her to take an IQ test, though she obviously was unable to read or write English, forcing her to fill in the blanks. She recalls that she only guessed and could not have done well.

As several of our respondents have indicated, people who contract cross-racial or cross-cultural marriages usually do not consider such differences important. They continue to hold these positions after they have children. Furthermore, they often make decisions for their children based upon this assumption. However, this can create problems for the children when they go into the larger community, including school. Jeff's experience is an example. Since his parents were not religious and did not consider religion important, they sometimes placed their children in multi-religious settings which were unpleasant. In particular, his parents placed a high value on education, and selected a junior high and high school for him because of its high academic standing. However, the school was a private Episcopalian institution. About his school experiences, Jeff says:

> I didn't like it. ... Because I was a poor Democratic Jewish boy surrounded by rich Protestant Republicans. ... I basically had no friends. ... first of all, I couldn't dress in the style that they could dress in. ... We had to take a religion class and I didn't want to learn the Nicene Creed, which we were all supposed to learn and believe in. ... As far as I know I was the only Jewish boy there. ... There were some Catholic kids, I know that. ... I don't think they were all Episcopalian, but they were all Christian. ... I knew the kids visited back and forth with each other in their homes. I was never invited to anybody's home.

So from the outset, mixed background children were confronted with the realization that they were "different," a category which most children try very hard to avoid. Respondents' stories made it clear that the early racial and cultural distinctions made at the outset continued throughout their school years. The respondents had come to expect these incidents when they enrolled in school or filled out forms. These incidents could appear at the most unexpected moments. Teresa, for example, reported an occasion in which the class was required to write an essay on a topic of their choice. Teresa casually commented in the presence of the teacher:

> ...yeah, I should do one on mixed people, and our teacher turned around, and she goes, "That's a good idea, Teresa, you do mixed people." So it was like, first it was a choice, but after I said something, it was like, "Oh, you have to."

What began as an optional topic for her suddenly became a forced assignment, which was not true for other students.

School problems did not cease when these children became adults. They continued even in college. Anita, who treasured her Mexican heritage, related an incident which occurred in a university class:

> One of the guys challenged me about not wanting to admit that I was African-American, and I felt that I was being verbally attacked on the issues, and the instructor didn't say a word. He just sat back and watched the interaction. I remember being really, really angry and hurt. Because I thought, he feels that way too. ... Why would the instructor allow him to keep going at it? To keep insisting that I was denying being African-American? ... even after I explained that I wasn't? And I felt that that was ah – my interpretation of that was that the instructor felt the same way. ... that I was denying being African-American. And you know, that was pretty significant, 'cause I thought, "Man, even educated people are stupid!"

Hence in grade school through college, teachers remained detached when students abridged the rights of other students. As these incidents illustrate, mixed race or culture students often found that they were forced into situations as a result of their mixed heritage when other students had more options. This lack of concern for different cultures was reported by several respondents. Many of them found themselves in situations in which their diverse backgrounds were considered an oddity, or were not respected or honored, not only by the other students but by the teachers and administrators as well. Jeanette complained that when she was in school in the 1940s and 1950s, diversity was not formally discussed; but "...that always was there, what group you were from," usually in a negative manner." Jeanette also expressed the belief that "...now I guess people are very careful ...," about discussing different groups. However, the experiences of Anita, Deanna, and Teresa would suggest that little had changed by the 1980s and 1990s.

Conclusions

This chapter has attempted to place the identity formation of mixed background children in a community context. Since families do not exist in a vacuum, the larger community plays an important role in influencing the way in which children come to a definition of "who they are." We have described several levels of community which play a role in this process, as well as the ways in which these influences operate.

The communities which influence the identity formation include, at the highest level, the culture of the USA as a whole, and the manner in which it has defined the various racial and ethnic groups which are part of the country. This plays a major role in defining the ways in which children will see themselves in relation to their own and other groups. Requiring that individuals be classified into a single category is a major aspect of this influence, and many mixed background respondents were concerned about this process.

Community also includes groups at the local level. Some regions or cities seemed to be more open to persons from diverse backgrounds than others, and children from these different types of settings will experience identity formation in different ways. Neighborhoods, churches, schools, even the business community, can influence children's views of their ethnic or racial background, and, consequently, of themselves. Where there are substantial numbers of persons from a particular ethnic or racial group, the perspective of that community is also influential. The community created problems for mixed identity people in five different ways.

A major concern was the tendency of many people at various levels to assume that every person had a single identity, forcing people to "pick one," even if they preferred to identify with more than one of the parts of their backgrounds. This prevents mixed identity people from honoring all parts of their heritage. They were also forced to accept a designation from someone else as to what their identity was. Sadly, a major source of pressure to identify in a certain manner came from the ethnic communities themselves. Anxious to maintain their power in society by maximizing their numbers, leaders of some ethnic groups may pressure people to accept membership, even if they do not identify with or belong in that category. Some mixed heritage people experienced rude encounters with ethnic group members who felt they were disloyal to their heritage.

The tendency of most communities to identify people by outward appearances was another issue which bothered many of the respondents. Obviously, skin color and other racial characteristics are a major component of this dimension. Dark-skinned individuals were presumed to be Black, even if the individuals were actually Hispanic or Indian. Other factors, such as an ethnically identifiable surname or a foreign accent, could also be used in this manner. Particular problems were encountered when different aspects of an individual's identity did not "match," a factor which might well occur with mixed heritage individuals. So some respondents had problems because their surname would suggest one identity, while their appearance would suggest another.

While racial patterns are more easily observed than cultural ones, some respondents saw cultural differences as more critical problems than racial ones. Cultural patterns outline the ways in which people relate to each other. Respondents who were in a position to compare race and culture found that there were more family disagreements over the different cultural patterns, which determined the proper way of acting for the members of the family. In general, respondents were critical of the lack of respect accorded to cultural differences in American society. They observed that Americans expected everyone to follow the same pattern of culture and behavior. Differences were not accepted, including discrimination against immigrants, anyone who spoke with a foreign-sounding accent, or religion.

Multi-racial persons were more likely to experience the feeling that the community identification measures were usually exclusionary in character, that is, to define them as "outsiders." In contrast, multi-cultural Whites sometimes had trouble getting people to recognize their distinct culture; they resented being reminded they were "just White." Respondents found it particularly distressful when members of their own groups rejected them because of the other aspects of their heritage. Both multi-racial and multi-cultural respondents reported that sometimes they were rejected by one or another of their ethnic groups because they were "not really" members, by virtue of their mixed heritage.

Since a major component of identity formation occurs during the years a child is in school, the role of the school in identity formation is critical. Many schools were not hospitable to the needs of multi-racial and multi-cultural children. Constant demands that they "choose one" category with which to identify, and having others make the choice for them, were particularly irksome. Some recalled having other children ridicule them because of their mixed background. Even teachers or administrators engaged in this sort of unequal treatment, including not allowing some children to enroll in their school of choice. These incidents began with primary school enrollment and continued through college.

Several respondents commented that children might deal with these situations more effectively if they were better prepared by their families. Hence Jeff would have felt more comfortable with his mixed background had his parents explained some of the customs more openly. In Chapter 7, we will consider some ways in which the family could provide this assistance.

Chapter 7
Achieving Success in Multi-cultural Families

As noted at several points, managing the inter-racial and inter-cultural dimensions of American society has long been problematic. With its wide variety of racial, ethnic, linguistic, and religious differences, the American population lacks a common cultural pattern which can unite it. As we have indicated, this has contributed to the existence of numerous conflicts over social values. These differences were exacerbated by the extensive immigrations of the late 19th and 20th centuries (Gordon, 1964, 1978; Greeley, 1971, 1974). They have continued to increase as a result of the changes in migration law which occurred in the 1960s, as well as the migration patterns which results from these changes.

The diversity issues which ensue from these cultural differences are numerous: the need to bring people from different cultures together and promote joint projects in the face of basic cultural differences; the difficulty of understanding others' perspectives when language variations make communication difficult; the differences in beliefs and values which result from basic religious and cultural perspectives. Such problems occur frequently and in a variety of settings (Fritz, 1985; Fong and Gibbs, 1996; Gallagher and Nahan, 1997; Gills and White, 1997). There are, however, precious few suggestions as to how to manage these difficulties. Most participants in multi-cultural or multi-racial settings operate in the dark and hope for the best. For the most part, the "voice of experience" is lacking.

To some extent, we can consider the respondents in our study to be "experts" in multi-cultural and multi-racial relations. Unlike most members of American society, they have been intimately involved in multi-racial or multi-cultural relationships – or both – for most of their lives, through their relationships with their own families. At a very early age, they were exposed to people from different races or cultures and the ways they interacted. As we have seen in previous chapters, many

---

This chapter is a revised version of two papers: The first paper was presented to the Society for Applied Sociology, October 1999, Dallas, TX, and later published as "Multicultural Families – What Makes Them Work?" in *Sociological Practice: A Journal of Clinical and Applied Sociology*, Vol. 3: No. 1 (March 2001): 1–17. Revised and reprinted with the permission of the publisher, the Association for Applied and Clinical Sociology. The second paper was presented to the Unity Meeting of the Sociological Practice Association and the Society for Applied Sociology, Washington, D.C., August, 2001.

have experienced problems as a result of their multi-cultural or multi-racial relationships. No one is more qualified than they to tell us some of the ways in which multi-cultural or multi-racial relationships can be made to work – or which approaches do not work.

In Chapter 4, we discussed some of the ways in which these families presented problems for their children, and failed to help them deal with them. In this chapter, we focus on the families' successes, and recommend some approaches families might take to assist their children in dealing with the problems multi-racialism or multi-culturalism may present. What did these families do that helped their children deal with the diversity they encountered every day, both within the confines of the family and in the broader community?

Hopefully, these approaches might provide suggestions concerning the methods which could be used to improve multi-racial and multi-cultural relationships in other families today.

It will provide suggestions as to how multi-cultural families can make the process of multi-cultural socialization a positive one for their children, particularly in a society which still tends to view multi-culturalism in a negative light. It may also be useful to professionals who work with families, suggesting ways in which clinical sociologists and others who work with multi-cultural families can advise their clients. Finally, by extension, it may suggest ways in which multi-cultural and multi-racial relationships may be improved in larger communities, or in society as a whole.

The chapter will be divided into two parts. The first part will summarize the major problems these families faced. Three major problems will be addressed: The critical role of the social setting, varying roads which can lead to multi-culturalism, and the problems of developing an identity and dealing with social relationships.

The second part will focus on the strengths these families exhibited, and analyze some of the ways in which they dealt with the difficulties they encountered. These will include the critical role of parents, a "cafeteria approach" to culture, the focus on relationships and social ties, the view of culture as unimportant, the tendency to see similarities within differences, the advantages of multi-culturalism, and the extension of multi-culturalism to a new generation.

Recalling the Role of the Community in Defining Multi-culturalism

At this point, it is useful to recall the role of the community in making children aware of various cultures, as well as of the cultures to which they themselves are a part. As we described in detail in Chapter 6, several respondents had noted how the social environment in which they lived had influenced their lives. Those who had grown up in social settings in which religious or ethnic differences had been emphasized were much more conscious of these issues. Social setting also played an important role in determining which of the several cultural options an individual would choose – or be forced – to emphasize. People whom the respondents encountered in the community, school, extended family, or other social settings called attention to the various cultural options they had. Hence, each individual's choice among the several cultural options was largely dependent upon the social experiences she or he encountered.

In some instances, this played a role in determining which aspect of their cultural heritage they would choose as their dominant identity. In more rigid instances, their sense of identity was not really a "choice," but was forced upon them by a community which left them little alternative, as in the rural Southern community where Robert grew up. The town was rigidly divided between Blacks and Whites, and there was no question as to which group a person belonged. No one noticed nationality differences, so he never thought of himself as having a mixed nationality background.

Similarly, race was the basis for identification for Derek, who was often reminded of his Black and Caucasian heritage, often related to the social setting in which he lived at the time. His cousins often had more negative racial experiences than he did; he believed that living on a military base protected his family, to a degree, from racial discrimination in the surrounding communities. Derek also commented on the role of the ethnic community itself in defining ethnic or racial identity. Light-skinned and mixed heritage Blacks, like himself, were often the target of envy by darker skinned Blacks.

Although Derek recalls being called derogatory names, he did not consider most of these actions to be malicious in character. In this regard, he did not appear to be hypersensitive to the comments of others, a pattern which some other respondents did not share. Karen recalled the name-calling targeted at Asian heritage children in her northeastern US town as a highly negative experience, one which she hoped to spare her own child someday.

Other respondents also reported that people with their cultural background received more positive or negative treatment in varying settings. Sarah, to her surprise, found that a small rural community was more accepting of her as a non-Christian, immigrant child than the suburb of a major city. Peter felt his Native American heritage was more negatively received in Michigan than in California. Peter and Sarah also commented on the role of other ethnic communities in defining identity: Peter noting that it was the Black students in his school who would not accept him, and Sarah experiencing discrimination from Polish people in her suburban neighborhood. Similarly, Deanna and Anita both felt pressured by members of the Black community to admit they were "just Black," although both felt closer to their Korean and Mexican heritages, respectively.

We also noted that there were many ways, other than race and nationality, by which different cultural traditions entered the family or were encountered in the community. Both Peter and Carol indicated that social class distinctions often played this role. Regina's experience as a child of Polish parents who spent her early years in Brazil illustrates the fact that living for a period in another culture can also make one multi-cultural. Both Regina and Sarah commented on the fact that being an immigrant itself can expose a child to the realization that she is radically different from others in the community, and expose them to discrimination on that basis. Brian's experience showed how the introduction of a new stepparent can bring a different culture into the family, perhaps resulting in a dramatic change, as it did in his family.

In some of the examples discussed, the communities seemed to place severe limitations on the contact which could occur between members of different groups. However, in communities which allowed more contact among members of the various subgroups, respondents experienced more options as to their choice of an identity. For example, Vickie explained her sister's interest in Catholicism on the basis of her attraction to a neighbor woman who was a devout Catholic. In contrast, Vickie developed a close relationship to her Jewish grandmother, leading her to identify as Jewish. These broad options would not be available if the local community did not allow opportunities for people from these variant groups to interact on a regular basis.

In summary, respondents in this study were well aware of the problems of being multi-cultural, in a world which seemed to assume that everyone had a single-culture origin. Some remembered painful experiences from their childhood as a result of these factors. Those who had children were equally anxious that their children not experience the negative aspects of multi-culturalism and that someone be there to help them if they did. Hence, there is a clear lesson for professionals who work with families and children. Multi-cultural settings need to provide a sensitivity to the cultural differences and to the feelings of persons with cultural differences. They need to anticipate the possibility – indeed the probability – of negative encounters which create difficulties, and to be prepared with methods for minimizing their impact on the participants. As Karen and Sarah insisted, social support must be available for individuals, especially children, who encounter the hazards of a multi-cultural setting. We have suggested that adoptions are another means of producing multi-cultural and/or multi-racial families and that these families also need to recognize that their children will experience the kinds of problems our respondents mentioned. In the next section, we will summarize some of the problems they mentioned.

Identification and Relationship Problems: Ignoring the Self or Never Fitting In

Respondents differed in their opinion of the impact these experiences had on them. As indicated above, some, like Derek, tended to minimize the effect it had upon them. Others were not so sanguine. As we discussed in Chapter 4, when Jeanette discussed her family's cultural differences, she frequently referred to the term as "painful." One of the painful memories appears to have been a constant pressure to ignore or forget part of their heritage. Asked to discuss how she identified herself, Jeanette commented:

> ...I would just say it shifts, it shifts as I'm understanding this myself. ... When I was growing up, that I think was for me the most painful. Who are we? I don't think as a kid you think, who am I? Who are we, who are all these people? It was very confusing to figure out are we Syrian or Lebanese, and then there's the Irish father, and then we were in this extended house and then there were, I had a German uncle, Polish [e.g., others who were married into her mother's Middle Eastern family].

She also reported that negative comments were frequently made in her school about aspects of her background. Jeanette, as an adult, still had not developed a single identity pattern which she was comfortable using in a variety of contexts.

Anita, with a Puerto Rican and Mexican background, had great difficulty finding an identity with which she was comfortable. She finally settled on an acceptable definition:

> I identify myself as multi-cultural, multi-racial, of Hispanic, or of, you know, of Latin American background, or something like that. Because it is, I can't say that I'm Mexican, can't say that I'm Puerto Rican. I'm not Americanized enough that I feel comfortable saying I'm American. Um, and although my birth certificate says I'm white, I'm obviously not that. So I consider myself multi-cultural, multi-racial.

However firm she may be in her personal sense of identity, Anita also noted that a multi-cultural person is always aware of "never fitting in." She recalled the incident involving a favorite cousin. So even with relatives, she was an outsider. She also comments that, on visits to Puerto Rico, "...we were known as the Americans!" She concludes: "I never really fit – anywhere. . . . just a sense of never fitting. That's a real part of my experiences."

Other respondents could sympathize with her feelings. Teresa described a sense of always being "different":

> ...a lot of the times I would wish ... not that I didn't love my mother, and that I didn't love my father, but I wish I was just Black, or I wish I was just White. ... if I was with a Black group of kids around my school ... I'd wish I – how come I couldn't be Black? ... we would go to my aunt's house ... the majority of the people that live in [that town] are White, so I would think like, why can't I just be White? Uh, mixed feelings. Like that. ... I always felt weird around there. ... [in the White suburb] I always felt like ... I'm the only Black person here, and ... I feel out of place, uh, my hair's like doing this funky bush thing, and theirs would be laying straight.

If there is a common theme among these multi-racial and multi-cultural respondents, it is a sense of never really belonging anywhere, of never fitting, of always being the "odd one out," whatever the circumstances. They first encountered this as children, as we have indicated at several points. Some have come to terms with it, so that it no longer bothers them a great deal. Others, such as Jeanette, remain uncomfortable with their identity well into adulthood. In this chapter, we will focus primarily on their childhood experiences, with particular emphasis on what seemed to work well.

Successful Multi-cultural Families – What Did They Do?

It seems obvious that the nuclear family itself would have an influence on the identity patterns of its members. After all, these are the people who have the most contact with the child on a day-to-day basis. All of the respondents were part of a nuclear family. Some families seemed particularly effective in providing their children with a strong and healthy sense of identity, in spite of the negative perceptions they were getting from the larger community. How did they do it? What did they do that was different from the experiences of people like Karen and Jeanette, who report such negative memories?

Sometimes these influences were deliberate; in other instances they seemed unintentional. These different approaches seemed to produce very different patterns in their children's identification. In this section, we will discuss the way the manner in which families responded to the problems of their multi-racial and multi-cultural children. In analyzing the data, the initial approach was to search for "themes" which appear in several of the interviews. In this area, we looked for themes or patterns that appeared to characterize the families which exhibited these positive outcomes. We may view these as "success stories" of family multi-culturalism. Five themes found in these families will be discussed: the critical role of parents, presence of a "cafeteria approach" to culture, closeness of family ties, definition of cultural differences as "unimportant," the ability to find similarities in differences, and a recognition of the advantages in a multi-cultural family setting. Finally, we will discuss the fact that some of these families have continued a multi-cultural family pattern into future generations. Their willingness to do this suggests that it cannot be too negative an experience! The implications of each theme will be illustrated with examples from the interviews. Where appropriate, we will suggest ways in which these approaches could be applied to social settings other than the family as well.

The Critical Role of Parents

A complaint which many of the respondents expressed was the lack of support they received from adults in their lives, particularly parents. Jeanette received little explanation about the names she was called at school or the confusing array of nationality backgrounds which surrounded her. She was not just interested in who *she* was, but who "all these people" – her multi-national aunts and uncles – were. Questioning her mother produced little help. She merely told her to "...just say we're Irish." However, her darker skin clearly indicated she was not "just Irish." Jeanette was left in confusion.

Karen, with her Korean and German background, also felt that her parents provided little support to her and her siblings in an unwelcoming social setting. Her mother came to the USA in the wake of World War II and the Korean War, with the resulting negative attitudes toward Asian war brides. The family also lived in what she described as a "very White community." As a result, there was little discussion on their parts about the cultural differences. Her mother avoided speaking Korean, cooking Asian foods, wearing Asian style clothes, or speaking about her life in Korea. She says, "...no, my parents didn't deal with cultural issues...." Since her parents never discussed their cultural identity, Karen says "...we were told by the community how to identify ourselves. ... When you get ethnic slurs passed your way and you get told that you are not, kids are not very nice ... [sometimes] you weren't sure why you were being excluded ... then you had kids ... someone would call you a name like Chink. . . ." She also complained that adults would comment that they were "cute," when other children were not called "cute." She notes that she developed a distaste for the term "cute."

What did she wish her parents had provided for them? She wished they had provided some information and support. However, her father simply dismissed the idea of racial differences:

> My father kind of passed off the importance of race as being not very important, because it wasn't an important issue to him. . . . if we had been called names because of our racial backgrounds at school and we came home upset, my father's attitude was . . . "sticks and stones will break your bones, but names would never hurt it." Which is not what you need as a kid.

Hence, Karen received little support from her father. As an adult, however, Karen was able to understand that her parents were both incapable of providing much assistance, and has come to terms with her father's lack of social support. She says:

> My father didn't know that [i.e., that race was relevant issue in the community], and he didn't know how – it wasn't an ill attempt on his part or he wasn't making fun of our concerns, it was not knowing how to deal with it or how to be supportive through it. My mother was unable to be supportive . . . because it hurt her too. . . . it was like making fun of her, when you make fun of her children. And she had enough of these issues . . . of her own, and I don't think she knew how to deal with them either. . .. as we grew older, we realized that everyone has faults and you just have to accept them and love them the same. So my father was a good father in many ways. There were areas where he was not. The area of race was not the area that he was strong on.

While their parents may not have known how to handle the problems of raising their children in a multi-cultural setting, these respondents seem to be more aware and alert to the problems of their own children in multi-cultural settings. Most felt that things were now easier for multi-cultural children. Thus, Sarah thought her own daughter was less sensitive to multi-cultural issues than she had been, and Karen reported taking steps with her child's father to assist her in dealing with being part Asian. Are there hints which we can give to her and to parents in other multi-cultural families to assist them in providing the support to their children which they themselves lacked? In the next section, we will analyze some of the things the respondents reported that their families did that helped them to deal with the dilemmas of being multi-cultural.

A Cafeteria Approach to Culture

Many multi-cultural families presented a sort of "cafeteria approach" to culture. Obviously, the parents who founded these families were not enormously committed to the preservation of their respective cultures in their purest form. Had they felt that way, they probably would not have married someone from another race, nationality, or religious faith in the first place. At the same time, however, characteristics of each culture are present in the home and the children are introduced to them, at least in a peripheral manner. Hence, the children have presented two or more cultural options to them, with little pressure as to which culture should be preferred. Two examples of the "cafeteria approach" of the family in their children's identity formation can be found in the families of Anita and Vickie. What makes all of these families so interesting is that all of them included several children, and each child in the family appeared to experience different family influences on their sense of identity.

We will begin with Anita's family. Her mother was born and raised in Mexico, while her father was from Puerto Rico, which, as we already noted, Anita felt were "totally different" cultures. As our original hypothesis would have predicted, Anita was highly committed to her mother's Mexican heritage. She loved going back to Mexico to visit relatives there, and admitted that, "In my heart, I'm Mexican!" However, as our earlier description of Anita's family showed, her siblings were quite a diverse group. One brother married a Puerto Rican woman, visits there a great deal, and identifies as Puerto Rican; he has never been back to Mexico. Another brother identifies as Mexican, but is referred to as "the white boy," because of his fair complexion, his poor command of the Spanish language, and his assimilation into American society, which included marriage to a Caucasian woman and Anglicization of his name. Still another brother was also highly assimilated and married to an Caucasian woman, but had retained a great deal of his Spanish language skills for business purposes. In contrast, a sister lived with an aunt in Mexico and attended high school there; she was highly identified with the Mexican culture, but eventually married a man from a Caribbean island, and the similarity of her husband's culture to that of Puerto Rico resulted in her achieving a sort of "hybrid" culture, although her identification still tends to be Mexican.

It is apparent that Anita's parents presented their children with copious information on their respective cultures. They made frequent visits to both homelands, learned the language, customs, and other cultural patterns, and came to appreciate their background. The extended family was also involved, as they frequently spent time with relatives in both countries. If the parents attempted to impose pressure on their children to identify in any particular way, it certainly was not apparent. Each child seemed to feel free to select that aspect of their parents' culture and heritage with which they were most comfortable.

A similar story is told by Jeff, whose father was the son of an Orthodox Jewish rabbi, while his mother was the daughter of a Methodist minister. Jeff identifies closely with the Jewish culture and states that he was raised to believe he was Jewish, although neither he nor his parents were religious. He believes he was closer to the Jewish culture, although not the religion, because his father was the dominant one in the family. In contrast, one of his sisters is described as associating herself with both the Jewish and the Christian cultures: "[She] regards herself as both, whichever is appropriate at the time." A half sister, however, is a product of the mother's earlier marriage, and is Christian. Hence, this family setting includes three children, one who identifies as Jewish, another who identifies as Christian, and a third who feels free to select whichever she feels fits the occasion.

An even more dramatic example of the "cafeteria culture" approach appears in the interview with Vickie, whose parents did not practice their respective religions; nor were they committed to their nationality backgrounds. However, each of their three children had selected a different aspect of their parents' cultural heritage. Vickie was fascinated with Judaism from early childhood, even though religious ideas had not been stressed in the household. As an adult, she has continued to identify as Jewish and is a practicing Jew, much to the consternation of her nonreligious parents. She also resents being called "half Jewish," retorting: ". . . there's no such thing as half Jewish. You're either Jewish or you're not Jewish!" Her younger sister, in contrast, has converted to the Catholic faith. And their brother has followed their parents' nonreligious orientation. However, to quote Vickie, "He's so into the Irish thing." He has visited Ireland, learned the Irish language, and raised his child to describe herself as an Irish girl, even though her background is only one-fourth Irish. Clearly, each of these three siblings felt quite free to select from among the religious and cultural heritages of their parents to develop his or her own personal identity and culture.

Hence, the children from these families seem to have a remarkable ability to view the cultural models presented in their families as interesting and valuable options which are open to them. In these closest of social ties, a common culture was not an imperative. Like diners in a cafeteria line, members take those items which are most appealing. However, the options they choose not to accept do not pose a threat. They are viewed as interesting options which other members of the family enjoy. Other groups could take a lesson from their openness. Whether they be in classrooms, work settings, or social groups, people should be encouraged to view cultural differences as interesting alternatives which can be enjoyed by others, rather than seeing each as a threat to his/her own cultural views. As Vickie and Anita and their siblings learned, they can be supportive of each other, while remaining secure in their own cultural choices. Professionals working with multi-cultural groups, from families, to work and school settings, can encourage their members to discuss their cultural patterns and what they derive from them. Examples such as these can help multi-cultural participants to feel secure in their own cultural choices, and to view other cultural patterns with respect and interest, rather than as a threat to their own

Successful Families Focus on the Relationships – Close Social Ties

Those who believe that a common culture is absolutely essential to the development of a strong social tie might look unfavorably upon the cafeteria approach to culture which I have just described. Different patterns are often seen as a threat to the group; presumably the appearance of different cultural options will break the social bonds which members of the group feel for each other. The solidarity exhibited by these families is exceptional, however. These were people who continued to remain close to their families in spite of cultural and sometimes even geographic distance.

Anita's family, for example, holds a family brunch once a month, to which family members bring their special dishes. Each month, a different couple hosts the gathering. Anita stresses that the specialty foods for each nationality are quite different. So each family contributes the items which they are most accustomed to cooking. Anita finds she can make the Mexican foods "better and easier," so these are her contributions. However, there are Puerto Rican foods of which she is also fond, so "...when I really want some I call my sister-in-law who's Puerto Rican."

Here is a family which maintains extremely close social ties, even though some identify with their Mexican heritage, others with their Puerto Rican heritage, and still others are rather thoroughly assimilated into American society, to the point of being affectionately termed "White boys." Anita proudly exhibited a picture of her family, including her parents, brothers and sisters, brothers- and sisters-in-law, and all of their respective children. In addition to their cultural differences, they exhibited a wide range of skin colors, from very light to medium brown. Yet the family was characterized by extremely close social ties and personal relations.

Vickie's reports of her Irish-Jewish family are very similar. In response to a query about how frequently she communicated with her brother and sister and her parents, she replied:

Daily, mostly. . . . Yeah. Well, my brother's on email, and we talk, and my sister-in-law. We talk mostly everyday on email. And then I usually call them on the weekends 'cause they work regular 9–5 jobs and they're tired when they get home. Um, I call my sister everyday. She's got 3 little kids, and, I mean, she needs the company, but she also needs to – I have to hear the daily development of the babies and stuff. So, um . . . And uh, yeah, mostly talk to my parents everyday too. Yeah. We're yakkers. [laughs] My phone bills are unbelievable!

Vickie also comments on her family's common Jewish food patterns:

...my grandmother made a lot of Jewish food. You know, brisket, and ... we ate bagels before anyone else in America ever heard of them. I mean, we teethed on bagels as babies. ...all that New York Jewish food, deli sandwiches and knisches, and blintzes, and, and fried matzos ... we ate all that kind of stuff, you know. And actually, my sister, in spite of her move to Catholicism, still ... she can't wait for Passover so I can talk her through making fried matzos on the phone. . . . So yeah, we ate a lot of that, but Irish stuff was really limited, I mean, to St. Patrick's Day.

The importance of the contact with both sides, and the different ways in which each side was accommodated, is echoed by Derek, whose mother was German and whose father was Black and Native American from Louisiana:

We were talking about if I associate myself differently with either side of the family. . . . just thinking back of the times we visited my father's family, the Black side of the family, . . . we enjoyed our times there. . . . my father came from a large family. They were all very close . . . it was a blast. We went there, as kids, laughing and goofing off, listening to the parents having a good time. You know, there's kids playing around, . . . all having a great time. . . . Then when we would visit my mother's family in Germany, we enjoyed ourselves too, but a little differently. It wasn't wild, it was, . . . they were very close . . . kids, we played around a lot. The parents sat and relaxed, ate cake, drank coffee all the time. . . . We had a real good relationship with both families. . . . I can't say I had a favorite, you know, either way, I can't say that normally, that I associated myself more with one or the other more, based on cultural differences.

Hence, it is clear that these families retained close social ties in spite of different cultural or even racial characteristics. They were able to focus on the things they shared in common rather than their differences. They obviously cared a great deal for each other. They not only looked forward to getting together, they made deliberate efforts to bring about such occasions. Rather than defining others as "different" and avoiding them, they sought each other out. Of course, these were persons related by blood. Could this be replicated in a nonfamily setting? A useful venture for professional counselors would be to encourage members of multi-cultural groups to develop social ties across cultural lines, even to "engineer" such contacts through the development of multi-cultural work or study groups. If the experience of these families is relevant, participants may begin to focus on the importance of the social relationship, rather than the differences in cultural beliefs. In the next section, I will suggest some ways in which this may come about.

A New Cultural Pattern – Defining Cultural Differences as Unimportant

Since social interaction requires some type of common cultural basis, it is interesting to consider how these families managed to maintain the social relationship in spite of cultural variations. Social scientists and lay people alike generally assume that successful social relations require a common set of interactional dimensions. How can social interaction occur without these? A careful examination of the families in the study indicates that they do, indeed, share common cultural assumptions which provide an important foundation for their social relationships.

Anita, for example, may stress the undeniable differences between Mexican and Puerto Rican culture and resent the suggestion that an amalgamated "Hispanic" culture exists. She may prefer to stress and identify with her Mexican heritage and have brothers and sisters who prefer to stress the Puerto Rican culture or be largely assimilated into American society. However, they share a number of common cultural characteristics. One of these is language: all of Anita's brothers and sisters speak both English and Spanish, although some are less fluent than others. Furthermore, the family celebrated numerous festivals borrowed from the customs of both Mexico and Puerto Rico, such as an extended 12 days of Christmas celebration and celebrations of various milestones in the lives of family members, "...between weddings, and First Communions, and you know [the coming of age ceremony for 15 year old girls], and things like that." In a similar manner, Jeff stressed his family's emphasis on the importance of education, and Sarah's East European Jewish and Christian family was united in its common support of left-wing politics.

Perhaps the most important aspect of the culture which these families seem to share is a pattern which defines certain cultural differences as unimportant. Derek, for example, believes that his experiences with his mixed Black and German background gave him a broader perspective. Particularly illustrative in this regard are the families which involve religious differences. Vickie comments that her Jewish-Irish parents were constantly asked to comment on mixed marriages:

> ...people would ask them all the time – it was almost a steady stream of people they knew coming into the house to ask them how you make a mixed marriage work. And their answer was always, and they'd say this to us, "If religion matters to you, a mixed marriage won't work. But since it didn't matter to us, it's fine."

Hence, one dimension of the culture of these families is that they define certain cultural dimensions as unimportant. This goes much deeper, however, than Vickie's parents' definition of religion as unimportant. In fact, it may include defining a specific focus as *very important*, but one in which *differences* are unimportant. Again, Vickie's family provides an illustration. Vickie and her sister remain very close, in spite of the fact that Vickie is a practicing Jew, her sister, a practicing Catholic. Their relationship is highly supportive, going far beyond mere tolerance of each other's religious beliefs. Indeed, they are mutually supportive of each other's religion:

> ...so I just always identified [as Jewish], and it's gotten more serious as I've grown older. And I also think it's grown more serious the farther I've gotten away from my family. Because it does bother my family that I'm now a practicing Jew. And it's in a weird sort of way, because my sister, who has converted to Catholicism defends me. Because if she doesn't defend me, then she can't defend herself.

In short, these multi-religious families define religious differences as unimportant. They focus on some aspects of culture which they share, and de-emphasize others which they do not share. Vickie and her sister, for example, stress their shared interest in having a religious focus for their lives, in contrast with their parents and brother, who are not religious. Their religious focus is a bond, even though they have chosen to follow different religions. In effect, the approach of these two families to religion and ethnicity is similar to the approach which people in the industrial world take to occupations. Most American families, for example, consider a person's choice of an occupation a matter of personal preference, not an issue over which the family should be concerned or which members of a family need to share in common.

In these multi-religious and multi-ethnic families, this personal preference approach extends to religious and ethnic issues as well. These families' lack of emphasis on ethnic or religious traits is also illustrated by the fact that many of them are involved in multi-religious or multi-ethnic marriages like their parents. Jeff, for example, continues to identify as a Jew, but had married a Christian woman. Anita had a long-term relationship with a Black man. And Derek had married a Filipino woman. His view illustrates the multi-ethnic, multi-racial view of these respondents:

> ...my wife is Asian, from the Philippines. Our children are all now Asian and part Black and part German too. ... So they're gonna be confused when they grow up! Look at all the college scholarships they'll qualify for! ...again, that's not something I planned on. It's not something I thought about. I just hoped that someday I would find somebody I could truly love and have a family with. And I happened to find somebody from the Philippines. My brother is married to a Mexican-American. My sister is married to a White American who's half British. ... So we're a very mixed family. ... And I don't think that we set out to do that. [laughs] To conquer the world, but ... That's just something that at least maybe we appreciate, that we appreciate people of other races because of our background.

Two lessons appear in these experiences. One is a focus on the importance of the social relationship, not the external characteristics of the cultural patterns each exhibited. By building social relationships which cross cultural lines, people learn to focus on the importance of their bonds with each other, rather than external cultural differences. Professionals can encourage the identification and development of such social ties.

Finding Similarities Within Differences

An important lesson from these families is the inevitable presence of cultural similarities, even in the midst of numerous cultural differences. Respondents' families had very considerable differences, from religion and language to race and nationality. However, they also had some clear similarities and were able to focus on these commonalities, rather than the differences. The Spanish language and religious festivals united Anita's family; the importance of religion united Vickie and her sister; Sarah's and Jeff's families were both united by common political views. Such commonalities exist in the wider world as well. In multi-cultural community settings, the community's needs provide a common cultural focus. Although Jews and the many varieties of Christian denominations are clearly different, they share many aspects of the Judeo-Christian culture. Professionals can assist multi-cultural groups by encouraging them to focus on these commonalities.

Even families which appeared to have difficulty dealing with differences exhibited some of these characteristics. Jeanette's family, for example, provided little support to their children in dealing with the many nationalities which were included in the household. However, she was quick to point out that, for her family, "...what was important was that he was Catholic, and ... my father was very good friends with my mother's older brother." Hence, there were two reasons why a marriage between two quite different nationalities was acceptable. There was a commonality of religion, which was considered extremely important in both the Irish and the Lebanese communities. In addition, however, the man was not really a stranger, but had been a friend of the family for quite some time. Indeed, this particular brother actually functioned "like the head" of the family. Furthermore, the brother was known for being involved in radical politics and somewhat of a hothead. Only her father could "calm him down."

Hence, it is clear that an impetus for this intergroup marriage was the fact that this outsider had already been accepted into the family, and was seen as useful to them for many reasons. Although less attention was given to the Irish side, it appears that they also believed the religious similarity was the most important issue. Jeanette also described two aunts who had married a Protestant and a Greek Orthodox, respectively. In these cases, considerable family fighting, scandal, and even an attempt to kidnap the bride ensued. Hence, the Catholic Church played a pivotal role in the family, but ethnic divisions were less important.

Sarah's description of the interreligious contact in her family is far less negative than Jeanette's. Asked whether her family ever discussed these differences, she laughed cheerfully and responded, "Yes, at length!" She then proceeded to describe some of the discussions which surrounded her. Her family had been in Europe prior to World War II, so there were numerous discussions which centered on religion:

Well, I was not baptized, because neither of my parents was observant, and so they've never
... it was never much of an issue, but ... my father ... told my mother that he felt that there
was a rising tide of anti-Semitism ... And he told her that for my protection he thought it
would be a good idea if I got baptized. And his sister, my aunt, and my grandmother, his
mother, entered into this with a great deal of fervor and enthusiasm, which began to bother
my mother a great deal. ... so preparations were going forward and my mother saw that
this was taking on a religious caste, other than the way of protecting me. I think she and my
father had a talk – I never heard the talk, but ... I knew that they were sitting down to talk
one evening, and after that, I heard no more about my baptism.

Sarah obviously was surrounded by a great deal of cultural difference, much of
it centered on religion, specifically, the rather dramatic difference between being
a baptized Christian and a Jew. Yet her memories seem to carry none of the negative overtones which characterized Jeanette's memories. Without rancor, indeed,
with considerable humor, she described many of these interactions. Multi-cultural
contacts – even conflicts – she obviously had in abundance. But for Sarah, they
lacked the distressing impact they had for Jeanette. It is possible that her family's
openness about their differences played a role in her comfortable perceptions. Jeff,
who shared Sarah's Christian-Jewish background, commented that the cultural differences in the family were easier to deal with if the family explained what they did
and why.

Sarah's comfortable approach to her mixed heritage was shared by other respondents. Like Sarah, Grace found considerable humor in the situation:

My dad is English, Irish; my mom's Indian and I'm not sure what else. I know it's Cherokee.
... I'm a jokester anyway; I like playing around, so I consider myself Heinz 57. I tell them
I'm English, Irish, and Indian, which I am. But I usually go Heinz 57 because that's what
most people say, so that's what I tell them.

Hence, for both Grace and Sarah, having origins in several different cultural
groups was not confusing or disturbing. It was something to laugh about. Ken and
Derek also reported making jokes when others made rude comments about their
mixed heritage. All were quite comfortable with their mixed origins; if others were
not, that seemed to be their problem!

Like Grace, Nicole's family included several different nationalities. She was Irish
through her mother but had a French surname because her father was French. Her
family thought of itself as Irish. In addition, she encountered other nationalities
in her community, which she describes as "mixed," but with a large component
of Germans. However, she recalls that: "No, where I grew up I don't remember
nationalities or any of that being terribly important. You were just whoever you
were and had nothing to do really with nationality."

Peter also seemed to take his multi-cultural contacts in stride. Although he frequently complained about the "meanness" of some of the students in the schools
he attended, he attributed these problems to economic differences and class-related
lifestyles, rather than to ethnic differences. In fact, he reported being more comfortable when he attended a multi-cultural school. He says:

...there was a large majority of African-Americans. Kind of a small part was Chaldean [a Christian Iraqi group]; another part was Filipino; and then a very small portion was Euro-Americans. I really couldn't identify with anybody else. ... but I was more at ease because my clothes were not a big issue anymore. That was becoming a low point for me in high school, the matter of my clothes. I couldn't dress the way I wanted to. When I came here my clothing wasn't that important, it was more who I was friends with. Because I knew how to surf, I picked up skate boarding and I kind of met up with the group that knew how to skateboard. And these were different types of people, one guy was Filipino, one guy was Irish, and the other guy was African-American. We were all kind of like inter-racial.

Clearly, the diversity which Jeanette found so confusing was actually comforting to Peter. A similar response came from Derek, who had a German mother and an African-American and Native American father. At one point, he commented that he and his siblings had "...experienced uh, name-calling and stuff like that ... People called us zebras, uh, crows, things like that. Weird names, because of our mixed heritage." The use of pejorative terms such as "zebra" or "oreo" for persons of mixed background was mentioned by other respondents as well, such as Theresa. However, Derek insisted that "...it was nothing really malicious." And at the end of the interview, he could sum his childhood experiences in very positive terms: "I love both my parents. Everything was a great time. We had a great relationship with my German grandparents and our American relatives. That's what we had."

This comfort with diversity was shared by several other respondents, including Peggy, Gary, Vicki, and Regina. While they all reported that they had received negative comments about their mixed backgrounds, they all shared the view that these had not created major problems for them. Instead, they enjoyed the experience of being mixed, and, like Peter, actually found more comfort in diversity than in a single cultural pattern.

Advantages and Assets of Growing up in a Multi-cultural Setting

While the respondents were keenly aware of the problems they encountered in growing up in a multi-cultural setting, there were also some advantages which they recognized. Chief among these was the appreciation of differences and other cultures which they gleaned from their experiences. As a group, the respondents seemed to feel that they had a keener sensitivity to the diversity of cultures than others who lacked their experiences with different races or cultures. Many of them expressed their annoyance with people who did not appreciate or understand people whose racial or cultural backgrounds were different from theirs. A few even mentioned specifically that they believed their backgrounds made them more sensitive to different cultures.

Their views are best expressed by Derek, who grew up in a multi-racial family, lived in multi-racial neighborhoods, and attended multi-racial schools. He discusses the impact of these experiences:

...if I'd been born, you know, pure Black, whatever that means. . . . I don't think I would have experienced . . . different cultures like what I've experienced . . . living in Germany, and knowing Germans, things like that, learning the language. . . . I guess I've gotten the best of both worlds. . . . I got to see things from both sides. . . . I think more tolerant. Right! . . . I think if I had grown up in different circumstances, if I were both Black parents, or all Black neighborhood . . . I might have picked up things, or . . . developed prejudice. . . . Whereas, you know, you can't generalize. I think you see things on both sides. I love both my parents. . . . . We had a great relationship with my German grandparents and our American relatives. That's what we had.

Hence, Derek felt it was difficult to develop prejudices against people you had lived with and known as well as he had known his relatives, schoolmates, and neighbors.

This belief that multi-cultural and multi-racial experiences helped one develop a more tolerant attitude was a common theme in the interviews. In these instances, the parents are, perhaps inadvertently, sending a message to their children that there are a wide variety of cultural patterns which are available for selection, much as a diner would select items from a cafeteria lineup. All are available; none are better than the others; they are just different. And the children apparently feel free to select and pursue those which they find most agreeable. Peggy provides a suggestion as to how this process might work. Although she was raised Catholic and educated in Catholic schools, she was constantly introduced to other points of view through long conversations with her non-Catholic mother:

There was one thing that my mother did . . . because of the religious difference, and I guess maybe the cultural difference between her and my dad . . . that I think had a profound effect on me . . . throughout my life. I had gone to Catholic school . . . I would come home and tell her what the priests and nuns had said. . . . And . . . she would listen, and then she would say, "oh, that's interesting, and some people think . . ." And then she would go on to talk about the fact that other people took a different point of view. And it was never nasty. There was no rancor in this. It wasn't mean. It wasn't telling me I shouldn't believe that. She was just very quietly presenting a different point of view. And one of the things I learned from her as I was growing up was that people could disagree about very important things like religion and not be mad at each other. . . . I think that this led me as an adult to have an appreciation for cultural differences that I would not have had, and that most of my friends didn't have . . . didn't appreciate the fact that other people could be different, and other people could . . . have different points of view, and that was all right.

In all of these families, the existence of different cultures was an obvious and accepted component of the family structure. While there was no apparent attempt to impose any one of the cultural patterns on the children, neither was there an attempt to hide their existence. The children in all of these families were quite aware of their parents' racial, nationality, and/or religious characteristics, as well as the fact that their parents did not share the same cultures. In presenting their various cultural patterns in this manner, these families also seemed to be telling their children that different cultures presented the individual with free options.

As a result, the children apparently felt free to choose their own sense of identity, and each selected a somewhat different manner of identification. Anita and her siblings chose different parts of their parents' culture with which to identify. Vickie and her siblings did the same. Peggy chose to identify with both her parents' cultures, and Derek chose to see himself as Black, largely on the basis of his appearance. The cafeteria approach also apparently provided their children with an openness to different cultures, whatever cultural tradition they chose to follow. Both Peggy and Derek seem to be saying that their multi-cultural families made them more appreciative of different cultures and more accepting of people different from themselves.

Continuing a Multi-cultural Tradition in a New Generation

The multi-cultural respondents in this study were largely united in their feelings that the setting in which they were situated played an important role in whether or not they recognized their multi-cultural character and felt discomfort with it. When they felt discomfort, it was largely a result of feeling that they never "fit in" with their peers, and that "fitting in" required that they reject one or more parts of their chosen identity. Data analysis also revealed that having parents from different cultures was not the only road to multi-culturalism; having a stepparent, being adopted by someone from another culture, or belonging to a family which moved to another setting were other ways in which respondents encountered the multi-cultural experience. Parents in these families clearly played an important role in their children's comfort with their multi-cultural origins. When parents explained their varying origins effectively, their children were more comfortable with their multi-cultural status as well.

Perhaps the most positive aspect of these respondents' experience is their comfort level with diversity and their willingness to continue the multi-cultural trend into adulthood. As noted, two of the respondents have recently become involved in multi-cultural adoptions. Several of them have been involved in multi-cultural or multi-racial relationships above and beyond those that occurred in their families of origin. Obviously this is a pattern with which they are comfortable, and they search for additional situations in which this can occur. Thus, Anita comments that she has "dated every color under the sun." Derek provides a good example of continued multi-culturalism, in a statement quoted above.

Perhaps multi-racial and multi-cultural individuals represent the wave of the future – persons who can extend themselves beyond the narrow boundaries of race, nationality, religion, and social class, to accept and associate comfortably with people from a wide range of racial, ethnic, economic, and social backgrounds.

Recommendations to Another Generation

Having experienced the negative dimensions of a biased environment as children, some of these multi-cultural and multi-racial respondents were particularly anxious to ensure that the problems they encountered be dealt with more effectively with their own children. Karen reports going to a counselor with her daughter's father, and emphasizing the importance of parents' being sensitive to their daughter's needs and supportive in any problems she might encounter. She explains:

> . . .it became very important to me to make sure that [he] understands . . . . My father kind of passed off the importance of race as being not very important, because it wasn't an important issue to him. . . . My mother was unable to be supportive, or she just didn't want to be because it hurt her too. . . . times have gotten a little bit better. She [her daughter] is only a quarter Asian. . . . you know kids make fun of people all the time, and race is another category to make fun of . . . it was important to me that my significant other understand that if these issues do rise up in the community and are directed at her, that he can not pass them off as being unimportant because he loves her and so everyone else should and if they don't too bad – he has to deal with this issue and the problems it creates.

Similarly, Sarah expressed satisfaction that her daughter appears more able to deal with reactions she gets from her classmates than Sarah had been able to as a child:

> . . .I think things are opening up, in American society, to some extent. . . . She [her daughter] is seen as, well, unusual . . . But the thing about her is that she seems to negotiate these things with great ease. The response of other people doesn't seem to concern her a great deal. And she's been able to, to have friends, and um, she's less responsive to the kind of interest that she generates than, than I would have been certainly.

From their own experience, these respondents were well aware of the problems of being multi-cultural in a world which assumed that everyone ought to be just like them. Some remembered painful experiences from their childhood as a result of these factors. Those who had children were equally anxious that their children not experience the negative aspects of multi-culturalism, and wanted to ensure that someone be there to help them if they encountered problems. Multi-cultural settings need to provide a sensitivity to the cultural differences and to the feelings of persons with cultural differences. Parents and counselors need to anticipate the possibility – indeed the probability – of negative encounters which create difficulties, and to be prepared with methods for minimizing their impact on the participants.

Summary

In this chapter, we have focused on the "success stories" of multi-cultural and multi-racial families. Throughout this entire section, we have described numerous problems which multi-racial and multi-cultural children have in developing an identity, particularly in the light of a social environment which is not hospitable to persons who do not "fit in" the way the community as a whole expects. They are forced into a single identity, although their heritage and experiences clearly are derived from multiple cultures or races. Many of them report highly negative experiences, including being rejected, called names, and reminded that they do not belong.

Yet many, indeed most of the respondents, were quite content with their backgrounds and preferred to be identified with their mixed backgrounds. Something must have worked right for them. For many it was apparently a matter of individual resilience. However, to a great extent, it was the effectiveness of their families which placed them in this position. Apparently some of these families were able to assist their children in dealing with the near insurmountable difficulties faced by multi-cultural and multi-racial children in a hostile environment. We have described them as the "success stories" of family multi-culturalism.

A number of themes or patterns appeared in these families. One was the critical role of parents in providing support to their children. We also noted the presence in these families of what we called a "cafeteria approach" to culture, which allows for the possibility that a number of different ways may be an appropriate focus of identification. We noted that these families often had particularly close family ties, bringing the members together in spite of dramatic cultural differences. These families were also capable of defining cultural differences as "unimportant." They also exhibited the ability to find similarities in their differences. Many also seem to recognize the advantages of living in a multi-cultural family for their success in a multi-cultural world. Finally, we discussed the fact that some of these respondents have continued a multi-cultural family pattern into future generations, a suggestion that they did not see their experience as totally negative. We will conclude with a list of suggestions for multi-cultural success. They might be effectively used to bring success to future multi-cultural families, as well as to other types of groups which bring together people from a variety of racial and cultural backgrounds.

Lessons to be Learned From Multi-cultural Family Experiences

A number of lessons can be learned from these multi-cultural families. These include techniques of dealing with a multi-cultural setting and ways which multi-cultural groups can use to make their relationships more effective. These can be used not only in multi-cultural families, but also in other multi-cultural groups.

Ability to Focus on the Shared Similarities

Respondents and their families seem to have developed ways for accentuating their common cultural patterns and minimizing the importance of their differences. While there were doubtless many differences in culture within these families, there were also numerous cultural similarities. Most shared a common language (perhaps more than one); many shared religious beliefs and rituals; and others shared such patterns as common political ties or emphasis on education. Some shared an emphasis on the importance of religion, although their religions differed. All of them placed great emphasis on their close personal ties with other family members. Other multi-cultural groups could follow their example by focusing on those patterns which are critical to the group's success, while choosing not to emphasize the patterns which are not critical. Most multi-cultural groups also have similarities on which clinical sociologists can help them to focus.

The Importance of Distinguishing Between Important and Unimportant Differences

With regard to the actual differences, these families shared an ability to distinguish between cultural dimensions which were important and those which were not. When the differences were unimportant, respondents and their siblings felt free to adopt whatever each found most appealing from their parents' heritages, sometimes resulting in quite divergent patterns among the siblings. However, they were also quite accepting of their siblings' choices, with the result that families could accommodate to their members' having very different cultural patterns and still remain an integral part of the family. Where aspects of culture are not critical to the relationships of group members, it makes sense to ignore them. Similarly, those cultural components which the members share can be emphasized, much as Vickie and her sister stress their common interest in *religion*, without focusing on the fact that they follow *different* religions. In this manner, other multi-cultural groups may be able to develop the strong social ties which these families possess, in spite of their cultural differences. The goal should be to provide each individual with a dual focus: a comfort with his/her own unique cultural patterns and identity, and a recognition of the broader cultural patterns which the entire group shares in common.

The Value of a Supportive Social Setting

Finally, a supportive social setting is particularly critical to the development of good multi-cultural relationships. Respondents whose social environments had been positive and supportive were more comfortable with their multi-culturalism than those who experienced less supportive environments. In this regard, it comes as no great surprise to a sociologist that several of the respondents, both those who were multiracial, and those who were from a single race, were painfully aware that many of the difficulties which multi-cultural groups and/or individuals experienced in various settings were the result of their *racial* identity, not their cultural identity. Being multi-cultural, or even multi-racial, was not so difficult in some settings as being a member of an unfavored racial group. Another common theme, even among persons from different racial groups, was that multi-culturalism was more acceptable today than had been true when they were young, and they hoped to be able to provide a more supportive environment for their children than they had experienced. In their work with multi-cultural groups, clinical sociologists can help to provide the same support which these respondents were providing for their members.

Accentuating their common cultural characteristics and minimizing their differences, distinguishing between those cultural dimensions which are important and those which are not, searching for the commonalities in their relationships, and establishing a supportive social setting all can engender the development of positive relationships in multi-cultural and/or multi-racial settings in the family, at work or school, or in communities. The experiences of these families can help clinical sociologists to foster these ventures.

Part III
Applying Our Knowledge: Incorporating Multi-Culturalism Into Social Policies and Programs

In this Section we will draw upon the experiences of respondents from multi-cultural families to suggest ways in which a multi-cultural society such as ours can accommodate the diversity of its members more effectively. This section will focus on social relations at all levels: micro level groups, such as the family; meso level groups, such as communities and schools; and the macro level, structures of society as a whole.

Micro-Level Recommendations – Individual Interactions (Chapter 8)

Chapter 8 will begin at the level with which the multi-cultural respondents were most familiar: the family. This chapter will summarize the problems which the multi-cultural respondents had in their formative years, and the ways in which families could assist them in the process. This chapter will focus on micro-level relations, suggesting ways in which families could deal more effectively with their mixed background children. It will also discuss ways in which outside agencies could also provide assistance in the difficult process of "growing up multi-cultural," by providing suggestions for family or individual counselors to use in their work with multi-cultural clients. These recommendations could also be extended to professionals of various types, such as counselors, teachers, and the health professions, for their use in work with individuals and families from mixed racial and cultural backgrounds. Chapter 8 will also describe ways in which the approaches of schools, communities, and government agencies might incorporate multi-cultural-friendly approaches into their policies and procedures.

Meso-Level Recommendations – Community and Institutional Programs (Chapters 9 and 10)

Chapters 9 and 10 move the emphasis to the meso level of social structure: the level of community development and social institutions. These chapters describe programs which illustrate how multi-culturalism can be incorporated into programs at the level of communities and institutions. Since schools are a major institution in which multi-culturalism is incorporated, and since so many of our respondents specifically mentioned the school as a problematic institutions in their childhoods, we will provide examples of multi-cultural programs in schools, together with their advantages and difficulties. We will also discuss the impact which multi-cultural programs may have on multi-cultural individuals.

As we have suggested, altering social institutions and communities cannot depend upon people of good will operating on an individual-to-individual level. Special programs must be developed which assist these groups and institutions to deal with the problems and difficulties they face. In this instance, we are dealing with the special problems which occur in communities and institutions which encompass persons from a variety of racial and cultural backgrounds. As we suggested at the outset, the experiences of our mixed background respondents provide a useful basis on which to recommend the way in which racial and cultural diversity can be handled in social settings. In this chapter, we will describe two programs which attempt to accommodate the community institutions to the needs of multi-cultural and multi-racial backgrounds. Both programs focus on the school setting. However, both could be adapted to other social institutions, such as religious groups or business organizations, as well as to residential communities, if they sought to achieve improved relations among the diverse ethnic and racial components which make them up.

Choice of the school setting as our example is appropriate for two reasons. First, and most obvious, public schools are responsible for educating all children in their communities. Consequently, the schools are often the first institutions to encounter the problems of diversity, in the person of new groups of entering children. While other groups and institutions can often avoid the problems of diversity by ignoring them, the responsibility of the schools to educate the community's children means they do not have the same option. As we noted with the case of Regina, private schools, like other nonpublic institutions, have the option of turning down students they wish to avoid. Public schools, however, are required to accept all children and provide them with the required educational experience, whether they like it or not. Hence schools are more likely to have developed techniques for dealing with the problems their diverse student populations present.

Second, as we have indicated at several points, children from diverse backgrounds often find school to be a particularly daunting experience. Numerous respondents recalled negative encounters from their school days. Children like Regina were refused entry into their chosen schools, apparently because an administrator believed they did not fit into the school population, or thought they might create problems for the school. Teachers and administrators often pressured students into choosing an identity other than the one they preferred. Many respondents reported hearing other children make derogatory comments, sometimes with the tacit or explicit consent of teachers.

These reports came from respondents who were students in the 1940s and 1950s, as well as those whose school days were more recent. Such occurrences are not likely to promote a satisfactory learning environment. It is difficult for children to devote their attention to learning if they are worried about being ridiculed or rejected by their teachers or classmates. As Title I of the "No Child Left Behind Act" specifies, it is critical that children from minority and disadvantaged groups be accorded the same educational opportunities as children from the dominant and more advantaged groups:

> ...to ensure that all children have a fair, equal, and significant opportunity to obtain a high-quality education and reach, at a minimum, proficiency on challenging State academic achievement standards and state academic assessments. ... [including]:
> ...(2) meeting the educational needs of low-achieving children in our Nation's highest-poverty schools, limited English proficient children, migratory children, children with disabilities, Indian children, neglected or delinquent children, and young children in need of reading assistance;
> (3) closing the achievement gap between high- and low-performing children, especially the achievement gaps between minority and nonminority students, and between disadvantaged children and their more (advantaged peers. ... (NCLB, 2001: Title I).

Hence public schools are faced with the challenge of dealing with a diverse student body.

In Chapters 9 and 10, we describe two quite different programs which were designed for use in the public setting. While the two programs are quite different, both are focused on the objective of improving the school experience for children from diverse racial and cultural backgrounds, an issue which our multi-cultural and multi-racial respondents found so painful. The two programs differ not only in their specific objectives but also in their format.

The first example, presented in Chapter 9, describes and analyzes an educational program at the high school level which specifically included aspects of racial and cultural diversity within the curriculum. The program, referred to as the "Diversity Program," encompasses the entire high school program, and attempts to include diversity-related issues within the entire school curriculum. The Diversity Program is the topic of the author's Ph.D. dissertation. The author describes the structure and content of the program, and evaluates it from the perspective of both the teachers and the participating students. The Diversity Program attempted, with some success, to develop and implement educational approaches which were more accommodating to the needs of children from diverse racial and cultural backgrounds. One dimension of this program was to include the child's family in the development of educational goals and objectives, and to involve family members in the assessment process as well.

It stands to reason, however, that major racial or cultural differences between teachers and children may create problems in the interaction process between the family, the child, and staff members. In such instances, it is likely that family and staff members may have difficulty communicating and understanding each other's points of view. In this section, we focus on a different type of program, also located in the school setting, which attempts to improve communication between the family and the school, specifically in the case of children who are recent immigrants to the USA.

As we discussed in Chapter 2, recent immigrant children frequently require special programs, particularly focusing on English as a foreign language, to assist them in adapting to the US school setting. Once they have learned English at a sufficient level, they no longer require special treatment and can be "mainstreamed," or included within the student body as a whole, for the majority of their classes. As we also discussed in Chapter 2, immigrants who entered the USA during the late decades of the 20th century and the early 21st century tend to be more diverse, in terms of race and religion, than earlier waves of immigration. Consequently, the children of these immigrants present an unfamiliar set of problems to the American school setting.

Chapter 10 focuses on the second program, a series of coordinated workshops which were designed by the author, and which make use of "Parallel Socialization" as an approach to improving the educational experience of immigrant children in American Schools. The workshops are established to enlist cooperation among the three sets of participants in the educational experience of immigrant children: the students, parents, and teachers. The author describes the structure and process employed in the workshops, and suggests techniques likely to ensure their success.

Hence Chapter 10 continues to focus on the development of institutional and community programs which can enhance diversity. Again, an educational program is the example. However, this is a very different type of educational program, although it too focuses on improving the educational experience of children who are "different." In the case to be described, the children are immigrants to the USA, and are caught, in many respects, between the culture of American society and school, on the one hand, and that of their immigrant parents which pervades their home life. This program was developed to increase the rate at which today's immigrant children could be "mainstreamed," or included in the student body as a whole. The program consists of a series of workshops with teachers, parents, and students, with the intent of bringing them together in a coordinated effort to improve the educational environment for these immigrant students.

A unique aspect of the program is the *coordination* of the workshops. That is, each workshop does not operate independently. Instead, the workshop organizer meets with each group, explaining to each group the concerns of the other participants in the process. Members of each set of workshops were expected to commit to working together, to achieving a mutual understanding of the problems, and to achieving a better educational environment for the children's education. It is this coordination among the workshop participants which makes this program particularly useful in attaining mutual understanding among persons from different cultural backgrounds.

Macrolevel Recommendations – Different Structures at the National Level (Chapter 11)

Our concluding chapter focuses on macro-level multi-culturalism. Chapter 11 will examine the manner in which several different societies in the world today have dealt with a multi-cultural and/or multi-racial population. This chapter will compare multi-cuturalism in the USA with other nations which are notably multi-cultural. This will give us an opportunity to examine varying ways in which different societies have coped with cultural variations, and the impact these varying approaches are likely to have. Among the societies to be included are Canada, Australia, Trinidad and Tobago, and France. This chapter will analyze the different approaches taken to their diverse cultural components by each of these modern societies. Attention will be paid to the possible consequences of each of these approaches, and suggestions will be made as to which approaches are likely to achieve different national objectives.

Chapter 8
Improving Personal Relations for Multi-cultural People

At this point, it is perhaps important to review the original purpose of this study. As we noted at several points, previous studies of multi-culturalism have essentially examined multi-culturalism at the meso- or the macro-levels. That is, they have focused on the several different cultural and racial groups which make up a multi-cultural society. As a result of these efforts, we have numerous works which examine the characteristics of the many groups which have entered into the USA over the course of its history, and which comprise American society as it exists today. Chapter 1 provided a summary of some of the studies of these varying immigrant groups, from early colonial days through the mid-20th century.

However, as we have shown throughout, this approach to multi-culturalism omits a major category of participants in any multi-cultural population: the *individuals* who are themselves multi-cultural. These individuals are the true experts in multi-culturalism. Persons who are simply participants in the various subgroups in a multi-cultural society experience multi-culturalism in a different way. They participate as members of a *single* cultural or racial group, all of whom interact with members of other groups from that unitary cultural perspective. Certainly, they have multi-cultural experiences, particularly if their cultural group is relatively small. In such instances, they must interact with members of other cultural groups in many settings. Members of larger ethnic groups, however, have often been able to contain their activities within the bounds of their own culture for extended periods of time.

Included among participants in multi-culturalism are members of the so-called dominant group, the "White" population, which does not like to view itself as a "subgroup." However, as we showed in Chapter 2, the so-called White population is itself multi-cultural, and has been so for most of its history, including persons of different religions and dramatically variant national origins. Furthermore, American multi-culturalism is increasing dramatically since the mid-20th century, as the American population includes a greater proportion of non-White and foreign-speaking persons. This means that the dominant White population increasingly encounters

---

This chapter is a revised version of a paper presented to the Sociological Practice Association annual meeting in Atlanta, GA, August, 2003.

representatives of cultures other than its own, at work, at school, in community settings, and so on.

In contrast to most participants in multi-cultural societies, multi-cultural *individuals*, such as those included in our sample, constitute a truly unique population. These are people who are themselves representatives of two or more cultures. They originated in families in which the parents were from distinctly different races or cultures. By virtue of their heritage, they encountered multi-culturalism on a daily basis within the family. Unlike members of monocultural groups, they never faced the world as members of a single cultural group, but always as representatives of two or more groups. Many reported experiences in which they were even rejected by members of their own groups, which often considered them outsiders because they were not "Black enough," not "Polish enough," or not "Chinese enough," due to their mixed ethnic heritage. As a result, multi-cultural individuals are in the unique position of understanding what it means to be "between cultures," in ways which no one from a monocultural background can understand.

As noted previously, persons who are multi-cultural or multi-racial and are aware of this status are relatively rare. An ethnic group must have been in this country for a relatively long period before they have become acculturated and assimilated sufficiently to contract marriages across ethnic lines. Their children will hold the status of multi-cultural or multi-racial individuals. Hence, there will be few recent immigrants represented in this category, since the group has not been in the USA long enough to have multi-cultural adult offspring. Furthermore, this may be present for only a single generation, since the children of these multi-cultural individuals are very likely to accept their mixed heritage without question. Hence, we depend upon the few individuals from each generation of multi-cultural and multi-racial individuals who are sufficiently aware of the uniqueness of their heritage to provide us with a description of the way multi-culturalism and multi-racialism is experienced.

Now that we have heard the stories of the multi-cultural and multi-racial respondents, what can we learn from them? What can they tell us about the experiences they had? How can their experiences make it easier for the multi-cultural or multi-racial people of today – or the future? As indicated earlier, these individuals can serve as a sort of a "natural experiment," to illustrate the manner in which intercultural social exchange can operate successfully. Our sample of multi-cultural and multi-racial respondents who have lived their entire lives in intercultural settings can provide these guidelines.

As our analysis has shown, living in a society which assumes that everyone originates from a single racial or cultural group can be problematic for persons from multi-cultural backgrounds. As Chapter 4 indicated, respondents encountered numerous settings which made their lives difficult. Some of these problems originated within the family itself. Others had their origin in the wider social environment, both the local community and the broader society as a whole. In this chapter, we will revisit some of these difficulties the respondents raised, and attempt to suggest ways in which families, communities, and the larger society might be made more accommodating to the needs of multi-cultural families and individuals.

Several respondents mentioned special problems which they had encountered as a result of the manner in which multi-cultural or multi-racial issues had been handled by particular institutions or agencies. Chapter 6 focused on the impact of the local community in creating problems for multi-cultural individuals. Particular reference was often made to school policies. Chapter 7 paid particular attention to the ways in which families dealt with the problems their children encountered in the process of growing up as multi-cultural individuals; we also noted that some families were not very effective in this regard.

In this chapter, we will bring together these various issues which multi-cultural individuals and families confronted, and attempt to suggest some ways in which their experiences can be useful in developing multi-cultural-friendly programs and policies on a broader scale. The lack of attention to multi-cultural/multi-racial persons presents problems both for the individuals themselves and for the larger community. From the standpoint of these individuals themselves, one wonders how the issue of diversity and multi-culturalism relates to those who are already multi-cultural, by definition. From the standpoint of the larger community, these are persons who are quite familiar with diversity and its problems. Their experience could provide valuable insights to the nature of multi-culturalism for the rest of us to ponder, and perhaps use in developing programs for a diverse society.

As noted above, this chapter will focus primarily on the micro-level of analysis. That is, the focus will be on the individuals themselves, and the difficulties they faced growing up as multi-cultural individuals. We will discuss ways in which their socialization experience might have been improved had the environment in home, school, and community been more hospitable to their needs. In particular, we will attempt to provide advice to parents and families regarding ways they could improve family relations and help their multi-racial and multi-cultural children adapt to their environment more easily. By extension, we will also provide suggestions as to ways in which communities and the broader society could minimize the difficulties of multi-cultural socialization. A special section will focus on counselors, teachers, and other professionals who work with multi-cultural and multi-racial individuals and families. We will suggest ways in which their work with multi-cultural and multi-racial individuals and family could be more effective. Because societal and community issues have an impact upon the family as it attempts to help children cope with the wider world, we will begin our discussion with these broader "macro" issues.

Macro-issues – Societal Issues Which Multi-cultural Families Must Confront[1]

As we showed in Chapter 6, families are unavoidably impacted by community and societal factors. These are factors which are generally referred to as "institutional racism," which ". . .refers to the practices, procedures, and culture of social

---

[1] Appendix D contains a brief summary of issues families with diverse backgrounds may confront.

institutions that deprive racially identified groups from equal access, opportunities, and treatment" (Rockquemore and Laszloffy, 2005: 44). Because these attitudes and relationship patterns are deeply imbedded in the social institutions and structures of society, they are presumed to be appropriate and unchangeable. Consequently, they are generally unquestioned. However, they have the same impact as individual racist acts (Knowles and Prewitt, 1967). Indeed, they may be more destructive because these discriminatory actions hold the status of well-accepted traditions.

A major issue mentioned by several respondents focused on restrictions on their preferred identification patterns. This was particularly true of multi-racial persons, who were faced at every turn with requirements that they identify themselves in a single factor system. The US Census, questionnaires, a wide variety of forms, particularly in school, constantly required them to identify themselves. In nearly all instances, they were pressured to "pick one," an option which many of them deeply resented. For multi-racial individuals, the requirement that they "pick one" option was a constant demand that they choose one parent and one heritage over the other. Since these have long been accepted as an appropriate query on the census, on questionnaires, and on forms of various types, the requirements are assumed to be appropriate. They are also imbedded in the education institution, which also gives them legitimacy. For many multi-racial respondents, it was their first introduction to a school environment which many found harsh and inhospitable.

Not only were they forced to select a single category, but the categories often over-generalized the options. Thus, persons from Puerto Rico, Cuba, or Mexico were constantly forced into the "Hispanic" category. Japanese, Chinese, Koreans, Filipinos, and Vietnamese were categorized as "Asian." And "Black" included anyone who had any Black genetic background, including American-Blacks, Caribbean-Blacks, African-Blacks, even those who appeared dark skinned. Even Whites complained that the general category of "White" did not allow them to claim their ethnic heritage.

Multi-racial individuals were also faced with the realization that they had to select the option which the questioner expected. If they made what others considered the "wrong choice," the questioner simply answered the question for them, or altered what they considered to be an incorrect response. Even family members were often complicit in the forced identification process. The reader will recall that Leslie resented the fact that her Caucasian mother enrolled her in school as "Filipino," without giving her the opportunity to be involved in the decision.

Summary

Hence, American institutions, policies, and traditions impose a three-fold burden on multi-cultural and especially multi-racial individuals concerning their self-identification. First, they are required to select one aspect of their heritage over the others. Second, the options they are given are extremely general and often fail to take account of the diversity within each category. Third, the options provided are not truly options; if the individual makes an unexpected selection, the official requesting the information often feels justified in recoding the response into a category considered more appropriate. Hence, multi-cultural and multi-racial individuals are constantly reminded by various social processes and traditions, and by persons in authority, that they do not really know who they are!

To deal with these difficulties, action on two levels is necessary. First, on a societal or community level, the plight of multi-cultural and multi-racial individuals would be eased considerably if questionnaires, forms, and the census included the option of choosing multiple categories or included a category for "other" or "mixed." The census has already accommodated this to a degree, by allowing respondents to indicate two or more races in their responses (U.S Census, 2006). Other agencies, such as survey researchers and schools, should follow the Census Bureau's example. And, of course, the individual's selection should be honored, not recoded if others consider it unacceptable. However, this process of change is likely to take some time. Given the history of American management of multi-culturalism, it might even take several generations. Hence, our second suggestion is aimed at parents of multi-racial and multi-cultural children, as well as professionals who work with them. At a later point, we will suggest ways they can prepare children for the categorization experiences they are likely to encounter.

Meso-level Issues – the Local Community's Impact

As we indicated in Chapter 6, the community is also heavily involved in defining the status of multi-cultural and multi-racial individuals. The institutional requirements, such as forms and census questions, are not the only means by which people of mixed backgrounds are reminded that they are "different," or do not belong. As we pointed out in Chapter 3, Karen said "the community" told her and her siblings they were Asian, to the extent that she always felt out of place until she went to Hawaii, where most people were even more "mixed" than she was.

Again, school was a particularly difficult setting, with other students questioning respondents' mixed ethnic or racial heritage and the identity choices they made. Teresa, Peter, and Karen all recalled that children's comments were often "mean." Teachers and administrators rarely helped the situation, often allowing or even encouraging students' confrontations of each other on ethnic and racial issues, as Anita and Regina found.

As we have shown, it was not only the so-called dominant White community which reminded multi-racial members that they did not belong. The ethnic and racial communities themselves often made a point that "mixed" persons were not acceptable. Many respondents reported feeling that both ethnic groups, even members of their own extended family, consistently made a point that their mixed heritage made them unacceptable, as Anita's cousin told her to "hide" her Mexican heritage when she was around his Puerto Rican friends. Some ethnic communities actually took contradictory approaches: on some occasions they would insist that mixed individuals had an obligation to recognize their identification with the ethnic group, only to remind them at a later point that their mixed background meant they were not really entitled to full membership.

Ideally, we would suggest that communities be more sensitive in their treatment of multi-cultural and multi-racial people. However, simple exhortations of this type are likely to do little good. Instead, programs to develop greater sensitivity and respect for cultural and racial diversity might be appropriate. We will suggest some programs of this type in Chapter 9. However, this chapter will also suggest ways that families and counselors can make efforts to prepare multi-racial and multi-cultural children for the reactions they may receive.

For Parents and Families – How to Ease the Process of "Growing Up Mixed"

If there were only one piece of advice which could to be given to parents of mixed race or mixed ethnic children, it would have to be a reminder to talk about the issues. Nearly all respondents who were comfortable with their heritage and with their choice of a focus of ethnic identity came from families in which the racial and ethnic origins of their parents were discussed openly. In contrast, families in which this topic appeared to be taboo produced children who were very confused.

Whether the parents agreed about their ethnic heritage was less important than whether they provided information about the different groups. The information they wanted varied from general information about the customs of the groups to ways in which others might treat them because of their membership in a group. Some parents apparently believe, however, that the less said about such issues, the better. Particularly annoying were families which provided little information, but still expected their members to participate appropriately in various activities of their ethnic communities. Jeff, for example, complained that his Jewish father never taught him anything about Jewish tradition. On occasion, however, he would be taken to Jewish festivals and expected to participate in an appropriate manner; when he failed to do so, his father would criticize and ridicule him.

Karen was more interested in learning about who Asians were and how they would be received by the community because of being Asian. However, her father considered racial differences no more important than having "big ears," so he never discussed them; and her mother was apparently too sensitive to the discrimination she and her children faced as Asian-Americans to discuss these issues. However, as Karen pointed out, it is quite obvious that the majority of the American population does not concur with his views on racial differences. Inevitably, their children will learn of their unusual heritage from the comments they receive from teachers, schoolmates, and other community members (Rockquemore and Laszloffy, 2005: 51).

Neither Jeff nor Karen received much assistance from their families. Instead, they generally learned about their ethnic origins and traditions through making errors, as Jeff did, or from the community as a whole, as Karen did. Receiving information in this manner is usually a particularly painful process. Respondents whose families were secretive about their differences created many problems for their children, as evidenced by the fact that both Karen and Jeanette reported having serious social psychological problems as adults. Jeanette's experience was the most dramatic, as she spent most of her childhood and much of her adult life wondering who the Lebanese were and how they differed from the Irish. Hence, it is critical that parents in multi-racial and multi-cultural families provide their children with information about their heritage and answer any questions the children may have.

Other families provided much more assistance. Anita's family provided a great deal of information about both Puerto Rico and Mexico, even to the point of making visits to both places. Their children grew up with considerable awareness of the variant dimensions of their heritage and each felt free to identify with some aspect of it. Sarah recalled that her parents discussed their religious and political views at great length. Peggy even mentioned that the discussions of the religious differences in her family were extremely helpful to her in shaping her perspective on life.

What are some of the issues multi-racial and multi-cultural parents should be prepared to deal with? Many of them are issues which are faced by any family which has children who appear "different" from others in the community. Some are unique to multi-cultural and multi-racial children. Based on the experiences of our respondents, we will discuss both types of issues and suggest ways of dealing with them.

General Issues Shared with Single Racial and Cultural Groups

Obviously, the first issue which children will have to deal with in the community is the fact that they may "look different" from others in the community, and, as a result, are likely to find they, as well as their families, are not accepted by others in the community. While parents may wish to spare their children by not discussing these issues and hoping they will "just go away," the fact is that this is unlikely to happen. Children are very observant; hence other children will be quick to notice any differences they observe in their classmates or neighborhood. They may even be sensitized to these differences by comments they hear from their own parents and other children. Hoping these comments will never occur is futile. It is best for parents to discuss racial and cultural differences prior to having their children encounter them in the outside world. As Rockquemore and Laszloffy (2005: 52) point out, parents who are aware of the ways in which American social discrimination operates are better prepared to assist their children in dealing with the problems they may encounter.

What are some of the types of issues multi-cultural and multi-racial children may encounter? As Chapter 4 showed, many of these are issues which are shared with any ethnic group which is different from the majority of the local community in any way. Children generally want to be like their peers. Parents should become aware of any factors which the family exhibits which would place their children in a situation where they are unlike their peers.

Physical differences of any kind are clearly the most obvious difference which must be confronted. Black children in a predominantly White neighborhood, or the reverse; or Asian children in most American communities, both White and Black, are certain to generate questions and comments on the part of other children. While racial differences are clearly the most obvious and the most likely to generate questions, they are not the only source of difficulty. As indicated at several points, even subtle physical differences were often the focus of attention. Sam and Jeanette were questioned about their dark skin, typical of Mediterranean peoples, although both preferred to be identified with the dominant American majority.

In addition, parents should consider whether there are any cultural patterns which may place their children in an uncomfortable position relative to their peers. Does the family exhibit social class patterns which may differentiate the family from others in the community? Are there ethnic traditions not commonly seen in the region? For example, Muslim or Sikh children in a largely Christian community should clearly be provided with explanations of their religious traditions and restrictions which differentiate them from other families and children in their community, just as Jewish children had to be prepared to respond to questions about their religious tradition in previous generations. Even children whose version of the Christian faith varies from that of other Christian denominations in the community are likely to be questioned about their religious practices. Confronting these issues is particularly critical when the specific ethnic group is targeted by the community for some reason. American animosity toward Arabs is an example of a group which has been targeted for some time – Jeanette experienced animosity toward Arabs in the 1940s; this has only exacerbated with the increase in Arab immigrants since the 1965 laws, and especially the attack on the World Trade Center.

Does the family speak a foreign language at home which other children will ask about? Do parents – or the children themselves – speak with a distinctive-sounding accent which is unfamiliar in the community? Are there any school or neighborhood activities which the children are unable to participate in due to certain family religious or ethnic traditions or requirements? For example, Muslim children should clearly be prepared to answer questions about why they fast during Ramadan, or why the girls and women wear the *hijab*. Clearly, children should understand and be prepared to explain such traditions should the question arise.

This would also be true of any other customs or practices which make the children "stand out" from their peers. Different age or gender requirements which made the family seem different from other families in the community were particularly difficult for some of our respondents. Jeanette was distressed by what she viewed as the excessive demands on girls and women in her Lebanese family; both she and Robert felt the desire of children to excel in school met with little sympathy on the part of their parents.

With regard to some of these issues, parents might want to consider whether there are issues on which the family culture might allow for accommodations to allow their children to conform more closely to the surrounding community. In effect, they may want to decide which traditions are of extreme importance and must be followed, and which others are less critical and might be reduced. In effect, this was the approach of some of the multi-religious families in our sample. Hence, Sarah's parents brushed aside both families' assertions that Sarah be forced to practice a particular religious tradition, and Vickie's family made it possible for each child to find his or her own religious tradition, while remaining a "member in good standing" of the family. Similarly, some of the families in our sample could have decided that the gender restrictions or family responsibilities might have been eased somewhat to allow their children to participate more comfortably in school and community activities. At the least, families could provide their children with a more comprehensive explanation as to what the family or ethnic traditions are and why they exist.

Specifically Multi-racial and Multi-cultural Issues

The issues discussed above are similar to those confronted by everyone who originates from a cultural or racial group which differs from that of the surrounding community. They are not unique to multi-cultural or multi-racial individuals, who have additional problems as a result of their mixed backgrounds. What are these additional problems? As we have discussed at several points throughout this book, a major problem encountered by everyone with a mixed background is the need to understand the diversity of their environment.

As Jeanette asked, "Who are we? Who are all these people?" It is unlikely that she and her sisters came up with these questions on their own. Rather, it was brought to their attention by hearing the questions from others – other children at school, parents and teachers, neighbors, even by the adults in the family. Jeanette noted that the household and visitors included numerous aunts and uncles, who constantly made comments about each other's varying ethnic origins. Unfortunately, they did not explain these issues to the children, leaving them with unanswered questions, "Who are all these people?" And how do we fit together? As she said, "It was very confusing. . . ." How could they respond to questions from teachers and schoolmates when they themselves were confused about their heritage? Consequently, children from mixed backgrounds need to be prepared for the questions they will inevitably hear from others in the community. They must be told at an early age about the diverse racial origins or cultural traditions which are present in the family.

As we pointed out in Chapter 5, children from single racial or cultural origin receive a unified answer to the questions "Who am I?" and "Who are we?" Parents, siblings, extended family members, perhaps neighbors as well all provide the same answer. "We are Black" (or Polish, or Irish, or Muslim, etc.), and so are you!" By definition, mixed background children do not receive a unified response. They hear a different answer from everyone around them. Teresa learned that Mom was White and Dad was African. Vickie knew that Dad was Irish and Mom was Jewish, even though neither was close to their parental heritage. Jeanette learned, after years of struggling, that Dad was Irish; Mom and her aunts were Lebanese; her uncles came from a wide variety of ethnic origins.

However, this still leaves the key question unanswered? "Who are WE?" And "Who am I?" There is no name for our family, as a group, or for me, as an individual. Rockquemore and Laszloffy (2005: 61) make a critical point in their book of advice for parents of multi-racial children:

...unlike most single-race children, mixed-race children have no parent with whom they can directly identify with [sic] as a mixed-race person. In other words, unless one's parent is also mixed-race, the majority of mixed-race children are learning about race from one or more adults who have not directly experienced their social reality.

This can be said as well for all those generations of mixed religion and mixed nationality individuals who have gone before. It is also true of the children of immigrants who are being socialized in a different society from that of their parents. Most parents model their parenting behavior on the only experience they have observed: the approach of their own parents. However, multi-cultural or multi-racial children, except for those few whose parents are themselves multi-cultural or multi-racial, are being socialized by parents who are totally unaware of their children's reality. An analysis of the experiences of some of our respondents will illustrate this.

We have frequently discussed the situation of Jeanette, who recalled her childhood in more negative terms than most other respondents. She was being reared by her Lebanese mother in typical Lebanese family tradition, with the expectation that she would adhere to the patriarchal family patterns of Lebanese culture. Her mother most likely believed she was rearing her daughter in the same manner in which she and her sisters were reared. However, there were dramatic differences between the childhood experiences of Jeanette and her sisters and those of her mother. Jeanette had two sets of expectations and role models which her mother never encountered. The first set of expectations came from the schools she was required by law to attend; these settings impose requirements that children learn about American society and have the expectation that they study. Hence, Jeanette and her sisters, like all children of immigrants, were exposed to different cultural requirements from their mother. Furthermore, Jeanette's discomfort over her Lebanese family's demands was exacerbated by her observation of her Irish cousins' relative freedom. Similarly, their father was familiar with the cultural expectations of an Irish family, and could not sympathize with the Lebanese cultural patterns to which his daughters were being exposed.

The presence of family members who are of a different race and/or culture is a major component of being raised multi-cultural and multi-racial. Inherent in this process is the possibility, perhaps even the likelihood, that some of a child's own relatives will reject dimensions of that child's identity. Leslie noted that her White relatives made derogatory comments about her Filipino aunt, who had Asian features like her own. Evelyn was made clearly aware that her Korean and Chinese relatives each looked down on members of the opposite side of the family. Anita's Puerto Rican cousin warned her to forget her Mexican heritage when she was around his Puerto Rican friends.

As we have noted at several points, some respondents dealt with the identity issue by eventually defining themselves as a single ethnic entity. Hence, Derek and Adam concluded they were Black because they looked Black, or because most of their contacts were Black, or because most people thought of them as Black, or some combination of those factors. Some respondents selected among the options their parents' culture allowed, with several siblings choosing different options, as in the families of Vickie and Anita. Different children responded to these issues in different ways. Hence, Teresa took offense at being called a "zebra," while Derek thought it was just good-natured "joking around."

Identity problems were particularly difficult when there were major disputes within the family over cultural or identification issues. In these instances, children often felt they were forced to "pick sides." All of them were in a position of being socialized by parents whose experience growing up was completely different from their own. Their parents have never experienced their reality and can never totally understand it. Deanna was reared by a Korean mother and worked in a Korean business; however, she also spent considerable time in the Black culture of her father. Neither her Black father nor her Korean mother could understand what it was like to be exposed to these two dramatically different cultures as a small child. Karen experienced being both Korean and White; neither of her parents could sympathize with what it meant to be exposed to both cultures and have interactions with relatives who were from a different race and culture. Yvonne feared she was going to hell if she went to church with her Protestant father. Sam's parents clearly disagreed over the relative value of his mother's Irish culture as opposed to his father's Italian heritage. And Evelyn's family was fraught with conflict over the relative value of Korean and Chinese culture.

In some cases, the conflict was so severe as to create a total family split. As a Korean-American child, Karen and her siblings had a Caucasian grandmother who rejected her part-Asian grandchildren. And Jeff's Jewish grandfather was never told that his son had married a gentile woman. Still many respondents took pride in their "mixed" racial heritage and wanted to be identified in that manner. To do otherwise was to reject a part of themselves, an issue which their single-race or single-culture parents never had to confront.

Such rejection by relatives has been reported in other studies of multi-racial and multi-cultural children as well (Rockquemore and Laszloffy, 2005: 144). It is difficult for single-culture or single-race parents to comprehend the impact that these experiences are likely to have on their mixed race and mixed culture children. Since they share the culture and/or race of the rejected relative, these experiences are likely to cause the children themselves to feel rejected. Indeed, experiences of rejection are likely to be shared by all children who live in multi-cultural or multi-racial settings. In short, people who are of mixed origins must cope with the question of who they are in a manner which is different from that of their parents.

Meso- and Macro-level Issues – Moving into the Larger Community

As we have indicated at several points, special problems exist if there are clearly observable differences between the two sides. As described in Chapters 2 and 6, racial differences are characteristics which cannot be hidden and are easily observed by others. In such cases, problems are exacerbated because they extend into the community as a whole. Hence, children are more likely to hear comments or be questioned or confronted by others, a complaint mentioned by nearly all the mixed race respondents. As Rockquemore and Laszloffy (2005: 52) indicate, parents of mixed race children must "take a proactive role" in sensitizing their children to the role of race in American society and preparing them to deal with it. The same is certainly true of more subtle physical differences, such as Jeanette's "Lebanese" skin. It may also be true of some cultural differences, like wearing the Muslim "hijab."

If children do not have information about the various components of their background, they will experience the problems Karen was concerned with, that is, that the *community* defined who they were, not their parents. Children can be "mean," as several respondents indicated, and teachers and administrators often do not help. Indeed, at times they were part of the problem. It was, after all, a principal of a Polish-speaking Catholic school who rejected the Polish-born Regina's application for admission.

Parents should also prepare their children for possible confrontations with members of their own racial or ethnic groups. As we have shown at several points, many ethnic and racial groups can be duplicitous about their approach to mixed background persons. On the one hand, some Blacks insist that "anything mixed with Black is Black," or "You have to be Christian because religion follows the father." However, these demands may also be followed by contradictory comments: "You're not really Black – you're part White," or "If you were really [Greek/Polish/Italian/etc.], you would speak the language." Respondents' experiences showed that these confrontations occurred in Black–White, Asian–Asian, Black–Asian, White–White, and interreligion combinations. Children should not have to be surprised by such attacks, but should be warned they may occur.

If there was one issue which many respondents considered particularly important, it focused on the issue of self-identification on forms and questionnaires. Most multi-racial and multi-cultural individuals insisted on this right. The requirement that they "choose one" of a group of predetermined options was particularly abhorrent. Some also objected to the over-generalized character of the categories, such as the use of "Hispanic" to apply to the broad range of Spanish-speaking communities. Most wanted a "mixed" alternative, or the option of checking two or more alternatives. Having teachers or other officials correct them or alter their responses was equally offensive. Mixed background people feel this should be their decision, not someone else's. Parents of multi-racial and multi-cultural children need to prepare them for the possibility that they may encounter such requests, and should discuss with them how they might respond to them. Furthermore, children should be assured that their parents will help them confront the issue if teachers or administrators do not understand.

Dealing with Issues Which Confront Multi-cultural and Multi-racial Children

In the previous sections, we have listed a number of issues which mixed background children face; we have also indicated that parents should be proactive in helping their children deal with these issues. How should families deal with these issues? In such situations, parents should clearly take the advice of Rockquemore and Laszloffy (2005) that they become "proactive" in helping their children deal with their mixed background.

This "proactive" stance involves a variety of dimensions. First, of course, it means parents should provide their children with knowledge to understand their parents' respective racial and cultural traditions, and how they share in both traditions. Second, it means they should be provided with a frank and honest analysis of the manner in which American society and its various components deal with people who are "different." Coming from loving parents, these lessons can be provided in a loving and supportive manner. Children should not be left to learn these difficult lessons from strangers, who may very well be cruel and inconsiderate in their approach. Finally, children should be able to count upon their parents to come to their assistance in dealing with any problems they may encounter as a result of their racial, cultural, or mixed heritage background. It should be obvious that parents of mixed background children should be prepared to become acquainted with their children's teachers, and to visit their children's schools on a fairly regular basis!

How should these discussions occur? We don't want parents to start a problem where none exists, to frighten their own children, or to cause them to engender racial or ethnic discrimination of their own. We do want them to be prepared for the prejudice and discrimination they encounter. Rockquemore and Laszloffy urge parents to "...take a proactive role" in discussing the nature of racial discrimination and prejudice (2005: 52). This includes pointing out to their children the ways in which social institutions as well as individuals may engage in discriminatory or unfair actions and prepare them for incidents which may occur.

Parents might, for example, begin by focusing on some issues which are known to be present and likely to be problematic. Inevitably, biracial children will be asked to list their identity on a school form, usually early in the school experience. Parents would do well to discuss this issue with their children *before* the incident arises. They might take the opportunity to discuss what the child perceives to be his or her ethnic identity. How does the child view him or herself? Is the child aware that mom and dad are different? How would the child want to be viewed? Like our respondents, most children are likely to choose to be identified with both parents. Parents can discuss with their children ways they can ensure that this desire is accommodated by the school or other agency. Parents should also assure their children that they will assist them in achieving whatever resolution of this issue the children choose. Had Leslie's mother held such a discussion with her daughter prior to enrolling her in school, Leslie would not have felt her mother and the school had conspired to deprive her of a choice in her self-identification.

Similarly, "Who are you?" is a question which children – and adults – constantly ask each other. They also comment on other members of the family. As several respondents reported, other children would ask questions such as, "How come your mother's White?" Or "What's this Black man doing with this White lady?" It should be obvious to multi-racial parents that their children will be asked such questions. When parents openly discuss the racial differences within the family, they place the issue in the context of a family which is bound together by love and respect. This will prepare their children to respond to these questions honestly and comfortably: "My Mom and Dad are different [races/religions/nationalities/etc.]. But they got married because they loved each other and they love me." If children have been prepared for questions about their heritage and have been assured that their parents do not find their mixed background odd, they will be less likely to be distressed at the questions.

Neither Jeanette nor Sam had the advantage of having a family which discussed these issues openly. Both might have profited from discussions which enabled them to see the contributions of the cultures from which both their parents originated. Unfortunately, many ethnic communities consider such discussions inappropriate or a violation of the authority of the family or the ethnic group. The reader will recall from Chapter 4 that Jeanette's mother never discussed who the Lebanese were, and told her daughter to "Just say you're Irish." Similarly, Evelyn reported the high degree of conflict that occurred in her family; in particular, the children were constantly reminded that parents held the authority, and children were expected to conform. There should be "...no arguing back at your parents." Hence, many ethnic communities consider it a violation of the culture for children to question community or family requirements. However, these demands place children at a disadvantage in their attempts to negotiate the differences between ethnic and American culture. In Chapter 9, we will discuss some programs which might be introduced into schools and communities to provide information to parents and teachers on how to deal with these kinds of issues.

Raising children in this kind of setting requires greater sensitivity on the part of the parents if they are to help their children cope. Parents need to be able to place themselves in the shoes of their children to understand what they are experiencing. This is what sociologists call "taking the role of the other" (Mead, 1934). Parents of mixed background children must be alert to the impact that exposure to their varying racial and cultural backgrounds may have on their children. They have to attempt to understand the confusion this may engender, and try to assist their children in dealing with the problems. Simply announcing that they are the parents and insisting their children follow their orders will be likely to create even greater confusion and will not help their children cope.

If children are to deal with these problems effectively, parents need to help. As most respondents indicated, the problems would be eased if family members discussed the issues more openly. The religious disputes within Sarah's extended family would have engendered similar difficulty had her parents not been united in their resolve not to allow her religious upbringing to become an issue. Since Sarah's family discussed issues "at length," she grew up with a clear understanding of the religious differences in the family, together with an understanding of her parents' resolution of the problems. In all such disputes, parents should be prepared to explain the family traditions in a manner which children can understand and which they can perceive in a positive way. This includes recognizing that there are racial and cultural differences within the family. While parents, like Karen's father, may not consider these differences important, others in the community are likely to consider them very important and are likely to mention them to the children. If parents have not discussed them, children will be confused.

Hence, parents should make a determined effort to discuss the family racial and cultural backgrounds with their children, and to prepare them for the reality that some outsiders, as well as some persons within the family, may have negative views of one race or culture or another. They should make it clear that all races and cultures have value, and that they should not allow the comments of others to affect them. Respondents, such as Vickie, Anita, and Sarah, whose parents generally made the effort to discuss the varying cultures and races present in the family, were much more comfortable with their mixed backgrounds.

There are several dimensions which these discussions should take. First, the varying cultural patterns in the family can be recognized without indicating that one race or culture is "better" than the other. Children will be exposed to such critical evaluations of their background by the outside world. Within the family, they should be assured that all aspects of their heritage are valuable: each individual race or culture is valued and respected, and the mixture itself is valued and respected as well. Children should be encouraged to appreciate their multiple heritages, even if they choose to view themselves as "belonging" to one group more than the other. After all, there must be some reason why parents have chosen to marry a person from another race or culture; they saw something of value in each other. These desirable qualities are derived from their respective races and cultures, and this is evidence of the valuable traditions they have inherited.

Children should definitely be prepared for the fact that others outside the family may not share the respect the family has for their multiple identities, either singly or in combination. They should be aware that others in the community, and particularly in the school, may make derogatory remarks. They should be prepared for the nature of these remarks. They should be warned that the remarks may focus primarily on one group; children whose racial or cultural background includes a group specifically targeted for discrimination, such as Blacks, Asians, Native Americans, or Arabs, should definitely be prepared for the prospect of comments and actions they may encounter. They should also be prepared for negative comments they may receive, both from the community as a whole and from members of the individual groups as well, concerning the mixture of races or cultures. While parents may want to protect their children from these attitudes and may wish they were not there, they must recognize that they do, in fact, exist. Learning about them in the loving center of the family is preferable to hearing them from rude, inconsiderate outsiders. Children should receive assurance from family members that their worth does not depend on the degree to which outsiders accept them.

It is clearly preferable if parents can enlist other relatives in the process of sensitizing their mixed background children to their unique heritage. As we indicated earlier, children were more negatively affected if their own relatives made derogatory comments about one aspect or another of their heritage. Unfortunately, many family members will not be cooperative with such plans, and may even add their own negative comments. Parents should be prepared to deal with these issues as well, without being rude or insulting. For example, Karen's father could have told her:

Your grandmother doesn't like Asian people. So she didn't want me to marry your Mom.
But she didn't bother to get to know your Mom very well. Isn't she a wonderful example
of a great Mom? So your grandmother is wrong about your Mom and about Asian people.
There are lots of people who are like that. But we know better. We know Asian people are
wonderful – like you and your Mom and your brothers and sisters!

In effect, parents need to know that some people, even their own relatives, may be prejudiced. But that does not make those views correct. They must make these views clear to their children in order to prepare them for what they will unquestionably encounter in the outside world.

What should children do if people make fun of their mixed background? Grace felt that being firm about who she was helped her to avoid being upset when negative comments came her way. Some also indicated that keeping a sense of humor about one's mixed background was helpful. Hence, Grace also joked about being "Heinz 57 varieties." And Derek chose to perceive the negative comments about "zebras" or "yellow" as good-natured kidding or a "term of endearment," rather than taking them seriously. Parents can assist in this regard as well, helping children to avoid taking negative comments to heart.

There was one final issue which stood out as extremely important in the interviews of several respondents. That was a strong attraction to multi-culturalism or multi-racialism on the part of several of them and a yearning to be around other people of mixed backgrounds. This is a critical aspect of their children's lives which single-culture or single-race parents can never understand. Single-culture or single-race individuals can be quite comfortable in a community made up entirely of persons who share their own background; indeed many prefer it. This is why people seek to live in ethic neighborhoods, focus their lives around their church, synagogue, or mosque, or send their children to ethnic schools. Many parents recall these congenial childhood experiences and want them for their own children.

Mixed background children have different needs, however. They are likely to have negative encounters in single-race or single-culture settings (Rockquemore and Laszloffy, 2005: Chapter 5). A few, such as Adam and Peter, may find them satisfying. Hence, Peter found his place in the Native American reservation of his father, and largely ignored his mother's Caucasian background. Adam, who never knew his Caucasian father, was raised in the African-American community of his mother and did not think of himself as White at all. And Robert hardly viewed himself as mixed because the community in which he lived only recognized racial differences as important.

Whatever the source of the diversity, most mixed background children need the presence of others like themselves. Hence, Deanna had a close friend who was Asian and Black, like herself. Anita reported that she had "...dated every color under the sun." Karen felt comfortable for the first time on a trip to Hawaii, where most people were more "mixed" than she was. It was made clear to Regina that she was not welcome in the Polish school her father chose for her; she found the public school more hospitable. Peggy was more comfortable with classmates who were from diverse ethnic origins. And Derek reported that he had fewer negative experiences in the diverse Washington, DC, area. Several respondents had contracted multi-cultural or multi-racial marriages. Jeff considered himself Jewish, but had married a Christian woman. Derek was Black and Caucasian, but had married an Asian woman. Somehow, many of them recognized that they had more in common with persons who shared their mixed cultural or racial experience. This pattern of preference for other mixed background people has also been noted in other studies (Williams, 1992: 288–295).

Hence, parents should allow their children to interact with others who share their multi-cultural or multi-racial heritage. Indeed, they should make deliberate efforts to provide their children with such social contacts, which validate the appropriateness of the mixed background experience. Such settings might even be cultivated on a community-wide basis in order to bring together persons from different backgrounds and attempt to develop a greater sense of community among them. In Chapter 9, we will discuss some sample forms which such programs might assume.

Multi-cultural Issues for Professionals[2]

One impact of the increased level of multi-culturalism in America is the increased number of institutions which have introduced programs to recognize or heighten awareness and appreciation of the racial or cultural groups represented in their midst. Schools, for example, have been encouraged to develop programs to recognize the culturally diverse nature of their student bodies (Alba and Nee, 2003; Roberts et al., 1994; Locke, 1992). Counselors and other professionals are encouraged to consider the racial or cultural backgrounds of their clients in order to perform their roles effectively (Coleman, 2001: 117–119; Rebach and Bruhn, 2001; Ponterotto et al., 1995).

Most works on multi-culturalism perform admirably well in the task they have set for themselves, namely, to provide teachers and counselors with information on the myriad of racial and cultural groups which make up American society. As we discussed in Chapter 1, most of these works are based on the assumption that the only special information which teachers or counselors need is information about individuals who are members of one of the identifiable racial or cultural groups in society. In short, it is generally presumed that if people cannot be identified as African-American or Hispanic or Asian, then they can be approached as though they are among the majority of persons who follow the generalized "American" culture.

As we have been discussing throughout this book, this approach totally fails mixed background individuals. Some authors recognize the diversity within the major subgroups, and that African-American, European-American, Hispanic, Asian, and South Asian are all categories which subsume within them an enormous variety of cultural differences; these works provide special information about cultural characteristics and counseling patterns for each of the varying categories

---

[2] Appendix E contains a summary of advice for professionals dealing with persons from diverse backgrounds.

(McGoldrick et al., 2005a). Again, however, these works generally assume that an individual or family coming for counseling can be categorized into one of the groups delineated.

One of the most comprehensive works on multi-cultural family therapy provides a summary of five guidelines which should be followed in order to work with families of divergent backgrounds. While these guidelines are specifically designed for family counselors, they could easily be adapted to the needs of professionals in other fields which work with either individuals or groups. Health care providers, for example, are often aware of the need to consider the cultural and racial backgrounds of their patients in order to provide effective health care. They too could profit from the use of these guidelines, as well as other suggestions we will make in this chapter.

Listed are the following assumptions on the part of counselors: a family's racial, cultural, and economic characteristics impact upon their behavior; appreciation of one's background plays a positive role in mental health; negative attitudes toward one's background is probably due to pressures to suppress it; full understanding of another's culture is impossible, but counselors should attempt to understand their own culture in order to communicate better with their clients; most clients have probably adopted the values of their own groups, whether dominant or marginal (McGoldrick et al., 2005b: 36–37).

While these are all valuable assumptions, they still miss the major issue related to multi-racial and multi-cultural people, who fall between the cracks of racial and cultural background and identity. Extremely rare is the author who provides information about counseling or assessment with mixed background individuals. One chapter of a work on multi-cultural counseling treats this issue to some degree, focusing specifically on eradicating the myths regarding the identity development of biracial individuals (Kerwin and Ponterotto, 1995).

However, a broad perspective on the issue remains to be written. In this section, we will not attempt to duplicate the advice provided in these earlier works on counseling with diverse cultures, nor will we presume to provide a thorough treatment of the problem of working with mixed background individuals. We will, however, make some specific suggestions which apply to the special population of people from ethnically or racially mixed backgrounds. These will be based largely on the experiences reported by our respondents.

Guidelines for Professionals Regarding Mixed Background People and Families

Guidelines for professionals must begin with the process of assessment. Whenever a new patient enters a doctor's office, a new student enters a school setting, or a new client enters the office of a counselor, the first task of the professional is to assess the status and difficulties of the client. While handbooks on multi-racial or multi-cultural counseling provide advice on the process of working with persons whose culture or race is different from that of the professional, they provide little assistance in the process of assessment.

This assessment process begins with the initial encounter between client and professional. If professionals are to be culturally sensitive, this encounter must include a determination as to which racial or cultural group the client represents. As we have indicated throughout this work, this is not an easy process. The USA includes a wide variety of racial and cultural groups. A simple process of distinguishing among the major groups of "White," "African-American," "Asian," or "Spanish-surnamed" is by no means sufficient. The early assessment process must distinguish among the many variations of these major categories.

Even groups which are assumed to represent a single culture may not be so unified. African-Americans include a wide variety of cultures based on social class, urban or rural origin, long-term residence in the USA versus recent immigration from Africa or the Caribbean islands, and so on. "Hispanic" also includes a wide variety of cultures from Mexico, Central America, Spain, and Puerto Rico, to mention a few. The same can be said about the wide variety of nations from which East Asian and South Asian immigrants originate. Even Whites, or "European-Americans," include a broad spectrum of nations which vary greatly in history, language, and culture. And all of these cultures provide quite different guideposts for family and individual behavior which can impact significantly on the manner in which social attitudes and behavior are patterned, as well as the ways in which professional advice is sought and working relationships are established. Major professional manuals now recognize the necessity of making these distinctions (McGoldrick et al., 2005a; Rebach and Bruhn, 2001; Ponterotto et al., 1995). Hence, professionals should resist the tendency to over-generalize about groups. They should resist the temptation to assume that all Blacks or Hispanics have had the same experiences or accept the same cultural patterns.

Furthermore, professionals cannot assume that the recognized ethnic groups are the only ones that play a role in determining individual behavior, attitudes, or getting assistance from professionals. As most manuals will suggest, these differences may be derived from a wide variety of dimensions, including race, religion, national origin, and social class. Certainly, professionals should be aware of such distinctions. However, they should also be aware that these patterns may persist for a much longer time than previously assumed. As we discussed in Chapters 1 and 2, descendants from British, Polish, Italian, or Irish heritages often continue to follow aspects of their ancestral cultures. Remnants of these cultures may continue to affect the manner in which their adherents deal with family, education, medical care, or other aspects of life many generations after their ancestors immigrated to the USA.

Indeed, the individuals themselves may think of themselves as "just American" and not even be aware they continue to follow these ethnic traditions. Professionals who make assumptions that these families and individuals are "just White" or "European-Americans" may make serious errors about their clients' attitudes, values, and behavioral assumptions. Most Whites obviously enjoy the status which accrues to being members of the White race. However, this generalization provides little information about the historical and cultural patterns which they have inherited from the diverse nations, religions, and languages which make up the European-American population.

All of these cautions about assessing cultural patterns apply to all clients, whatever their racial or cultural background, and regardless of whether they have a unitary or a mixed background. Special cautions apply, however, to multi-cultural and multi-racial individuals and families. As our respondents illustrated, the same family may include two or more cultural patterns. The presence of these varying patterns is not likely to be obvious at the outset. Professionals will need to be very observant in order to discern these differences. For example, a father brings his child for medical care in an emergency room or seeks counseling in a psychological clinic. Their dark skin strongly suggests they are Black. They may even state their race as "Black" on forms provided to them. However, prematurely making this assumption can cause professionals to miss important information.

Perhaps the child is Deanna, our respondent whose mother was Korean and who also lived in Korea the first five years of her life. Hence, she is biologically and culturally part Korean. Her first language was Korean. Her earliest years were spent imbedded in her mother's Korean culture. Professionals who make a premature assumption that Deanna is African-American may waste valuable time pursuing dead-end alternatives. For example, a physician who attempts to treat her might miss diagnosing a genetically based illness which is common in Asian people but little known among American Blacks. Or a family counselor may fail to recognize the existence of important family traditions which have been passed down from her Korean mother.

If an individual's parents were of different races or cultures, professionals should attempt to determine which group the individual identifies with and which culture s/he follows. The temptation is to assume the most obvious characteristic, such as racial appearance or family surname, determines the identity and culture of the family and its members. As so many of our respondents illustrated, these external characteristics are not the only cultural and identification sources for multi-cultural and multi-racial people. Indeed, some persons may deliberately identify with more than one. Mixed race or culture individuals may be deeply offended if others refuse to recognize the various aspects of their identity. Furthermore, professionals who fail to recognize clients' or patients' hidden cultures may miss important cultural patterns they observe.

Since mothers do much of the child-rearing in the family, persons of mixed cultural backgrounds may actually be more influenced by the mother's culture. This may be true even if they identify with the father's culture, and there is reason to do so because of the father's surname. Hence, major assumptions about the individual's life patterns based on the surname can be inaccurate. An obvious example was Deanna, who was more associated with her mother's Korean culture than her father's African-American culture. Her family also illustrates the fact that various members of the same family often follow different cultural patterns; Deanna's brother felt closer to his father's African-American heritage, a pattern which was also seen in the families of Vickie, Anita, and several others.

While the cultural origins of the biological mother and father represent the most obvious sources of cultural identities, individual identities may also arise from other, less obvious aspects of life, such as the presence of stepparents, foster parents, or adoptive parents, or the individual him/herself having lived for some time in another country or culture. Regina's early life in Brazil made her more Brazilian in culture than her Polish surname and parents would suggest. And Brian, whose parents were both Irish, who identified as Irish, and appeared to follow the family traditions and values of his parents, had a German stepmother for several years. She had a considerable impact on the family by imposing a German sense of structure on her unruly Irish stepsons. He may well have become accustomed to some of these more authoritarian family patterns. If Brian were to marry and raise children of his own, he might impose some of these patterns on his own family. A family counselor who attempted to work with Brian's family might assume they were Irish, based on his surname and reports of his Irish parentage. However, this assumption would miss the cultural tradition of structure imposed by the introduction of a German stepmother.

Cultural patterns affect a wide variety of aspects of life. Aside from obvious characteristics, such as race or religion, cultural differences affect such subtle dimensions of life as beliefs of about child-rearing, attitudes about family visiting or community participation, and the individual's tendency to express or repress emotions. All of these have a considerable impact on both the family's internal social patterns as well as the manner in which they would approach professional intervention into family matters. These issues are the matter on which counseling manuals focus their attention (McGoldrick et al., 2005a; Rebach and Bruhn, 2001; Ponterotto et al., 1995). Professionals who fail to discern, at an early point, which culture a family and its several members follow, do so at the risk of failing in their goal to assist their clients.

As noted at several points, some persons from multi-cultural or multi-racial backgrounds specifically reject the option of selecting a single identity. They take pride in being of mixed heritage. Some are so committed to their mixed heritage that they are determined to continue this tradition into future generations, preferring others with a mixed heritage for their social contacts, and even as marriage partners. Insisting that clients with this type of background must accept some aspect of their rich heritage as their "real" identity represents a supreme personal insult. Professionals who take this approach are likely to doom any efforts they might make with these clients.

These cautions suggest that the presence of multi-racial and multi-cultural families imposes extremely complicated requirements on the work of professionals. What they remind us is that professionals cannot assume the race or the culture of their patients and clients. This issue becomes a matter for investigation in the early stages of professional work. Careful inquiry is necessary to determine the racial and cultural heritage, not only of the patient or client, but also of his or her parents and grandparents, as well as other relevant family members. Stepparents are an example, but so are other extended family members, such as grandparents, who may have played an important role in their upbringing. As we have indicated, Americans are increasingly adopting children from other nations. They also bring in the heritage of other races and cultures which must be considered by professionals who work with them and attempt to understand their illnesses and social psychological problems.

When dealing with families which include varying cultures and races, professionals need to be aware that persons from different cultural backgrounds in the same family may have different role expectations. Hence, the family problems of an Asian husband and a Caucasian wife may be derived in large part from the fact that each parent has different expectations about husband–wife roles and the proper demeanor of parents and children. Expectations of the role of in-laws in their children's lives are likely to be different. Their children may receive conflicting role definitions from each parent. The counselor who attempts to work with such families must discern the important cultural dimensions of family expectations. This may seem an enormous expenditure of time; however, it is absolutely critical to an effective working relationship.

More than this, the family's multi-cultural and multi-racial dimensions may be a matter not just for assessment but for counseling itself. Many multi-cultural or multi-racial families, or their members, may not be aware of the nature of their cultural orientation. As our respondents illustrated, some families may not even be aware what their family culture is or what expectations it imposes. Jeanette's parents deliberately kept their children in the dark regarding the cultural dimensions of their family. Members may not even know whether more than one tradition exists in the family. They may need help in determining what these cultural traditions are.

Clients in counseling may also need help in determining how their problems may relate to their multi-culturalism. Karen was keenly aware that her community's perspective on the Asian race played a major role in the manner in which she and her siblings, even her Caucasian stepbrother, defined who they were. Her father, however, would probably require considerable persuasion to understand that everyone did not share his view that racial differences were unimportant and that his ignorance of this fact had greatly impacted upon his children's welfare.

Special cautions pertain to professionals who work with groups. This would include teachers with their students and counselors who conduct group work. They will need to exercise particular caution in assigning racial or ethnic identity to members of these groups. As we have shown at several points, the racial or cultural identity of any single individual may not be obvious. Many may have multiple identities and may vigorously insist on their right to this diversity. Professionals should check the backgrounds of their students/clients/group participants to determine whether they might have more than one ethnic or racial origin. Again, this may be difficult, but it is imperative to successful work with multi-racial and multi-cultural clients. Most important, professionals must always respect the views of their clients regarding their views of themselves. It is the utmost arrogance of professionals to attempt to impose their own judgments in place of the clients' own preferences. This was the one tactic which the majority of multi-racial and multi-cultural people found most objectionable.

Summary

In this chapter, we have focused on the micro-level of analysis: the difficulties which multi-racial and multi-cultural individuals faced in growing up. We attempted to suggest ways in which this process could be made less difficult. These suggestions were aimed at society as a whole, at the families of multi-racial and multi-cultural individuals, and at professionals who provide services to families and individuals. While most of our suggestions have been directed at family and individual counselors, they are equally appropriate for health care professionals, educators, or any other professionals who deal with persons from diverse races, cultures, or mixed backgrounds.

At the societal level, we focused upon the three-fold burden which American society places on persons of mixed backgrounds, particularly multi-racial individuals. First, they are often forced to choose a single identity on various forms and questionnaires. Second, most options are extremely general and do not allow people to select from among numerous subcategories, with which they actually identify. Third, these are not really free options, because the questioner frequently feels free simply to change a response if it is considered inappropriate. In effect, these requirements constitute what is known as "institutional racism," because they are so imbedded in our social institutions that they are presumed to be acceptable. In the long run, society should alter these procedures, as the USA has already begun to do. Until this change occurs, it is critical that families prepare their children to confront these situations.

At the community or meso-level, communities and institutions, particularly schools, need to alter their programs in ways which are sensitive to the needs of persons from multi-racial and multi-cultural backgrounds. Particularly offensive to some mixed background people is discrimination on the part of other minority groups, many of which attempt to pressure persons of mixed backgrounds to identify with the group they represent. While it is fruitless to urge that people simply "act nicer," it is incumbent upon officials, especially school teachers and administrators, to establish procedures which discourage such action in public settings.

Our major focus has been to suggest ways in which multi-cultural and multi-racial families can assist their children in dealing with the problems they are likely to face. Most important is the recommendation that they openly discuss the cultural and racial differences within the family. Inevitably, they will learn about these differences from the community. Children are generally more comfortable if they receive this information from the family first.

The most important characteristics for families to discuss with their children were those which differentiated them from the local community. Racial differences are obvious, but some physical differences can be very subtle, such as variations in skin color. Children should also be aware of any cultural differences, such as language or religious practices, which others may observe, and should be prepared for possible questions or comments they might engender. This is particularly important for mixed background children, since they must understand the diverse origins of the family, not only a single ethnic or racial background. Families may also want to consider whether they might distinguish among their traditions, delineating those which are critical to maintain, and others which might be reduced to allow their children to adapt more easily to their mixed heritage or to the community as a whole.

Mixed background children have a particular problem related to defining their own identity. This involves not only the question of "Who am I?" as an individual, but also the issue of "Who are we?" as a family group. There is no easily understood name for a mixed heritage family. Some children resolved the issue by choosing one aspect of their parents' identity possibilities; others chose a mixed identity option. They need assistance from their families in resolving this issue.

To complicate matters, multi-racial and multi-cultural individuals are in a unique position, in that most cannot identify racially or culturally with either parent. Neither do their parents understand the problems of their multi-cultural or multi-racial children; most probably grew up in a single-race or single-culture setting. They cannot understand the many difficulties of a mixed background family, such as the possibility that some relatives may reject individuals or culture of the other side.

Identity problems are particularly difficult when outsiders injected their views. These outsiders can include the community as a whole, the various ethnic groups with which the family is associated, even members of the family itself. All of these groups consider it their place to inform the child who he or she is, and often these messages are conveyed in particularly nasty ways. Children are most comfortable when their parents help them understand and deal with these issues. Thus, an important role for parents is providing this information before their children hear it from outsiders, including members of the extended family or the broader ethnic group.

Experts have suggested that parents should "...take a proactive role" in discussing discrimination and prejudice their children are likely to experience (Rockquemore and Laszloffy, 2005: 52). This involves several dimensions: providing information about the family's various cultures, explaining the nature of racial and ethnic prejudice and discrimination, and assuring their children they will be available to assist them when they encounter problems. This is particularly important in the school setting. Parents need not be confrontational in their conversations with their children, but should focus on the positive aspects of each culture which initially brought their parents together. Parents need to make an effort to view these issues from their children's perspective, what sociologists call "taking the role of the other." This may not be easy, since the parents themselves are probably not multi-racial or multi-cultural.

In particular, parents should make a deliberate effort to express value for all aspects of the family's culture, and to encourage children not to demean one aspect or the other, even if they come to choose a single identification. They should also help their children understand that their self-worth, as well as the worth of the family, is not dependent upon the opinions of others. Viewing negative comments in a joking manner helped several respondents to cope with these issues.

Many mixed background individuals prefer to identify with their mixed heritage than with either individual dimension. They may also feel more comfortable associating with other persons who are also of multi-racial or multi-cultural backgrounds. Their parents, not being multi-cultural themselves, may not understand this sentiment. However, they should attempt to understand and accommodate this desire on the part of their children.

We have also attempted to provide advice to professionals who attempt to work with mixed background individuals and families. Many aspects of advice to parents could apply to them as well. Recent works have provided good advice to professionals about working with persons from different racial or cultural backgrounds. However, some have focused their attention on the major racial and cultural groups; many fail to recognize the diversity which exists within these groups. More critically, they have not generally focused their attention on the individuals who themselves have mixed origins.

The assessment process is particularly important for professionals working with mixed background individuals. The first task in dealing with such clients or patients is to determine which racial or cultural groups constitute their background. This should be followed by an attempt to determine which groups these individuals identify with, and which culture they follow. To complicate matters, these may not be the same. Hence, a considerable amount of time in the early phase of consultation will be expended in this process. While it may appear to be a waste of time, it is preferable to spending time and effort based on an invalid assumption about personal culture and identification. Discerning such underlying family characteristics is also critical for medical professionals; failure to uncover the existence of such family patterns may cause them to miss relationships which suggest the possibility of genetically based characteristics or illnesses.

Dimensions of racial and cultural backgrounds are not simply a matter for assessment, however. Some clients may seek counseling to deal with problems that stem from their mixed heritage, and a major component of counseling may focus on problems they have encountered as a result of their background. The counselor's task will be to assist these clients in defining who they are and how they fit into their families or communities.

Finally, we suggested special care must be taken in working with groups, whether these are counseling settings, schools, or communities. It is tempting to assume that members of these groups are members of and identify with the groups which appear most obvious. Again, professionals must take pains to determine the real identity preferences and cultural patterns of the groups. They cannot assume that any single individual views him/herself as others assume. In the next chapter, we will move directly into the groups and community issue, providing some examples of programs designed to assist communities and schools that deal with a diversity of races and cultures.

Chapter 9
Incorporating Diversity at the Community Level – Example 1: Developing a School Program Which Encourages and Supports Racial and Ethnic Diversity

Obviously, if racially and culturally diverse children are to be provided with a valuable educational experience that prepares them for a useful future and enriches their lives, it is important that they be provided with a school environment in which they are able to learn in safety and comfort. Many schools in the past have not provided such a setting. This section will describe and evaluate a program which proposes to enhance the school learning environment, particularly with reference to diversity-related issues. We will first describe the program itself; this will be followed by an analysis of teacher and student evaluations concerning its success.

About the "Diversity Program"

The program on which we focus our attention follows the pattern of the "Senior Academy," which is one of the programs developed by the Edison Project (Chubb, 1997). It will henceforth be known as the "Diversity Program."[1] Edison Schools were founded in 1992 by a diverse group of individuals from the USA and the UK; the group's goal was to improve public education (Edison Schools, 2008a). The Edison school design was the culmination of three years of research and development. The team which conducted the research included experts in the areas of teaching, school administration, school finance and management, technology, and educational research. Participants in the project believed that the educational structure was antiquated, and children were being taught in the same way their parents and grandparents were taught, and that this did not prepare them for life in the modern, technological world. Hence, a major goal of the group was to ensure that modern technology was included as a part of the educational experience for children in elementary and high school (Edison Schools, 2008b, c). Edison Schools claim particularly high achievement on the part of their students, and indicate that 86% of Edison parents rate their children's school as an "A" or "B," as compared with 69% of parents in traditional public schools (Edison Schools, 2008h).

This chapter is contributed by Sonya Berkley

[1] As with all specific references in this chapter, the title of the program is a pseudonym.

M.C. Sengstock, *Voices of Diversity*, Clinical Sociology: Research and Practice, DOI 10.1007/978-0-387-89666-3_9, © Springer Science+Business Media, LLC 2009

The Edison Program claims to blend the educational principles of a tradi-tional liberal arts education with skills which prepare students for the 21st century. Accordingly, the program:

> ...focuses on the essential academic disciplines, including: reading, writing, literature, mathematics through calculus, history, government, economics, the sciences, and social science. Students also enjoy an enriching program of fine arts, world language, health and fitness, and an emphasis on practical skills from technology to teamwork that are crucial to success in the workplace (Edison Schools, 2008b).

The program also claims to build a partnership between the faculty, student, administration, and family to improve the learning process. To achieve these goals, the Edison Programs include extensive assessment programs and intensive profes-sional development for teachers. The curriculum was designed to help students see connections between knowledge and its practical applications. As a charter school, it is expected that Edison Schools will "...meet or exceed all state standards" (Edi-son Schools, 2008e); Edison officials also claim that their on-going assessment pro-gram is well adapted to conforming with the requirements of the "No Child Left Behind" Act (Edison Schools, 2008j). Edison also aims to include the development of responsible citizenship as "an integral part of the Edison curriculum" (Edison Schools, 2008e).

For our purposes, particularly critical is the Edison Program's focus on diversity. The Edison Program claims to be dedicated not only to providing a high-quality education, but also to diversity:

> We believe that the qualities of talent and leadership know no boundaries. Talent and lead-ership are found in individuals with different backgrounds, cultures, genders, ages, race, sexual orientation, and ethnicities. Edison's diverse staff reflects the many communities that we serve and helps to deepen our culture of respect and achievement. Our diversity drives not only the academic achievement of our students but also our business success (Edison Schools, 2008i).

Furthermore, Edison Schools specifically indicate that their schools and teachers are expected to infuse a culturally diverse orientation into the curriculum:

> A spirit of multiculturalism infuses the Edison curriculum. Students explore their own cul-tural heritage and that of other ethnic groups through a literature-based approach to teaching and learning. Teachers foster cultural awareness and understanding as students explore var-ious values, customs, and lifestyles within a broad study of the human experience (Edison Schools, 2008e).

As a result of this focus, the Edison school approach has frequently been sought by school districts in which there is a predominance of minority students (Frontline, 2003a, b). The website of the Edison Schools (2008f) takes pains to illustrate the multi-cultural character of its faculty, staff, and student population by including photographs of a broad spectrum of the races represented in its schools.

Toward these ends, the Edison Programs help teachers to develop a supportive environment in the classroom that will help students feel they belong. Special train-ing programs on the development of a supportive learning environment are a part of ongoing professional development for teachers in Edison Schools. Edison Schools are required to set aside sufficient time and other resources to provide their teachers with the opportunity and support they need to establish the desired learning environment. Included is an intensive training program prior to the teacher's first assignment in an Edison School; such programs are offered at various sites throughout the country. New teachers are also provided with on-going support in classroom management and instructional techniques. Prior to each school year, an intensive summer conference for all Edison teachers sets the stage for the professional development activities, which continue on a monthly basis throughout the school year. This includes periodic visits from national resources personnel, as well as on-going Internet resources, and the opportunity to attend periodic leadership programs at the national level (Edison Schools, 2008f).

The specific program, which we are calling the "Diversity Program," was established as a component of a high-school program in a county in southeastern Michigan, an area adjacent to the City of Detroit. Within the community, it was usually referred to as the "Edison Program," or the "Edison School." Like all Edison Programs, the Diversity Program was established as a "charter school" within the local school district (Edison Schools, 2008d). As is true of charter schools, the Diversity Program was publicly supported, and was open to all students who resided within the county in which the school was located. The location of the Diversity Program was particularly apt, since the student population of the school district in which it was located consists of 48% minority students. The Diversity Program was required to meet the same academic standards as traditional public schools. However, like most charter schools, the Diversity Program was permitted to operate without many of the bureaucratic and regulatory constraints placed on traditional public schools.

This resulted in an atmosphere which was more like that of a private school than a large public school. While the Diversity Program was housed within the same building as the traditional public high school, it occupied a separate section of the building. Students in the Diversity Program were kept separate from the student body in the traditional high-school program, except for elective classes such as typing or physical education, or during the lunch hour. Diversity Program classrooms were physically larger, while the class size was smaller: approximately 15–20 students per classroom, as opposed to 35–40 students in the traditional public high-school classes down the hall. Program classrooms were also more pleasant: they were carpeted and painted each year, while the regular high-school classrooms were not. Program students had access to a student computer in their classrooms, an advantage which students in the traditional program did not have. The Diversity Program also had an extended school day and a longer school year. Even the terminology was different: Diversity Program participants were consistently referred to as "family," in order to provide students with a feeling of belonging.

In keeping with the philosophy of the Edison Schools, the Diversity Program maintained other program components which distinguished it from the public high school as a whole. Every student was provided with a computer for use at home. There was an attempt to maintain an effective alliance among the various components of the student's environment: the child, the teacher, and the family. This was achieved through the use of quarterly conferences, which included an assessment of the student's achievement during the previous period, the setting of goals for the coming quarter, and the development of plans to meet these goals. Teachers in the Diversity Program, like teachers in all Edison Programs, participated in on-going professional development. One area of this development was an on-going seminar in diversity.

The Diversity Program began its operation in the fall term of 1999 and operated for four academic years. It was terminated at the end of the 2002–2003 school year, allegedly for lack of funds. It was also alleged that teachers and students in the traditional school setting were resentful of the special resources allocated to the Diversity Program. Thus, teachers would learn that a diversity seminar or other professional development opportunity was being offered, but they were not eligible since the seminar was open only to Diversity Program faculty. It is also easy to surmise that students in the traditional high-school program, not to mention their parents, must have been annoyed by the presence of freshly painted, carpeted classrooms, equipped with computers, in the Diversity Program classrooms, as compared with the lack of resources in their own section of the school. Following the closure of the Program, both teachers and students were transferred back into the traditional high-school program.

What Made the Diversity Program a Resource for Multi-cultural Education?

As noted above, the Diversity Program was different from the traditional public school in several ways. One area that set it apart was the commitment to ongoing education development training for faculty; this training was not available to educators in the traditional public setting. Another area was the availability of technological resources as a core component of the students' learning process. The program also stressed constant accountability and professionalism. In contrast, traditional public schools are frequently confronted with financial difficulties. These difficulties led to overcrowded classrooms, lack of ongoing educational development for teachers, and frustrated principals and administrators who cannot move their schools in ways they need to go without district commitment and financial support. Most important, in contrast with traditional public school, the Diversity Program was part of a nationally developed program which aimed to include multi-cultural dimensions in the educational setting. As such, the Diversity Program provides a valuable example on which to base our analysis of the manner in which an educational program can provide a more secure environment for racially and culturally diverse students in a school setting.

Data for Evaluation of the Diversity Program

The data on which the analysis is based were collected by the author in three different phases, beginning in 1999 and terminating in 2004. All aspects of the study were conducted under the requirements of the Wayne State University Human

Investigation Committee. Data included participant observation of the author in the program in which her daughter was a student, as well as feedback from educators and students who participated in the Diversity Program.[2] The three phases of data collection with faculty and students were as follows:

> Phase one consisted of interviews with five members of the faculty and staff of the Diversity Program during the 1999–2000 school year. All interviews were qualitative in nature;
>
> Phase two consisted of narratives collected from 34 students in the Diversity Program during the 1999–2000 school year;
>
> Phase three consisted of ten interviews with teachers and administrators from the Diversity Program which were conducted following the demise of the Program, after they had been transferred back into the traditional high-school program. Again, the interviews were qualitative in nature.

Phase One – Diversity Program Teachers Describe Their Backgrounds and Their Program Activities

The first set of interviews with educators in the Diversity Program focused on the educational backgrounds of the instructors and administrators, their commitment to racial and cultural diversity, and the activities they attempted to carry out in the classrooms. The purpose of this section of the analysis was to discern what skills the educators brought to the diversity segment of the program, and how they carried out the commitment to diversity in the classroom.

Initially, it is interesting to note that few of the educators had been exposed to a racially or culturally diverse setting early in life. Three were White males (E1, E3, and E5). One (E1) was born and reared in Europe; he was not even aware that racial differences were a problem until he moved to the USA at the age of 15. The others had lived most of their lives in White neighborhoods, and attended primarily White schools. Educator 2, an African-American female, also lived in a racially segregated area and attended primarily Black schools; her first contacts with Whites in college were not pleasant. The only respondent with a diverse background was Educator 4, a White female, who grew up in New York City, who said she missed the diversity of New York when she moved away. Most encountered persons from other races and cultures for the first time late in their college years or in their initial teaching experiences.

Since diversity was not a part of their early life experience or education, where did they get their interest in this area? Several of the teachers in the Diversity

---

[2] Throughout this section, study participants will be referred to by a code letter and their respondent number. Thus Educators will be referred to as Ex; and Student will be referred to as Sx, where "x" represents the respondent number. In the discussion of Phase 3 teachers, new respondents will be referred to by the code, NEx (New Educator). Where appropriate, the race and gender may be specified following the respondent number, using the following codes: F = Female; M = Male; A = Asian; B = Black; W = White.

Program indicated that members of their families had influenced them to view diversity in a positive manner, an issue very similar to comments discussed in Chapter 7. One (E3) reported that his mother was Jewish and a convert to Christianity, "...so we were always very tolerant and very open, especially since she was an educator." He also reports that his closest friend in high school was African-American. Another educator (E5) also reported that his family had provided the example of being open to persons from other races. Another teacher said she always "...wanted to be a teacher that would help kids that seemed to be suffering a lot" (E2).

All reported having few opportunities for formal training in diversity in their teacher training programs, although one (E5) mentioned he had sociology and history courses which discussed "...the impact of race and culture on history and various concepts that were impacted by them." Hence, none of these five educators had formal training or experience with multi-culturalism or multi-racialism. For most, their introduction to teaching children from diverse backgrounds apparently occurred when they actually began teaching. Although they came to their interest in diversity education by a variety of roads, all seemed to have developed a concern for people from a wide variety of backgrounds, and a strong desire to work with children from such settings. They were attracted to a program which clearly expected the faculty to include racial and cultural diversity as an important part of the curriculum. On the surface, their lack of diversity training and experience did not suggest they would be successful in this arena. However, it does suggest that if they can perform well in this setting, other teachers ought to be able to do the same.

When they thought about diversity, what did they mean by it? Two types of definitions appear, one general, the other more specific. The general definition was summarized by one as follows: "...I think diversity means that we're all equal and unique and we all have something to offer" (E1). Another adds: "To me diversity means to make sure everybody is included. Being accepted, coming together and working together in harmony" (E2). To be more specific, another focused on different groups as well as the teaching environment: "...When I started student teaching ... I realized the kids were from a variety of racial and ethnic backgrounds and seemed to have different needs" (E5). Hence, these educators did not define diversity in terms of specific racial, religious, or ethnic groups. Rather, they recognize that there is a broad spectrum of groups in society, and that an effort must be made, particularly by educators, to ensure that everyone is included, and their needs are fulfilled.

We now turn to a discussion of what they did in the classroom and how they did it. For the answer to this question, we turn to the program details they described. We begin with the overall outlook of the Diversity Program as a whole. One of the educators, an administrator within the program, made a point of the fact that diversity was supposed to be a *general orientation* to programming, rather than a specific mention of one racial or cultural group or another:

> ...I've told my staff not to celebrate Black History Month or Cinco de Mayo. No! we're not gonna take a month to celebrate. Unless you're been doing it all year, don't celebrate diversity apart. ... Don't come to me saying it's a special project. It is not special. This is life (E1).

Furthermore, this philosophy, that diversity is to be a part of the on-going program, is embedded in training and program planning, through weekend in-service programs, as well as discussions among the teachers to determine the effectiveness of their approach (E1).

How is this philosophy carried out in the classroom? The teachers indicated that they really attempted to include references to various racial, ethnic, religious, and gender segments of the population within the day-to-day school program. Some sample comments illustrate this approach: "...In my classroom, all my board displays, racial and gender-wise, was as equitable as I could make them" (E1).

Some fields, such as English or social studies, seem particularly adapted to this approach. Hence, one would expect that history and literature classes could include diversity-related materials. An English instructor included folktales in her classes; this enabled her to "...discuss that country and that culture ... [a]nd find it on the map..." (E4). In her language arts class, students participated in a "Celebrate Diversity" program, for which they "...presented a drama skit, song, or dance related to their race and ethnic group." A social studies teacher said he used his background in American history and Black history "...to incorporate different historical events into my curriculum that talk about different cultures" (E5). He felt that the current textbooks helped, because they "...include visual illustrations of various races, ethnic groups and their way of life in each unit discussed" (E5). This teacher also mentioned the fact that students from various ethnic groups, particularly Black males, had different problems in the learning process; he made an effort to accommodate these needs.

Cultural inclusion is used even in courses which one might not expect to have a diversity dimension. Thus, a mathematics teacher reports: "The textbook I use ... tells you about different multi-cultural issues. There are different facts in the book that help out with the problems. Some of the problems relate to the kids' backgrounds" (E2). The science teacher reports a similar attempt to include material of interest to different groups: "I try to bring in many ethnic type backgrounds. In 10th grade [science class] we were just talking about genetics. We're talking about sickle-cell anemia, which is a predominant disease in Afro-Americans. So I try to bring anything that might be of interest to any specific culture into the class" (E3).

Two teachers mentioned that the physical structure of the classroom also played a role in the way they dealt with diversity in the classroom. One teacher said she "...put two Blacks and two Whites at a table to make sure they are not the same" (E2). Another also said she tried to achieve "...a good mix as far as the students' gender and race" (E4). Others mentioned the need to decrease gender biases, and the importance of considering the impact of economic disadvantage in education (E3). One teacher summarized the overall approach of the faculty: "...In a nutshell, diversity just means appreciating differences and not letting it become an issue. Just realizing that people are different and accepting them for who they are instead of judging them or having preconceived notions about them. Just make an effort to understand where they're coming from" (E4). For her, this included another dimension of diversity, children from broken homes; she believed they required special assistance "...because of the emotional burdens many of them carry."

At the administrative level, program leaders reported that they looked for multi-cultural experience when reviewing applications for the faculty. In that regard, one noted, "We don't have as much diversity on the staff as I would like" (E1). Administrators also made an effort to review conflicts or problems which might occur between teachers and students. One said, "I also take a look at discipline referrals being sent for different groups of students. I try to make sure we don't have a problem there. You know, some educators may not be consciously aware of it [i.e., differential treatment by race]" (E1). Consequently, he organized a series of in-service workshops with a conflict resolution consultant to assist teachers in handling these situations. Similarly, teachers reported noting interracial problems among students, and bringing them in to "...talk about it" (E3).

In summary, several aspects of the program accommodate diversity. These are worth delineating for the use of other programs:

- The over-riding assumption is that all persons deserve understanding and respect. This includes all racial, religious, gender, and ethnic groups, as well as economically disadvantaged children, those who have special learning problems, and those who come from broken homes.
- The commitment to diversity should not be a special project a few times each year, but should be a regular component of the program on an on-going basis.
- Relevant diversity issues should be included in all classes, from social studies and literature to science and math.
- Efforts should be made to hire a racially and culturally diverse faculty.
- Attempts should be made to bring together members of diverse groups through such techniques as multi-racial and multi-cultural seating arrangements in classes, and inter-group activities of various types.
- Efforts should be made to ensure that social interrelations among teachers and students occur in ways which are respectful of persons from all racial, religious, gender, and cultural groups. Conflict resolution techniques can be useful in this regard.
- In-service training programs should be conducted on a regular basis to ensure that faculty members have the proper training to carry out these programs.

Had the respondents in our study attended schools which implemented such policies, they might not have experienced the negative school patterns which they reported. In particular, one would hope that teachers and administrators in a diversity-focused school would not have rejected children based on their ethnic or racial origins, insisted that mixed background children "choose sides" in defining their identity, or forced them to accept a predetermined identity choice.

How did the educators view the Diversity Program? Were they satisfied with it? Or were there changes which they thought were necessary? Generally, teachers seemed to feel that the Edison Program was committed to working with children from diverse groups and was doing well in that regard, although some felt there should be more in-service training on various issues (E2, E3, and E5). However, an unexpected criticism of the program also appeared. As indicated earlier, the

Diversity Program was housed in the same building as the traditional high school, and some teachers reported that relations between the two schools were not cordial. One teacher wanted to start a photography class, but "...because of politics between the two schools we can't get that done because it's in the other part of the school" (E3). Another teacher, an African-American woman, commented: "...The changes I would like to see is the school right over there [i.e., the traditional high school]. ... There's a lot of clashing between the two schools" (E2). She attributed the "clashing" to the animosity of teachers in the traditional school to the success of African-American teachers in the Diversity Program. Hence, there appeared to be problems which the program faced which were unrelated to the way in which they conducted the program, and were likely to lead to problems in the long run, a situation which did indeed occur, as we shall see.

Phase Two – Diversity Program Students Reveal Their Views on the Program

We move now to the students' views of the Diversity Program. The student phase of the data collection consisted of "jointly told tales," a narrative ethnography approach in which the interviewer assists students in reporting their experiences in the school setting. Students participating in the project were asked to write a narrative focusing on one or more of three questions presented to them. The three issues the students were asked to discuss were any attitudes or behaviors they had observed by teachers or administrators which included what the students perceived to include racial or cultural bias, whether their experiences with teachers or administrators had been positive or negative, and how the positive or negative experiences with educators or administrators had made them feel.

Student responses indicate that several had problems with teachers in the past. One student, a female with a mixed Black and White heritage, reported that a teacher in early elementary school had suggested she draw a picture of a zebra, "...because you relate to them" (S20). At the time she was too young to realize the racist nature of the comment. She also felt the teacher was unfair in her grading policies. The same student also related an incident in middle school in which she was not permitted to go on a trip with the school band because the teacher claimed that "...'we need more boys, because girls are too much to handle'" (S20).

In contrast, several students felt that the Diversity Program was more supportive (S8; S22). One girl spoke for all when she said: "In this school [the Diversity Program] I've mainly had good experiences with all the teachers, black, white, male or female" (S21). A mixed race student told of a teacher who developed "...a program at her home called the sisters circle which was a group of girls who discussed their problems." She felt that several girls in the group were discouraged from early entry into parenthood due to the interest of this teacher (S5). Two students, a Black female (S24) and a White female (S26), both expressed appreciation to teachers who had encouraged their educational achievement when other teachers in the past had not done so. One commented: "...My experience with the Edison Program was fine with me" (S26).

Several students pointedly mentioned incidents in which teachers had effectively dealt with various aspects of discrimination (S26). One young woman reported a negative incident with a teacher who made a rude comment on her weight; another teacher, whom she described as "...very kind and strict about discrimination...took that teacher aside and explained to him his role as a teacher" (S33). Similarly, a White male who revealed his homosexuality during high school reported that most of the teachers "stood up for me when anyone tried to pick a fight" (S7).

In contrast to these positive incidents, however, this same student reported a highly negative experience with a counselor, who "...decided to tell mother about the fact that I was gay without talking with me first about it. That ruined my relationship with my mother and I lost my trust with him as a counselor" (S7). Several female students reported negative experiences in physical education classes with teachers who did not consider girls to be qualified for sports. Conversely, a Black male was concerned because he felt teachers thought of him as just a basketball player; he said, "...I wish other people would get to know me for more than just a tall kid who can hoop" (S28). Some White students also expressed an awareness that some teachers discriminated against Blacks (S33). And one Asian student (23) complained that few Asians were in the school, nor were Asians mentioned much in the program, only Whites and African-Americans. Another student also mentioned being the target of negative responses because of her religion (S27).

In general, however, most students felt that the Diversity Program had accommodated their needs better than other schools they had attended. One commented: "No matter what happened our teachers are always there for us" (S25). A White male summarized the opinions of most when he wrote: "...we have an amazing amount of diversity here [in this community]. We have people from all different races, cultures and backgrounds, a melting pot of color and tradition. Because of this unique advantage, prejudices and apprehensions that our parents and grandparents may have had are not distilled into us. ... I count myself lucky and all the wiser to be able to experience this first hand, an education no book can teach us or make us understand" (S31).

Finally, it is important to note that several students reported the same negative relationships with the traditional school with which they shared the building. A White female student described the relationship well:

> ...what is demonstrated most widely is the barrier between traditional high school and the Edison senior academy. The school within a school factor we have here ... was a bad idea. The segregation here is much worse than any I've ever witnessed first hand. The sad part is that it starts with the adults and spreads to the children (S3).

This student went on to discuss how she wanted to work on the school newspaper but only students in the traditional school were accepted. Two other students were excluded from the yearbook for the same reason (S2 and S12). Another student was told by other students that she had to leave the building by the back door because she was walking through a "traditional hallway" (S10). Others complained that program students were not properly informed about cap and gown fittings and class rings

(S3). One student commented it was like they were "...labeled as Scarlet 'E' for Edison" (S12). Perhaps the most dramatic demonstration of the conflict between the two programs involved an administrator from the traditional school, who stopped to talk with a small group of Diversity Program students who were studying without a teacher present. The student commented, "...This would have been normal except she was practically yelling at us. Before she left, she looked up at us and said..., 'I'm the new assistant principal, and you're Edison!'..." (S3).

To summarize, most students and teachers in the Diversity Program felt that multi-racial and multi-cultural issues had been handled relatively well. They were not perfect; indeed, some serious diversity-related problems occurred, such as the gender discrimination in physical education and the counselor's handling of the homosexual student. However, intergroup relations were probably better than what occurred in most traditional schools. Any benefits that might have been gained from the special approaches of the program were diminished, however, by the conflicts which existed between relations between faculty, administrators, and students in the two programs. As one student commented, having a "school within a school ... was a bad idea." As we suggested earlier, it is probably not surprising that traditional school participants would be well aware of the special resources available to the Diversity Program down the hall, and this undoubtedly played a major role in creating the poor relations.

Phase Three – Educators Look Back on the Diversity Program After Its Closure

As we noted above, funding difficulties brought about the closure of the Diversity Program after four years. What role the negative relations between the two programs played in its demise is not clear. Following the Program closure, additional interviews were held with faculty and staff, both the original respondents and some new ones.

These interviews focused on the educators' impressions of the two different programs and how they differed from each other. In responding to queries about the demise of the Diversity Program, teachers in the program attributed its closure to the budgetary problems of the district. One suggested that the Edison Program had been delinquent in paying the program's bills. It is interesting to note that none mentioned the animosity between the two programs which had been evident in the earlier research with both the educators and the students.

Here, our main emphasis will be on a comparison of the diversity aspects of the two programs. Did the educators view the Diversity Program as having any advantages? How did they perceive the traditional program? This is particularly important from the point of view of those who had the earlier experience of the Diversity Program. These interviews provide us with a valuable opportunity to compare the educators' perception of the effectiveness of the Diversity Program with the more traditional high-school program into which they had been transferred.

Teachers from the Diversity Program disagreed about whether the emphasis on diversity had diminished; one said, "...I think there was more emphasis on diversity with the Edison Program. Right now the focus in on MEAP, MEAP, and MEAP.[3] ... the overall picture is on how to bring everybody up to speed is the main focus and less emphasis on diversity" (E3). Most, however, either thought there had been an improvement since the program change, or saw little difference. One had positive feelings about the way the school was handling the issue; he said there was: "...more inclusive diversity programming. And anything related to diversified cultures ... the Administration has been good about approving" (E5). An African-American female teacher (E2) also said she thought there was more emphasis on diversity, largely because she thought "that everybody is comfortable..." with diversity programming now, as opposed to earlier. She also believed staffing better reflected diversity at the later point. Others saw little change from one program to the other. Students still had problems with insensitive teachers (E3), and diversity activities were approved, but apparently with little enthusiasm (E8). Some were sympathetic with the administration, recognizing that any unusual approaches were difficult, given the district's "...drastic budget cuts" (E2).

A particular concern mentioned by seven teachers was the need for in-service training of all types, but particularly related to diversity. One said, "I have not had any diversity training in the school since I've started teaching" (NE2). Another agreed, and added that "The focus right now is on 'No Child Left Behind' " (NE4). Others mentioned special animosity expressed toward African-American teachers if they attempted to take a leadership role or make suggestions. This teacher thought it was difficult for teachers to serve as models for children when they themselves were not accepting of diversity (NE3). Another teacher felt there was a particular need for training about the Muslim religion, due to the international situation, coupled with an increasing number of Arabic students, who often received negative reactions from their classmates (NE8). Most teachers had little hope there would be any change in diversity programming, due to funding restrictions and the increased emphasis on student assessment ("No Child Left Behind" and the MEAP test).

One must consider the possibility, however, that any diversity emphasis which remains may be due, in part, to the efforts of the Diversity Program over the four years of its operation. Certainly, the approaches they developed could be valuable suggestions for other schools to use in the future to improve learning conditions for children from a variety of cultural and racial backgrounds, including children of mixed heritage.

Summary and Conclusions

This chapter has described a program which attempted to make racial and cultural diversity an integral part of the curriculum, indeed, of the entire structure, of a high-school educational program. The Diversity Program was based on one of several

---

[3] "MEAP" refers to the Michigan Educational Testing Program (see Michigan Dept. of Education, 2008).

programs developed by the Edison Schools. It was formulated on the assumption that all persons, whatever their ethnic, racial, gender, or religious background, and whether or not they have special problems of various types, are deserving of respect and understanding.

Integral to the program was the assumption that diversity should be imbedded in the structure of the educational program; it should not simply be an occasional supplement to the daily school program. The institution should make deliberate efforts to hire a racially and culturally diverse faculty. It should attempt to bring children from different backgrounds together through various mechanisms, such as seating arrangements or intergroup activities. It should ensure that all have an opportunity to learn about different cultures, as well as to describe their own culture to others. Special efforts were made to ensure that interrelations among students and teachers exhibited this respect for others. There were frequent training sessions for teachers and administrators to ensure that they were properly prepared to carry out these goals.

In general, data collected from teachers and students indicated that both groups believed the Diversity Program had attained its objectives. Teachers reported making considerable effort to include diversity in their classroom programs. For the most part, students reported that the Diversity Program was more hospitable to children from different racial and cultural backgrounds than they had experienced in other school settings. There was some suggestion, however, that gender differences and homosexuality were not always handled with understanding and respect.

Unfortunately, the Diversity Program was not continued after four years, allegedly for financial reasons. However, it is likely that the negative relations that existed between the Diversity Program and the adjoining traditional high school could have also played a role in its demise. There was disagreement among the teachers as to whether the program's sensitivity to diversity had been adopted in the traditional high-school program following its closure.

The Diversity Program could serve as a model for other schools that hope to provide a hospitable approach to diverse racial and cultural groups within the school curriculum and environment. The program could also be adapted to other community environments. For example, community centers, senior centers, or other community level social settings could adapt the approaches taken by the Diversity Program to the needs of their members.

Chapter 10
Incorporating Diversity at the Community Level – Example 2: Mainstreaming Immigrant Children Through Coordinated Parallel Socialization Workshops

Theoretical Background for the Parallel Socialization Workshops

Social environment plays an important role in a child's definition of self. Cooley (1922) used the analogy of a "looking glass" to describe the process by which a child developed his/her idea of "who s/he is." Hence Cooley saw young children as looking at themselves through the "mirror" of the social groups around them. In a similar vein, Mead (1934) went so far as to say that the views of the society actually become part of the individual's sense of self, a component of the self-concept which he called, the "ME."

Since the social environment is of critical importance in the development of a child's perspective on himself/herself and the world, it is equally critical that parents and teachers keep that perspective in mind as they discharge their duties of socializing the children under their care. They will not be effective in their tasks unless they keep at the forefront of the minds the various influences which will impact on these children as they move throughout their lives, both at home and in school. Both play a critical role in children's views of themselves, and of the expectations that others have of them.

The immigration process is always problematic, even for adults, who presumably have made a conscious choice to migrate. For children, however, it is even more traumatic. In a few short months, or even weeks, immigrant children are transported from the familiar environment in which they have lived their entire lives, often separated from extended family members and friends, and are transported to a new and unfamiliar social setting, half a world away. Recognition of these varying cultural traditions is essential to the success of these children in school. They need assurance that their needs are being recognized while they make efforts to move into the mainstream.

As they enter the American school setting, immigrant children, usually for the first time, encounter an environment in which the expectations of different parts of their worlds are at odds with each other. In the pre-immigration environment, all aspects of their social group – parents, siblings, extended family members,

---

This chapter is contributed by Arifa K. Javed

M.C. Sengstock, *Voices of Diversity*, Clinical Sociology: Research and Practice,
DOI 10.1007/978-0-387-89666-3_10, © Springer Science+Business Media, LLC 2009

neighbors, and teachers – had the same expectations. In the USA, however, they are faced with two different sets of expectations. Often these expectations are at odds, or may even be diametrically opposed to each other. Consideration of both these sets of perspectives is critical to a successful achievement of educational objectives for children. Having teachers and parents operate with quite different sets of assumptions, without consideration of the perspectives of the other side, is likely to result in misunderstanding, even conflict, between parents and teachers, resulting in considerable confusion for the child.

Because of this unique background, immigrant children need to be approached differently from other students. As Mead and Cooley would suggest, the immigrant family and the school staff are both playing critical roles in defining immigrant children's view of the world: who they are; how they should behave; how they should relate to the rest of society. In order to avoid confusion in the school, as well as in the children's minds, it is essential that representatives of the two parties responsible for their socialization reach an understanding of the perspectives of each side, as well as a consensus concerning the goals and objectives to be achieved in the school setting. The workshops we will describe are an attempt to assist in achieving this census.

Description of the Setting for the Workshops

Beginning in the mid-1990s, the author worked with several school districts in the Detroit Metropolitan Area, as well as with social agencies which focused on the problems of immigrants, to bring teachers and parents together. The goal of the workshops was to establish a less-threatening, more harmonious school setting for immigrant children. Numerous workshops were presented in a variety of settings, and this chapter is a description of those workshops, together with an analysis of the degree to which they were successful, as well as an analysis of the ways in which they might be improved. Workshops were conducted with participants in all three sectors of the school setting: the teachers, the parents, and the children. The focus of the workshops involved three different dimensions: positive parenting in two cultures, diversity training, and teen conflict.

Immigrant families included in the workshops were primarily from among the new waves of immigrants coming to America. They included largely groups from the Middle East and South Asia. There were several Muslim groups, including Arabs, Bosnians, and Bangladeshis. Some Middle Eastern groups were Christian, including Iraqi-Chaldeans, a Roman Catholic sect from Iraq. From the Asian subcontinent were Hindus and Muslims from India, as well as Muslims from Pakistan. The majority of these workshops were non-White and non-Christian, with the exception of the Bosnians, who are White, and the Chaldeans, who are Christian. It should be noted that these immigrants presented a portrait of diversity which was dramatically different from anything previously experienced by the neighborhoods in which they lived, and in the schools which the children attended. These were children and families with pronounced racial, religious, and cultural differences.

Most had never before been placed in a position in which they were forced to interact with persons from a racial, religious, or cultural group other than their own. Similarly, the teachers who worked with the immigrant children and their families were also lacking in experience with persons from such radically different racial, religious, and cultural groups. Thus it is not surprising that neither the parents nor the teachers were even minimally prepared for the challenges they were likely to encounter.

In considering the adaptation of the immigrant family into the new environment, agencies which attempt to assist them must bear in mind the intensity of the change involved in the immigrant setting. To return to the description of the socialization process, as described by Mead and Cooley, immigrants, both parents and children, have experienced their entire socialization in the context of an entirely different social environment. They have been totally immersed within a social culture and role in a completely different society. Most things they were trained to do in the preceding society is relevant any longer; anything they are expected to do in this strange, new environment is new and unfamiliar. The parents as well as their children must learn to function in a completely different way. Since the adult learning process is usually slower than that of children, parents often run the risk of role reversal in the new society: many children adapt to the new environment more quickly than their parents.

The experience of immigration in the 21st century is dramatically different from the immigration of a century earlier. Until the mid-20th century, most immigrants left their homeland and its culture behind forever. While they may have held nostalgic reminiscences of their homeland, they were largely separated from their country of origin and its culture on a day-to-day basis. A few immigrants paid a visit to their homeland once or twice before they died, but most never returned to the land of their birth. This pattern has completely changed with the advent of globalization, coupled with the digital revolution that has enhanced communication. As a result, immigration is a very different experience from what it had been in the past. The ability of immigrant families to reconnect to their old culture via phone, television, and the Internet has changed their approach to integration into mainstream American society. This has also greatly influenced immigrant practices of socialization with children. Contacts with the country of origin are now more frequent, and result in more immigrant families being influenced to maintain cultural patterns from the homeland, and to attempt to influence their children to do the same.

Characteristics of Socialization with Immigrant Children

The socialization process for immigrant children is necessarily different from that of children being reared in their own culture. Immigrant children are essentially reared in two different worlds, and are forced to struggle to live up to the expectation of both these worlds. At home they are socialized into the culture of their homeland; when they attend school, they are expected to conform to the expectations of the receiving society. The process by which an individual learns and adopts dimensions of a culture in which s/he was not reared is called "acculturation" (Gordon, 1964). This process is essential for immigrants if they expect to participate in the new society.

What is less frequently realized is that both sides of the cultural divide must be involved in the acculturation process, at least to some degree. Hence participants from both cultures must find ways of communicating effectively. Not only must children and their families learn the expectations of the host society, but teachers, as representatives of the host society, must also become acquainted with the cultural elements the new families bring with them, and take these into account in their interactions with immigrant children and families. For interaction to occur, both sides must develop some mechanisms for understanding each other. In effect, children, parents, and teachers must become acquainted with their respective cultural differences and similarities. This process can be referred to as "reciprocal acculturation." This concept is the key to understanding the two-way communication approach that is used in the coordinated workshops. Under this concept, the two parties involved in the interaction approach each other from their respective viewpoints and progress to a mutual cultural exchange.

Acculturation is actually a highly complex process, and the various components of the process may occur at different rates, as Gordon (1964) has illustrated. The two major components of the process are acculturation and assimilation. In the acculturation process, elements of the different culture are learned and adopted; this includes such items as language, economic patterns, and religious traditions. The other major dimension involves assimilation, in which members of the incoming group merge into the social groups and associations of the receiving society. As Gordon (1964) pointed out, social assimilation proceeds more slowly than acculturation. This is, in part, because of the reluctance of new immigrants to relinquish their lifelong patterns of association. However, members of the receiving society frequently resist the inclusion of new members as well.

An example of the differential rates of acculturation can be seen in some of the Arabic families who participated in the workshops. They were willing to learn the language and culture, but were concerned with maintaining their own social patterns and cultural traditions as well. Parents, in particular, exhibited a willingness to acculturate but not to assimilate. Their children, on the other hand, were bilingual and bicultural, as well as highly functional in the mainstream society. They were fluent in Arabic and spoke English without an accent, which was frequently an asset for their parents' business. They were active at local mosques and practiced their religion and maintained their identity. They went through the public school system and were culturally competent to deal with the peer pressure and popular culture comfortably. They enjoyed a sense of dual anchorage to both cultures and took pride in their hyphenated identity.

This disparity of culture on the part of the two sets of adults, the parents and the teachers, creates serious problems for the socialization of immigrant children.

A major component of the child's socialization process is imitation: children model themselves on the behavior of the adults in their lives. However, for immigrant children, the adults in their lives are presenting conflicting role models. Teachers are presenting a model of American society and culture. Their parents, who are themselves going through a process of resocialization into American society, present a model culture based on the culture of the homeland. Since parents preferred to use their native language at home, bicultural and bilingual children are required to speak two different languages, one at home and the other at school.

Immigrant parents have special problems serving as role models to their children, because they are experiencing a process of *resocialization* into American society, while their children are going through the normal socialization process of childhood. Resocialization is a more complicated process than socialization, because it involves unlearning the original culture, as well as relearning the new culture. Consequently, it is slower than socialization alone. Hence the pace at which immigrant parents acquaint themselves with the new society tends to be slower than the rate at which their children adapt. As a result, immigrant children often become bicultural more rapidly than their parents.

To summarize, immigrant children are socialized concurrently in two different learning environments – at home under the guidance of parents, and at school under teachers who represent the host society. In the development of the workshops, this was referred to as *parallel socialization*, in which the children are actually undergoing two independent and often conflicting socialization processes, and living with two sets of norms and values, one at home and another at school. Because parents and teachers have different frames of references, children are raised with conflicting role models. In order to adapt, immigrant children grow up balancing the expectations of the two sets of adults in their lives. Conversely, the two sets of adults have no experience of their own to deal with the unique challenges bicultural children face, and have difficulty understanding the challenges from the children's perspective. The workshops were developed as an attempt to assist the two sets of adults in communicating more effectively with each other, and through this increased communication, to alleviate the difficulties which conflicting communications might have upon the children.

Nature of the Workshops and How They Were Conducted

The workshops were conducted by the author, who acted in the capacity of an acculturation specialist. The author's experience working with these different groups was used to assist the participants in dealing with the problems of interacting with persons from other cultural and religious groups. Parents who participated in the workshops included both mothers and fathers; their ages ranged from 25 to 42.

These methods target a two-way communication approach, rooted in the ideology of acculturation and reciprocal acculturation, as a process of becoming part of American society. For the workshops, *acculturation* refers to a process by which immigrants strive to learn the ways of the new culture in their new society, while still retaining some aspects of the old culture. *Reciprocal acculturation* is a process of cultural exchange between the immigrants and the hosts, in which the immigrants learn the new culture of the hosts, but at the same time, the hosts cannot escape the impact of the immigrant culture. Thus reciprocal acculturation is a two-way communication process between the immigrants and the representatives of the host society, who interact as though they are two different parties at opposite ends of a bridge. Their approaching and meeting with each other can be accelerated if both make efforts to move toward each other. The attainment of this goal was the objective of the workshops.

Parallel Socialization as the Basis of Successful Acculturation

The basis of the workshops was the concept of *parallel socialization*, as described above. Several dimensions of the process can be delineated. First is the notion of *becoming bicultural*. In the workshops, this concept applied to a condition initiated by immigration and the biculturalism that follows. However, it can also apply to all families in which a culture prevails at home which is different from that of the mainstream society, as presented in the school. Hence it applies to other multi-racial and multi-cultural individuals, and can be broadly used for minorities in general. This approach recognizes that such individuals can also be bicultural, even though they have never migrated and were born and raised in the same society. Hence these workshops could be used with any groups which experience the phenomenon of living up to the duality of cultural expectations. The Amish or Mennonites, who have lived in the USA for several generations, are examples. Duration of contact and interaction with the mainstream society does not matter if an ethnic group chooses to maintain a cultural distance. However, parallel socialization is all the more difficult for non-European immigrants because of certain physical, cultural, and religious differences.

- *Duality of Expectations:* Duality of expectations refers to the lack of cultural consistency between the host society and the family, with the host society represented by teachers, and the parents representing the culture supposedly left behind, but still influencing a great deal of the family's social and cultural patterns. Patterns at home have a different point of reference than those at school, and both have their own expectations. This causes duality of expectations, and children learn dual compliance. As a result bicultural children often are more flexible, and are functional in more than one cultural environment.
- *Conflicting Role Models:* Because the adults do not share the same cultural tradition, they are of little assistance as role models to the children. Neither presents a complete picture which the children can imitate, and neither teachers nor parents can ever have a firsthand experience of this duality. As a result immigrant children grow up with conflicting role models both at home and at school. Parents

and teachers both have limitations in socializing the children, and neither is capable of understanding the nature of cultural duality, and the challenge it presents for the children. The best they can do is to attempt to understand the possible dilemmas, and try to alleviate the conflicts the children are likely to experience. This can be accomplished if each tries to understand the other cultural world and envision the possible problems that may develop.

- *Dual Anchorage:* As a response to the dilemma they face, most immigrant children work out a mechanism that they consider compatible with both sets of expectations, and acquire flexibility in adjusting to the cultural differences. They move on to being bicultural and bilingual, speaking both English and the home language fluently without any accent. This enhances their own cultural competence and helps them develop a *dual anchorage* and sense of belonging to both cultures. As we have suggested, immigrant children are often more effective in developing a dual anchorage in the two cultures than their parents.
- *Consequences of Parallel Socialization at School and at Home:* Parallel socialization provides the children with a dual anchorage in the two cultures. This can sometimes result in role reversal, an issue which will be discussed shortly. Children who do not navigate the process effectively may experience negative impacts. These may include marginalization at school and within the family and community, as well as identity crises, low self-esteem, and isolation. Children are caught between the demands of the school, which expects them to study and perform well, and the family, which may have additional family obligations.

A particularly serious difficulty arises in the numerous instances in which the children become more facile than their parents in maneuvering the cultural divide. Because they are the only ones who are familiar with both sets of cultural norms, they often act as mediators between the two sets of socializing agents. Only through the children can these two sets of adults communicate effectively and understand each other's authority. In effect, through the process of parallel socialization, children are acting as ambassadors of their parents' culture at school, and of the host culture at home. Only through the children do the two sets of adults generally get any information about each other. However, children will vary in their ability to handle this process effectively, which will cause misunderstandings between home and school. When the parents have limited knowledge of English, children are often entrusted with the task of translation. In all such instances, children are in the position to conceal some information if they wish, giving them considerably more power and control than either set of adults.

- *Role reversal:* As we have suggested, parallel socialization increases the cultural competence of children at a pace that is faster than their parents. They learn the norms and acquire functional independence in the American society. Initially, parents often take pride in the fact that their children are able to handle American social processes well. In many instances, parents also rely on their children to navigate the adults' adjustment, as in cases in which the children advise their parents on financial matters or provide translation in medical emergencies. As time goes by, however, many parents become embarrassed that they are unable to provide leadership and be role models. In effect, parents and their children have reversed roles, with the children taking charge in the interchange between the family and the broader society, and parents depending upon their children's leadership. Consequently, parents come to feel they are lacking in their roles as parents.

This process produces a wider generation gap between parents and children, as compared to nonimmigrant parents, and children are forced to perform responsibilities far beyond their level of maturity. However, parallel socialization can also enhance the self-esteem of children and provide them with a stronger sense of understanding of the culture of their new society. They become bicultural with a sense of enhancement and enrichment, enjoy a sense of dual membership and identity, and acquire a cultural flexibility which is an asset in a heterogeneous environment. This gives them an edge over mainstream children, who are often used to homogeneity at home and at school. In fact, these children do exceptionally well academically and help facilitate their parents' acculturation. However, for these advantages to be accomplished, it is necessary that the two agents of parallel socialization mutually recognize and appreciate each other's input. The two sets of adults must be knowledgeable and comfortable dealing with the cultural differences.

Describing the Workshops

We now move to a description of the Parallel Socialization Workshops. Three sets of workshops were designed, each targeting a different group of participants in the parallel socialization process: the parents, the teachers, and the children. All workshops shared four major objectives:

- Immigrant families and their children should be mainstreamed into American society more rapidly but with mutual understanding.
- A smoother transition to American society should be promoted, but with the maintenance of ethnic pride, minimal culture shock, fewer dropouts, and a decreased level of juvenile delinquency.
- The newcomers and their children should be assisted in achieving the American Dream without compromising their social and psychological health.
- Immigration should be made a positive experience for both the immigrants and the hosts.

Toward these ends, three distinct sets of workshops were developed, each targeted specifically at one of the three participating groups: the parents, the teachers, and the children. These workshops will be described in detail below. However, a critical aspect contributing to the success of the workshops consisted of the development of a set of components which were necessary if the workshops were to be successful. We will begin by describing the strategies that were employed in the workshops, as a means of bringing the three groups of participants together.

Applied Strategies of Two-Way Communication

Providing various training programs for teachers, parents, and children when school problems occur is not a unique process. However, if these discussions remain independent, they do little to deal with the most critical aspect of the home–school relationship: the need to promote communication among the three groups. Lacking such communication, each group of participants may continue to operate independently, often unaware of the expectations of the others. Hence a major objective for these workshops was to mediate between the three participant groups and help them understand the perspectives of the others. There were five important strategies that were developed in order to improve communication among the three groups:

- *Coordinated Simultaneous Workshops:* The most important factor in communication between the three groups was to ensure that parents, teachers, and children understood the positions of the others. Toward that end, the workshops for the three groups were not conducted independently, but were coordinated with the discussions being held with the other groups. Hence each group met in a separate meeting, a few days or weeks apart, to discuss the same issue. The same leader conducted all three of the workshops, and was well aware of the content of each of the other workshops. Consequently, the leader was able to explain to each the perspectives of the other two groups, and assist them in understanding each other more effectively.

The workshop leader quickly became aware of the fact that each group was surprisingly unaware of the perspectives of the other two groups. We will describe these different perspectives below. As a result, there were communication gaps and misunderstandings that delayed acculturation and reciprocal acculturation. The strategy of coordinated simultaneous workshops helped overcome these shortcomings by addressing the same issues from three different perspectives, and assisting the participants in appreciating the viewpoints of the others.

- *Needs Assessment:* Participation in the workshops involved multiple ethnicities. Hence it was important to assess the acculturation needs of each group, including its sociohistorical background, social class, language skills, job skills, ethnicity, and religion. Based on such factors, parents from varied backgrounds had different acculturation needs. What worked for Bosnian immigrant parents did not work for Chaldean or Bangladeshi immigrant parents. Similarly, the needs of teachers in the process of reciprocal acculturation varied from one school district to another, depending on which immigrant groups were enrolled. The sets and subsets of workshops had to be tailored to the specific needs of each setting.

- *Prologue to the Workshops:* This strategy required parent, teacher, and teen groups to meet separately with the workshop leader. In this preliminary meeting, participants were asked to list three problems they encountered with the other participants. In these early sessions, each group spent considerable time complaining and blaming the other(s) for their irrationality. These sessions were very important because they helped groups to vent their feelings against the others, and helped the leader to determine the problematic issues that needed to be addressed in the main workshops.
- *Diplomatic Addressing of Concerns and Reaching Compromises:* Once all sides had been heard, the leader played the role of mediator in each session, helping the participants understand the views from the other sides. Participants were encouraged to compromise in order to facilitate a two-way communication, rather than simply point fingers of blame. Each party was made to feel equally responsible for promoting a mutual understanding.
- *Resocializing Both Socializing Agents:* The most important purpose of the whole project was to promote an entirely new approach to understanding the perspectives of the other participants. A prerequisite for a successful process was that all participants had to "unlearn" the previously held approaches of values and behavior, and "relearn" a new approach focusing on two-way communication. This required that all accept mutual responsibility for promoting understanding and acculturation.

All of the above were necessary approaches contributing to the success of the workshops. Perhaps the most important was the conduct of the "Prologue" – preliminary meetings held to conduct the "Needs Assessment" of the three component groups, as well as set the ground rules for the workshops. In the next section, we will provide a brief description of the results of the Needs Assessment, detailing the concerns raised by each group.

Results of the Needs Assessment – Case Analysis and Sample Lists of Concerns

As indicated above, the initial meeting of each group involved a needs assessment, in which participants were encouraged to provide information about the concerns they had in the school setting. This assessment was critical to the success of the workshops. In this section a description of the results of each needs assessment is provided.

Parents' Perspective

Parents' concerns focused on three major areas:

1. *Maintaining Cultural Boundaries:* Being alienated and reduced to a minority is a strange experience. Immigrant parents go through a phase of acute insecurity

in the initial stages of immigration, when they see themselves as a part of the "other" in the new society. They feel pressured to turn bicultural in order to acquire functionality in the new society and enter a new phase of resocialization. It is easy to feel overwhelmed and lose confidence at this stage. Parents realize that they have to pick and choose because not all aspects of their old culture can be retained. This critical phase makes them feel threatened about losing their children to the new culture, making them hold more strongly than ever to aspects of the old culture they might otherwise set aside.

2. *Schooling as a Partial Package of Academic Learning:* Most immigrant parents are fascinated by the opportunities of education their children have in this country. They take schooling very seriously, but tend to focus only on academics. They generally fail to see the importance of extracurricular activities like sports, music, or volunteering. In addition, there is a fear that their children might pick up deviant behaviors from their peers in the after-school environment, which is less formal than the classroom.

3. *Maintaining a Traditional Pattern of Socialization:* Recent immigrants have not yet become comfortable in the new society. They seek to maintain their traditional patterns of culture and behavior for themselves, and to maintain traditional socialization patterns for their children. They are hesitant to adopt new practices because these approaches are unfamiliar, and they lack confidence in those methods, as well as in their own ability to carry them out effectively. This aspect of immigration seems the most challenging one for parents, often making them feel incompetent. The insecurity makes them possessive about their traditional pattern of socialization.

Teachers' Perspective

Teachers' mentioned two major concerns, both of which were diametrically opposed to the goals of the parents:

1. *Breaking Cultural Boundaries:* The teachers are eager to make immigrant students blend in with others as quickly as possible. They rarely consider the transitional phase these children and families experience while struggling to adjust to the new environment. Rather than accelerating the mainstreaming process, this overzealous approach of teachers can sometimes have the opposite result. An example of such a negative outcome occurred during the conduct of one set of workshops, which included several Muslim families. Some Muslim girls in the local school wore the traditional headscarves (hijab), while others did not. Some girls expressed to their teachers their wish that they could remove their headscarves like their friends. The teachers encouraged them to remove their scarves at school, suggesting they could replace them before returning home. Shortly thereafter, some of the girls who removed their headscarves were no longer in school. Hence the teachers' eagerness to accelerate the acculturation process only served to abolish the opportunity completely.

2. *Expecting Immigrant Students to Adapt to Mainstream Socialization:* Teachers exhibited little awareness of the historical and cultural past of their students. Most had no realization of the reasons why their immigrant students failed to meet the same expectations they had of an average student. They rarely understood the extreme differences between the upbringing of these children, who were from another culture and had parents born and reared in a different society. Teachers had to be taught to examine the situation from the students' perspective.

The Children's Perspective

Most students who attended the workshops were teens, and were experiencing a normal adolescent identity struggle. They were in the process of determining who they were and how they fit into their world. This was especially challenging for them because they were bicultural and their generation gap with their parents was wider than the usual parent–adolescent divide. As we discussed earlier, parents often relied on them to take up the more mature role of mediation between them and the new society; yet they still expected their children to exhibit the traditional obedience to their parents. Hence several issues were mentioned by the immigrant children. Four of these are listed below:

1. *Identity Crisis:* Immigrant children often have serious issues of identity. The acuteness of this crisis varies with the degree of dissimilarity they have from the mainstream, in terms of race, religion, and ethnicity. Among the students in the workshops, those students who were lighter-skinned had an advantage compared to darker-skinned children or Asians. Children who were from Christian backgrounds also had an advantage over Muslims, because of the similarity of their religion to the mainstream. Those groups with the least in common with the mainstream had the most difficult time of all.
2. *Peer pressure and "Fitting In":* The children in immigrant families were seen struggling with their differences to deal with peer pressure and the challenge of fitting in. Some students, especially Indian and Pakistani immigrants whose parents were in high-level professions, but also including Bangladeshis whose parents were not highly educated, look to academic excellence as a way to deal with these issues. This approach helped them gain the respect of both their parents and teachers. At times, however, they were bullied and ridiculed by their fellow students for their focus on academics.
3. *Balancing Dual Expectations and Parallel Socialization:* The process of balancing dual expectations and parallel socialization is easier in the preteen stage, in which children follow adults at home and school without question. But as children grow up and start questioning the adults, they face problems with both sets of adults. Hence the problem was more serious for teenaged children.
4. *Mediating Between the Two Sets of Adults:* Some bicultural children complained about the necessity of mediating between the two sets of adults they had to deal

with, one at school and the other at home. As indicated above, parents and teachers often could not communicate directly due to language and cultural barriers. Both were dependent upon the assistance of the children. Furthermore, if anything was communicated incorrectly, the children bore the blame. This was an unfair burden to place upon children, whose level of maturity was inadequate for the demands placed upon them.

The Workshops

The next section moves to a description of the format of the workshops themselves. The focus of each set will be described.

Parent Workshops

Positive Parenting in Two Cultures: Workshops aimed at the parents were designed to educate parents about the major change they had brought into their families when they moved to a new society, as well as to sensitize them to some of the basic elements which were part of this transition. Three subsets of workshops were part of the parenting training:

1. *Parenting Workshop Set 1: "Culture Talk – Broadening Frames of Reference":* This workshop was designed to help the newcomers acquire a sense of balance between their old values, and the new values they would encounter in America. It also attempted to engender a positive approach to cultural differences, as well as an acceptance of diversity in society. This was particularly important in view of the fact that many came from societies in which ethnic, racial, or religious diversity was not a major component of the social experience. Hopefully, these new perspectives would provide the immigrants with the skills necessary for faster acculturation. This workshop focused on acculturation issues, highlighting the basics of adjustments in a new environment and acquiring a lifestyle to successfully achieve the American Dream.
2. *Parenting Workshop Set 2: "The Public School System in America":* This workshop was designed for parents from varied cultural backgrounds, and attempted to describe the goals of the American school system, particularly in promoting individualism and competition, concepts with which many new immigrants are unfamiliar. Such awareness helps parents understand what is expected from them as parents, and from their children as students. The workshop also addresses how sociocultural practices and parenting style can affect children's growth and development. It provides parents with information about the prevalence of peer pressure, popular culture, and the need of children to feel they "fit in" with their peers. It alerts parents to the perspective their children are likely to experience, as they struggle to balance their ethnic identity, while also feeling the need to

"blend in" to the mainstream. It acquaints parents with issues of discipline, homework, class performance, and extracurricular activities.

3. *Parenting Workshop Set 3: "Accepting Parallel Socialization":* This workshop was designed to help parents understand the dual socialization process that is unavoidable for their children, as they grow up in a new society and cope with two distinct cultures, one at home and the other at school. Parents are helped to realize that their children cannot escape being bicultural, and they must accept the impact of mainstream culture in the socialization of their children in a multicultural pluralistic society. Although they have the freedom to maintain their heritage, they need to acquire the flexibility to adapt to the rhythm of life in this fast-moving, postmodern society, if they are to successfully attain the dreams which they sought when they immigrated.

Teacher Workshops: Sensitivity and Diversity Training for Teachers

The teacher workshops were designed to help teachers to understand the problems their students confronted, being from diverse cultural backgrounds and reared by parents whose total experience is from another society. The basic goal of this set of workshops was to create culture sensitivity and enhance the cultural competence among the teachers to deal with bicultural and bilingual students. There were three sets in this group of workshops:

1. *Teacher Workshop Set 1: "Culture Talk – Approaching Diversity":* As its title indicates, this workshop parallels the cultural diversity workshop given to the parents. It attempts to promote an understanding of different cultures, customs, and religious practices among teachers, and to help them come to acknowledge social and cultural differences without being judgmental. Hopefully this will lead them to accept and celebrate all diversity as one of the strengths of the American social fabric. It also helps teachers understand their importance as one of the first contacts immigrant families have in American society. Teachers play an important role in presenting the host culture. In this workshop, they were taught to do so in an inviting manner, and to view the newcomers as constructive and contributive members of American society. This workshop also focused on acculturation issues, highlighting the basics of adjustments between mainstream hosts and the ethnic influx of the immigrant population. The approach emphasized a "salad bowl" approach, in which the various components are allowed and encouraged to exhibit aspects of their distinctive cultures, rather than as a "melting pot," which required them to give up their cultural characteristics and merge into American culture as a whole.

2. *Teacher Workshop Set 2: "Serving Bilingual and Bicultural Students":* This workshop helped the public school teachers to understand the challenges of their

role in working with students who are first-generation immigrants and whose parents were not educated in American society. It helps to identify the different needs such bicultural students might have, as they confront the need to "unload" parts of their cultural baggage and develop a new rhythm of life better adapted to their new society. Teachers were also helped to empathize with the pressures of adjustment these young minds endure while living in two different cultures at home and at school.

3. *Teacher Workshop Set 3: "Recognizing Parallel Socialization":* This workshop helped teachers recognize the fact that their bicultural students cannot avoid a dual socialization, with their cultural training at home running parallel to what they learn at school. It was intended to sensitize teachers to the fact that, in this era of globalization, biculturalism is a permanent feature of their growth and development. It also helps teachers understand that bicultural students are going to be integrated into the mainstream in the model of the "salad bowl," rather than the "melting pot."

Teen Workshops: Teen Challenges and Conflicts in a Diverse Society

The final set of workshops was designed to address the needs of bicultural teens growing up in two different cultures. Their position is particularly difficult in view of the fact that they are the only participants in the process who have knowledge of both cultures, but their experience and understanding in both cultures is minimal. At the same time, they are being pressured to avoid compromising either cultural pattern. The workshops attempt to address their dilemma as they try to balance both worlds.

1. *Teen Workshop Set 1: "Culture Talk – Balancing Multiple Frames of Reference":* This workshop emphasized promoting confidence and ethnic pride among bicultural teens, faced with the dilemma of maintaining their cultural heritage, while encountering the challenges of pressure from their peers. The workshop attempts to assist the children in becoming comfortable with ethnic and cultural differences, as well as recommending ways they can be successful at school. It helps them acquire a sense of pride in being who they are, while respecting others who are different from them. The workshop stresses understanding the concepts of individual freedom and pluralism, without feeling either inferior or superior to others in the society.

2. *Teen Workshop Set 2: "Challenges at School and Peer Pressure":* This workshop expanded on the earlier workshop, by focusing more specifically on the challenges of academic requirements, school discipline, and peer pressure, in conjunction with the dual expectations of their parents and teachers. It helped the children understand the privileges a secular education and the public school

system might provide to them, as well as make them aware of the resources available at school to help them. This workshop in particular focused on ways students could excel in school, and stressed the importance of higher education as a means of upward social mobility in the new society.

3. *Teen Workshop Set 3: "Balancing Parallel Socialization":* This workshop helped the teenagers balance the dual expectations of their home and school environments and the conflicting role models they had. The objective was to assist them in growing up with ethnic pride and confidence. It helped them to develop a dual anchorage in both cultures, to be proud of their heritage, as well as acculturate themselves to the new culture. The workshop emphasized ethnic pride and an acceptance of cultural differences, without feeling inferior to their mainstream classmates.

Communication Strategy of the Workshops

Three characteristics of the workshop leader were used to advantage in attempting to work with the immigrant groups and their contacts in the host society. First was the leader's professional education and expertise, as holding a doctoral degree and being employed at a University. These were helpful in winning confidence and credibility with teachers and parents. Even teachers who may have had issues with the leader being a woman of color and a foreign accent, tended to recognize these credentials. For the parents, the leader's experience as an immigrant parent helped to establish credibility. Parents identified with the leader as someone who had faced the same parenting challenges. Some parents also identified with the leader as one who shared their minority race and religious status. Reaching the children was somewhat more difficult, since they did not understand such credentials. The fact that the workshop leader also had children helped somewhat, and most eventually developed a unique confidence in the workshop which they were yet to attain with regard to their own parents and teachers.

Major Hurdles for the Acculturation Program and Two-Way Communication

The most daunting hurdle for the program was its cost in terms of time and money. School districts involved in the workshops were different in many ways. However, all were generally united in their financial constraints. Most schools did not have a budget for dealing with the new needs of different types of students and teachers. As a result they had difficulty following the schedule of simultaneous, coordinated workshops, even if they appreciated the holistic nature of the program. Most schools sought out the services only when an incident of some kind occurred and they needed a quick solution.

Each time a diversity-training workshop for teachers was planned, the school had to find and pay substitute teachers, a cost few districts can bear on numerous occasions. Moreover, some administrators who had been brought up in the world that idealized a "melting pot" society were not easily convinced about "reciprocal acculturation." Efforts to convince them of this new ideology were not always persuasive. Some always remained unconvinced, and regarded the new ideology of reciprocal acculturation as an affront to traditional American ideals. They believed in the ideology of assimilation, and felt it had withstood the test of time. They were convinced this one-way process had worked in the past, and should continue to be followed.

However, the changing pressures of globalization, coupled with the influx of new and different immigrants, as detailed earlier, have fundamentally altered the way in which acculturation must be handled. What is more important is to educate many community and institutional leaders in American society about more effective ways of bringing new immigrants into the mainstream, as well as mechanisms to assist the next generation of immigrants in becoming as successful as their predecessors.

It is clear that some communities and institutions have learned to adapt to these new challenges. This can be seen in some schools in the Detroit Metropolitan Area, which is home to a large concentration of Arab immigrants from the Middle East. In this area, several school districts have adopted procedures which are evidence of reciprocal acculturation on the part of both the ethnic communities and the dominant community institutions. Some school districts and colleges have become more conscious about dietary restrictions of Muslim students, and have begun offering foods which accommodate those requirements. The broader community has also become aware of Muslim holidays, such as *Ramadan* (the Muslim month of fasting). Such accommodations inevitably produce more cordial relations among members of the community.

Summary and Conclusions

This chapter has focused on an approach to improving interaction between agents of American society, in the person of teachers in the public schools, and recent immigrant families who are unfamiliar with American culture and its school system. The program consists of a series of coordinated workshops which make use of the concept of "parallel socialization." The workshops provide a mechanism by which teachers can work more effectively with immigrant parents and their children to improve relations between the school and the family, and thereby enhance the effectiveness of the children's learning experience. They could be useful as models for other school settings in which such difficult relationships occur.

While the workshops described here were specifically designed for use in schools, the techniques they employed could lead to similar success, not only in school settings, but in other community settings in which people from diverse cultures interact. The broader focus of the program was the elimination of misunderstandings which exist between representatives of the dominant society and the immigrant newcomers who are unfamiliar with American culture. The coordinated workshops are an approach to resolving such misunderstandings. Hence they could also serve as models for other institutions and communities which seek to improve inter-racial and inter-ethnic relations within their midst.

Chapter 11
Models of Multi-culturalism in an International Context

Every society wrestles with its own cultural issues. Wherever multi-culturalism exists, it presents an extraordinary challenge to the society. Where heterogeneity of one kind and degree or another exists, it requires the society to deal with a unique set of challenges. These include the need to legitimize the incorporation of ethnic diversity among its members, as well as to create a sense of national unity among the members of these diverse ethnicities (Kallen, 1982). As part of this process, it is also necessary to invite and increase citizen participation in civil society (Tiryakian, 2004). Without these participatory processes, cultural diversity produces social fragmentation, rather than a unified society.

How can such "unification within diversity" be achieved? In an attempt to answer this question, this chapter provides a discussion of the multi-cultural models used in five societies. It analyzes the similarities and differences of these models, as well as some of the problems and promises of multi-culturalism present in each society. The analysis will include an examination of the ways in which these societies wrestle with multi-culturalism, together with their successes and mixed results in adopting this approach to diversity. Finally, the chapter offers some suggestions on improving intergroup relations at the macro-level.

The word multi-culturalism was first used in 1957 to describe Switzerland, but it became more common when Canada used the term in the late 1960s. Use of the term quickly spread to other English-speaking countries, where its use and discussion is more prominent (Kallen, 1982). This chapter transcends a predominantly "Anglophone" focus by referring to other countries that have adopted a multi-cultural approach.

First, multi-culturalism in the USA, an Anglophone nation, is discussed. This is followed by an analysis of cultural dualism in Canada. In particular, Canada's official multi-cultural public policy, designed to create national unity within a diversity context, is highlighted. A discussion of Australia's multi-racial identity, together with its impact on multi-culturalism, will follow. Australia's multi-culturalism merits attention, as this nation has been successful in bringing together people from well over 100 ethnic backgrounds.

This chapter is contributed by Brenda I. Marshall.

M.C. Sengstock, *Voices of Diversity*, Clinical Sociology: Research and Practice,
DOI 10.1007/978-0-387-89666-3_11, © Springer Science+Business Media, LLC 2009

239

Moving outside of the Anglophone format, the French model of multi-culturalism is then discussed. Finally, as an interesting contrast to these societies, with their western European origins, Trinidad and Tobago's multi-culturalism is examined. Trinidad and Tobago is considered by several scholars to be the most ethnically, religiously, and culturally diverse of all the islands in the Caribbean (Yelvington, 1993; Cornwell and Stoddard, 2001). The role of multi-culturalism and ethnicity is often used to explain the country's national culture. Examining multi-culturalism in Trinidad and Tobago serves to give a brief example of the present scope of Caribbean multi-culturalism. All five societies have been shaped throughout their histories by wide-scale immigration. Further, they provide the basis for a comparative discussion of multi-culturalism, with sufficient scope for an analysis of its present state.

Multi-culturalism – The Case of the USA

The USA – How Multi-cultural is Its Population? Chapters 1 and 2 provided some basic historical background concerning the diverse immigrant populations that have entered the USA throughout its history, and continue to do so into the present. These chapters described the ways in which immigrants were initially accepted, how they progressed, and the degree to which they were eventually assimilated into American society. This sociohistoric reality of the USA allows for a more accurate discussion of the present state of multi-culturalism in the American society. Throughout the entire period, a succession of immigration laws has been enacted. Immigration legislation continues to be enforced in the USA; that immigration, together with considerable religious tolerance, creates the ethnic and religious diversity which now exists in the USA.

Relations between natives and newcomers have long been a mixture of confrontation and accommodation in the USA. How did this population of diverse people come to constitute a single society? And how do they presently coexist? America has been described as probably the most diverse society on earth, although some debate the claim (Schuck, 2003: 3). America's multi-culturalism encompasses both ethnic/racial and religious diversity. Understanding the sociohistoric reality of the cultural, linguistic, and racial diversity of America's past allows for a better understanding of the present multi-culturalism in the American society.

With a few notable exceptions, the US population can be categorized as either migrants or offspring of earlier migrants. Those exceptions include Native Americans, who were already present when the first Europeans came to America; native Hawaiians, whose lands were overtaken and annexed by the USA; and many persons of Mexican origin, who lived in border areas when they were taken over by the USA. The influx of 5 million immigrants in 1820–1860 and 26 million between 1870 and 1920 was noted earlier. American immigrants originated from a vast array of countries, with the largest numbers originating from various locales in Europe, Latin America, and Asia (Parillo, 1994; Kivisto, 2002). Each successive wave of immigrants has contributed to America's ethnic history in some unique way.

"Acceptable" and "unacceptable" Europeans have long been identified in US society. Jews, Catholic, Slavs, Mediterranean peoples, and Nordic peoples from Western Europe were all seen as inferior and therefore threats to the Protestant majority. Grant (1916) commented that these diverse new arrivals were filling the jails, insane asylums, and almshouses, and generally devaluing American life. The Europeans who entered the USA during the late 19th and early 20th centuries were instrumental in the invention of the conception of the White race, and their inclusion in this definition is functional to their American identity (Allen, 1994). The Irish are an example here. In their early years, they were categorized as "white" and often considered to be similar to Africans. To rid themselves of this stigma, the Irish embraced White culture and identity. They distanced themselves from outsider groups and supported White supremacy oppression practices (Kivisto, 2002: 46).

Turning from White immigration to African-American identity, four historical time periods provide insight into their status: forced immigration and institutionalized slave labor; emancipation and institutionalized segregation; the great migration and development of urban ghettoes; and the civil rights movement of the 20th century. Even though the laws have changed, an ambiguous status remains, and African-Americans are still marginalized. After coming through a Civil War that freed them, African-American history was profoundly affected by the events of the 1950s and 1960s. Following the Civil Rights Movement that abolished legal segregation, African-Americans still struggle with the same issues that obtained previously. This has served to confuse and add uncertainty about their national identity with America.

With regard to the most recent waves of immigration, considerable debate surrounds the immigration reform law of 1965 and its role in defining America's diversity. Some scholars suggest that the Act realized unanticipated multi-cultural consequences, which were never intended by the framers of the initial legislation (Chinn, 1996). The Immigration Act opened the doors of the USA to an international influx of immigrants. Migrants from Cuba, El Salvador, Nicaragua, the Caribbean, Asia, Guatemala, and other countries in the Western Hemisphere continue to come to the USA; their impact on America's demographic diversity is unparalleled. The 2000 census reported that more than 31 million foreign-born individuals live in the USA. This is 11.3 million more than in 1990 (Schmitt, 2001). The USA is described as the leading immigrant-receiving nation in the world (Kivisto, 2002: 73). Foreign-born comprise 9.0% of the total population.

Figures from the US Census Bureau (2001) show that Latinos, comprising Mexicans, Puerto Ricans, and Cubans, and representing 12.5% of the population, are the largest of the new immigrant groups. It is predicted that they will soon replace African-Americans as the largest racial minority (Census Bureau, 2001: 1). Out of this well-established ethnic community, demands for ending discrimination and a greater voice in social and political life are being heard.

Often termed the "model minority," Asians in the USA have also grown considerably (Takaki, 1989). Though a numerical minority, Asians often are held up as a model of success. They enjoy higher per capita incomes and educational attainment levels and lower levels of poverty than other ethnic groups. In some cases they are perceived to do even better than Whites. The term "model minority," however, is often used to denigrate the status of Latinos, Blacks, and American Indians, by comparing them unfavorably with the Asian success story. The term is intended to convey the need for these other groups to imitate the industry of the Asians to attain success (Takaki, 1989: 474–484). Despite their alleged success, however, Asians continue to confront exclusionary policies and practices that prevent their full incorporation into the mainstream (Tuan, 1998).

The religious affiliations of new Americans and recent immigrants present another significant component of cultural pluralism in America, an issue which has implications for the American religious sphere (Schuck, 2003; Parillo, 1994). The presence of Asians and Middle Easterners has added three major world religions, Islam, Buddhism, and Hinduism, to religious diversity in the USA (Warner and Wittner, 1998).

To summarize, American multi-culturalism includes overtones of race, religion, and date of arrival. In general, the closer one can trace one's history to the White race, Protestant religion, and early colonial settlers, save, of course, for the status of the Native Americans, the higher one is thought of in American sociocultural history. Recent arrivals, dark skin, and non-Christian religion are the least acceptable sociocultural categories. With this background in mind, we move to a discussion of the model which multi-culturalism takes in the USA at the onset of the 21st century.

Multi-culturalism – The US Model

In its zeal to preserve "American culture," despite the diverse composition of immigrants, America has formulated several policies to maintain its unique cultural identity over the years. These approaches to multi-culturalism combine to create America's model for dealing with diversity. In its essence, the original American model primarily included the concept of a monocultural identity, derived from the original British culture. This approach has been secured by a succession of varying legal acts and discrimination policies. Subsequent models included assimilation, the "melting pot" approach, and more recently, multi-culturalism (Gordon, 1964, 1978).

Monoculturalism in America

Initially, America was committed to a monoculture, aimed at racial preservation, as well as the promotion of the original British culture from which the majority of the earliest colonists came. Gordon (1964) has called this approach, "Anglo-Conformity." While the early British settlers did not want to be ruled by Britain, they certainly wanted to preserve its traditions, governmental structure, and culture. They held strong sentiments about which foreigners should be admitted and eventually allowed to attain citizenship. At an early point, the 1790 Nationality Act gave citizenship rights to "free white persons"; it further controlled citizenship by excluding those Whites who were indentured and lacked property. Later measures used to promote and ensure a monocultural approach included the Quota Act of 1921 and the Immigration Act of 1924, both aimed at restricting immigration to the "desirable races" of Western Europe, while limiting the number of immigrants from Eastern and Southern Europe. The major objective was to ensure that immigrants could be easily assimilated into the existing population; hence preference was given to persons who were part of the White, Anglo-Saxon, Protestant tradition. Consequently, immigrants from Great Britain, and secondarily, Germany (also with White, Anglo-Saxon, Protestant origins), were favored. Alterations were also made in other naturalization and citizenship measures (U.S. Immigration History, 1998; Jacobson, 1998).

Since the maintenance of White supremacy was a goal, citizenship rights were not extended to persons of other racial descent, such as Native Americans, Mexicans, and Africans. In the case of Africans, the debates did not include them; instead, they were legally excluded from the national identity process. In addition to legal action, segregation, racial discrimination, and even deportation were used to ensure that Blacks, Mexicans, and persons of other races did not share in this identity. In the case of persons with African descent, it was not until 1870, with passage of the Fourteenth Amendment to the US Constitution, that citizenship rights for Blacks were a theoretical possibility. However, for Blacks, emancipation still did not mean inclusion into the American national identity. Actual attainment of such rights had to wait until the Civil Rights Movement of the 1950s and 1960s.

The Shift to Assimilation

When the several measures aimed at continuance of the British model seemed to have failed, assimilation became the tool of choice in the USA. Assimilation is the process by which members of one cultural group are expected to "blend" into a second group (Gordon, 1964). In the case of the USA, immigrants were expected to blend into the extant American pattern, such that their cultural beliefs, attitudes, values, customs, traditions, language and accent, and personal identity, resembled closely that of the American model. Assimilation was considered a means of ensuring that immigrants adopted the American identity without contaminating the nation. Alexander (2001: 243) refers to assimilation as a process by which members of groups generally considered inferior are allowed and encouraged to "pass" into public life.

Many people believed, however, that the cultural assimilation of new immigrants would be difficult. Consequently, they advocated the development of measures to ensure that "foreign" ways would be shed rapidly. To achieve this goal, ethnic minorities were pressured to rid themselves of all that made them distinctive and become carbon copies of the ethnic majority (Alba, 1999: 7). Assimilation was not necessarily one-sided. It allowed two or more groups to enter civil life, provided that the out-group members shed their polluted primal identities (Alexander, 2001: 243).

Rise of the "Melting Pot"

When assimilation failed, the "melting pot" notion became the model of choice for integrating the millions of new immigrants. Soon after its introduction, however, this model also became a metaphor for assimilation. The melting pot model assumed that immigrants of diverse origin would acquire the American creed, while retaining old rituals of their ethnic heritage. In large part, the notion of the melting pot promoted the notion that popular culture could be enriched, without threatening the core of American culture and identity (Citrin et al., 1994: 7).

In reality, however, melting pot ideology was synonymous with the concept of assimilation, in which various groups of new immigrants affect the values of the dominant group to eventually produce a distinct new breed of people. Further, this aspect of the melting pot idea has long been considered to be of doubtful value. Most authorities believe that the melting pot process really did not result in the development of a new identity and culture. Instead, the result was actually assimilation, with immigrants actually required to shed "native" or "ethnic" customs, learn to speak English, adopt a political creed, improve personal hygiene, avoid alcohol, and adopt American style religious beliefs (Higham, 1985). Group identities often persisted beyond the first generation; the rapid shedding envisioned was not attained. The failure of the approach was solidified by the fact that the dominant society had little interest in fulfilling its part of the bargain, namely, by accepting some new approaches into the dominant cultural stream. Hence the "melting pot" concept never became a reality.

Multi-culturalism

"Multiculturalism is the quest to achieve equal recognition and inclusion for the diverse cultures which constitute the United States," according to Long (1997: vii), who sees this as an unmistakable feature of present US society. Multi-culturalism, often called "cultural pluralism" or "social pluralism," also sparks heated discussions, since it tends to challenge the validity of the "American" identity (Long, 1997, vii). Multi-culturalism as a movement in America has been seen as a significant and recent reflection of the long-continuing politics of identity (Spencer, 1994: 547). American identity is still considered to be that which was established by the White, English-speaking Protestants at the time of the Revolution (Steinberg, 1989: 7). Some still accept the initial belief that immigrants are inassimilable, and that their customs and manners constitute a threat to the American cultural identity (Spencer, 1994: 549).

In contrast, decades of practice in the USA have produced a different reality. Makedon (1996: 2) asserts, "In the United States, multiculturalism is couched inside legal, political and psychological 'protective shields' that make it more than just a theory of social existence. Thus, based on legal decisions handed down by the U.S. Supreme Court, which are in turn based on the court's interpretation of the Federal Constitution, minority ethnic or cultural groups may not be unreasonably discriminated against." This legal protection gives such groups the opportunity to coexist with all their rights intact, even if a real or hypothetical "majority" were to prefer that they did not.

A core assumption of multi-culturalism in the USA is a recognition that individual identity rests on two bases: their shared and equal status as American citizens, and their ethnic origins, both of which play important roles in shaping their values and interests. Consequently, there must be assurances that racial, cultural, or language inequality do not exist; nor should these be the basis for claims for larger shares of society's goods (Citrin et al., 1994: 9). Multi-culturalism in the USA covers a wide range of practices. These include educational practices which make American students more aware of world history. Bilingual education is another aspect of multi-culturalism in the USA. Beginning in 1960, bilingual education was introduced. The Bilingual Education Act (BEA) of 1968 provided a framework that advocated respect and toleration for cultural differences, globally, internationally, locally, and individually. This could be done via education at all levels, including more television coverage of various groups' ethnic cultures, promotion of more ethnic festivals, and celebrations. However, establishment of bilingualism has been vigorously resisted in the USA.

Multi-culturalism is criticized for tending to promote unequal distribution of power and cultural incompatibility between the minorities and the majority society. For example, it can be seen as advocating unequal distribution of goods and services through policies such as affirmative action, in which minorities may benefit from preferential treatment because of their classification. Moreover, Joppke (1996: 454) raises questions concerning the commonly held assumption that US multiculturalism is related to the recent waves of non-European immigrants. Instead, he sees the growth of this approach as the direct consequence of America's unresolved race problem.

In summary, the US model for dealing with diverse cultures and groups has long been a composite of three different perspectives on other cultures which have appeared throughout American history. The current approach itself represents a blending of these three views. The "English First" movement and the continued emphasis on tenets of the Protestant religion represent a force for maintenance of the Anglo-Conformity approach. Commonly heard assertions that ethnic groups ought to "blend" into the American mainstream represent a continuation of the belief that the concept of the "Melting Pot" can, and should, still be achieved. Finally, the "multi-cultural" or "cultural pluralist" approach is a recognition of the continued presence of immigrants and their descendants, many of whom maintain some cultural patterns of their ancestors, sometimes several generations after their arrival in the U.S.

State Sponsored Multi-culturalism: The Case of Canada

Brief History

Canada is one of the more significant advanced industrial nations which have been shaped by wide-scale immigration. However, unlike Americans, Canadians more readily view themselves in pluralistic terms. Canada fits John Porter's (1965) metaphor, *"The Vertical Mosaic,"* as used in his analysis of class structure and power. In this view, Canadian ethnic groups not only view themselves as *different* from each other, but also as *hierarchically arranged*, such that the various groups perceive themselves as "better than" other ethnic groups (Kivisto, 2002: 85). Unlike the USA, Canada confronts not only high levels of immigration, but also issues related to mobilized ethnic nationalism, with each group attempting to maximize its own identity and culture to a greater degree than in the USA.

Canada's history began with the efforts of the French explorer, Jacques Cartier, who claimed the land for the King of France in 1534. This was followed by British incursions into the region later in the century, which resulted in Britain claiming large expanses of land. After four wars, from 1689 to 1815, leading to the signing of the Treaty of Paris, the British managed to gain control of a large area of Canada from the French. Although the French were the original founding group, they became a minority after the establishment of British control, and were politically and economically inferior to the English in the Anglophone areas (Kivisto, 2002: 86). The two groups differed not only in language but also in religion, since the English were Protestant and the French minority was Catholic.

This divergence was accentuated after the American Revolution, when approximately 40,000 American colonists who were loyal to the crown moved to Canada. This produced an even greater population disparity between the French and the English, with the French reduced to a politically and economically subordinate position (Kivisto, 2002). Hence from a very early period, Canada has been confronted with a culturally diverse population, the major differences focusing on language and religion (Lower, 1977).

Diverse Population

Like other, long-standing nation states, Canada deals with an increasingly diverse population. At the time of Confederation in the 1860s, Canada's population was divided almost entirely among three groups: the indigenous people, the French, and the English. A very small stream of Chinese and European immigrants began to enter during this period as well. Growing demands for labor led the Canadian government to embark on a program of structured immigration (Hawkins, 1989: 4–21). To realize this objective, the Immigration Acts of 1910 and 1919 established the basis for a "White Canada." Europeans were welcomed, while people of color, particularly the Chinese and other Asians, were barred entry into Canada. In the aftermath of the Depression and Second World War, further large-scale immigration occurred, resulting in the arrival of large numbers of Italians, Greeks, Poles, and Portuguese (Elliott, 1983). The Europeans who migrated to Canada during this period eventually became a "third force," an odd term in view of the fact that there already were three components to the Canadian population. However, the indigenous population was never viewed as a major force within Canadian society (Canadian Heritage, 2008).

During the 1950s, further efforts were made to open Canada's doors to new immigrants. This was done largely to allow the nation to realize economic expansion and compete successfully in the world market. In the words of Prime Minister John Diefenbaker, the nation's choice was to "populate or perish" (Hawkins, 1989: 38). Immigration laws were revised to encourage mass immigration. With reference to this period, Fleras and Elliott (1996) point out that the increased immigration had a profound effect on the Canadian demographic makeup. Although the number of immigrants entering the USA during this period exceeded that entering Canada, the Canadian population at the time was only one-tenth the size of the USA. Consequently, the increased immigration had a much more extreme impact on Canada. By the 1990s, there were 8.8 immigrants per 1,000 residents in Canada, compared with only 2.5 per 1,000 in the USA (Fleras and Elliott, 1996).

In 1962, the government put an end to "White Canada" policies. Racial discrimination in immigration law effectively ended that year (Kivisto, 2002: 97). This move was carried out to provide workers, as well as to enhance Canada's reputation as a non-White Commonwealth country. Due to the change in immigration laws, countries of origin for immigrants also changed. Three decades later, even though Europeans continued to come, around three-quarters of all newcomers arrived from Asia, the Caribbean, and Central America (Kelly and Trebilcock, 1998). Referring to the impact of the arrival of these newcomers in Canada, Kivisto (2002: 97, quoting from Samuel, 1990) states "...The new arrivals have within the course of three decades changed the character of multi-cultural Canada."

Multi-culturalism – The Canadian Model

As a result of these influences, three components exist in Canada's multi-cultural model. The next section will focus on these three components.

Mononationalism

First, and quite similar to the US model, Canada's initial model was a mononational one, in which British superiority, laced with English as the language of choice, was the main goal. The ideology of the dominant British group was encouraged and supported by the use of state power. Even though there was a French presence, the English-speaking majority dominated, and the idea of a dual society (Anglophone and Francophone) was not entertained. To ensure this dominance, laws passed between 1763 and 1867 restricted immigration exclusively to British Isle immigrants. This bias in favor of British immigrants continued until 1945. Only a small number of Slavic immigrants represented any deviation from the norm of the dominant British population. The intent was to guarantee that English-speaking Canadians would outnumber the French-speaking Canadians, so as to ensure English language dominance, and hence, British power.

The scene changed somewhat by 1896, with the arrival of rich Chinese business-men, Jews, Ukrainians, and Polish immigrants. This was followed by the Quota System in 1923 that allowed a limited number of Asians from India to enter the country. The English–French duality continued, and the use of French was acknowledged at some levels. However, immigrants from Northern and Western Europe were assimilated to the dominant British population, not the French. Consequently, English remained more or less the language of choice. This leads to the second major component of the Canadian model, assimilation.

Assimilation

As has just been noted, Canada encouraged assimilation to ensure that immigrants conformed to British expectations of behavior, language, and culture. Similar to the USA, persons who were non-English speaking and/or non-British were expected to adopt the culture and language of the dominant group. The intent was to ensure that non-English-speaking Canadians would be assimilated into British culture, that English would remain the primary language, and that British culture would retain its dominance. Over the years, the French language and culture have declined, while the use of English has increased, even though the proportion of English/British residents has significantly decreased.

Official Multi-culturalism

Multi-culturalism became a component of the Canadian model only recently. At the beginning of the 20th century, Canada was in many ways a conglomerate, in which the dominant ethnic and cultural makeup was easily identifiable. Dupont and Lemarchand (2001: 315) note that the Canadian society at that time comprised: "A French Canadian majority and an English minority in Quebec, an English and a mixed-English population in Ontario, a dominant Slavic population in the Prairies, the Loyalists in the Maritimes, and a French-speaking minority in New Brunswick." The regions at that time were linked by the will of the colonial power to unite its colonies and territories, along with the political determination of Canadian political leaders to act in accordance with that preference, as established in 1867 (Dupont and Lemarchand, 2001: 315).

This situation left Canada with a problematic task: the need to search for a way to define its ethno-cultural diversity and its new ethnic plurality (Dupont and Lemarchand, 2001: 322). The desired "ethnic mosaic" of national identity called for the recognition of ethnic diversity, while seeking to overcome decades of ethnic particularism (Breton, 1986; Kivisto, 2002; Roy, 1995). The English-speaking majority, which now included descendants from the original British settlers, as well as immigrants who had been assimilated into the English-speaking majority, backed official multi-culturalism in Canada. French-speaking Canadians, however, rejected the notion of multi-culturalism.

Consequently, there was no unified support for multi-culturalism at the time it was introduced. Nonetheless, the government introduced an official policy, which asserted that all Canadians had the right to make a choice concerning whether to retain their original cultures. All cultures were given a universal right to be celebrated. The idea of multi-culturalism and the mosaic concept was sold to Canadians, and the policy adopted in 1971. Thus official multi-culturalism became a state policy in Canada before multi-culturalism, as a philosophy or an ideology, had become widely accepted (Dupont and Lemarchand, 2001: 322). The notion helped to project the idea of a Canadian unified identity. It has been suggested that the goal of multi-culturalism in Canada was to keep the country together and derive a sense of a shared Canadian identity and loyalty to the nation-state (Wilson, 1993; Harles, 1997). The concept also served to move Canada from its former British model, and allowed the values, political ethos, and symbols defined as "British" to change. It also afforded Canadians an opportunity to consciously differentiate themselves from the US image (Kivisto, 2002: 309). During its first decade, Canadian multi-culturalism was a work in process. The government established ministries and provided funding to promote a multi-cultural approach. Various ethnic organizations were established; diversity-related publications were supported, and educational programs were developed to promote diversity (Burnet, 1981).

Multi-culturalism moved into a new stage during the second decade of Canada's multi-cultural movement (Reitz and Breton, 1994). The second stage of multi-culturalism in Canada occurred in the 1980s, and was marked by the conservative government's passage of the Multi-culturalism Act in 1988. This Act raised multi-culturalism to the legal level of bilingualism (Fleras and Elliot, 1996). It also established the principle that the constitution (1982), and the Charter of Rights and Freedoms (1985), both emphasized Canada's essential multi-culturalism (Liodakis, 1998). Two articles of the constitution (15/1 and 27) stressed the multi-cultural nature of Canada. Article 15/1 affirmed that no discrimination should exist on the basis of race, national or ethnic origin, color, religion, gender, or age. Article 27 asserted that The Charter of Rights should be interpreted so as to maintain, support, and increase the value of Canada's multi-cultural heritage (Dupont and Lemarchand 2001: 324). Multi-culturalism was further legitimized in light of its potential economic benefits. The allure of international trade and the comparative advantage of such trade were envisioned as a result of the varying languages and cultures present in Canada's plethora of diverse populations (Fleras and Elliott, 1996: 332).

By the 1990s, the third stage of policy development had arisen. Civic multi-culturalism, characterized by society building, was fostered. Canadians became concerned about integration. Rightist groups saw multi-culturalism as a waste of money and insisted that the government stress more "true" Canadian values. This debate was intensified in the 1993 federal election, with the Reform Party promising to abolish official multi-culturalism (Harrison, 2008). The conservative government, while still supportive of multi-culturalism, enacted a new law on multi-culturalism in 1988. This law linked folklore, multi-culturalism, and citizenship under the minister for multi-culturalism (Kaplan, 1993; Liodakis, 1998: 38).

During this period, serious attempts were made to include all Canadians in national institutions, and to foster a sense of belonging and identity (Fleras and Elliott, 1996: 334–335). The role of the "third force" was more visible, and can be noted in the 2000 election of Ujjal Dosanjh, an Asian Indian, as premier of British Columbia, and the first provincial premier of Asian background in Canadian politics (Kivisto, 2002: 99). The integration of new immigrants into the political and social mainstream is noted during this stage of multi-cultural development.

Referring to Canada's state of multi-culturalism, Dupont and Lemarchand (2001: 326) claim: "In the 1990's, English Canada looked more like the United States: a White melting pot surrounded by visible minorities. The history is not the same, the picture is different, but the problems and issues are alike." There is a growing geographical divide in Canada between its three metropolises (Toronto, Montreal, and Vancouver), which are multi-racial and multi-cultural, and the rest of the country, which is mostly white, slightly multi-cultural, and with few visible minorities.

During the last part of the 20th century, Canada had become a pluralist country. Immigration laws were freed from prejudices, so that individuals from varying cultural backgrounds have made Canada their home. Fleras and Elliott (1996) summarize multi-cultural development in Canada in terms of three stages: the folkloric (1971–1980), the institutional (1981–1990), and the civic (1990–2009). Each stage had its own objectives and employed different means to realize them. The folkloric stage of multi-culturalism is seen as that associated with "song and dance" activities of cultural groups; this stage placed an emphasis on "celebrating differences." All culture was seen as equal and contributing to the Canadian mosaic. Of this period it is claimed:

> The years of Anglo-conformity were behind us. God, King and the Empire could no longer be the cultural imperative of all Canadians. All culture was seen as equal and all contributing to the Canadian Mosaic. To this end there was a shift from that of the "two founding nations" cultural model towards a more bilingual but multicultural vision that included "the third force" of non-British and non-French ethno-cultural groups. In this stage individuals were protected from discrimination as a result of their cultural "choices"; instead, they were encouraged to cultivate these choices, while participating in Canadian life generally (Fleras and Elliott, 1996: 331).

Diversity has become a fact of life, especially in the three metropolises mentioned above. This diversity is based on the acceptance of cultural differences. However, official multi-culturalism, while able to forge cultural acceptance of differences, has been unable to remove the old symbolic order, in which Her Majesty the Queen of England occupies the pinnacle position. Canadians continue to operate under the hierarchy of British rule, with its English symbols. The structural organization of power in the cultural and political landscape remains, despite the introduction of official multi-culturalism (Dupont and Lemarchand, 2001: 329). Liodakis (1998: 1) refers to Canada's state of Multi-culturalism as a Canadian demographic reality. Canadians remain fragmented on the issue of multi-culturalism. Public debates criticizing the policy are not uncommon. A major theme seems to be that Canada, in its eagerness to be seen as a diverse nation, has failed to establish a clear culture of its own. Canada has become a nation of hyphenated identities. Some apparently believe that ethnic interests have been placed ahead of national inter-ests, and individual rights have been subordinated to group rights (Dupont and Lamarchand, 2001: 309).

In conclusion, multi-culturalism in Canada has been criticized on five counts. First, some commentators see Canadian multi-culturalism as helping to reproduce stereotypes of ethnic groups (Bissoondath, 1994). It is claimed that the approach places individuals into preconceived stereotypes, accentuating what people are, and not who they are. A country of hybrids is seen as the outcome. As Bisoondadth (1994: 73) contends: "We are so many colors, that we are essentially colorless."

Second, Canadian multi-culturalism is accused of undermining social cohesion (Bibby, 1990: 7–8). Promoting peaceful coexistence based on cultural relativism is seen as supporting the break down of group life. Excessive individualism and cul-tural relativism have led to the construction of "mosaics within mosaics"; as a result, Canadians have lost a sense of community and moved away from the collectivism that characterized Canadian life in the 1950s (Bibby, 1990: 7–8). Some Federal political parties also present this view, stating that it is the obligation of Canada's Federal government to first preserve and promote "national" culture, and second, to encourage ethnic cultures to integrate into it (Reform Party of Canada, 1989).

Third, multi-culturalism is accused of ghettoizing ethnic groups: ". . .ethnic com-munities appear so busy preserving and promoting their own culture that they have no time, resources or incentives in participating in national institutions" (Liodakis, 1998: 6). While a correction of this problem was one of the objectives of the civic stage in the 1990s, it has yet to bear fruit (Abu-Laban and Stasiulis, 1992: 376; Li, 1988).

Fourth, multi-culturalism is criticized for undermining the special claims of Fran-cophones and Native people (Liodakis, 1998: 7). Some critics, as well as native representatives, are of the view that Canadian multi-culturalism undermines the legitimacy of Quebec nationalism (Abu-Laban and Stasiulis, 1992: 367). And native people and their representatives feel multi-culturalism in Canada reduces them to "just another minority," undermining their self-government aspirations, reducing them to an insignificant people, endangering their survival. They favor negotiating their future in a framework that recognizes their unique status (Fleras and Elliott, 1996: 343).

Lastly, Canadian multi-culturalism is accused of depoliticizing and disguising social inequality (Liodakis, 1998: 7). The argument here is that, in its early stages, multi-culturalism focused on "song and dance," and did little to challenge the domi-nance of the French and British in political, economic, and cultural realms (Roberts and Clifton, 1982; Lewycky, 1992). Cultural groups are always described by eth-nic adjectives; consequently, members of these groups tend to be clustered together and marginalized, rather than being treated as individuals (Liodakis, 1998: 8). Bar-riers remain to full participation in national institutions, the result of Canadian class structure, patriarchal ideologies and practices, and cultural differences (Merhgi, 1990). Despite the above criticisms of Canada's multi-culturalism, ethnic diversity, together with a sense of shared Canadian identity and loyalty to the nation-state, continue to be Canada's hope as moves into the 21st century.

Australia – A Multi-racial Empire?

Brief History

Australia, like Canada and the USA, is considered to be a significant advanced industrial nation, whose history has been shaped in major ways by large-scale immigration (Kivisto, 2002: 84). Since 1945, more than 5 million settlers from different countries have come to Australia, leading to great cultural diversity. In this regard, Australia may be described as a "classical country" of immigration (Castles, 1992: 549). Moreover, Australia has been described: "As the only continent with a multi-ethnic population to be governed as a single political entity" (Smolicz, 1997: 171). Though some Australians may not agree with the idea, Australia has been likened to a laboratory for multi-culturalism, because of the way it has "managed" its internal pluralism, and its ethnically diverse immigrant groups (Smolicz, 1997: 171). This portrayal is particularly interesting in view of Australia's history. Its current approach, which favors multi-cultural diversity, follows an earlier stance which has been described as explicitly racist, favoring a "White Australia," and an assimilationist approach to immigration (Smolicz, 1997; Jupp, 2002).

A study of the history of Australia reveals that for the first two-thirds of the 20th century, Australia had defined itself legally and culturally as "White Australia." This stance was supported by The Immigration Restriction Act of 1901, which codified this understanding of national identity by erecting a racial divide between those deemed to be capable of assimilation into Australian society and those who were not (Smolicz, 1997: 107). It was the belief of policy makers that the "inferior" races would lower the quality of life, and that miscegenation was a distinct threat that was to be prevented. To ensure the purity of the nationals, only white immigrants were allowed to enter Australia. Immigrants from Britain were the most desired.

The situation changed during the postwar period. By the late 1960s, it was difficult to attract western and southern European workers to Australia. This shortage of immigrants forced the Australian government to relax some of its immigration policies. Castles (1992: 551) describes these policies as, "A series of measures to attract and retain immigrants: further liberalization of family reunion, recruitment in Yugoslavia and Latin America, and some relaxation of the White Australia Policy." The world recession of the 1970s contributed to some drastic changes in Australia's immigration policies. The Australian Labor Party (ALP) government abolished The White Australia Policy, introducing entry criteria which did not discriminate on the basis of race, ethnicity, religion, or national origin (Collins, 1988: 26). Even though the immigration program was intended to maintain the Anglo-Australian image, the reverse had occurred, and great ethnic diversity prevailed. The Australian government replaced its assimilation practices with those of integration and radically inclusive policies toward immigrants. Integration became the official policy from the mid-1960s until 1972. This was considered the stepping-stone to multi-culturalism in Australia (Murphy, 1993: 164).

Multi-culturalism – the Australian Model

Australia's multi-cultural model developed as a consequence of the new immigration policies that saw the entry of immigrants from over 100 nations. A series of approaches were taken to deal with the large number of immigrants. First, assimilation was attempted. Second, they experimented with integration. When this failed, Australia toyed with multi-culturalism. These three stages will be described.

Assimilation

Assimilation was used by Australians until the mid-1960s as the first official process to help retain a racially pure nation. New immigrants were expected eventually to become a part of the Australian way of life and enjoy the same treatment as others. The policy was originally geared toward British immigrants, but was eventually extended to include other Europeans, since the demand for migrants grew beyond the British supply. Extension of the policy was based on the belief that other Europeans would discard their culture and languages and be assimilated into that of the host population, and these differences would eventually be lost. The Whites who entered were expected to assimilate. It was assumed that they would adopt the British cultural model which prevailed in Australia. The English language was particularly important (Stratton et al., 1998).

It is clear that the initial immigration program in Australia was not designed to bring about ethnic diversity. The White Australian policy kept out all non-whites, including the Asian wives of Australian soldiers (Wilton and Bosworth, 1984). Assimilation as cultural and social absorption remained the main objective of immigration policies during the postwar period. Immigrants were viewed as potential New Australians. Labor unions, employer organizations, churches, and schools all helped in the assimilation process (Kivisto, 2002). Organizations specifically designed for this purpose were established to assist in the assimilation process, and to encourage newcomers to assimilate (Murphy, 1993: 140–141). The process of assimilation also involved some government measures, such as providing Basic English courses, jobs, and provisions for initial settlement (Jakubowicz, 1989). Naturalization was possible after five years; this was later reduced to three years, and eventually to two years. Children born to immigrants were granted Australian citizenship, and bringing family members to Australia was simplified (Martin, 1978, Department of Immigration and Ethnic Affairs, 1986).

Assimilation remained the main objective of immigration policies during the postwar period. Nevertheless, by the late 1950s, doubts were raised regarding its success. Maintaining the homogeneity of the Australian society remained paramount; however, realization of the contributions made by other migrants began to develop. Consequently, by the 1960s the assimilation process was deemed unsuccessful. Many immigrants felt isolated from mainstream Australian culture; poor living conditions and poor schooling for immigrant children prevailed in many immigrant populations (Department of Immigration and Ethnic Affairs, 1986: 31; Galligan and Roberts, 2003). Assimilation was discontinued as a workable policy during the 1960s, and was replaced by integration.

Integration

Integration became an official policy in Australia in the mid-1960s, and lasted until 1972. In Australia, the process of integration was considered to be different from assimilation. While assimilation required total emersion into another culture and language, integration implied that the other cultures should cause the dominant culture to be altered as well. In the Australian context, integration implies what others have called "two-way assimilation." In integration, cultural diversity was not encouraged. Instead, the newly formed "altered" culture was the one that all Australians were expected to adopt. The movement from assimilation to integration called for an awareness of the usefulness of acculturation, and required more awareness of the difficulties faced by newcomers, such as the acquisition of English language proficiency (Kivisto, 2002: 110). To enable the integration process to work, the Australian government recognized the need to reduce the rate of departure of immigrants who might have problems with acculturation, including the need to learn and use English, and remedial action was taken in this regard.

Following the adoption of nondiscriminatory immigration policies, the White Australia Policy had effectively ended. This resulted in the admission of well-qualified Asians, as well as a change in the criteria to allow them to attain lawful residential status. However, not all Australians were willing to adopt a culture influenced by immigrants, leading to the demise of the integration policy. Nevertheless, the new force created by these new ethnic groups in the political arena helped to influence the move from integration to a new phase of "multi-culturalism."

Multi-culturalism

By the 1970s, the number of immigrants had increased so drastically that political leaders began to see them more as political assets than hindrances, especially since they comprised a significant proportion of working-class voters. Collins (1988: 135–137) reports that the Australia Labor Party (ALP) set up Greek and Italian sections, advertised in the ethnic press, and selected some migrants as candidates. The 1972 elections saw the victory of the ALP as a consequence of pursuing migrant candidates (Collins, 1988: 135–137). The entrance of other "ethnic" minorities into politics created a new force in Australian politics that led to a greater need to recognize ethnic diversity while helping migrants settle and maintain their cultural identities.

Influenced by the example of Canada, the Australian government in 1972 discarded the integration approach and embraced multi-culturalism. This new method was applicable to all of Australia, including the aboriginal community. To ensure that racism did not interfere with the smooth implementation of multi-culturalism, the government passed antidiscriminatory legislation, including the Race Discrimination Act in 1975. This Act allowed the government to play a greater role in the protection of minorities. Multi-culturalism meant viewing the Australian national identity as a fluid, open, and future-oriented identity (Kivisto, 2002: 110). In this regard, the Australian government was committed to ensuring that cultural preservation occurred – including the preservation of non-English languages and cultures.

In 1983, after the election of the Hawke ALP government, multi-culturalism was continued for a short time. By 1984, following the "Great Immigration Debate," pressure from racist groups and others in the nation caused the government to conclude that multi-culturalism was losing its popularity. In 1986, several of the multi-cultural agencies were closed, and funds were decreased for others. The Institute of Multicultural Affairs was abolished, and funding was cut for English as-a-Second-Language teaching and for the Multi-cultural Education Program. This move resulted in ethnic unrest that threatened the ALP hold on marginal seats in Sidney and Melbourne (Castles, 1992: 556).

In 1987, there was a rapid reversal of the previous year's cuts in multi-cultural programs. The ALP government advocated the economic benefits of multi-culturalism. It was argued that multi-culturalism was a positive contributor to international trade and communication. More important, multi-culturalism was seen as a way of providing an opening to Asia, which was regarded as crucial to Australia's future (Castles, 1992: 556). New policies and institutions to promote multi-culturalism were introduced, including policies related to language. Commenting on these changes, Castles (1992: 556) states, "The National policy on Languages, adopted in 1987, has the aim of encouraging bilingualism, including the learning of 'languages of economic and strategic significance,' as well as maintaining the 'community languages' of migrant groups." It should be noted that the issue of language has been a major point of contention in striking the multi-cultural balance. While English is included as a shared language for all people, it does not exclude other languages that are spoken in the community (Smolicz, 1997: 175).

A 3D multi-cultural policy was launched by the Prime Minister in 1989, which appeared in the National Agenda for a Multicultural Australia. This National Agenda is seen: "As a system of rights and freedoms which are limited by an overriding commitment to the nation, a duty to accept the Constitution and the rule of law, and the acceptance of basic principles such as tolerance and equality, English as the national language, and equality of the sexes" (Castles, 1992: 557). The Office of Multicultural Affairs (OMA), which is federally charged with a wide range of multi-cultural policy-related tasks, outlines the three dimensions of the policy as follows:

- cultural identity: the right of all Australians, within carefully defined limits, to express and share their individual cultural heritage, including their language and religion;

- social justice: the right of all Australians to equality of treatment and opportunity and the removal of barriers of race, ethnicity, culture, religion, language, gender, or place of birth;
- economic efficiency: the need to maintain, develop, and utilize effectively the skills and talents of all Australians, regardless of background (Castles, 1992: 557).

The Australian government has clearly shown its stance concerning multi-culturalism. It has defined Australian national identity to be open, fluid, and diverse – a marked difference from the past. By seeking to preserve and support ethnic identities, the government had redefined the Australian national identity fairly successfully. Multi-culturalism has been able to provide a shift from a racist and isolationist national identity to one of diversity, one that is open to new cultures and new challenges.

Despite these apparently positive ventures, the Australian model of multi-culturalism has several flaws, which raise numerous questions. First, entry regulations into Australia are easy to enforce due to its geographical location, together with the fact that white immigrants still predominate. If these controls should falter, it is not certain whether the Australian nation will be so willing to accept migrants from more diverse origins into their society.

Second, ethnicity still appears to be a marker of class position for certain groups. "Members of certain ethnic groups (particularly southern Europeans, Latin Americans, Lebanese, Turks, and Indo-Chinese) tend to have lower occupational status, lower incomes, higher unemployment rates and a variety of special health and educational needs" (Department of Immigration and Ethnic Affairs, 1986, Australian Bureau of Statistics, 1989). Commenting on this situation, Castles (1992; 560) states, "By providing general services to migrants, some special needs and perpetuating structural discrimination may result." The question that arises here is: How does this serve to support social justice – the second of the multi-cultural policies as set out by the OMA?

Third, the National Agenda advocates rights for all Australians. Nevertheless, the ethnic group model of the 1970s made use of ethnic associations in the construction of culturally based definitions of needs (Castles et al., 1990). Ethnic organizations and ethnic leaders were used to support certain political ideologies. This helped to maintain the image of harmonious and permanent ethnic communities with common needs. Some government programs, such as migrant welfare, were issued through grants to ethnic organizations, rather than through the mainstream social system. This approach to funding allowed for preferential or selective funding, based on the government's perception of the political usefulness of the particular ethnic organization (Castles, 1992: 560). However, some criticized this move as "welfare on the cheap," since pay and staffing levels could be lower in these organizations than in government agencies (Jakubowicz et al., 1984: 81).

Fourth, the major Australian institutions are based on British, USA, or European models. How does this organizational structure affect people who are culturally or ethnically different in their appearance, speech, values, or behavior? What is being done to change central institutions to really reflect the "true" Australian multi-cultural society? Policies that reflect cultural pluralism and diversity are still being debated. Australia's journey toward multi-culturalism remains incomplete, however, and is still seeking general support from the nation. In 1999 and 2003, the government proposed new multi-cultural agendas, aimed at making multi-cultural policy relevant to all Australians. The aim of these proposals was to ensure that the social, cultural, and economic benefits of diversity were fully maximized, and to encourage equity, productive diversity, community, mutual respect, and harmonious relationships among all Australians. However, both attempts were tabled (Stormfront White Nationalist Community, 2005).

Despite this long-term commitment to the pursuit of multi-culturalism in Australia, the policy continues to generate mixed sentiments. Consequently, its future in Australia seems uncertain at this time.

France and Multi-culturalism

Brief History

In our discussion of France, we will confine ourselves to what the French call "Metropolitan France," that is, the area located in Europe, and excluding French territories elsewhere. This area originally was occupied by the ancient Gauls, a Celtic tribe, whose territory was conquered by Julius Caesar around 50 BCE (De Sauvigny and Pinkney, 1977). As the Roman Empire was losing is power, what is now France came under the control of the Germanic Franks, who gave France its name. The French tribes were converted to Christianity at an early date, and established a special relationship with the Roman Catholic Church. After the fall of the Holy Roman Empire, France largely operated as a monarchy. The actions of some French kings brought war, economic distress, and chaos to their subjects. The monarchy reached its height in the 17th century. During this period, France was known for its intellectual life, had great influence in European culture, and established colonies in many parts of the world (Yonge, 2005).

Modern France essentially traces its origins to the French Revolution of 1789, which eliminated the French monarchy. While there were attempts to return the monarchy to power, by the mid-1800s, the French Republic was well established (Crook, 1993; Sauvigny et al., 1977). All of these early influences have left dramatic marks on French culture as it exists today. However, it should also be noted that France has also suffered numerous wars which have also altered its social, cultural, and political structure. These include the many wars during the monarchical era, the French Revolution, and two World Wars.

In the late 1800s, France began to emerge as a democratic society. The industrial revolution and the migration of peasants to the urban areas helped to change the economic structure of France, giving considerable power to the peasants, who controlled the agricultural labor on which the French economy depended. Political leaders were highly dependent on their vote (Charle, 1991: 111). The middle classes or petty bourgeoisie (retail tradesmen, small craftsmen, employees, and minor officials) also constituted a significant force in French society. Professionals, including doctors, lawyers, teachers, clergy, intellectual, and artistic professions, were highly respected and enjoyed professional freedom (Charle, 1991: 169). A notable component of French democracy was introduced in 1852, when the Republic established universal manhood suffrage, giving voting rights to all adult males, regardless of income, property, religion, race, or any other qualification (Crook, 1993; Sauvigny et al., 1977). France was also one of the first European nations to recognize the Jews, who were emancipated and given legal equality following the French Revolution.

Diverse Population

As we have seen with the other nations discussed, immigration is one of the main contributors to creating diverse populations. However, France's immigration history largely began in the mid-19th century, when industrialization brought about a demand for labor. From its inception, France's immigration policies have allowed for easy acceptance of foreigners, even to the point of allowing citizenship. This is reflective of the French brand of republicanism, which has long stressed popular sovereignty, citizenship, and human rights (Cornelius et al., 2004). The French population retains remnants of these many themes which have played a role in its history. These include the early Celtic, Latin, and Teutonic heritage, as well as Slavic, North African, Indo-Chinese, and Basque minorities. The religious composition of the country is predominantly Roman Catholic (83–88%). Religious minorities consist of Muslims (5–10%), Protestants (2%), Jews (1%), and unaffiliated persons (4%) (CIA the World Fact Book, 2008).

Following the Second World War, France was the only European country which encouraged permanent migration. At this time, France sustained a period of economic growth and an availability of new jobs; this led the French government to encourage immigration, with dramatic results. Noiriel (1988: 21) states that immigrants in France accounted for a larger share of the French population than did immigrants in the USA. The role of immigration in the population composition of France cannot be overemphasized. Of all the European countries, France has the most immigrants (Dignan, 1981). Further, France strongly supports asylum-seeking persons and allows immigration for this reason.

Three main reasons are presented for France's immigration: the pattern and timing of industrialization, slow population growth, and political changes arising from republicanism. The republican model helped with the integration of new immigrants into the society. The new immigrants played an important role, satisfying the need for labor (Cornelius et al., 2004: 184). Immigration policies during the 1950s and 1960s were largely established in terms of economic and demographic planning. They were based on universalistic, republican ideals, and included respect for the civil and human rights of foreigners, as well as underlying social democratic traditions based on Catholic principles. This is largely what is encompassed in the concept which the French call "republicanism."

Schain (2004) contends that immigration to France occurred in four waves. The first wave consisted of Italian and Belgian immigrants; they were followed by Polish immigrants; immigrants from Portugal followed; the final wave consisted of immigrants from French colonies of North Africa. Immigration into France was initially intended for European preservation. For example, immigration from Italy and Spain was encouraged with the aim of introducing culturally compatible immigrants from neighboring states. It was assumed this would reduce the impact on French society and culture, and allow France to continue its tradition of exchange with other Catholic countries (Cornelius et al., 2004: 185).

By the late 1960s, "immigration" from within had become the norm. During this time, the immigration control system had been privatized, giving the employees of the system a considerable degree of control over the process. Rather than following previous processes, they boycotted the institutional route, recruiting foreign workers mainly from Spain, Portugal, and former French colonies. These workers were brought into French society, and immigration status for the preferred persons was sought after they had entered the country (Hollifield, 1992: 45–73). However, some postwar policies were intended to discourage certain nationalities. Efforts to stop the flow of immigrants started as early as 1973. However, this did not affect those seeking political asylum, or certain categories of professionals and highly skilled personnel.

The most dramatic impetus for immigration change occurred in the late 1960s, with the arrival of hundreds of thousands of Algerian immigrants from France's North African colonies (Morocco, Tunisia, and West Africa). Since they were predominantly Muslim, their arrival brought about radical changes to the French population, causing Islam, though still a minority, to become the second largest religion in the country. Hence the arrival of the Algerian immigrants also provoked issues of religious tolerance. Steps were taken to control this flood of immigration, including control of free movement and inflexible laws for housing and care of foreign workers. Some employers objected to these regulations, because they feared the workers would make greater demands for wages. However, numerous factors supporting immigration remained. There continued to be a high demand for labor; the immigrants were from former French colonies, which gave them a certain sense of entitlement; and France had a long-standing tradition of respect for foreigners' civil and human rights. Consequently, immigration was allowed to continue (Cornelius et al., 2004: 190). In the minds of the public, "immigration" was equated with unskilled labor; the influx of skilled or professional workers was largely ignored.

The situation became volatile during 1984, when the extreme-right National Front, which advocated a complete cessation of African immigration and the separation of races, won the municipal elections in the city of Dreux. As a result of this election, immigration requirements for Africans were altered, such that they had to wait longer to gain naturalization status. Later legal changes targeted foreigners and challenged the earlier republican model of due process. Foreigners were denied the possibility of appealing for asylum, and access to the social security system, especially health care, ceased. Police were also given stricter orders to detain and deport foreigners.

To summarize, during the latter decades of the 20th century, a significant number of immigrants entered France from Third World societies. They were drawn there because numerous characteristics of French society made immigration attractive: a better quality of life; possibilities for employment; opportunity to reunify families; freedom to practice religious beliefs; and ability to assist persons remaining in the homeland through remittances. The resulting flow of immigrants into French society affected the structural composition and social relations of the population.

Multi-culturalism in France

Monoculturalism

France's historical background plays an important role in the way it addresses multi-cultural policies. Its political ideology, based on republicanism, assures that all cultural groups share in civil liberties. France has adopted varying ways of addressing multi-cultural issues; these have included assimilation, integration, selective immigration, and discrimination. In some cases, there has been outright rejection of certain ethnic groups. In France, prior to the mid-20th century, a relatively homogeneous society existed. During this period, a monocultural national identity, focusing on "Frenchness," was encouraged, and was easily achieved by most immigrants.

Selective Immigration and Integration

Immigrants who entered following the Second World War were of a different type. Refugees in search of asylum, and immigrants allowed into the country to provide labor challenged the monoculturalism which France's political republican stance encouraged. In an effort to retain its homogeneous republican image, France introduced the concept of integration, which was largely equated with assimilation. France was concerned with maintaining its existing identity, culture, and political ideologies. Refugees seeking asylum were encouraged to integrate; they were expected to become assimilated into the culture and were readily granted naturalization status.

To address the shortage of labor, selective European immigration was encouraged. The Ordonnance of 1945 prevented immigration restrictions based on ethnic or national origins. Nevertheless, France continued to base its search for immigrants on their nationality. Preservation of the "French" monocultural republican identity remained the ultimate goal (Cornelius et al., 2004). European immigrants posed no threat to the established French order, since immigrants from Italy, Spain, and the other feeder countries already resembled the dominant ethnic group in numerous ways, particularly in the area of religion. The issue of cultural pluralism did not present a threat.

An interesting aspect of the French approach to immigration is its policy concerning the designation of immigrants in official records. Under a policy which has been termed, the "official disappearing act," children of foreign birth, upon reaching the age of majority, are automatically listed in census records as having been born in France (Tribalat, 2004). This allows their foreign origins to disappear without a trace. This "disappearing act" is also applicable to children and grandchildren born to foreigners. This approach automatically integrates the immigrants into French society: after a specified period of time, they are simply recorded as being French (Hargreaves, 1995).

Concerns about Assimilation

The immigration of French African nationals from Africa began in 1962, as a consequence of independence in those countries. This signaled a new era in France's multi-cultural policies. The Africans introduced a new ethnicity, religion, and cultural orientation into France. Not only were they different, but their differences were obvious. For some, the color of their skin was different. More critically, the wearing of the headscarf clearly marked them with what has been described as "A visible marker of the identity of Islam" (Wiles, 2007: 1; Jennings, 2000). These were differences that no policy could make disappear. The presence of these immigrants challenged the feasibility of France's cultural pluralism due to their perceived inability to be easily assimilated into the republican culture, and their use of identifiably foreign words (Safran, 2003).

The Africans' arrival in France created a renewed effort for assimilation. A number of policies were initially introduced to assist with the assimilation of these new immigrants into the French society. Some of these policies were initiatives to renegotiate the free movement of Algerian nationals; denial of visas; tightening of border controls; improved control of labor markets to avoid the increase of undocumented workers; and decrees to terminate immigration completely.

Discrimination and Rejection of Individual and Group Rights

In spite of these restrictions, immigration of Africans to France, especially from Algeria, continued. This continued infiltration of new members into the society challenged the established norms of the society and inevitably led to conflict. To address these challenges, new state policies were quickly implemented. Unlike the USA, which traditionally allowed for a relatively slow assimilation process, France preferred rapid assimilation (Safran, 2003).

The French continued to view these diverse groups as a danger to the republican image (Safran, 2003). Hence its political leaders embarked on discriminatory practices and the rejection of basic human rights. In many instances, the laws enacted were constitutionally questionable, had racial underpinnings, and were prone to enrage immigrants. As a result of these harsh measures, multi-cultural relations were eroded. One policy, which received considerable criticism on the international scene, was the ban on the wearing of headscarves by Muslim girls in French schools (Wiles, 2007). These incidents also led to conflict between the Africans and the political leaders, and between political leaders with different perspectives. Some even escalated into violent confrontations.

To summarize, multi-culturalism in France has been highly divisive. Although some value it highly, others are inalterably opposed. In some instances, the state has blatantly overstepped its previously self-imposed political and constitutional mandates regarding the civil rights of immigrants and French nationals, since most of the Africans held this status prior to their arrival in France. France exhibited a lack of toleration for cultural pluralism, as well as for the presence of groups that appeared to challenge the Catholic-based religious unity and the French language orientation of French culture.

Consequently, when the issue of multi-culturalism is raised with regard to France, one is tempted to ask, "What multi-culturalism?" The nation seems committed to its long-standing monocultural approach: some anti-multi-cultural laws remain; most holidays continue to be based on Catholic religious festivals; restrictions on other religious practices remain in force; and French is the only language permitted in public communication. Thus the case for multi-culturalism in France still remains an open question.

Multi-culturalism in Trinidad and Tobago

Brief History

Trinidad and Tobago is a unitary, parliamentary, democratic nation in the Caribbean that gained independence from the British in 1962, and became a Republic in 1976. The nation is made up of two separate islands, Trinidad, which is 1,980 square miles, and Tobago, which is 120 square miles. Hence, this is by far the smallest nation under discussion here. Trinidad was one of the islands that Columbus discovered for the Spanish during his second voyage in 1498. Similar to most of the other societies discussed in this chapter, Trinidad and Tobago was also part of the British Empire for an extended period of time.

Through Trinidad and Tobago's history, it has been characterized by a highly diverse group of people, racially, religiously, and linguistically. The dominant religious groups are Roman Catholic (30%), Hindu (25%), Anglican (12%), and other Protestant (14%). The remainder of the population consists of other religions or no religion; one significant group practices Orisha, which is an old established form of worship in Nigeria and its environs. In Trinidad the religion is somewhat modified and borrows from Hinduism, Spiritual Baptist, African, Catholic, Protestant, and Kabbalah[1] religions to form an "Afro-American" religious complex network of religious activities (Houk, 1995: x).

The official languages are Hindi, French, Spanish, and Chinese (Trinidad and Tobago Facts and Figures, 2008). The original inhabitants of Trinidad were the Arawaks, an Amerindian tribe given the name to denote their peaceful nature. Early colonizers of Trinidad were Spanish, who brought priests with them to convert the indigenous population. These efforts led to the Arena Massacre of 1699, which accounted for the death of several Amerindians in Trinidad. Other Amerindians who feared capture committed suicide by jumping off cliffs (Newson, 1976). Some Amerindians were also devastated by new epidemic diseases introduced by outsiders, such as measles, smallpox, malaria, and dysentery (Meditz and Hanratty, 1987). As early as 1797, several villages had virtually "disappeared," and the remaining Indians were brought under colonial control (Brereton, 1981: 7, 16, 20–21).

During the early years, Spain largely neglected the area, due to its relatively limited development. However, the Spanish enslaved the Amerindians, who by 1783 comprised about 74% of the total population of 2,763; African slaves comprised 11%, and the remainder consisted of freed non-Whites and Whites (Meditz and Hanratty, 1987). Unlike some other Caribbean countries, Trinidad did not become a major sugar producer until late in the 18th century, at which time the Spanish encouraged non-Spanish immigrants to enter the island (Birth, 1997). The government of Trinidad at the time sought immigrants to fill the labor shortage. Immigrants were required to be Catholic and subjects of one of the countries that were friendly with Spain. The Haitian revolution, and the unrest in other French territories, prompted French migration to Trinidad during this period. Immigrants came to Trinidad accompanied by their "Creole" slaves. "Creoles" included persons who were born in the Caribbean, or were of African background, from Haiti, Martinique, Guadeloupe, and other French territories in the region, or had some combination of these origins. Initially most of the new arrivals planted cotton, cocoa, and coffee. Commenting on the population composition, Naipaul (1884, 1969) identifies white immigrants (predominantly French speaking), free African slaveholding populations, and their slaves as comprising the population in Trinidad by 1783. Consequently, even though Trinidad was a Spanish colony, a French-speaking population dominated. Other European powers were constantly challenging Spain's colonial grasp on the Caribbean.

In 1797, the British took control of the island of Trinidad, and English, Scots, and Irish owners won control of the sugar plantations from the Spanish. By this time, the price of sugar in Europe made it the most important crop, such that it was called "King Sugar," and formed the mainstay of the Caribbean economy (Leonce, 2004). This demand for sugar resulted in an increase in plantations, which in turn spiked population growth. The demand for more laborers resulted in an increase in the slave

---

[1] Kabbalah refers to forces of a higher order, which act while remaining hidden to the believers. It is common throughout the Caribbean, especially in Trinidad, and is part of the Orisha beliefs. It is believed to have originated in the oral laws of Judaism.

trade, importing African slaves from countries such as Yoruba, Hausa, Congo, Ibo, Rada, Mandingo, Kromanti (Koromantyn), and Temne (National Library and Information System Authority of Trinidad and Tobago, 2008). African slaves increased to 20,464 by 1803; there were also 5,275 free non-Whites, and 2,261 Whites. French continued to be the language of choice for most slaves and free people, while the remainder of the population spoke either Spanish or English. Several of the African-descended persons entered Trinidad as free persons, during slavery, or just after it ended. Those who came after slavery ended brought with them and preserved the Yoruba language and religion throughout the 19th century (Warner-Lewis, 1991).

At this time, with the immigration of thousands of free non-Whites, French Catholic planters and slaves, Trinidad's demography had changed significantly. About 56% of the population consisted of slaves. This increase came as the Amerindian population was declining, for the reasons mentioned earlier. Amerindians eventually came to represent only 6% of the total population (Meditz and Hanratty, 1987).

Unlike Trinidad's history of a peace-loving native population, the Caribs, a warlike Amerindian tribe, originally occupied the island of Tobago. Little development occurred there in the early colonial years. The island changed hands 22 times, moving among the French, Dutch, and British. Slave labor in Tobago derived mainly from the slave trade from Africa. In 1814, the British eventually took control of the island of Tobago. In 1888, the British incorporated Tobago and Trinidad into a single colony (Birth, 1997).

Slavery continued in Trinidad and Tobago until 1838, when the emancipation of slaves occurred. In both Trinidad and Tobago, several of the freed slaves moved away from the plantations, causing a shortage of much-needed labor. Those who remained bargained at exorbitant prices with plantation owners, who often could not afford to pay these wages. To fill this shortage, several indenture schemes brought Portuguese, Chinese, Syrians, Lebanese, and Africans to the islands. Financial incentives were offered to African-Americans, but they found the climate too hot. Indentured laborers were also sought from Madera, England, and Germany, but they could not cope with estate work. The search to find suitable laborers continued until India was identified as the best place from which to seek the needed labor (Leonce, 2004).

East Indian indentured labor (also called Indian indentured labor) began in 1845 and continued until 1917. Indentured workers were brought in to work for a specified period of time in exchange for passage to a colony. Laborers from India were called "Indians," Indo-Trinidadians, or "Coolies," the Hindi word for laborer, which was traditionally used in Trinidad in a derogatory manner. These East Indian laborers were considered more profitable to planters, since they were willing to supply free labor and work harder than the former "creoles" or African slaves.

The year 1834 marked a turning point in Trinidadian history. The new arrivals were not welcome. Instead antagonism quickly became manifest in bitter confrontation between blacks (the "Negro") and East Indians (the "Coolie"). "They [East Indians] came to form a large and separate sector, separated from the other three tiers or groups of ex-slave society by culture, religion, language, ethnicity and (until 1971) legal restrictions" (Brereton, 1993: 36). The three tiers referred to here were the Africans and their locally born descendants, which were the majority population and formed the base; people of mixed descent and "free-blacks," comprising a middle tier; and the elites, primarily of European descent (British, French, and Spanish) situated at the apex. Hence the East Indians entered the society after the tier system had been well established. In addition, the circumstances under which they came generated great animosity on the part of the ex-slaves. Not only were the East Indians "outsiders," but they were also perceived to be obstacles to the ex-slaves' newly found opportunity to exact payment for their labor. With the arrival of East Indian indentured workers, plantation owners no longer needed to hire the newly freed workers. The East Indians were willing to work harder, and for free, and were disdainfully labeled "Coolies" by the freed slaves.

The East Indians' status as outsiders was further highlighted by their non-Christian religious beliefs (primarily Hindu and Islam), as well as their strong resistance to acculturation into Trinidadian society. The Blacks were mainly Protestants or Catholics, who viewed the East Indian religions (especially Hinduism) with disdain, considering it to be "pagan" or "heathen." The East Indian style of dress, in which the loincloth was used, was another invitation for ridicule; these all served to intensify the Blacks' hostile treatment and isolation of the Indians (Munasinghe, 2001: 9). This contempt was manifest in the economic and political arenas as well.

As a result of these factors, Blacks gravitated toward more urban jobs, such as teachers, civil servants, and constabulary workers, while East Indians were largely employed in the rural agricultural sector, or pursued jobs as store clerks, domestic servants, huskers, and farmers. Blacks dominated the political scene and made most of the political decisions. Unlike the other former British colonies previously discussed, a British role in defining national identity was not crucial to Trinidad and Tobago's identity. More critical was the status of being "creole," which refers to one who was born in the region, and hence was an "insider." Creole is, therefore, synonymous with the terms, African, Afro-Trinidadian, Negro, and Black (Reddock, 1995). The term also encompasses French Creole, which is a mixture of White, and African Trinidadian; they are also referred to as Negro or Black. Hence Creole is a mixture of African elements with Spanish, French, and English colonial culture. The long-standing animosity between the Black population and the East Indians is critical for the discussion of Trinidad and Tobago's model of cultural diversity and national identity.

Kaleidoscopic Population

Trinidad's population is truly colorful. Cornwell and Stoddard (2001: 30) refer to Trinidad and Tobago as "the most ethnically varied, religiously and culturally heterogeneous of all the Caribbean islands." Munasinghe (2001) uses the tantalizing metaphor, Callaloo, or "tossed salad," in referring to Trinidad, while Khan (2004) calls it the "Callaloo Nation." Several other writers also refer to the multi-ethnic nature of the Trinidadian population (Rouse, 1992; Naipaul, 1984; Moodie-Kublasingh, 1994). The proximity of the island to the South American mainland enables the migration of diverse groups into the Caribbean (Rouse, 1993).

Venezuelans migrated during the 19th century (Khan, 1993). A flood of people came in search of the mythical city of El Dorado in the Orinoco river basin (Naipau, 1984, 1969). Finally, the sugar plantation system, and, to a lesser degree, the cocoa plantations, attracted workers from various countries under slavery or varying indenture schemes, also adding to the diversity of the population (Birth, 1997). As a result, the country's population claims descent from various mixed origins: European, African, East Indian, Amerindian, Portuguese, Chinese, Lebanese, and Syrian, among others.

Several races and mixtures of races are present. Forty percent are East Indians (descendants from India, also called Indians, Coolies, and Indo-Trinidadians); 40% are Africans (those who trace their ancestry back to Africa; also called Negro, Black, Creoles, Afro-Trinidadian). Slightly under 20% identify as "mixed," as will be discussed later (Trinidad and Tobago Facts and Figures, 2008). (2001: 36–37) comparing race in Trinidad and Tobago to race in the USA Stoddard and Cornwell contend, "Phenotype (especially color), class, and cultural identification are more important in Trinidad than race as understood in the U.S. context." They further comment, "In the U.S. context race is commonly treated as a metaphysical essence that is inherited and carries with it a cultural identity. The notorious one-drop rule categorizes anyone with any hint of African ancestry as Black or African American." In Trinidad, however, like Guyana and other Caribbean countries, color was closely linked to class. The lightest person occupied the top, and the darkest person, the bottom. Thus, as Segal (1993: 92) has noted, during the British colonial period, some groups could alter their status by achievements, education, and by speaking and behaving properly. However, this did not apply to Blacks.

Trinidad's racial definitions are highly varied. Knowing the categorization schemes helps to comprehend the differences in the society, and how they intersect in defining a national culture. In Trinidad, "White" may often include Chinese, Syrians, and Lebanese persons. The definition of "White" in Trinidad varies significantly from that used in the USA, Australia, France, and Canada. "White" does not denote the ancestral or ethnic phrase, "European heritage" (Stoddard and Cornwell, 2001). However, the definition of "White" is not very important in Trinidadian discussions, since they constitute a very small percentage (1%) of the total population. Yet they control 85% of the capital, while the remaining 99% of the population compete for only 15% (Parmasad, 1997).

This method of categorizing Whites dates back to the White owner-class during the country's earlier history. The Spanish and the British played minimal roles earlier in defining Trinidadian culture. However, when the French Creole planters entered the society, they established the dominant culture and religion in Trinidad. All Whites born in Trinidad after the French Creole planters established themselves were assimilated into the French Creole ethnic group (Segal, 1993: 83). It is noteworthy that the designation, "White," does not play a dominant role in Trinidadian discourse, in spite of their massive control of the local wealth (Parmasad, 1997).

As indicated above, another categorization present in Trinidadian discourse refers to persons of Mixed, Spanish, Light, or Amerindian identity. This group comprises about 20% of the population, though some researchers believe this number may be greater (Shand, 1997; Reddock, 1994). Combinations of mixed persons are numerous including, but not limited to, European and East Indian; White and Black; European and Chinese; Black and Chinese; and Indian and Chinese. As noted above, persons of light complexion tend to have more power and privileges, and make up most of the middle class. The pattern is linked to the legacy of colonialism, and is often referred to as having the "colonial mentality." Trinidad tends to have considerable commentary on lightness of colors, and the specific category of "mulatto," or mixed White and African race; in Tobago, this is not part of the discourse (Stoddard and Cornwell, 2001: 36).

A prominent element of Trinidadian racial discussion is the "Dougla," a Hindi term for "bastard" or "miscegnate," which refers to descendents from the union of African and East Indian parents (Khan, 1993; Puri, 1995; Reddock, 1994; and Shibata, 1994). "Douglarization," a metaphor for Indo- and Afro-Trinidadian mixing, is used interchangeably to refer to biological and sometimes cultural hybridization (Stoddard and Cornwell, 2001: 40). This mix carries negative connotations in Trinidad. While various mixed races exist in Trinidadian society, the mix between persons of African and Indian descent did not enjoy the same status as those between other races.

In some cases, the Douglas experience social rejection from both sides, perhaps more strenuously from the East Indian side. There is considerable scholarly analysis of the perceptions that Indians, particularly those with a Hindu religious background, have toward "Dougla" unions (Stoddard and Cornwell, 2001; Reddock, 1994; Parmasad, 1997). They view the union as contaminating the women, their color, and caste endogamy. Others fear extinction of their race (Reddock, 1994: 115–116). In several cases, ethnic tension forces persons of Dougla background to reside with African or Creoles, though they are still viewed as Douglas.

The "Dougla" position in Trinidadian society has been worsened by political movements in Trinidad, in which Africans and East Indians have become the two dominant racial categories in the political arena. "Douglas" are, therefore, caught between the political tensions of the two dominant political groups. Some Trinidadians see them as adding confusion to the political battles waged by the two dominant groups, since the Douglas are perceived to have conflicting loyalties. Others perceive the Douglas as the promise of a new regime, a means to establish unity in the political arena. Still others believe that Douglas have been largely silenced in the political debates of the nation (Hernandez-Ramdwar, 1997). The tensions between the two dominant races and the concept of "Douglarization" are critical to understanding Trinidad's national culture.

Trinidad's Search for a National Culture

National Identity

Trinidad's national identity is particularly important to persons of East Indian origin, who are constantly treated as "Outsiders" by the Africans, who claim native status.

In many ways, Trinidad's situation is similar to that of Canada, where the introduction of new groups had a great impact. Trinidad's population is significantly smaller than that of Canada; hence the introduction of new groups has an even greater impact on race relations. This impact is particularly obvious in the relationship between the Africans and the East Indians.

To ensure that East Indians played no part in mainline society, their rights were reduced under the Immigration Ordinance of 1854. Under their contracts, their mobility was severely curtailed, and their interaction with other society members was minimized; they spent most of their time tied to rural sugar estates. This situation was intensified by the actions of planters, who used every means possible to curtail East Indian mobility. By 1917, the system of East Indian indentureship had been eliminated. However, East Indians were still positioned outside the "National Self" (Munasinghe, 2001: 1).

The early decades of the 20th century represented a period of considerable turmoil for Trinidad. There was considerable unrest, particularly by Africans, who resented their lack of representation in various levels of government, including voting limitations. Several actions were taken by the British government, beginning in the 1920s, to remedy these problems. Included were constitutional changes, efforts to increase the number of people who had the franchise, and increased local powers. The culmination of these efforts occurred in 1962, when Trinidad and Tobago gained independence and joined the British Commonwealth (Commonwealth Observer Group, 2001: 4). This only partially resolved the problem, since control remained vested in the middle-class Creoles, who jealously guarded their power over economic, social, and cultural spheres.

Further change occurred in the 1970s, with the acquisition of oil, which led to the migration of many East Indians from the rural areas, exchanging their previous agricultural pursuits for business ventures. This increased the Indians' sense of ethnic consciousness, and led them to search for an increased role in the political and economic structure of the nation. Similar to the pressure from Africans in the early 1920s, East Indians sought inclusion in Trinidadian national identity during the late 1980s and early 1990s. African and Creole Trinidadians saw themselves as representing the national culture. East Indians questioned this perception and sought a role for themselves in this issue. However, they were still viewed as "outsiders," and the ruling majority resisted their inclusion.

A critical part of this dispute was the East Indian association with the Hindu religion, which provided grounds on which the Afro-Creoles could base their opposition (Munasinghe, 2001). This exclusionary behavior of Afro-Trinidadians has been equated to Eurocentrism, making it similar to the model that persists in societies like the USA, Australia, Canada, and France (Cornwell and Stoddard, 2001: 41). The question of national identity became the overriding concern of East Indians in the late 1980s and early 1990s. They accused the government of marginalizing them, even as Afro-Creole Trinidadians continue to perceive of themselves as representing the national culture. It is interesting to note that "East Indians in the Trinidadian society seek national inclusion by changing the nation symbolism and not 'their' peculiar identity. They sought to insert their community into the definition of the 'national self'" (Munasinghe, 2001: 1). Hence they were not content simply to be included within the structure of the society and its government. Rather, they sought to alter the symbolism of Trinidadian society, such that it would reflect East Indian culture as well as the culture of the other groups. While they have not achieved all of these goals, they have realized some political recognition, with the election of an East Indian majority to Parliament in 1995, and again in 2000. In 1995 Basdeo Panday became the first East Indian Prime Minister (Munasinghe, 2001).

Establishing a national identity for Africans in the Trinidadian republic was realized quite early and rather easily. They sought educational advancement as a means by which to overcome low income and status. This was supported by the race, class, and culture of the society. Initially, East Indians escaped through agricultural expansion, later turning to commerce and domestic jobs. But for them, inclusion in the national identity has been a difficult struggle. As the 21st century begins, the situation is more tolerable. Africans and East Indians in Trinidad rely on each other economically, and may incorporate elements of each culture in some cultural or religious activities. For the most part, however, each ethnic group continues to retain its cultural individuality. This pattern has been called coexistence without assimilation (Augelli and Taylor, 1960).

Multi-culturalism

Kivisto (2002) provides an in-depth examination of multi-culturalism in Trinidad and Tobago. He refers to everyday life in Trinidad and Tobago as filled with many examples of its shared cultural norms. Almost everyone eats the same food, and engages in the same festivals and traditions. These are influenced by each of the ethnic groups that comprise the population. It is not uncommon for members of each group to cook foods originating in the other groups. Carnival, derived from African and European traditions, is celebrated by all races. Divali, a Hindu religious holiday, is also a national holiday. And some musical forms enjoyed by most Trinidadians are a fusion of Indian and African styles (Reddock, 1995: 132). Despite the apparent mixing in these areas, however, Trinidad continues to experience high levels of controversy on other levels, as evidenced in the continued strong sentiments about intracultural marriages, still highly opposed by both Indo- and Afro-Trinidadians.

This hostility is often vented via the vehicle of music. "Africanness" and "Blackness" are present in calypso, which has its roots in African songs. However, calypso has also become diversified as a consequence of the socioeconomic status and political power of East Indians, as well as an increase in their numbers (Stoddard and Cornwell, 2001). Hence Trinidadian music, particularly calypso, operates both as an expression of cultural division and as a unifier. The "Carnival" spirit allows calypso to be used in ways in which everyday language may not allow. It is used to project, criticize, incite, and support one ethnic group against the other. Language, accusations, and sexual license, which are inappropriate under normal conditions, become appropriate (Cornwell and Stoddard, 2001: 40). Examples are the racial slurs used in calypso, especially between East Indians and Afro-Trinidadians (Kivisto, 2002). It should also be noted that in calypso, the text represents more than the explicit words. Calypso lyrics often have deeper meanings that are culturally understood by Trinidadians.

Trinidadians simultaneously rebuke themselves for "racialism" and warn themselves against copying the kinds of ethnic and racial tendencies noted in other societies. For example, they are aware of the undertone of racial tension which exists in their own society, but believe they have risen above the level of overt, ongoing, racial division that exists in the USA. They are succeeding on many levels in advancing multi-cultural democracy (Cornwell and Stoddard, 2001: 47). To this end, Trinidad has created a unique identity by engaging in intercultural democracy, which involves mixing cultures in such a way that they influence each other and create a unique Trinidadian culture. This uniqueness does not lessen pluralism, however. On the contrary, differences are honored and celebrated in common. Further, while there is still distrust, conflict, and disagreement among academic, governmental and political bodies, there is simultaneous tolerance, communication, and celebration. Trinidadians strive to remember the importance of the project: maintaining a multi-cultural Trinidad and Tobago.

Throughout this entire discussion, it should be obvious that the major focus has been on ethnic and racial conditions in Trinidad. Tobago has barely merited a mention. This is due to two characteristics of Tobago: its small population, relative to Trinidad, and its largely monocultural composition. Tobago represents only about 2% of the nation's population, and most are part of the African racial group. Hence there is little ethnic strife within Tobago itself, and within the larger national scene, they are politically allied with the Africans.

Oostindie (1996: 7) suggests that pluralist societies contain great potential for diverseness and ethnic hostility. To ensure national unity, he suggests the implementation of "cultural homogenization" and miscegenation as recipes for multi-cultural nation building. However, multi-culturalism in Trinidad and Tobago takes a radically different approach. Trinidad and Tobago may be seen as encouraging cultures to exist in a parallel manner, with each of the two dominant groups endeavoring to express power in different social arenas (Cornwell and Stoddard, 2001: 17–18). This is similar to the manner in which the French and English have coexisted in Canada for several hundred years.

In this way, a national culture may be defined, and there is no dominant group exploitation. Instead a parallel model exists, in which the two dominant groups both strive to create a pluralist society. Although there are other minority groups, they do not operate as a major force in national identity. As for persons of mixed race, they are often forced to choose one racial identity or the other, since defining oneself as being "mixed" often leads to stigmatization. Being "mixed" is seen as breaking down the barriers of the two dominant groups, an issue perceived to be a major taboo in Trinidad. However, it is also widely recognized that some amount of accommodation for each group is necessary. Through these mechanisms, internal diversity is recognized, together with the goal of defining a national identity that comprises these different ethnic entities (Cornwell and Stoddard, 2001: 17).

Hence Trinidad and Tobago continues to be an unequal nation. Race and color continue to determine status as well as income and wealth. The control of the country continues to be based on the unevenness of opportunities. Africans continue to be poor in Trinidad, and seek their advancement through education and civil service positions. East Indians have largely improved their position by turning to commerce.

Summary of International Multi-culturalism

We have looked at five different nations and their approaches to managing their increasingly multi-cultural populations. What do these societies tell us about multi-culturalism? Do they have any messages to give us as to what works – and what does not? A brief review of the five nations and the models they pursued is in order.

The USA began as a European colony, primarily of Great Britain. Original immigration consisted primarily of Europeans, especially Protestants and persons who were English speaking. Modern America continues to be plagued by problems inherent in the diversity resulting from the presence of two additional groups from this era: the Native Americans, who were largely eliminated, displaced, or ignored; and the extensive slave trade, which brought in Africans as early as the colonial era. Immigration in the late 19th and early 20th centuries brought in a greater variety of nationalities and cultures, and restrictions were introduced when these became problematic. Changes in immigration law in the late 20th century generated greater diversity, probably as an unforeseen consequence. The US approach to its diverse population has vacillated over time, beginning with attempts to select immigrants who could be easily assimilated into the English model (Anglo-Conformity). It later moved to the ineffective "melting pot" approach. At the present, it seems more appreciative of its internal diversity, attempting to implement programs which focus on social or cultural pluralism. In the American model, overtones of race, religion, and date of arrival have played a role in determining which groups are preferred. To a great extent, the US model remains a composite of the preceding themes, all of which continue to prevail, or rather, to compete with each other in structuring US society. Generally the US government prefers not to interfere in matters related to intergroup relations unless major problems occur, such as intervention in cases of school desegregation or job discrimination. Such actions often generate a public reaction against them. One might describe the American situation as "de facto multi-culturalism," which exists in the USA whether Americans like it or not.

Canada is what might be called "state-sponsored multi-culturalism." The government officially established a policy of encouraging a multi-cultural approach. To a great extent, this approach is a natural consequence of Canada's origin as a dual culture society from the outset, with two languages (English and French) spoken from its earliest colonial days. Recently the "third force," made up of the new immigrants brought into Canada as a result of its dire need for workers, represents another dimension of multi-culturalism. Canada's smaller population ensures that these diverse immigrants will have a greater impact on the country than is the case in the USA. Native Americans who lived in Canada prior to European colonization are largely ignored in this pattern. Canada continues to seek official mechanisms by which to achieve the goal of a national identity, encouraging its many diverse cultural groups to develop a commitment to Canadian national citizenship and identity while still continuing their individual cultural traditions. However, many believe that little sense of shared identity has developed. Furthermore, the French and Native Americans are resentful that multi-culturalism does not recognize what they perceive to be their unique status in Canada.

Australia originally pursued a "White Australia" stance and a racially restrictive immigration policy, which preferred persons who would be easily assimilated into Australian society, and gave preference to Whites, particularly British. Australian aborigines were largely ignored in this picture. This approach lasted until the last third of the 20th century, when Australia, like the USA, introduced more liberal immigration policies, with entry criteria which did not discriminate on the basis of race, ethnicity, religion, or national origin. As in the USA, this approach produced a far more diverse population than originally anticipated. Because of its smaller population size, these diverse immigrants have had a greater impact on Australia than is true in the USA. Australia's response was the development of the policy of integration, by which they meant what others call "two-way acculturation," in which both the incoming cultures and the dominant culture are altered to develop a single national culture. However, resistance from the dominant culture makes this pattern difficult to achieve, as Australia soon learned, leading Australia to join Canada in embracing multi-culturalism. This policy has vacillated, depending upon public sentiment and the party in power at a particular time. And it is clear that some groups do not share in national benefits to the same level as others.

France is unlike the other societies analyzed because it was, until the mid-19th century, a monocultural society, not just by aspiration but also in reality. While its history includes several different cultural groups, long centuries of French history and culture had produced a monocultural society, with one language and commitment to a single religion, Roman Catholicism. This monoculturalism was cemented by the French Revolution and its republican values. Hence French multi-culturalism is truly a recent phenomenon, beginning when the French republic became the first European nation to grant equal rights to Jews. Increased in-migration in the late 19th century brought about a society with a greater variety of classes and occupations, which were given greater rights in society. However, the emphasis on maintaining French culture remained, since most immigrants came from nearby countries with similar religious and cultural traditions. Only after the Second World War did France experience immigration of persons from diverse backgrounds, primarily from France's former colonies in North Africa, who brought their Muslim religious beliefs, and the associated cultural practices, with them. Yet France appears determined to continue its insistence on the acceptance of French culture and identity for all newcomers. Considerable opposition to the new arrivals has been reported. France's multi-culturalism is thus a new phenomenon. It can best be described as a work in progress. It remains to be seen how successful its resolution will be.

Trinidad and Tobago is different from all of the others for two major reasons. It is much smaller, and it has had a diverse population throughout much of its history: diverse in race, religion, language, and national origin. Hence it has had long experience with the problems of acculturating, assimilating, or integrating persons from a wide variety of backgrounds. What it illustrates is that this process is by no means easy. Some groups have been assimilated into each other (Creoles and Douglas). Some of the mixed backgrounds are accepted; others are derided. To a great extent, Trinidad and Tobago society is multi-cultural. But it is a form of multi-culturalism which cannot be described either as assimilation or a melting pot. Most groups remain separate, leading to the analogy of a "tossed salad." All the same, some groups, primarily the East Indians, remain "outsiders," and do not share in the social advantages to the same extent as others. However, one lesson which Trinidad and Tobago can teach us about multi-culturalism is that race is not an inevitable divider. While light skin color is still a mark of higher status there, darker skinned persons can achieve higher status through advancement in education or other achievements. Trinidad and Tobago also illustrates the manner in which collective humor and celebration can help release the stresses of a multi-cultural society.

An Overall Review

So what is the overall future of multi-culturalism? As we have said at several points, it appears always to be a "work in process." In every instance, it has experienced numerous setbacks of various kinds. Even when national governments adopt policies which encourage and promote multi-culturalism, there is no assurance that these will be maintained over time. Opposition may develop, leading to changes in government, and, consequently, in its policies. All of the nations analyzed began with the same goal: development of a single national identity and culture. All started with a simple approach: to continue the cultural pattern with which they started. For Australia, Canada, Trinidad and Tobago, and the USA, this approach was a form of Anglo-Conformity. In each case, it also assumed that White culture would prevail. France's experience was essentially the same, except that it was based on what might be termed "Franco-Conformity," rather than Anglo-Conformity. Many have also toyed with something akin to the "melting pot" approach, and most have tried to implement social or cultural pluralism, in which groups are allowed or encouraged to remain separate from each other, while still participating in the advantages of the large society. All have worried about their ability to retain a strong sense of national identity and allegiance in the context of diverse peoples and cultures.

After several years of effort on the part of these several nations, the only clear answer is ... that there is no clear answer. We do know that one-way assimilation, which forces people to accept the dominant culture, as Anglo-Conformity or

Franco-Conformity require, may work for some groups, but is ineffective on a large scale. We know that the "melting pot" approach is ineffective as well. As Australia found, the dominant group is largely unwilling to make alterations in its culture, and it has the strength of numbers to enforce its resistance. Some form of cultural or social pluralism is probably the most feasible model, but it remains to be seen how effective any of these or other nations will be in establishing an effective working model. As we move into 21st century, new policies and laws will undoubtedly be formulated and implemented to address immigration issues, both those which already exist, and others not yet identified. Hopefully we can use previous examples such as these as a guide, to ensure that the undesirable attitudes and behaviors of the past are not perpetuated into the future.

Epilogue

What does a diverse world mean for the people who inhabit it? To understand this viewpoint, one must assume their perspective. Many apparently fear that it means an end to the world as they know it, and in many respects, it does. More frequently they will see persons whose skin color and racial backgrounds are radically different from their own. They can no longer assume that most people they encounter share their values. Frequently they will hear strange and incomprehensible languages. They are more likely to observe unfamiliar patterns of dress, and witness religious traditions radically different from their own. For traditional Protestants, whose ancestors considered Roman Catholics to be pagans, the specter of sharing their world with Muslims, Hindus, and Sikhs is simply incomprehensible!

It is a normal human emotion to fear the unknown. And for many, a diverse society represents the vast unknown. How can the substantial numbers of people who fear the specter of diversity be led to view it in more positive terms? Perhaps the first movement in this direction is to allay their fears. Diversity in America, or any nation, does not require that anyone must abandon his or her own culture. For the most part, all can continue to speak their own language, practice their preferred religion, and interact primarily with others very much like themselves. On a daily basis, most people's lives will change little.

So how will their lives be different? What does constitute the greatest component of change for them? The greatest change for most will occur at a distance: signs in Spanish or Arabic in local businesses; pictures of other races or religious groups on television; perhaps even seeing persons from these groups running for political office – all events which occur today on a fairly regular basis. Closer to home, some may work with a man who wears a Sikh turban, or a woman in a Muslim veil. Their children may attend school where immigrant children take classes in English as a Second Language. Occasionally they may hear a foreign language spoken on the street or in a store.

Over time, these patterns can be accommodated. As Dr. Javed has indicated in Chapter 10, residents of the Detroit area have become accustomed to the presence of a large number of Middle Eastern immigrants who speak Arabic and practice the Muslim faith. Gradually, they and their neighbors have accommodated to each other, and more congenial relations have begun to develop.

More critically, many people fear that these new and different groups represent competition for scarce resources, resources which they would rather retain for themselves and those like them. Dollars spent on English as a Second Language courses drain funds from school district resources – dollars which might otherwise be spent on Advanced Placement classes or job training or sports, to be enjoyed by their own children. Services for new immigrants, or other unfamiliar groups, require the expenditure of tax dollars they do not wish to pay. Newcomers compete for jobs they may wish to have, or scholarships they want for their children. These competitive issues have arisen, not only the USA, but in other diverse nations as well, as Brenda Marshall has illustrated in Chapter 11.

While one might sympathize with their fears and understand their desire to return to an earlier era in which such problems were not even imagined, one must also recognize that the world has undergone an irrevocable change. Whatever some might wish, a return to a monocultural past is beyond the range of possibility. The influence of a multi-cultural world is as near as one's airport, television set, computer screen, and cell phone. The era of "One World" is at hand, and all must adapt to the presence of people from a broad range of cultural perspectives. Learning to accommodate to this world is inevitable.

But how do we do this? Based on the experiences of the multicultural individuals in our study, this book has suggested some mechanisms by which such accommodations can occur. These experts on multiculturalism bear the components of two or more different races or cultures within their very being. They know, better than anyone, the difficulties of living cross-culturally or cross-racially. They are the "Douglas" of the USA, to use Trinidadian terminology. Yet most of them came to recognize that being multicultural had its advantages as well as disadvantages. They had a strong, confident sense of personal identity, and a feeling of comfort in dealing with others from a different background. Hence the key to successful multicultural societies is to learn to minimize the problems and draw upon the advantages which multiculturalism brings. In Part III, we made these several suggestions aimed toward these ends, on three different levels. While the original recommendations were directed specifically at *persons* who were multi-cultural or multi-racial, they apply equally well to any situation in which such differences occur.

On the interpersonal level, Chapter 8 outlined ways in which families could prepare their mixed background children for issues they were likely to encounter in the broader community. Suggestions for professional counselors who work with such persons were also made. The core of these recommendations focused on the need for *individual respect*. The right of the individual to choose her or his own destiny formed the core of the issue. This respect should be maintained at all levels of society. Government level programs should not force persons to "choose one" racial category when they wished to claim their identity with the background of both their parents. Neither should schools or ethnic communities or family members force individuals to "choose sides."

The same respect is illustrated in successful multi-cultural programs at the community or institutional level. The Diversity Program described in Chapter 9 by Sonya Berkley showed that schools can achieve educational objectives with children from diverse backgrounds when they recognize and celebrate that diversity. Cultural diversity becomes a part of the daily routine. Children in such settings learn to understand and appreciate not only their similarities, but also their differences. They come to accept the fact that people can have different traditions, but still have cordial relationships and appreciate each other's perspectives. Dr. Javed's workshops provide an alternate approach for achieving similar objectives. These same approaches could be introduced in other community and institutional settings as well.

Finally, at the societal level, we had the opportunity to compare five different societies, all modern democratic nations, and all highly diverse in race, religion, language, and national origin. All had long histories of in-migration. All had experienced their own levels of turmoil as a result of their diversity. And all faced, and continue to face, the same dilemma encountered by every multi-cultural society: How does a free society develop and maintain a sense of national unity and identity – while respecting the rights of its several racial and ethnic components, both majority and minority? Australia, Canada, France, the USA, and Trinidad and Tobago – each nation was engaged in developing its own unique response to this question. And all responses can best be described as "works in progress." Hence at this point, there is no clear answer as to which solution is "best."

What is common to all these issues, at all levels, however, is a single dimension: intergroup respect. Every group, whatever its race or culture, is entitled to be viewed for what it is: a valued component of the human condition. Every culture is the sum total of a people's accumulated experience and learning. As such, each cultural or racial group must be accorded the right to exist and practice its traditional ways, so long as each also agrees to recognize the same right in others.

What does this mean for persons living in multi-cultural and multi-racial societies? Does it mean they are forced to relinquish their beloved cultural traditions? Must they learn another language? Turn their backs on the religious beliefs they cherish so dearly? Must they accept a secondary status for their race?

In fact, multi-culturalism and multi-racialism requires none of these things. What it does require is that all persons accord to other races and cultures the same respect and appreciation they want others to give to them. While no one is asked to relinquish his or her treasured race and cultural traditions, neither should they ask others to relinquish theirs.

Are any aspects of culture prohibited? To some degree, the answer is, "Yes." The one component of culture which all are asked to reject is any cultural belief which contends that others must be conquered, converted, or extinguished. This is the single dimension on which the modern, multi-cultural, and multi-racial nation cannot afford to compromise. Mutual coexistence on this dimension is essential.

So what does the diverse society require of us? And what does it permit us?

- No one is required to accept another's religion ...

  ○ But all must accept others' right to practice their religion.

- No one can be forced to speak a different language ...

  ○ But the right of others to speak their language must be accommodated.

- No one should accept a view that says his or her race is inferior ...

  ○ But neither should they treat other races as inferiors.

- No one can be forced to accept someone else's definition of their personal identity ...

  ○ But all should respect others' definition of themselves, even if they disagree.

Thus the demands of the diverse society are few: respect others, and accord them their right to maintain their lives and cultures in the manner which we would want them to respect us. To do otherwise is to destroy the very basis on which a diverse society must rest. To observe these requirements will help us deal with the challenges which a diverse society presents, and in turn, will ensure for all the abundant rewards which the rich cultural heritage of a diverse society can provide.

Appendix A
Outline of Questions for Interview

Cultural Background and Identity

Tell me something about your cultural background. What are the cultural origins of your father and mother?

How do you usually identify yourself? Do you identify with one of these cultures? Which one? Why? [If not, why not?]

Do you usually identify *yourself*? Or do *other people* identify you? How do they identify you? How do you feel about that?

Did your parents ever talk about their cultural backgrounds or differences? If so, what did they say?

Child Rearing

Are there any experiences from your childhood that are particularly salient to you? What are they? What do you remember about them? Why?

Who spent more time with you during your childhood?

- helping with school work?
- going to the school to see teachers?
- doing the disciplining?
- type of discipline:

    - did you ever get spanked?
    - by whom – father or mother?
    - have privileges taken away?
    - by whom – father or mother?

Social Patterns

Have you ever lived with members of your extended family?

Was a foreign language ever spoken in your home? Which parent's?

Whose relatives did you see more – your father's or your mother's?

Which relatives did you live nearest to – your father's or your mother's?

Do you see your relatives as an adult? How often? Whose – your father's or mother's?

Were ethnic festivals celebrated in your home? Which ones – your mother's or your father's?

Were ethnic foods ever eaten in your home? Which ones – your mother's or your father's?

Siblings:

Do you have siblings? In general, do you think their experiences and reactions were similar to or different from yours?

Appendix B
Description of Sample Respondents

Multi Racial Respondents ($n = 10$)

Black and Caucasian ($n = 3$)

#27 Teresa (Female; 18; African father, White mother)
#30 Adam (Male; 33; self-employed; African-American mother, Caucasian father)
#25 Derek (Male; 40; Black father, German mother)

Black and Asian ($n = 1$)

#14 Deanna (Female; 24; student; African-American father, Korean mother)

Caucasian and Asian ($n = 2$)

#20 Karen (Female; 40; German father, Korean mother)
#24 Leslie (Female; c 30; Filipino father, Caucasian mother)

European and Native American ($n = 3$)

#02 Peter (Male; mid-20s; student; French/English mother, Paiute father)
#03 Grace (Female; mid-40s; English/Irish Father, Cherokee and Caucasian mother)
#26 Carlos (Male; Salvadorean/Spanish father, German and Native Central American mother)

Black and Native American ($n = 1$)

#17 Ken (Male, c. 25; Guatemala/Black/Native American)

Multi-Religious Respondents (All Christian-Jewish) ($n = 3$)

#07 Sarah (Female; c. 50; teacher; Greek/Polish/Catholic/Orthodox father, Jewish/European/Rumanian mother)

#09 Vickie (Female; 38; teacher; Irish father, Jewish mother)

#12 Jeff (Male; 70; teacher; Jewish father, Methodist mother)

Multi-nationality Respondents ($n = 14$)

Different European Backgrounds ($n = 9$)

#04 Robert (Male; mid-60s; teacher; English father, Scottish mother)

#05 Nichole (Female; c. 40; Irish Mother, Father "other")

#06 Peggy (Female; mid-60s; teacher; Irish father, Belgian mother)

#13 Betty (Female; c. 45; Polish, Irish, German, English parentage)

#15 Ted (Male; c. 50; Austrian, Irish, and general European parentage)

#16 Francine (Female; Father Czech, mother Italian)

#18 Margo (Female; 22; Sicilian/French Canadian/Austrian)

#22 Sam (Male; 39; Irish mother, Italian father)

#29 Yvonne (Female; c. 50; Scottish and Swedish father, French-Canadian mother)

European and Middle Eastern Backgrounds ($n = 2$)

#01 Jeanette (Female; 57; graduate student; Lebanese mother, Irish father)

#21 Ida (Female; British father and Lebanese mother)

Different Parts of the Americas (or Native American and European) ($n = 2$)

#08 Gary (Male; 23; Mexican mother, Lithuanian & Polish father)

#10 Anita (Female; c. 45; Mexican mother, Puerto Rican father)

Different Asian Backgrounds ($n = 1$)

#11 Evelyn (Female; 30; Chinese father, Korean mother)

Other Sources of Multi-culturalism ($n = 3$)

Parentage V. Residence

#19 Regina (Female; c. 40; Polish parents; raised in Brazil)

Social Class Differences

#23 Carol (Female; father working class, mother southern aristocracy)

Presence of Stepparent

#28 Brian (Male; c. 60; Irish parents, raised by German stepmother)

Appendix C
Definition of Terms

Acculturation: the exchange of cultural features that results when groups come into continuous firsthand contact; the original cultural patterns are altered, but the groups remain socially distinct. Only the incoming group may change (one-way acculturation) or both groups may alter their cultures somewhat (two-way acculturation; also called reciprocal acculturation).

Anglo-Conformity: a theory about cultural interchange between people from two different cultures, one of which is English-speaking, in which the non-English-speaking group is required to adopt the English language and culture.

Anglophone: culture that is largely from the legacy of the British, English.

Assimilation: the process whereby members of a minority group gradually become part of the dominant group, being accepted in its social relationships and institutions. Specifically applies to the social dimensions, but usually also implies that the cultures change.

Calypso: A style of Afro-Caribbean music that originated in Trinidad and Tobago.

Civic multi-culturalism: a stage in the development of a multi-cultural society in which the goal is to build a unified society by linking multi-culturalism and citizenship. Used in Canada.

Coolies: the Creole name given to East Indians in Caribbean nations; a negative term, reflective of their rural and lower class origins.

Creole: a term that was applied to all persons of White and Black extraction, who were born in the Caribbean or Africa; it excludes East Indians.

Conflicting Role Models: refers to the problem experienced by children from minority races and cultures, who are faced with the presence of two different patterns of behavior exhibited by the adults who surround them, one model being presented by members of the dominant group, the other model coming from the minority racial or ethnic group.

Cultural Pluralism: a term used when small groups within a larger society maintain their unique cultural patterns, including attitudes, values, and behavior patterns, even if they are functional and participate socially in the larger society.

Dougla: a Hindi word for "bastard." In Trinidad society it refers to the mixed identity resulting from unions between persons of African and East Indian descent.

Dual Anchorage: refers to the fact that members of minority races and cultures, once they have been successfully socialized, can be securely established as members of both groups, and comfortable participating in interactions in both cultures, and sharing a sense of belonging to both cultures.

Duality of Expectations: refers to the fact that members of minority racial or cultural groups have two sets of expectations placed upon them: one by the dominant culture, and the other by their own racial or ethnic community.

East Indians: an ethnic group, originating from the area in and around the city of Bombay, India.

Ethnic, Ethnic group: a group of human beings whose members are distinguished from others in the society on the basis of common cultural, linguistic, ancestral, religious, or behavioral traits, real or presumed, and who share a sense of identification with each other on this basis. Ethnic groups may or may not share common biologically observable traits.

Francophone: culture that is largely from the legacy of the French.

Integration: inclusion of all racial and ethnic groups into the social structures of society; often used as synonymous with assimilation. In Australia, integration implies two-way acculturation, such that all groups, including the dominant group, alter their culture to establish a new national culture. Integration is also sometimes used as a legal term.

Melting Pot: a theory about cultural interchange between two or more groups, in which it is assumed that all groups will adopt each other's patterns of culture, at least to some extent.

Metropolitan France: the part of France located in Europe, including Corsica, as opposed to the overseas departments and overseas territories,

Mixed Race: in Trinidad, it refers to the mixed identity resulting from the union of two or more different races (except in the case of an African and an East Indian).

Monocultural: a society which has a single cultural pattern.

Mononationalism: the concept that a country can have only a single nationalistic approach and culture; used in Canada to describe what the USA has called Anglo-conformity.

Multi-cultural: a state of racial, cultural, and ethnic diversity within the demographics of a specified group, usually at the scale of a nation, city, neighborhood, or organization, such as a school or business.

Multi-culturalism: a policy that allows and encourages members of a society to continue to maintain and practice their own individual cultures. Often used synonymously with social pluralism or cultural pluralism.

Parallel Socialization: refers to the fact that children who are members of a group other than the dominant group in society learn two different social and cultural patterns in tandem: the dominant one, and the pattern of their own ethnic or racial group. It is a process of simultaneous socialization that bicultural children undergo at home and in school and the larger society, as a part of their experience growing up in a pluralistic society with a dominant culture distinctly different from their own.

Race, Racial group: usually refers to the concept of dividing humans into populations or groups on the basis of various sets of characteristics, usually traits which are physically visible, especially skin color, cranial or facial features, and hair texture. Such groups often share a sense of identity on this basis, and may also share traits also associated with Ethnic Groups. Conceptions of race, as well as specific ways of grouping races, vary by culture and over time, and are often controversial, for scientific as well as social and political reasons.

Reciprocal Acculturation: the process in which members of two cultural groups meet and both engage in mutual acceptance of some beliefs, traits, and behaviors of the other group. Also called two-way acculturation. To be distinguished from one-way acculturation, in which a minority group adopts habits and language patterns of the dominant group, which makes no changes to accommodate the newcomers.

Social Pluralism: a term used to refer to the fact that small groups within a larger society tend to remain separate from social participation in the larger society, even if they do not continue a distinct cultural pattern.

Third Force: the wave of new ethnocultural groups which have come into Canada in recent years, following the British and French founding groups.

Trinidad and Tobago: a unitary, parliamentary, democratic state, composed of two islands in the Caribbean, formerly a British colony.

Two Founding Nations: in Canada, refers to the two original European nations which settled in Canada: Britain and France.

Two-way Communication: involves a reciprocal, mutual cultural exchange between two individuals or groups. The critical issue is that both parties in the communication must make an honest attempt to understand the other, as well as make their own needs and expectations known.

Vertical Mosaic: a multi-cultural social structure in which ethnic groups not only view themselves as different from each other, but also as hierarchically arranged; sometimes this term is applied to Canada.

Appendix D
Advice for Parents and Families Which Include Diverse Racial and Cultural Origins

- Parents and other family members should recognize the differences that exist within the family and discuss them with their children. While the parents may not consider these differences important, others in the community might and may mention them in public. If the parents have not discussed them, it will be confusing to the children.
- The different cultural patterns in the family can – and should – be recognized without indicating preference of one over another.
- Children can be encouraged to appreciate their multiple heritages, even if they feel they "belong" to one more than the other.
- Children should be prepared for the fact that others outside the family may not recognize their multiple identities. They should receive assurance from family members that their worth does not depend on the degree to which outsiders accept them.
- All parents should be aware that children who are in any way "different" from the surrounding community are likely to encounter criticism and comments from others. They should be sensitive to these problems, and prepare to assist their children in dealing with them.

Appendix E
Advice for Professionals: Approaches to Individuals and Families From Diverse Backgrounds

- There are many different cultural groups in the USA, all of which have an impact on identity and behavior. These include a great many groups, not just those which are the most obvious ethnic groups, such as racial or Spanish-surnamed groups.
- These differences may be derived from a wide variety of dimensions, including race, religion, and national origin.
- Even groups which are assumed to be a single culture may not be. For example, African-Americans include a wide variety of cultures based on social class, urban or rural origin, long-term residence in the USA versus recent immigration from Africa or the Caribbean islands, and so on. "Hispanic" also includes a wide variety of cultures from Mexico, Central America, Spain, and Puerto Rico, to mention a few.
- Do not assume that the recognized ethnic groups are the only ones that play a role in determining individual behavior. There are a wide variety of groups which continue to have different cultural patterns – even after long periods in the USA. Descendants from British, Polish, Italian, or Irish heritages may continue to exhibit remnants of these cultures in the way they deal with family, education, medical care, or other aspects of life – many generations after their ancestors immigrated to the USA.
- Professionals should resist the tendency to overgeneralize about groups. The terms "Hispanic" or "Spanish-surnamed," or "African-American" or "Black," are applied to people with a great many cultural differences. Professionals should resist the temptation to assume that all Blacks or Hispanics have had the same experiences or accept the same cultural patterns.
- A single individual may have several different racial and/or cultural origins. Professionals should check the backgrounds of their students/clients/group participants to determine whether they might have more than one ethnic or racial origin.
- Religion and nationality are important determinants of individual behavior. The national or religious backgrounds of individuals are not always obvious. Generalized "European" background is rarely a meaningful identity or culture. Neither is a generalized "Asian" or "African-American" background.
- If an individual's parents were of different races or cultures, professionals should attempt to determine which culture or group the individual follows or identifies

with. It cannot be assumed that it is always the most obvious – such as racial appearance or surname. Indeed, some persons may deliberately identify with more than one.

- Mixed race or culture individuals may be deeply offended if others refuse to recognize the various aspects of their identity. Professionals should take care not to offend them in this manner.
- Cultural patterns affect a wide variety of aspects of life. Aside from obvious differences such as race or religion, cultural differences affect such subtle dimensions of life as beliefs of about child-rearing, attitudes about family visiting or community participation, the individual's tendency to express or repress emotions, and so on.
- Since mothers do much of the child-rearing in the family, persons of mixed cultural backgrounds may actually be more influenced by the mother's culture – even if they identify with the father's culture or if it is more obvious due to the presence of the surname. Major assumptions about the individual's life patterns based on the surname can be inaccurate.
- While the cultural origins of the biological mother and father represent the most obvious sources of cultural identities, individual identities may also arise from other, less obvious aspects of life, such as the presence of stepparents, foster parents, or adoptive parents, or the individual himself/herself having lived for some time in another country or culture.
- Some persons from multi-cultural or multi-racial backgrounds are quite proud of the mixed identity – and determined to continue the tradition into future generations. They may consider the failure to recognize their multi-culturalism a supreme personal insult.

Bibliography

Abu-Laben, Y, & S Stasiulis, 1992. "Ethnic Pluralism Under Siege: Popular and Partisan Opposition to Multiculturalism." *Canadian Public Policy*, 27:365–386.

Abudabbeh, N, 2005. "Arab Families: An Overview." In M McGoldrick, J Giordano, & N Garcia-Parto, Eds. *Ethnicity and Family Therapy*. 3rd Ed. New York: Guilford. Chap. 23, pp. 423–436.

Adams, BN, 1968. *Kinship in an Urban Setting*. Chicago: Markham.

Alba, R, 1999. "Immigration and the American Realities of Assimilation and Multiculturalism." *Sociological Forum*, 14:3–25.

Alba, R, & V Nee, 2003. *Remaking the American Mainstream*. Cambridge, MA: Harvard University Press.

Alexander, JC, 2001. "Theorizing the "Modes of incorporation": Assimilation, Hypenation, and Multiculturalism as Varieties of Civil Participation." *Sociological Theory* 19:237–249.

Allen, TW, 1994. *The Invention of the White Race: Racial Oppression and Social Control*. London: Verso.

Allen, JA, Jr., 2007. "Opinion Divided on Mass Decision." *National Catholic Reporter* (July 20): 5.

Allen, KR, & BK Beitin, 2007. "Gender and Class in Culturally Diverse Families." In BS Trask, & RR Hamon, Eds. *Cultural Diversity and Families: Expanding Perspectives*. Thousand Oaks, CA: Sage. Chap. 4, pp. 64–79.

Almeida, R, 2005. "Asian Indian Families." In M McGoldrick, J Giordano, & N Garcia-Parto, Eds. *Ethnicity and Family Therapy*. 3rd Ed. New York: Guilford. Chap. 28, pp. 377–394.

Almond, GA, RS Appleby, & E Sivan, 1995. *Strong Religion: The Rise of Fundamentalisms Around the World*. Chicago: University of Chicago Press.

Alvarez, J, 1998. "A White Woman of Color." In CC O'Hearn, Ed. *Half and Half: Writers on Growing Up Biracial and Bicultural*. NY: Pantheon Books. pp. 139–149.

Americans United for Separation of Church and State, 2007. "Lest We Forget: The Jerry Falwell Saga." *Church & State* (Aug.): 7–9.

Anderson, CH, 1970. *White Protestant Americans: From National Origins to Religious Group*. Englewood Cliffs, NJ: Prentice-Hall.

Ankerberg, J, & J Waldon, 1995. *Protestants & Catholics: Do They Now Agree?* Peabody, MA: Harvest House Publishers.

ARI, 2008. "Accent Reduction Institute." http://www.lessaccent.com/. Accessed July 22, 2008.

Augelli, JA, & HW Taylor, 1960. "Race and Population Patterns in Trinidad." *Annals of the Association of American Geographers*, 50(2) (Jun., 1960), pp. 123–138.

Australian Bureau of Statistics 1989. *Overseas Born Australians 1989 – A Statistical Profile*. Canberra: Australian Government Publishing Service.

Baldwin, J, 1963. *The Fire Next Time*. Merchantville, NJ: Dial Press, Division of Doubleday.

Baca Zinn, M, DS Eitzen, & B Wells, 2007. *Diversity in Families*. 8th Ed. New York: Allyn & Bacon.

Bank, DP, & MD Kahn, 1997. *The Sibling Bond*. New York: Basic Books.

Barrett, JR, & D Roediger, 1997. "In Between Peoples: Race, Nationality and the 'New Immigrant' Working Class." *Journal of American Ethnic History* 16(3):3–44. Spring.

Behar, R, 2008. "The Anthropologist's Son." *The Chronicle Review*. Dec. 5: B12–13.

Berkley, S, (Forthcoming). "Bridging the Gap through Diversity Educational Programming." Detroit: Wayne State University: Unpublished Ph.D. dissertation.

Bendixen & Associates, 2006. "Multilingual Poll of Legal Immigrants on U.S. Immigration Policy." New American Media. http://www.americanprogress.org/kf/imm_policy_poll.pdf (accessed 7/31/07)

Berger, P, 1967. *The Sacred Canopy: Elements of a Sociological Theory of Religion*. New York: Doubleday.

Bernstein, M, 2005. "Identity Politics." In KS Cook & DS Massey, Eds. *Annual Review of Sociology*, 31:47–74.

Bibby, R, 1990. *Mosaic Madness*. Toronto: Stoddart.

Billingsley, A, 1968. *Black Families in White America*. Englewood Cliffs, NJ: Prentice-Hall.

Birth, K, 1997 Most of Us are Family Some of the Time: Interracial Unions and Transracial Kinship in Eastern Trinidad." *American Ethnologist* 24:585–601.

Bisoondath, N, 1994. *Selling Illusions: The Cult of Multiculturalism*. Toronto: Penguin.

Black, L, & V Jackson, 2005. "Families of African Origin: An Overview." In M McGoldrick, J Giordano, & N Garcia-Parto, Eds. *Ethnicity and Family Therapy*. 3rd Ed. New York: Guilford. Chap. 5, pp. 77–86.

Bloomberg, M, 2006. "Mayor Michael Bloomberg Delivers Slate 60 Dinner Keynote Address At William J. Clinton Presidential Library." Nov. 12. http://www.mikebloomberg.com/en/issues/education/mayor_michael_bloomberg_delivers_slate_60_dinner_keynote_address_at_william_j_clinton_presidential_library.htm (accessed July 30, 2008).

Bollinger, LC, 2007. "Why Diversity Matters." *The Chronicle of Higher Education*. (June 1): B20.

Boston, R, 2006. "The Religious Right and American Freedom." *Church & State*, June: 4–9.

Bosworth, AR, 1967. *America's Concentration Camps*. New York: WW Norton & Co.

Boulet, J, Jr., 2001. "Assimilation, Not Amnesty." Guest Comment on National Review Online (Aug. 21). http://www.nationalreview.com/comment/comment-boulet082101.shtml (accessed 7/21/07).

Brereton, B, 1981. *A History of Modern Trinidad 1783–1962*. London: Heinemann.

Brereton, B, 1993. "Social Organization and Class, Racial and Cultural Conflict in Nineteenth Century Trinidad." In K Yelvington Ed. *Trinidad Ethnicity*. Knoxville: University of Tennessee Press. pp. 33–55.

Breton, R, 1986. "Multiculturalism and Canadian Nation Building." In P Kivisto Ed. *Multiculturalism in a Global Society*. MA: Blackwell Publishers, Ltd.

Brezosky, L, 2007. "Texas Governor Signs Compromise Border Security Bill." AP NewsWires. (June 6). http://www.mysanantonio.com/sharedcontent/APStories/stories/D8PJJA0O0.html (accessed 8/2/07)

Brislin, RW, & T Yoshsida, Eds., 1994. *Improving Intercultural Relations: Modules for Cross-Cultural Training Programs*. Thousand Oaks, CA: Sage.

Brown, NG, & RE Douglass, 1996. "Making the Invisible Visible: The Growth of Community Network Organizations." In MMP Root, Ed. *Racially Mixed People in America*. Thousand Oaks, CA: Sage. Chap. 20, pp. 323–340.

Bruce, S, 2000. *Fundamentalism*. Malden, MA: Blackwell.

Burnet, J, 1981. "Multiculturalism Ten Years Later." *History and Social Science Teachers* 17: 1–6.

Canadian Heritage, 2008. "Canadian Diversity: Respecting our Differences." http://www.pch.gc.ca/progs/multi/respect_e.cfm. (Accessed September 17, 2008).

Caribworldnews.com, 2008. "French Creole, Spanish Among Languages Now Mandated." July 23. http://www.caribbeanworldnews.com/middle_top_news_detail.php?mid=1114 (accessed July 30, 2008).

Castles, S, 1992. "The Australian Model of Immigration and Multiculturalism: Is it Applicable to Europe?" *International Migration Review*, 26: 549–567.

Castles, S, B Cope, M Kalanzis, & M Morrisey, 1990. *Mistaken Identity – Multiculturalism and the Demise of Nationalism in Australia*. 2nd Ed. Sydney: ANZ Publishing Co.

Cauce, AM, Y Hiraga, C Mason, T Aguilar, N Ordonez, & N Gonzales, 1992. "Between a Rock and a Hard Place: Social Adjustment of Biracial Youth." In MRP Root, Ed. *Racially Mixed People in America*. Thousand Oaks, CA: Sage. Chap. 15, pp. 207–222.

Central Intelligence Agency. 2008. "France" The World Factbook. https://www.cia.gov/library/publications/the-world-factbook/geos/fr.html (Accessed September 25, 2008).

Charle, C, 1991. *A Social History of France in the 19th Century*. Oxford: Berg Publishers.

Chaves, M, & PS Gorski, 2001. "Religious Pluralism and Religious Participation." In KS Cook & J Hagan, Eds. *Annual Review of Sociology*, 27: 261–281.

Chick, JT, n.d. *Smokescreens*. Ontario, CA: Chick Publications.

Chinn, GJ, 1996. "The Civil Rights Revolution Comes to Immigration Law: A New Look at the Immigration and Nationality Act of 1965." In P.H. Schuck. 2003. *Diversity in America: Keeping government at a safe distance Massachusetts*. Cambridge, MA: The Belknap Press of Harvard University.

Christian Information Ministries, 2003. "Evangelicals and Catholics." http://www.christian information.org/article.asp?artID=15. (accessed 7/16/2007)

Chubb, J, 1997. *The Senior Academy*. New York: The Edison Project.

Citrin, J, EB Haas, C Muste, & B Reingold, 1994. "Is American Nationalism Changing? Implications for Foreign Policy." *International Studies Quarterly*, 38: 1–31.

Clarke, C, 1986. "East Indians in a West Indian Town: San Fernando, Trinidad, 1930–70." 2001. Quoted In GH Cornwell & EW Stoddard, Eds. *Global Multiculturalism: Comparative Perspectives on Ethnicity, Race, and Nation*. New York: Rowman & Littlefield Publishers, Inc pp. 29–50.

Clinton, HR, 1996. *It Takes a Village: and Other Lessons Children Teach Us*. Simon and Schuster.

CNN.com/living, 2007. "Could Mr. Right be White? More Black Women Consider Dating Out." CNN.com/living, Aug.6. http://www.cnn.com/2007/LIVING/personal/08/06/interracial. dating.ap/index.html (accessed 8/9/07).

Coleman, A, 2001. "Work with Families." In HM Rebach, & JG Bruhn, Eds., 2001. *Handbook of Clinical Sociology*. 2nd Ed. New York: Kluwer, Plenum. Chap. 7, pp. 113–132.

Collins, J, 1988. *Migrant Hands in a Distant Land: Australia's Post – War Immigration*. Sydney: Pluto Press

Commonwealth Observer Group, 2001. "The Trinidad and Tobago General Election, 11 December 2000." *The Report of the Commonwealth Observer Group*: Commonwealth Secretariat.

Connidis, IS, 2001. *Family Ties and Aging*. Thousand Oaks, CA: Sage.

Cooley, CH, 1922. *Human Nature and the Social Order*. Rev. Ed. New York: Charles Scribner's Sons.

Cornelius, WA, T Tsuda, PL Martin, & JF Hoffifield, 2004. *Controlling Immigration: A Global Perspective*. Second Ed. Stanford, CA. Stanford University Press.

Cornwell, GH, & EW Stoddard, Eds. 2001. "Introduction: National Boundaries/Transnational Identities." In GH Cornwell, & EW Stoddard, Eds. *Global Multiculturalism: Comparative Perspective on Ethnicity, Race, and Nation*. New York: Rowman & Littlefield Publishers, Inc. pp. 29–50.

Crawford, J, 2004a. *Educating English Learners: Language Diversity in the Classroom*. 5th Ed. Los Angeles: Bilingual Education Service.

Crawford, J, 2004b. "No Child Left Behind: Misguided Approach to School Accountability for English Language Learners." *Presentation to the Forum on Iedeas to Improve the NCLB Accountability Provisions for Students with Disabilities and English Language Learners*. Washington, DC: Center on Educational Policy (Sept. 14). http://users.rcn.com/crawj/langpol/misguided.pdf (accessed 7/21/07)

Crawford, J, 2006. "The Decline of Bilingual Education: How to Reverse a Troubling Trend? Forthcoming in International Journal of Multilingual Research Journal. (accessed 7/21/07) http://users.rcn.com/crawj/langpol/Crawford_Decline_of_BE.pdf

Crawford, J, 2007. "A Diminished Vision of Civil Rights." *Education Week*. (June 6). http://www.elladvocates.org/media/NCLB/EdWeek6jun07.html (accessed 7/21/07)

Crook, M, 1993. "French Elections, 1789–1848." *History Today*, 43: 41–46.

Cross, RD, 1973. "How Historians Have Looked at Immigrants to the United States." *International Migration Review* 7, 1 (Spring): 4–22.

Cushner, K, 1994. "Preparing Teachers for an Intercultural Context." In RW Brislin & T Yoshsida, Eds. *Improving Intercultural Relations: Modules for Cross-Cultural Training Programs.* Thousand Oaks, CA: Sage.

De Sauvigny, GDB, & DH Pinkney, 1977. *History of France: Revised and Enlarged Edition.* Arlington Heights: ILL: The Forum Press, Inc.

Democracy Now, 2005. "Governor Richardson Calls For Tighter Border Security." Democracy Now. Sept. 22. http://www.democracynow.org/article.pl?sid=05/09/22/1846255 (assessed 7/31/07)

Department of Immigration and Ethnic Affairs. 1986. "Don't Settle for Less: Report of the Committee for Stage 1 of the Review of Migrant and Multicultural Programs and Services." Canberra: Australian Government Publishing Service.

Dickerson, DJ, 2005. "The Great White Way." *Mother Jones*, Sept.–Oct.: 77–79.

Dignan, D, 1981. "Europe's Melting Pot: A Century of Large-Scale Immigration into France," *Ethnic and Racial Studies*, 4: 137–152.

DiPrete, TA, & GM Eirich, 2006. "Cumulative Advantage as a Mechanism for Inequality: A Review of Theoretical and Empirical Developments." In KS Cook & DS Massey, Eds. *Annual Review of Sociology*, 32: 271–297.

Doucet, F, & RR Hamon, 2007. "A Nation of Diversity: Demographics of the United States and Their Implications for Families." In BS Trask, & RR Hamon, Eds. *Cultural Diversity and Families: Expanding Perspectives.* Thousand Oaks, CA: Sage. Chap. 2, pp. 20–43.

Duncan, K, 2003. "Secularism's Laws: State Blaine Amendments and Religious Persecution." *Fordham Law Review*, 72 (Dec.): 493–593. http://law.bepress.com/cgi/viewcontent. cgi?article=1044&context=expresso (accessed 7/20/07).

Dupont, L, & N Lemarchand, 2001. "Official Multiculturalism in Canada: Between Virtue and Politics." In GH Cornwell & EW Stoddard, Eds. 2001. *Global Multiculturalism: Comparative Perspectives on Ethnicity, Race, and Nation.* Maryland: Rowman & Littlefield Publishers, Inc. pp. 29–50.

Edison Schools, 2008a. "About Edison Schools." New York: Edison Schools, Inc. http://www.edisonschools.com/edison-schools/about-us (Accessed 8/24/08.)

Edison Schools, 2008b. "About Our School Design and Curriculum." New York: Edison Schools, Inc. http://www.edisonschools.com/edison-schools/school-design-curriculum (Accessed 8/24/08).

Edison Schools, 2008c. "Technology Acquisition Plus Innovative School Design Transform Education Company." New York: Edison Schools, Inc. http://www.Edisonschools.com. (Accessed 8/24/08).

Edison Schools, 2008d. "What Is a Charter School?" New York: Edison Schools, Inc. http://www.edisonschools.com/edison-schools/faqs#q5 (Accessed 8/24/08).

Edison Schools, 2008e. "A Rich and Challenging Curriculum." New York: Edison Schools. http://www.edisonschools.com/edison-schools/school-design-curriculum/curriculum (Accessed 8/24/08).

Edison Schools, 2008 f. "Professional Development." New York: Edison Schools. http://www.edisonschools.com/edison-schools/school-design-curriculum/professional-development (Accessed 8/24/08).

Edison Schools, 2008 g. "Faces of Achievement." New York: Edison Schools. http://www.edisonschools.com/edison-schools/faces-of-achievement/facesofedison_popup_view (Accessed 8/24/08).

Edison Schools, 2008 h. "Student Achievement Results." New York: Edison Schools. http://www.edisonschools.com/edison-schools/achievement-accountability/achievement-reports (Accessed 8/24/08).

Edison Schools, 2008i. "A Commitment to Diversity." New York: Edison Schools. http://www.edisonschools.com/edison-schools/career-opportunities/diversity-statement/?searchterm=diversity (Accessed 8/24/08).

Edison Schools, 2008j. "Leaving No Child Behind." New York: Edison School. http://www.edisonschools.com/edison-schools/achievement-accountability/no-child-left-behind (Accessed 8/26/08).

Elliott, JL, Ed., 1983. *Two Nations Many Cultures*. Scarborough, Ont.: Prentice Hall of Canada.

ELT, 2008. Executive Language Training. http://www.eltlearn.com. Accessed July 22, 2008.

Emerson, MO, & D Hartman, 2006. "The Rise of Religious Fundamentalism." In KS Cook & DS Massey, Eds. *Annual Review of Sociology*, 32: 127–144.

English First, 2007. "Official Home Page of English First." Springfield, VA: English First, Suite 102, 8001 Forbes Pl. http://www.englishfirst.org/ (accessed 7/21/07).

Fallows, MR, 1979. *Irish Americans: Identity and Assimilation*. Englewood Cliffs, NJ: Prentice-Hall.

Farber, B, B Lazerwitz, & CH Mindel, 1998. "The Jewish-American Family." In CH Mindel, RW Habenstein, & R Wright, Jr., Eds. *Ethnic Families in America: Patterns and Variations*. 4th Ed. Upper Saddle River, NJ: Prentice-Hall. Chap. 17, pp. 422–449.

Farley, R, 1996. *The New American Reality: Who We Are, How We Got Here, Where We Are Going*. New York: Russell Sage Foundation.

Fernandez, CA, 1996. "Government Classification of Multiracial/Multiethnic People." In MMP Root, Ed. *The Multiracial Experience: Racial Borders as the New Frontier*. Thousand Oaks, CA: Sage. Chap. 2, pp. 15–36.

Fernandez, EC, 2000. *La Cosecha: Harvesting Contemporary United States Hispanic Theology (1972–1998)."* Collegeville, MN: Liturgical Press.

Finke, R, & R Stark, 1992. *The Churching of America, 1776–1990: Winners and Losers in Our Religious Economy*. New Brunswick, NJ: Rutgers University Press.

Fitzpatrick, JP, 1987. *Puerto Rican Americans: The Meaning of Migration to the Mainland*. Englewood Cliffs, NJ: Prentice-Hall.

Fleras, A, & Elliott, JL, 1996. *Unequal Relations: An Introduction to Race, Ethnic and Aboriginal Dynamics in Canada*. Toronto: Prentice-Hall, Canada; Prentice-Hall International (UK).

Fong, LG, & JT Gibbs, 1996. "Facilitating Services to Multi-Cultural Communities in a Dominant Culture Setting: An Organizational Perspective." *Administration in Social Work* 19 (2): 1–24.

Fong, E, & K Shibuya, 2005. "Multiethnic Cities in North America." In KS Cook & DS Massey, Eds. *Annual Review of Sociology*, 31: 285–304.

Frazier, EF, 1957. *Black Bourgeoisie*. Glencoe, IL: Free Press.

Fritz, J, 1985. "Communities: Making Them Work." In RA Strauss, Ed. *Using Sociology*. Chap. 8. pp. 136–152. Bayside, NY: General-Hall, Inc.

Frontline, 2003a. "Public Schools, Inc: Interview Sarah Horsey." New York: Public Broadcasting System, July 3. http://www.pbs.org/wgbh/pages/frontline/shows/edison/interviews/horsey.html (Accessed 8/26/08).

Frontline, 2003b. "Public Schools, Inc: Inside Edison's Schools: Baltimore, MD." New York: Public Broadcasting System, July 3. http://www.pbs.org/wgbh/pages/frontline/shows/edison/inside/ (Accessed 8/26/08).

Gallagher, BG, & N Nahan, 1997. "Cross-Cultural Parenting on Detroit's Eastside: Establishing Community-Based Parenting in Multicultural Neighborhoods." In P Nyden, A Figert, M Shibley, & D Burrows, Eds. *Building Community*. pp. 141–149. Thousand Oaks, CA: Pine Forge Press.

Galligan, B, & W Roberts, 2003. "Australian multiculturalism: Its rise and demise." Refereed paper presented to the Australian Political Studies Association Conference September 29-October1, 2003. Accessed September 16, 2006. http://www.utas.edu.au/government/APSA/GalliganRoberts.pdf

Gambino, R, 1974. *Blood of My Blood: The Dilemma of Italian-Americans*. New York: Doubleday.

Garcia-Preto, N, 2005. "Latino Families: An Overview." In M McGoldrick, J Giordano, & N Garcia-Parto, Eds. *Ethnicity and Family Therapy*. 3rd Ed. New York: Guilford. Chap. 11, pp. 153–165.

Gaskins, PF, 1999. *What Are You?: Voices of Mixed-Race Young People*. New York: Holt.

Gazelem, 2007. "Key Utah Legislators oppose The Border Security and Immigration Reform Act of 2007. May 21. http://gazelem.blog-city.com/utah_legislatures_oppose_immigration_act.htm (7/31/07)

Gerson, LL, 1953. *Woodrow Wilson and the Rebirth of Poland, 1914–1920*. New Haven, CN: Yale University Press.

Gerson, L, 1972. *Woodrow Wilson and the Rebirth of Poland, 1914–1920*. Hamden, CN: The Shoe-String Press.

Gibbs, JT, 1998. "Biracial Adolescents. In Children of Color: Psychological Interventions with Culturally Diverse Youth." In JT Gibbs & LN Huang, Eds. *Children of Color: Psychological Interventions with Culturally Diverse Youth*. San Francisco: Jossey-Bass. pp. 305–332.

Gibbs, JT, & AM Hines, 1992. "Negotiating Ethnic Identity: Issues for Black-White Biracial Adolescents." In MRP Root, Ed. *Racially Mixed People in America*. Thousand Oaks, CA: Sage. Chap. 16, pp. 223–238.

Gibson, M, 1988. *Accommodation Without Assimilation: Sikh Immigrants in an American High School*. Ithaca, NY: Cornell University Press.

Gills, D, & W White, 1997. "Chicago's Empowerment Zone and Citizen Participation." In P Nyden, A Figert, M Shibley, & D Burrows, Eds. *Building Community*. pp. 211–218. Thousand Oaks, CA: Pine Forge Press.

Giordano, J, M McGoldrick, & JG Klages, 2005. "Italian Families." In M McGoldrick, J Giordano, & N Garcia-Parto, Eds. *Ethnicity and Family Therapy*. 3rd Ed. New York: Guilford. Chap. 44, pp. 616–628.

Glazer, N, & DP Moynihan, 1963. *Beyond the Melting Pot*. Cambridge, MA: MIT Press.

Goldstein, S, & C Goldscheider, 1968. *Jewish Americans: Three Generations of a Jewish Community*. Englewood Cliffs, NJ: Prentice-Hall.

Gordon, M, 1964. *Assimilation in American Life: The Role of Race, Religion, and National Origins*. New York: Oxford University Press.

Gordon, M, 1978. *Human Nature, Class and Ethnicity*. New York: Oxford University Press.

Graham, IC, 1956. *Colonists From Scotland: Emigration to North America 1707–1783*. Ithaca, NY: Cornell University Press.

Grant, M, 1916. "The Passing of the Great Race: Or, the Racial Basis of European History." New York: Charles Scribner and Sons. Digitalized Version, 2007. (Accessed September 26, 2008) http://books.google.com/books?id=RmEnAAAAMAAJ&dq=the+passing+of+the+great+race &source=gbs_summary_s&cad=0

Greder, KA, & WD Allen, 2007. "Parenting n Color: Culturally Diverse Perspectives on Parenting." In BS Trask, & RR Hamon, Eds. *Cultural Diversity and Families: Expanding Perspectives*. Thousand Oaks, CA: Sage. Chap. 7, pp. 118–135.

Greeley, AM, 1971. *Why Can't They Be Like Us?* New York: E. P. Dutton.

Greeley, AM, 1974. *Ethnicity in the United States*. New York: John Wiley & Sons.

Hall, CCI, 1992. "Please Choose One: Ethnic Identity Choices for Biracial Individuals." In MRP Root, Ed. *Racially Mixed People in America*. Thousand Oaks, CA: Sage. Chap. 18, pp. 250–264.

Handlin, O, 1973. *The Uprooted*. New York: Little, Brown.

Hargreaves, AG, 1995. *Immigration, Race and Ethnicity in Contemporary France*. New York: Routledge.

Harles, JC, 1997. "Integration Before Assimilation: Immigration, Multiculturalism and the Canadian Polity." *Canadian Journal of Political Science*, 30: 711–736.

Harris, DR, & JJ Sim, 2002. "Who Is Multiracial? Assessing the Complexity of Lived Race." *American Sociological Review*, 67(4) (Aug., 2002):614–627.

Harrison, T, 2008. "Reform Party of Canada." *The Canadian Encyclopedia*. (Accessed September 29, 2008). http://www.thecanadianencyclopedia.com/index.cfm?PgNm=TCE&Params=A1ARTA0006737

Hart, AB, & HR Ferleger, Eds., 1989. *Theodore Roosevelt Cyclopedia*. Rev. 2nd Ed. New York: Theodore Roosevelt Association.

Hawkins, F. 1989. *Critical Years in Immigration: Canada and Australia compared*. Kingston and Montreal: McGill-Queen's University Press.

Henderson, TL, 2007. "The Compelling Realities of Diversity, Poltics, and Laws." In BS Trask, & RR Hamon, Eds. *Cultural Diversity and Families: Expanding Perspectives*. Thousand Oaks, CA: Sage. Chap. 13, pp. 228–243.

Hernandez-Ramdwar, C. 1997. "Multiracial Identities in Trinidad and Guyana Exaltation and Ambiguity." *Latin American Issues*, 13, (Accessed August 10, 2008). http://webpub.allegheny.edu/group/LAS/LatinAmIssues/Articles/LAI_vol_13_section_V.html

Higham, J, 1985. *Strangers in the Land: Patterns of American Nativism 1860–1925*. 2nd Ed. New York: Atheneum.

Ho, MK, 1987. *Family Therapy with Ethnic Minorities*. Thousand Oaks, CA: Sage.

Hollifield, JF, 1992. *Immigrants, Markets, and States*. Cambridge Mass: Harvard University Press.

Hongo, G, 1998. "Lost in Place." In CC O'Hearn, Ed. Half and Half: Writers on Growing Up Biracial and Bicultural. NY: Pantheon Books. pp. 1–11.

Hooyman, NR, & HA Kiyak, 2005. *Social Gerontology: A Multidisciplinary Perspective*. 7th Ed. Boston: Pearson Education/Allyn and Bacon. Chap. 14.

Horgan, ES, 1998. In CH Mindel, RW Habenstein, R Wright, Jr., Eds. *Ethnic Families in America: Patterns and Variations*. 4th Ed. Upper Saddle River, NJ: Prentice-Hall. Chap. 3, pp. 39–67.

Houk, JT, 1995. *Spirits, Blood, and Drums: The Orisha Religion in Trinidad*. Philadelphia, PA: Temple University Press.

House-Senate Commission on Immigration, 1910–1911. "The Dillingham Commission Reports." Washington, DC: U.S. Government: 61st Congress. http://library.stanford.edu/depts/dlp/ebrary/dillingham/body.shtml (Accessed 9/17/08).

Howard, JA, 2000. "Social Psychology of Identities." In KS Cook & J Hagan, Eds. *Annual Review of Sociology*, 26: 367–393.

Hudson, WS, 1961. *American Protestantism*. Chicago: University of Chicago Press.

Huntington, GE, 1998. "The Amish Family." In CH Mindel, RW Habenstein, R Wright, Jr., Eds. *Ethnic Families in America: Patterns and Variations*. 4th Ed. Upper Saddle River, NJ: Prentice-Hall. Chap. 17, pp. 450–479.

Invasion USA, 2005. "Texas Governor Hot Over Border Security." *World Net Daily*. Oct. 13. http://www.worldnetdaily.com/news/article.asp?ARTICLE_ID=46814 (accessed 7/31/07).

Jacobs, JH, 1992. "Identity Development in Biracial Children." In MRP Root, Ed. *Racially Mixed People in America*. Thousand Oaks, CA: Sage. Chap. 14, pp. 190–206.

Jacobson, MF, 1998. *Whiteness of a Different Color: European Immigrants and the Alchemy of Race*." Cambridge, MA: Harvard Univ. Press.

Jakubowicz, A, 1989. "The State and the Welfare of Immigrants in Australia." *Ethnic and Racial Studies*, 12: 1–35.

Jakubowicz, A, M Morrisey, & J Paker, 1984. *Ethnicicty, Classs and Social Welfare in Australia*. Sydney: University of New South Wales, Social Welfare Research Centre.

Jennings, J, 2000. "Citizenship, Republicanism and Multiculturalism in Contemporary France." *British Journal of Political Science*, 30: 575–597.

Jesus-is-lord.com, n.d.-a. "Alert!!!! The Roman Catholic 'Church' is Not Christian." http://www.jesus-is-lord.com/cath.htm (accessed 7/16/2007)

Jesus-is-lord.com, n.d.-b. "Jesus Christ is the ONLY Way to God." http://www.jesus-is-lord.com/cath.htm (accessed 7/16/2007).

John, R, 1998. "Native American Families." In CH Mindel, RW Habenstein, R Wright, Jr., Eds. *Ethnic Families in America: Patterns and Variations*. 4th Ed. Upper Saddle River, NJ: Prentice-Hall. Chap. 16, pp. 382–421.

Jones, MA, 1960. *American Immigration*. Chicago: University of Chicago Press.

Jones, A, 2000. "Hispanic Catholics Ignored." *National Catholic Reporter*, Feb. 11.

Joppke, C, 1996. "Multiculturalism and Immigration: A Comparison of the United States, Germany, and Great Britain." *Theory and Society* 25: 449–500. http://www.jstor.org/ (Accessed July 14, 2004).

Jupp, J, 2002. *From White Australia to Woomera: The Story of Australian Immigration*. New York: Cambridge University Press.

Jupp, J, 2006. "Terrorism, Immigration, and Multiculturalism: The Australian Experience". *International Journal* (Toronto), 61(3): 699–710.

Kallen, E, 1982. "Multiculturalism: Ideology, Policy and Reality." *Journal of Canadian Studies*, 17:51–63.

Kane, JJ, 1955. *Catholic-Protestant Conflicts in America*. Chicago: Henry Regnery Co.

Kane, MW, 2000. "Racial and Ethnic Variations in Gender-Related Attitudes." In KS Cook & J Hagan, Eds. *Annual Review of Sociology*, 26: 419–439.

Kanuha, VK, 2005. "Na 'Ohana: Native Hawaiian Families." In M McGoldrick, J Giordano, & N Garcia-Parto, Eds. *Ethnicity and Family Therapy*. 3rd Ed. New York: Guilford. Chap. 4, pp. 64–74.

Kaplan, W, 1993. "Belonging: The future of Canadian Citizenship." In GH Cornwell & EW Stoddard Eds. 2001. *Global Multiculturalism: Comparative Perspectives on Ethnicity, Race, and Nation*. New York: Rowman & Littlefield Publishers, Inc. pp. 29–50.

Karasik, RJ, & RR Hamon, 2007. "Cultural Diversity and Aging Families." In BS Trask, & RR Hamon, Eds. *Cultural Diversity and Families: Expanding Perspectives*. Thousand Oaks, CA: Sage. Chap. 8, pp. 136–153.

Katznelson, I, 2005. *When Affirmative Action Was White: An Untold History of Racial Inequality in Twentieth Century America*. New York: Norton.

Kelly, N, & M Trebilcock, 1998. *The Making of the Mosaic: History of Canadian Immigration*. Toronto: University of Toronto Press.

Kennedy, RJR, 1944. "Single or Triple Melting Pot? Intermarriage Trends in New Haven, 1870–1940." *American Journal of Sociology*, 49: 331–339.

Kerwin, C, & JG Ponterotto, 1995. "Biracial Identity Development: Theory and Research." In JG Ponterotto, JM Casas, LA Suzuki, & CM Alexander, Eds. *Handbook of Multicultural Counseling*. Thousand Oaks, CA: Sage.

Kich, GK, 1992. "The Developmental Process of Asserting a Biracial, Bicultural Identity." In MRP Root, Ed. *Racially Mixed People in America*. Thousand Oaks, CA: Sage. Chap. 21, pp. 304–230.

Kiely, K, 2006. "GOP Leaders Oppose Immigration Felony." *USA Today*. Apr. 12. http://www.usatoday.com/news/washington/2006-04-12-immigration-congress_x.htm (accessed 7/31/07).

Kim, BC, & E Ryu, 2005. "Korean Families." In M McGoldrick, J Giordano, & N Garcia-Parto, Eds. *Ethnicity and Family Therapy*. 3rd Ed. New York: Guilford. Chap. 26, pp: 349–362.

Kim, S, & T Woolfolk, 2007. "Women, Work, and Families." In BS Trask, & RR Hamon, Eds. *Cultural Diversity and Families: Expanding Perspectives*. Thousand Oaks, CA: Sage. Chap. 6, pp. 100–117.

Kivisto, P, 2002. *Multiculturalism in a Global Society*. MA: Blackwell Publishers, Ltd.

Kitano, HHL, 1969. *Japanese Americans: The Evolution of a Subculture*. Englewood Cliffs, NJ: Prentice-Hall.

Khan, A, 1993. "What is 'a Spanish'?: Ambiguity and 'Mixed' Ethnicity in Trinidad." In KA Yelvington, Ed. *Trinidad Ethnicity*. Knoxville, TN: University of Tennessee Press. pp. 180–207.

Khan, A, 1998. "Constructing Identities in Trinidad." *American Ethnologist*, 25: 499–500.

Khan, A, 2004. *Callaloo Nation: Metaphors of Race and Religious Identity Among South Asians in Trinidad*. Durham and London, Duke University Press.

Klein, JM, 2005. "Merit's Demerits." *The Chronicle of Higher Education*. (Nov. 4): B12–B13.

Knowles, L, & K Prewitt, 1967. *Institutional Racism in America*. Englewood Cliffs, NJ.

Krauthammer, C, 2006. "Why Is Border Security Conservative?" *Washington Post.* May 18, p. A21. http://www.washingtonpost.com/wp-dyn/content/article/2006/05/18/AR2006051801774.html (accessed 7/31/07).

Krysan, M, 2000. "Prejudice, Politics, and Public Opinion: Understanding the Sources of Racial Policy Attitudes. In KS Cook & J Hagan, Eds. *Annual Review of Sociology,* 26: 135–158.

Lee, E, & MR Mock, 2005a. "Asian Families: An Overview." In M McGoldrick, Giordano, & N Garcia-Parto, Eds. *Ethnicity and Family Therapy.* 3rd Ed. New York: Guilford. Chap. 20, pp. 269–289.

Lee, E, & MR Mock, 2005b. "Chinese Families." In M McGoldrick, J Giordano, & N Garcia-Parto, Eds. *Ethnicity and Family Therapy.* 3rd Ed. New York: Guilford. Chap. 22, pp. 302–318.

Leonce, H, 2004. "Shared Memory: East Indian Immigration." *International Congress on Archives.* (Accessed September 10, 2008). Leonce www.wien2004.ica.org

Leonetti, R, & DG Muller, 1976. "The Spanish-Surnamed Child and School." *The Elementary School Journal,* 76(4) (Jan): 246–255.

Leung, PK, & JK Boehnlein, 2005. "Vietnamese Families." In M McGoldrick, J Giordano, & N Garcia-Parto, Eds. *Ethnicity and Family Therapy.* 3rd Ed. New York: Guilford. Chap. 27, pp. 363–373.

Lewycky, L, 1992. "Multiculturalism in the 1990s and into the 20th Century: Beyond Ideology and Utopia". In Victor Satzewich. Ed. *Deconstructing A Nation: Immigration, Multiculturalism and Racism in '90 s Canada.* Halifax: Fernwood Publishing.

Leyburn, JG, 1962. *The Scotch-Irish: A Social History.* Chapel Hill, NC: University of North Carolina Press.

Li, P, 1988. *Ethnic Inequality in a Class Society.* Toronto: Thompson Educational Publishing, Inc.

Lindsey, LL, 1990. *Gender Roles.* Englewood Cliffs, NJ: Prentice-Hall.

Liodakis, N, 1998. The Activities of Hellenic-Canadian Secular Organizations in the Context of Canadian Multiculturalism Etudes *Helleniques/Hellenic Studies* 6(1): 37–45.

Liodakis, N, & Victor S, 1998. "Activities of Hellenic-Canadian Secular Organizations in the Context of Canadian Multiculturalism." *Hellenic Studies* 6: 37–58.

Lipset, SM, 1963. *The First New Nation.* NY: Basic Books.

Locke, DC, 1992. *Increasing Multicultural Understanding: A Comprehensive Model.* Thousand Oaks, CA: Sage.

Long, RE, 1997. *The Reference Shelf: Multiculturalism.* New York: Library of Congress Cataloging-in-Publication Data.

Lopata, HZ, 1976. *Polish Americans: Status Competition in an Ethnic Community.* Englewood Cliffs, NJ: Prentice-Hall.

Lopata, HZ, 1998. "The Polish-American Family." In CH Mindel, RW Habenstein, & R Wright, Jr., Eds. *Ethnic Families in America: Patterns and Variations.* 4th Ed. Upper Saddle River, NJ: Prentice-Hall. Chap. 6, pp. 128–152.

Lower, A, 1977. *Colony to Nation: History of Canada.* McClelland & Stewart Ltd.

Lucas, G, 2005. "SACRAMENTO: Border Security Debate Revived, Governor's Praise of Minutemen Leads to Talk of Costs, Benefits." *San Francisco Chronicle.* May 16. http://sfgate.com/cgi-bin/article.cgi?file=/c/a/2005/05/16/IMMIG.TMP (accessed 7/31/07).

Luongo, MT, 2007. "In U.S., Expatriate Professionals see 'Accent Reduction' as a Sound Investment." *International Herald Tribune,* Business, June 5. http://www.iht.com/articles/2007/06/05/business/accents.php. Accessed July 22, 2008.

Mailman, S, 1995. "California's Proposition 187 and its Lessons." *New York Law Journal.* Jan. 3. (p. 3, col. 1). http://ssbb.com/article1.html (accessed 7/31/07).

Makedon, A, 1996. "What Multiculturalism Should Not Be." Chicago State University. http://webs.csu.edu/⁻amakedon/articles/mutliculturalism.html (Accessed 6/05/2005).

Martin, J, 1978. *The Migrant Presence.* Sydney: George Allen and Unwin.

Massey, D, 1995. "The New Immigration and Ethnicity in the United States." *Population and Development Review* 21, 3 (Sept.): 631–652.

Mazzi, J, 2007. "Are Catholics Christian?" Malta: Trinity Evangelical Church. http://www.justforcatholics.org/a21.htm (accessed 7/16/2007).

McDermott, M, & FL Samson, 2005. "White Racial and Ethnic Identity in the United States." In KS Cook & DS Massey, Eds. *Annual Review of Sociology*, 31: 245–261.

McGoldrick, M, J Giordano, & N Garcia-Parto, Eds., 2005a. *Ethnicity and Family Therapy*. 3rd Ed. New York: Guilford.

McGoldrick, M, J Giordano, & N Garcia-Parto, 2005b. "Overview: Ethnicity and Family Therapy." In M McGoldrick, J Giordano, & N Garcia-Parto, Eds., 2005. *Ethnicity and Family Therapy*. 3rd Ed. New York: Guilford. Chap. 1, pp. 1–40.

McGrath, A, 2007. *Christianity's Dangerous Idea: The Protestant Revolution – A History from the Sixteenth Century to the Twenty-First*. New York: Harper-Collins.

McNamara, RP, M Tempenis, & B Walton, 1999. *Crossing the Line*. Westport, CN: Praeger.

McPherson, M, L Smith-Lovin, & JM Cook, 2001. "Birds of a Feather: Homophily in Social Networks." In KS Cook & J Hagan, Eds. *Annual Review of Sociology*, 26: 415–444.

Mead, GH, 1934. *Mind, Self, and Society*. Chicago: University of Chicago Press.

Meditz, SW, & DM Hanratty, Eds., 1987. *Caribbean Islands: A Country Study*. Washington: GPO for the Library of Congress.

Merhgi, A, 1990. "Keeping Ethnics on the Periphery." *The Toronto Star*, May 15, p A23.

Michigan Department of Education, 2008. "MEAP Michigan Educational Testing Program." Lansing, MI: Michigan Department of Education. http://www.michigan.gov/mde/0,1607,7-140-22709_31168—,00.html (Accessed 8/26/08).

Miller, RL, 1992. "The Human Ecology of Multiracial Identity." In MMP Root, Ed. *Racially Mixed People in America*. Thousand Oaks, CA: Sage.

Min, PG, 1998. "The Korean-American Family." In CH Mindel, RW Habenstein, & R Wright, Jr., Eds. *Ethnic Families in America: Patterns and Variations*. 4th Ed. Upper Saddle River, NJ: Prentice-Hall. Chap. 10, pp. 223–253.

Mindel, CH, RW Habenstein, R Wright, Jr., Eds., 1998. *Ethnic Families in America: Patterns and Variations*. 4th Ed. Upper Saddle River, NJ: Prentice-Hall.

Moodie-Kublalsingh, S, 1994. *The Cocoa Panyols of Trinidad: An Oral Record*. London: British Academic Press.

Moore, JW, 1970. *Mexican Americans*. Englewood Cliffs, NJ: Prentice-Hall.

Motomura, H., 2006. "Immigration: How 'They' Become 'Us.'" *The Chronicle of Higher Education*. (Sept. 8): B6–B8.

Mullavey-O'Byrne, C, 1994. "Intercultural Communication for Health Care Professionals." In RW Brislin & T Yoshsida, Eds. *Improving Intercultural Relations: Modules for Cross-Cultural Training Programs*. Thousand Oaks, CA: Sage. Chap. 10, pp. 171–196.

Munasinghe, V, 2001. *Callaloo or Tossed Salad?: East Indians and the Cultural Politics of Identity in Trinidad.*" Ithaca, NY: Cornell University Press

Murphy, B, 1993. *The Other Australia: Experiences of Migration*. Cambridge: Cambridge University Press.

Myers, DG, & LD Scanzoni, 2005. *What God Has Joined Together? A Christian Case for Gay Marriage*. San Francisco, CA: Harper San Francisco.

Nagel, J, 2000. "Ethnicity and Sexuality." In KS Cook & J Hagan, Eds. *Annual Review of Sociology*, 26: 107–133.

Naipaul, VS, 1984[1969]. *The Loss of El Dorado*. New York: Vintage.

Nakashima, CL, 1992. "An Invisible Monster: The Creation and Denial of Mixed-Race People in America." In MMP Root, Ed. *Racially Mixed People in America*. Thousand Oaks, CA: Sage. Chap. 12, pp. 162–178.

Nakazawa, DJ, 2004. *Does Anybody Else Look Like Me?: A Parent's Guide to Raising Multiracial Children*. Cambridge, MA: Perseus.

Nath, S, 2005. "Pakistani Families." In M McGoldrick, J Giordano, & N Garcia-Parto, Eds. *Ethnicity and Family Therapy*. 3rd Ed. New York: Guilford. Chap. 30, pp. 407–420.

National Library and Information System Authority of Trinidad and Tobago. 2008. "Emancipation Day." Accessed September 22, 2008). http://library2.nalis.gov.tt/Default.aspx? PageContentMode=1&tabid=216

Nelli, HS, 1980. "Italians." In S Thernstrom, A Orlov, & O Hanlin, Eds. Harvard *Encyclopedia of American Ethnic Groups*. pp. 545–560. Cambridge, MA: Harvard University Press.

Newson, L, 1976. *Aboriginal and Spanish Colonial Trinidad*. London: British Academic Press.

Ngai, M, 1999. "The Architecture of Race in American Immigration Law: A Reexamination of the Immigration Act of 1924." *The Journal of American History* 86(1): 67–92.

No Child Left Behind Act (NCLB), 2001. Washington, DC: U.S. Department of Education. http://www.ed.gov/policy/elsec/leg/esea02/pg1.html#sec1001 (Accessed Aug. 24, 2008).

Noiriel, G., 1988. "Le Creusetfrancais: Histoire de l'immigration XIX–XXe Siecles." In M Tribalat, 2004. An Estimation of the Foreign-Origin Populations of France 1999. Population (English Edition, 2002), 59: 49–79.

Noiriel, G, 1995. "Immigration: Amnesia and Memory." *French Historical Studies*, 19, 367–380. http://www.jstor.org/stable/286777 (Accessed September 24, 2008).

Obama, B, 1995. *Dreams from My Father: A Story of Race and Inheritance*. New York: Three Rivers Press.

O'Byrne, CM, 1994a. "Intercultural Communication for Health Care Professionals." In RW Brislin & T Yoshsida, Eds. *Improving Intercultural Relations: Modules for Cross-Cultural Training Programs*. Thousand Oaks, CA: Sage.

O'Byrne, CM, 1994b. "Intercultural Interactions in WelfareWork." In RW Brislin & T Yoshsida, Eds. *Improving Intercultural Relations: Modules for Cross-Cultural Training Programs*. Thousand Oaks, CA: Sage.

O'Hearn, CC, Ed., 1998. *Half and Half: Writers on Growing Up Biracial and Bicultural*. NY: Pantheon Books.

Olson, DVA, 1998. "Religious Pluralism in Contemporary U.S. Counties." *American Sociological Review*, 63: 759–761.

Oostindie, G, Ed., 1996. "Ethnicity in the Caribbean: Essays in Honor of Harry and Eve Hoetink." In GH Cornwell & E Stoddard, Eds. 2001. *Global Multiculturalism: Comparative Perspectives on Ethnicity, Race, and Nation*. New York: Rowman & Littlefield Publishers, Inc.

Papajohn, J, & J Spiegel, 1975. *Transactions in Families*. San Francisco: Jossey-Bass.

Parillo, VN, 1994. "Diversity in America: A Sociohistorical Analysis." *Sociological Focus* 9 (4): 523–545 (Dec.) Special Issue: Multiculturalism and Diversity.

Parillo, VN, 2000. *Strangers to These Shores: Race and Ethnic Relations in the United States*. 6th Ed. Needham Heights, MA: Allyn & Bacon.

Parmasad, K, 1997. "Personal Interview, September 29." In GH Cornwell & EW Stoddard, Eds. *Global Multiculturalism: Comparative Perspectives on Ethnicity,Race, and Nation*. New York: Rowman & Littlefield Publishers, Inc. pp. 29–50.

Peterson, P, 1994. "Multicultural Counseling." In RW Brislin & T Yoshsida, Eds. *Improving Intercultural Relations: Modules for Cross-Cultural Training Programs*. Thousand Oaks, CA: Sage.

Phinney, JS, & MJ Rotheram, Eds., 1987. *Children's Ethnic Socialization*. Newbury Park, CA: Sage.

Pillari, V, 2005. "Indian Hindu Families." In M McGoldrick, J Giordano, & N Garcia-Parto, Eds. *Ethnicity and Family Therapy*. 3rd Ed. New York: Guilford. Chap. 29, pp. 395–406.

Pinkney, A, 1993. *Black Americans*. 4th Ed. Englewood Cliffs, NJ: Prentice-Hall.

Ponterotto, JG, JM Casas, LA Suzuki, & CM Alexander, Eds., 1995. *Handbook of Multicultural Counseling*. Thousand Oaks, CA: Sage.

Porter, J, 1965. *The Vertical Mosaic: An Analysis of Social Class and Power in Canada*. Toronto: University of Toronto Press.

Portes, A, & RG Rumbaut, 2001. *Legacies: The Story of the Immigrant Second Generation*. Berkley, CA: University of California Press.

Poston, WC, 1990. "The Biracial Identity Development Model: A Needed Addition." *Journal of Counseling and Development*, 69 (2): 152–155.

Pottinger, JS, 1972. "Equality for Spanish-Surnamed Students." *Equity and Excellence in Education*, 10 (6) (Nov.): 48–53.

Puri, S, 1995. "Race, Rape and Representation: Indo-Caribbean Women and Cultural Nationalism." ISER-NCIC Conference on Challenge and Change: the Indian Diaspora in its Historical and Contemporary Contexts. University of the West Indies, St. Augustine, Trinidad.

Quillian, L, 2006. "New Approaches to Understanding Racial Prejudice and Discrimination." In KS Cook & DM Massey, Eds. *Annual Review of Sociology*, 32: 299–328.

Ramirez, DA, 1996. "Multiracial Identity in a Color-Conscious World." In MMP Root, Ed. *The Multiracial Experience: Racial Borders as the New Frontier*. Thousand Oaks, CA: Sage. Chap. 4, pp. 49–62.

Rebach, HM, & JG Bruhn, Eds., 2001. *Handbook of Clinical Sociology*. 2nd Ed. New York: Kluwer, Plenum.

Reddock, R, 1994. "Douglarisation and the Politics of Gender Relations in Contemporary Trinidad and Tobago: A Preliminary Exploration." *Contemporary Issues in Social Science: A Caribbean Perspective* 1: 98–127.

Reddock, R, 1995. "Contestations over National Culture in Trinidad and Tobago: Considerations of Ethnicity, Class, and Gender." *Contemporary Issues in Social Science: A Caribbean Perspective* 2, 106–145.

Reform Party of Canada. 1989. "Platform and Statement of Principles." In Y Abu-Laban & S Daiva 1992. Ethnic Pluralism Under Siege: Popular and Partisan Opposition to Multiculturalism. *Canadian Public Policy* 27: 365–386.

Reitz, JG, & R Breton, 1994. *The Illusion of Difference: Realities of Ethnicity in Canada and the United States*. Toronto: C.D. Howe Institute.

Robbins, T, 2007. "States Fret at Easing of Border Security Plan." National Public Radio: All Things Considered. May 23. http://www.npr.org/templates/story/story.php?storyId=10357984 (accessed 8/2/07).

Roberts, LW, & RA Clifton, 1982. "Exploring the Ideology of Canadian Multiculturalism." *Canadian Public Policy* 8: 88–94.

Roberts, L, & C Rodney, 1982. "Exploring the Ideology of Canadian Multiculturalism". *Canadian Public Policy* 8 (1):88–94.

Roberts, H, JC Gonzales, OD Harris, DJ Huff, AM Johns, M Lou, & OL Scott, 1994. "Teaching from a Multicultural Perspective." Thousand Oaks, CA: Sage.

Rockquemore, KA, & DL Brunsma, 1998. *Beyond Black: Biracial Identity in America*. Thousand Oaks, CA: Sage.

Rockquemore, KA, & T Laszloffy, 2005. *Raising Biracial Children*. Walnut Creek: Altimira.

Roediger, DR, 2005. *Working Toward Whiteness: How America's Immigrants Became White*. New York: Basic Books.

Roediger, DR, 2006. "Whiteness and Its Complications." *The Chronicle of Higher Education*. (July 14): B6–B8.

Roosevelt, T, 1919. "Letter to the American Defense Society." (January 3). http://urbanlegends.about.com/library/bl_roosevelt_on_immigrants.htm (accessed 7/23/07).

Root, MPP, 1992a. "Back to the Drawing Board: Methodological Issues in Research on Multiracial People." In MRP Root, Ed. *Racially Mixed People in America*. Thousand Oaks, CA: Sage. Chap. 13, pp. 181–189.

Root, MPP, Ed., 1992b. *Racially Mixed People in America*. Thousand Oaks, CA: Sage.

Root, MPP, 1992c. "Within, Between, and Beyond Race." In MMP Root, Ed. *Racially Mixed People in America*. Thousand Oaks, CA: Sage. Chap. 1, pp. 3–11.

Root, MPP, Ed., 1996. *The Multiracial Experience: Racial Borders as the New Frontier*. Thousand Oaks, CA: Sage.

Root, MPP, 2005. "Filipino Families." In M McGoldrick, J Giordano, & N Garcia-Parto, Eds. *Ethnicity and Family Therapy*. 3rd Ed. New York: Guilford. Chap. 23, pp. 319–331.

Rosen, EJ, & SF Weltman, 2005. "Jewish Families: An Overview." In M McGoldrick, J Giordano, & N Garcia-Parto, Eds. *Ethnicity and Family Therapy*. 3rd Ed. New York: Guilford. Chap. 48, pp. 667–679.

Rouse, I, 1992. *The Tainos*. New Haven, CT: Yale University Press.

Rouse, I, 1993. *The Tainos: Rise and Decline of the People Who Greeted Columbus*. New Haven, CT: Yale University Press.

Roy, PE, 1995. "The Fifth Force: Multiculturalism and the English Canadian Identity." *The Annals of the American Academy of Political and Social Science* 538(1): 199–209.

Rumbaut, RG, & A Portes, Eds., 2001. *Ethnicities: Children of Immigrants in America*. Berkley, CA: University of California Press.

Sachs, P, 2007. "How Colleges Perpetuate Inequality." *The Chronicle of Higher Education*. (Jan. 12): B9–B10.

Safran, W. 2003. "Pluralism and Multiculturalism in France: Post-Jacobin Transformations." *Political Science Quarterly*; 118: 437–465.

Santorum, R, 2005. *It Takes a Family: Conservatism and the Common Good*. Intercollegiate Studies Institute.

Schain, MA, 2004. "Politics, Immigration and Multiculturalism in France and the United States. "Transatlantic Tensions. From Conflicts of Interests to Conflict of Values?" Colloquium, CERI/GMF, February 2–3, 2004

Schmitt, E, 2001. "Census Data show a sharp increase in living standards." *New York Times*, A1 (August 6, 2001).

Schneider, DM, & GC Homans, 1955. "Kinship Terminology and the American Kinship System." *American Anthropologist* 57 (Dec.): 1197–1209.

Schuck, PH, 2003. *Diversity in America: Keeping Government at a Safe Distance*. Massachusetts: The Belknap Press of Harvard University.

Scott, JR, 2007. "Veiled Politics." *The Chronicle of Higher Education*. 54 (13): B10.

See, L, 1998. "The Funeral Banquet." In CC O'Hearn, Ed. *Half and Half: Writers on Growing Up Biracial and Bicultural*. NY: Pantheon Books. pp. 122–139.

Segal, D, 1993. "Race and 'Color' in Pre-Independence Trinidad and Tobago." In K Yelvington, Ed. *Trinidad Ethnicity*, Knoxville: University of Tennessee Press. pp. 33–55.

Segal, UA, 1998. "The Asian Indian-American Family." In CH Mindel, RW Habenstein, & R Wright, Jr., Eds. *Ethnic Families in America: Patterns and Variations*. 4th Ed. Upper Saddle River, NJ: Prentice-Hall. Chap. 14, pp. 331–360.

Sengstock, MC, 1976. "Importing an Ethnic Community." In J Gardner & R McMann, Eds. *Culture, Community, and Identity*. Vol. 2: 235–249. Detroit, Michigan: Wayne State University-University Studies, Weekend College.

Sengstock, MC, 1994. "Researching an Iraqi Community in the Midst of the U.S.-Iraq War: The Researcher as Clinician." *Clinical Sociology Review*, 12: 69–82.

Sengstock, MC, 1996. "In Search of the Mother Culture." Presentation to the Society for Applied Sociology. Atlanta, GA.

Sengstock, MC, 1999. *Chaldean Americans: Changing Conceptions of Ethnic Identity*. Staten Island, NY: Center for Migration Studies.

Sengstock, MC, 2001. "Multicultural Families – What Makes Them Work?" *Sociological Practice: A Journal of Clinical and Applied Sociology*, 1 (1) (March): 1–17.

Sengstock, MC, 2005. *Chaldeans in Michigan*. East Lansing, MI: Michigan State University Press.

Shakir, E, 1991–92. "Arab Mothers, American Sons: Women in Arab-American Autobiographies." *Melus* 17 (3) (Fall): 5–15.

Shand, T, 1997. "Mixing it Up." *Panache* 4, 1977. In GH Cornwell & EW Stoddard, Eds. 2001. *Global Multiculturalism: Comparative Perspectives on Ethnicity, Race, and Nation*. New York: Rowman & Littlefield Publishers, Inc.

Sherman, CB, 1965. *The Jew Within American Society*. Detroit, MI: Wayne State University Press.

Shibata, Y, 1994. "Neither 'African' Nor 'Indian': Douglaization, Creolization and Guyanization." Eighteenth Annual Conference of the Society for Caribbean Studies, St. Stephen's House, Oxford. July 1994.

Shibusawa, T, 2005. "Japanese Families." In M McGoldrick, J Giordano, & N Garcia-Parto, Eds. *Ethnicity and Family Therapy*. 3rd Ed. New York: Guilford. Chap. 25, pp. 339–348.

Shick, MJ, 2007. "Are Roman Catholics Christian?" Christian Apologetics and Research Ministry. http://www.carm.org/catholic/saved.htm. (accessed 7/16/2007).

Shipton, CK, 1936. "Immigration to New England, 1680–1740." *Journal of Political Economy*, 44 (Apr): 225–239.

Smith, CS, 1998. *American Evangelicalism: Embattled and Thriving*. Chicago: University of Chicago Press.

Smolicz, JJ, 1997. "Australia: From Migrant Country to Multicultural Nation." *International Migration Review*, 31: 171–186.

Song, YI, & EC Kim, Eds., 1993. *American Mosaic: Selected Readings on America's Multicultural Heritage*. Upper Saddle River, NJ: Prentice-Hall.

Spencer, ME, 1994. "Multiculturalism, "Political Correctness," and the Politics of Identity." *Sociological Forum*, 9: 547–567.

Spikard, PR, 1992. "The Illogic of American Racial Categories." In MMP Root, Ed. *Racially Mixed People in America*. Thousand Oaks, CA: Sage. Chap. 2, pp. 12–23.

Squiers, DA, & JS Quadagno, 1998. "The Italian-American Family." In CH Mindel, RW Habenstein, & R Wright, Jr., Eds. *Ethnic Families in America: Patterns and Variations*. 4th Ed. Upper Saddle River, NJ: Prentice-Hall. Chap. 5, pp. 102–127.

Steinberg, S, 1989. *The Ethnic Myth: Race, Ethnicity, and Class in America*. Boston, MA: Beacon Press.

Stephan, CW, 1992. "Mixed Heritage Individuals: Ethnic Identity and Trait Characteristics." In MPP Root, Ed. *Racially Mixed People in America*. Thousand Oaks, CA: Sage. Chap. 5, pp. 50–63.

Stewart, P, & KP Goldfarb, 2007. "Historical Trends in the Study of Diverse Families.' In BS Trask & RR Hamon, Eds. *Cultural Diversity and Families: Expanding Perspectives*. Thousand Oaks, CA: Sage. Chap. 1, pp. 3–19.

Stoddard, EW, & GH, Cornwell, 2001. "Miscegenation as a Metaphor for Nation-Building: The 'Douglarization' Controversy in Trinidad and Tobago." In GH Cornwell, & EW Stoddard, Eds. *Global Multiculturalism: Comparative Perspective on Ethnicity, Race, and Nation*. New York: Rowman & Littlefield Publishers, Inc., pp. 29–50.

Stormfront White Nationalist Community, 2005 "History of Australian Multiculturalism – Who was responsible?" http://www.stormfront.org/forum/showthread.php/history-australian-multiculturalism-responsible-255808.html (Accessed August 11, 2008).

Stormfront White Nationalist Community, 2008. "Abolition of the "White Australia" Policy." http://www.stormfront.org/forum/showthread.php/history-ausrralian-multiculturalism-responsible (Accessed September 16, 2008).

Stratton, J, & I Ang, 1998. "Multicultural Imagined Communities: Cultural Difference and National Identity in Australia and the USA." In D Bennet Ed. *Multicultural States: Rethinking Difference and Identity*. London: Routledge. pp. 135–162.

Strauss, AL, 1959. *Mirrors and Masks: The Search for Identity*. Glencoe, IL: Free Press.

Suarez-Orozco, C, & MM Suarez-Orozco, 2001. *Children of Immigration*. Cambridge, MA: Harvard University Press.

Sutton, CT, & MA Broken Nose, 2005. "American Indian Families: An Overview." In M McGoldrick, J Giordano, & N Garcia-Parto, Eds. *Ethnicity and Family Therapy*. 3rd Ed. New York: Guilford. Chap. 2, pp. 41–54.

Swift, M, 2007. "Those Who Sound Too Different Face Social or Career Barriers." *San Jose Mercury News*, April 15. http://www.mercurynews.com/valley/ci_7667096?nclick_check=1. Accessed July 22, 2008.

Tafoya, N, & A Del Vecchio, 2005. "Back to the Future: An Examination of the Native American Holocaust Experience." In M McGoldrick, J Giordano, & N Garcia-Parto, Eds. Ethnicity and Family Therapy. 3rd Ed. New York: Guilford. Chap. 3, pp. 55–63.

Takaki, R, 1989. *Strangers from a Different Shore: A History of Asian Americans*. Boston: Little Brown and company.

Tauro Synagogue, 2007. "Web Site of Tauro Synagogue: America's Oldest Synagogue." http://www.tourosynagogue.org/timeline/timeline.html (accessed 7/22/07).

Taylor, RL, Ed., 1994. *Minority Families in the United States: A Multicultural Perspective*. 2nd. Ed. Upper Saddle River, NJ: Prentice-Hall.

Thornton, MC, 1992. "Is Multiracial Status Unique" The Personal and Social Experience." In MRP Root, Ed. *Racially Mixed People in America*. Thousand Oaks, CA: Sage. Chap. 22, pp. 321–325.

Tiryakian, E, 2003. "Assessing Multiculturalism Theoretically: E Pluribus Unum, Sic et Non." *International Journal on Multicultural Societies* 5: 20–39.

Tiryakian, EA, 2004. "Assessing Multiculturalism Theoretically: E Pluribus Unum, Sic ET non.". In J Rex & G Singh, Eds. *Governance in Multicultural Societies*. USA: Ashgate Publishing Company.

Trask, BS, & RR Hamon, Eds., 2007. *Cultural Diversity and Families: Expanding Perspectives*. Thousand Oaks, CA: Sage.

Trask, BS, & JM Koivunen, 2007. "Trends in Marriage and Cohabitation." In BS Trask, & RR Hamon, Eds. *Cultural Diversity and Families: Expanding Perspectives*. Thousand Oaks, CA: Sage. Chap. 5, pp. 80–99.

Triandis, HC, 2002. "Subjective Culture." In WJ Lonner, DJ Dinnel, SA Hayes, & DN Sattler, Eds. *Online Reading in Psychology and Culture*. Unit 15, Chap 1. Bellingham, WA: Center for Cross Cultural Research, Western Washington University. www.wwu.edu/~culture

Tribalat, M, 2004. "An Estimation of the Foreign-Origin Populations of France 1999." *Population* (English Edition, 2002), 59: 49–79.

Trinidad and Tobago facts and figures, 2001. "The Trinidad and Tobago General Election, 11 December 2000: The Report of the Commonwealth Observer Group." Commonwealth Observer Group, Commonwealth Secretariat, Commonwealth Secretariat.

Trinidad and Tobago facts and figures, 2008. http://encarta.msn.com/fact_631504879/trinidad_and_tobago_facts_and_figures.html (Accessed August 5, 2008).

Tuan, M. 1998. *Forever Foreigners or Honoring Whites? The Asian Ethnic Experience*. New Brunswick, NJ: Rutgers University Press.

Uhlenberg, P, 1996. "The Burden of Aging: A Theoretical Framework for Understanding the Shifting Balance of Caregiving and Care Receiving vs. Cohort Ages." *The Gerontologist*, 36: 761–767.

Uhlenberg, P, 2004. Historical Forces Shaping Grandparent-Grandchild Relationships: Demography and Beyond." *Health and Medical Complete*. 24: 77.

US Census Bureau, 2001. "Diversity of the country's Hispanics highlighted." http://www.census.gov. (Accessed July 12, 2005).

US Census Bureau, 2006. 2006 American Community Survey. http://factfinder.census.gov/servlet/GRTTable?_bm=y&-geo_id=01000US&-_box_head_nbr=R0207&ds_name=ACS_2006_EST_G00_&-redoLog=false&-format=US-30&-mt_name=ACS_2004_EST_G00_R0207_US30 (Accessed Aug. 4, 2008.

US Customs and Border Protection, 2006. "On Track to Securing America's Borders." May 15. http://www.cbp.gov/xp/cgov/newsroom/highlights/news_highlights/ontrack.xml (accessed 7/30/07).

US English, Inc., 2005. "Making English the Official Language." U.S. English, Inc., Suite 1050, 1747 Pennsylvania Ave. NW, Washington, DC. http://www.us-english.org/inc/ (accessed 7/21/07).

Usita, PM, 2007. "Parent-Child Ties of Culturally Diverse Aging Families." In BS Trask & RR Hamon, Eds. *Cultural Diversity and Families: Expanding Perspectives*. Thousand Oaks, CA: Sage. Chap. 9, pp. 154–169.

Valverde, KLC, 1992. "An Invisible Monster: The Creation and Denial of Mixed-Race People In America." In MRP Root, Ed. *Racially Mixed People in America*. Thousand Oaks, CA: Sage. Chap. 11, pp. 162–178.

Warner-Lewis, M, 1991. "Guinea's other sums: The African dynamic in Trinidad culture." In GH
    Cornwell, & EW Stoddard, Eds. (2001). *Global Multiculturalism: Comparative Perspectives
    on Ethnicity, Race, and Nation*. Baltimore, MD: Rowman & Littlefield Publishers, Inc.
Warner, S, & J. Wittner, Eds. 1998. *Gatherings in Diaspora: Religious Communities and the New
    Immigration*. Philadelphia: Temple University press.
Waters, MC, 1990. *Ethnic Options*. Berkeley, CA: University of California Press.
Waters, MC, & TR Jimenez, 2005. "Assessing Immigrant Assimilation: New Empirical and Theo-
    retical Challenges." In KS Cook & DS Massey, Eds., *Annual Review of Sociology*, 31: 105–125.
Wiles, E, 2007. "Headscarves, Human Rights, and Harmonious Multicultural Society: Implications
    of the French Ban for Interpretations of Equality." *Law & Society Review*, 41: 699–736.
Williams, TK, 1992. "Prism Lives: Identity of Binational Amerasians." In MRP Root, Ed. *Racially
    Mixed People in America*. Thousand Oaks, CA: Sage. Chap. 20, pp. 280–303.
Willmott, P, & M Young, 1960. *Family and Class in a London Suburb*. London: Routledge &
    Kegan Paul.
Wilson, TP, 1992. "Blood Quantum: Native American Mixed Bloods." In MRP Root, Ed. *Racially
    Mixed People in America*. Thousand Oaks, CA: Sage. Chap. 9, pp. 108–125.
Wilson, VS, 1993. "The Tapestry Vision of Canadian Multiculturalism." *Canadian Journal of
    Political Science*, 26: 645–669.
Wilton, J, and R Bosworth, 1984. *Old Worlds and New Australia*. Ringwood: Vic: Penguin.
Winant, H, 2000. "Race and Race Theory." In KS Cook & J Hagan, Eds. *Annual Review of Soci-
    ology*, 26: 169–185.
Yelvington, K, Ed., 1993. *Trinidad Ethnicity*. Knoxville: University of Tennessee Press.
Yonge, C, 1998. *U.S. Immigration history*. http://www.rapidimmigration.com/usa/1_eng_
    immigration_history.html (Accessed June 24, 2008).
Yonge, C, 2005. *History of France*. New York: D. Appleton and Company.
Yonge, C, 2008a. *CIA the World Factbook*. (Accessed August 26, 2008). https://www.cia.gov/
    library/publications/the-world-factbook/geos/fr.html
Yonge, C, 2008b. *Trinidad and Tobago: Country Progress Report*. http://data.unaids.org/pub/
    Report/2008/trinidad_and_tobago_2008_country_progress_report_en.pdf (Accessed September
    27, 2008).

Index

A

Acculturation
  definition, 3, 224, 225
  differential rates of, 224–225
  ethnic, 37
  "multi-linear" nature of, 38
  parallel socialization as basis of, 226–228
  process of, 224
  program and two-way communication,
    hurdles for, 236–237
  reciprocal, 224, 225, 226, 229, 237
  two-way, 272
Advice
  for parents/families, diverse racial/cultural
    origins, 289
  for professionals, approaches to
    individuals/families from diverse
    backgrounds, 291–292
Affirmative action programs, 32, 36, 131
African-Americans
  culture, 107, 115, 200
  immigrants from eastern/southern Asian
    countries, 23–25
  immigrants from Middle East, 25
  native Americans, 21–22
Afro-Creole Trinidadians, 268
"American culture," 6, 7, 13, 29, 77, 80, 94,
    102, 136, 194, 197, 234, 237–238,
    242, 244
American multi-culturalism in 21st century
  America as multi-cultural society, future
    of, 36–38
  assimilation on micro-level, 38–40
  mixed cultural backgrounds, 47–49
  multi-cultural families as micro-analysis of
    assimilation, 40–43
  multi-cultural persons, 49–52
  research on persons from mixed racial
    backgrounds, 43–47

  resurgence of White identity
    and superiority
    English language movement, 30–31
    reassertion of Christian fundamental-
      ism, 33–36
    resistance to affirmative action, 31–33
    resistance to immigration, *see*
      Immigration, resistance to
American values, traditional, 29
American views of multi-culturalism, review of
  African-Americans, targets of prejudice
    and discrimination, 19–25
  Hispanics, 22–23
  immigrants from eastern/southern
    Asian countries, 23–25
  immigrants from Middle East, 25
  native Americans, 21–22
  cultural pluralism, part of, 7–8
  counseling handbooks, 7
  dominant white group as part of ethnic mix
    English Protestants, 8–9
    German Protestants, 9–10
    lessons from White Protestant
      immigration experience, 11–12
    Protestants from other national
      origins, 9
    Scandinavians, 10–11
    Scotch and Scotch-Irish, 10
  Irish, "really different" White immigrant
    group, 12–14
  Italian immigrants, 14–15
  Jews, white Americans, non Christian
    Polish, the, 17–18
  special position reserved for people of
    color, 19
  two hundred plus years of American
    multi-culturalism, 5–7
Anglo-conformity, 242, 245, 250, 271, 273
Anglophone, 239, 240, 246, 247

Breinigsville, PA USA
02 September 2009
223408BV00005B/85/P